BEYOND
the End of the Road

A Winter of Contentment North of the Arctic Circle

MICHAEL D. PITT

Agio
PUBLISHING HOUSE

151 Howe Street, Victoria BC Canada V8V 4K5

Thanks to Marsha and Bruce Batchelor of *Agio
Publishing House* for layout designs and editorial
counsel, respectively. Tracey D. Hooper also
provided much appreciated editorial insight. Special
accolades to the entire Fehr family for sharing their
home, and for advice regarding the tools, skills and
preparation necessary to enjoy an Arctic winter.

*For rights information and bulk orders, please
contact:* info@agiopublishing.com *or go to*
www.agiopublishing.com

Beyond The End Of The Road
ISBN 978-1-897435-36-6 (trade paperback)

10   9   8   7   6   5   4   3   2   1 - h

DEDICATION

To Kathleen, my companion in life and adventure.

People often tell me how lucky I am
to have a wife who shares my passion for 'roughing it' in
northern Canada. I usually smile, and simply nod my head
in agreement. For without Kathleen, I would not have
experienced this marvellous and profoundly satisfying Arctic winter.

TABLE OF CONTENTS

FOREWORD

Before I begin this book I would like to tell you a little bit about myself, and how it came to be that Kathleen and I spent the winter of 1999, from January 31 to June 20, in a one-room cabin 100 km north of the Arctic Circle. We were all alone, 40 km from the nearest community, 350 km from the nearest road. No running water. No electricity. A grand adventure shared with wintering caribou, proud Ravens, and one inquisitive mink. All around us, the boreal forest rested silently – waiting for the snow to recede – waiting for the rivers to thaw – waiting for spring to return. One hundred and forty-one days of complete satisfaction and contentment.

For you see, I have always been in love with the land that lies beyond the end of the road. I am drawn to this mystical place – like the moth is drawn to the flame – like the caribou are drawn to their summer calving grounds – like a young man is drawn to his first lover. My passion never subsides. I am never satisfied. I always want more. I dream always of the land beyond the end of the road.

These dreams began very early in my life. One of my earliest memories is perhaps at five years of age. It was early on a Saturday morning, in suburban Sacramento, California. My parents were sleeping, and the house belonged to me. I opened the cupboard and poured a box of cereal into a bowl. I sat at the kitchen table, looking out the window, beyond the walls and security of my house, beyond to the backyard. Light trickled across the lawn while morning shadows played in the shrubs lining the fence.

I opened the back door, carried my bowl and spoon across the threshold, and headed slowly over to my sandbox. I felt so very adventurous. I sat all alone in the morning stillness, and for the first time felt the warmth of the rising sun on my back. This memory remains very vivid to me, even now, more than half-a-century later.

At ten years of age, like other boys, I was reading and collecting comic books. The one that I remember most was an edition where Donald Duck's nephews, Huey, Dewey and Louie, along with Scrooge McDuck, were camped on the edge of a lake deep in the Canadian forest. The Beagle Boys had just broken out of prison, and were drifting through the trees around the ducks' campfire intending to steal Scrooge's money. The nephews were understandably worried about the impending attack. My interest in this story, however, focused not on the boys' predicament. Rather, I spent literally hours staring at the scene, studying the forest beyond the Beagle Boys, wondering what other mysteries lay beyond the reach of the fire's light. I wished that I were camping by that fire with Huey, Dewey and Louie. I wished that I could explore that pristine Canadian forest.

Our Sunday newspaper featured a colour comic strip titled *Prince Valiant*. I know today that the strip's setting was Arthurian, and Valiant himself was a Nordic prince from Norway. Early in the story, Valiant had come to Camelot, earned the respect of King Arthur and Merlin, and became a Knight of the Round Table. I wasn't aware of any of this at the time, though. In fact, I never even read the words. I simply enjoyed the drawings of Valiant on his horse, riding down lonesome and isolated trails, always seeking adventures beyond the next ridge. I wished that I were riding with Prince Valiant. I wished that I could penetrate that ancient English forest.

I began backpacking into the mountains of California with my father when I was 12 years old. We would leave after my father got off work on a Friday night, drive for several hours, and then set off down the trail by moonlight – just like Prince Valiant in the English forest. We would camp for two nights around the fire – just like Huey, Dewey and Louie in the Canadian forest. We would return late on Sunday night, and I would lie in bed, wishing that my father didn't have to be back at work on Monday morning. I wished that we were still camping and living in the mountains.

When I enrolled at the University of California at Davis in 1965 I entered the two-year pre-forestry program. I presumed that such a career would allow me to wander through California's mountains while also earning a living. An easy and obvious career choice for me. During these first two years I studied mathematics, physics, chemistry, geology, surveying and other technical subjects. The actual professional forestry program began in the summer between my sophomore and junior years, at the summer camp operated by the University of California at Berkeley. It was here that I learned that the forestry profession focused mostly on cutting down trees. There would be precious little walking along lonely trails or exploring pristine forests.

Other than two summer jobs, I never actually worked in the forestry profession. I wasn't interested in cutting down trees for profit, nor in managing blocks of even-aged monocultures masquerading as regenerating forests. Rather, after receiving my degree, I entered graduate school in grassland ecology. All the while I continued backpacking at every opportunity, always seeking more distant and more remote locations. Except for Alaska, however, true wilderness no longer existed in the United States. In fact, a 1975 report on the status of wilderness in America claimed that nowhere in the lower 48 states was farther than 16 km from a road of some kind. It seemed that I had been born at least a century too late to pursue my inherent passion and love for un-peopled and un-roaded landscapes.

When I graduated with my doctoral degree in 1975, I saw an advertisement for a teaching and research position at the University of British Columbia in Vancouver. I had visited central British Columbia once before, on a family vacation, when I was 16 years old. I remembered a heavily-forested landscape that seemed relatively undeveloped and less impacted by industrial forestry compared to my home of California. A little research revealed that Canada was the world's second largest country, yet had a population equal only to that of California. Moreover, nearly 90% of Canada's population lived within 160 km of the border, leaving most of the country relatively unpopulated. British Columbia was larger in area than California, Oregon and Washington combined, yet its population was less than one-tenth that of California's. Wow! British Columbia was obviously the place for me. I applied, and felt very fortunate to be offered the position.

I met my wife Kathleen in 1976, and she quickly came to share my passion for silent, empty landscapes. At first we pursued weekend hiking trips into the mountains of southwestern British Columbia. These short sojourns soon lengthened into week-long withdrawals to more isolated alpine retreats of northern British Columbia and the southern Yukon. We always sought those peaceful, special places that remained least insulted by noise, pollution and degradation.

Finally, perhaps inevitably, we discovered the pristine purity of Canada's Far North. For 10 summers we paddled, mostly alone, on month-long canoeing expeditions across the remote Barren Grounds of the Northwest Territories and Nunavut. Rarely did we see other people. Only the occasional bush cabin reminded us that we lived in a congested world of six billion other human beings.

Yet, my thirst for purer, more extended isolation remained unquenched. My hunger to experience the natural, pre-industrial world became more compelling and more irresistible with each additional expedition, and with each passing year. Short bursts of only 30 days beyond the end of the road were no longer sufficient.

By now Kathleen and I had also realized that we wanted to spend a winter in Canada's Arctic. Our experience on summer canoe trips seemed incomplete. We wanted to spend a winter in the North, where rivers, lakes and muskeg remain frozen for 7 to 8 months of the year. Summer is for visitors. Only by following the winter trail did we believe that we could truly understand and know the character and soul of Canada's seemingly limitless northern landscape.

We wished to immerse ourselves in cold. We wanted to be surrounded by snow and ice. We longed to know the exquisite joy of seeing the ice break apart in the warmth of spring. We yearned to witness the rivers burst through the frozen chains of winter to once again run free and sparkling in the sunlight. We shared an unfulfilled desire to hear the swans, the geese, the loons and the multitudes of ducks that would suddenly and joyously return to their northern nesting grounds.

These goals and visions were not possible to achieve in our home of Vancouver. The adjacent Pacific Ocean seldom allows temperatures to dip below -10 degrees. Snowdrops and crocuses normally bloom in their flowerbeds by late January. In Vancouver, it is not possible to even begin to understand what it means to live in Canada, a vast realm that for much of the year lies slumbering beneath snow, ice and frigid sky. [Note: Unless otherwise indicated, all temperatures are presented in degrees Celsius. For a simple but imprecise conversion to degrees Fahrenheit, multiply by two and add 30. For an accurate conversion to degrees Fahrenheit, multiply degrees C by 9/5 and add 32. Similarly, all distances are presented in kilometres. For an accurate conversion to miles, multiply by 0.62. For a simpler conversion, divide kilometres in half, and then add a few miles for good measure.]

We would need to find a true winter retreat. We would need to find some hidden place to which we could escape as soon as possible after the first snowfall. We couldn't arrive just a day or two before the ducks returned.

Where would be the excitement in that? We couldn't show up, like tourists, only a week or two before the rivers began to flow. Where would be the anticipation in that?

No, to truly experience the thrill of spring renewal, we needed to spend most of the winter in a remote, isolated cabin. Ideally, we would paddle down the headwaters of a western Canadian Arctic river in the fall. We would reach our cabin, north of the Arctic Circle, a few days before freeze-up. We would then spend the winter exploring our private domain. We would snowshoe down frozen rivers. We would set up our wall tent on the shores of ice-covered lakes. On most nights, we would hunker down in our cabin, reading quietly by candle light, waiting for the excitement of spring. When the ice finally broke, we would climb back into our canoe and paddle a month, maybe more, down to the Arctic coast. That would be the ultimate experience.

We began to formulate these plans in the spring of 1997, and serendipitously found our cabin at the north end of Colville Lake, on a tributary of the Anderson River, in the Northwest Territories. This book describes our life in that cabin during the winter of 1999. For those 141 days Kathleen and I lived my dreams that began so long ago in that suburban Sacramento sandbox. For those wonderful 141 days we lived a simple life of cutting wood, hauling water and travelling along our own snowshoe trails.

We also experienced and better appreciated how native people and the early European explorers of Canada could live and travel, seemingly in comfort, when the mercury fell below minus forty for weeks at a time. The history of northern Canada's early exploration is truly extraordinary. I particularly admire men like John Rae, an explorer, surgeon and Chief Trader for the Hudson Bay Company. Ken McGoogan details Rae's exploits in *Fatal Passage: The Untold Story of John Rae, the Arctic Adventurer Who Discovered the Fate of Franklin*. During the winter of 1844–45, Rae trekked nearly 2000 km on snowshoes between Manitoba and Ontario in only two months. Nearly a decade later, in the winter of 1851–52, Rae averaged 40 km per day on another 2000-km trek above the Arctic Circle in search of the lost Franklin Expedition.

Rae entered the wilderness lightly, on its own terms. Often accompanied by only a few companions, with virtually no food or supplies, Rae moved quickly and easily by dogsled or canoe, hunting caribou and other game for subsistence as he built a phenomenal reputation for winter exploration and travel. Rae invariably returned from his expeditions healthier and stronger than when he had departed civilization.

For me, John Rae lived like a man should live! Such a contrast to my life in Vancouver – a life of ties and suits – a life of meetings and walls – a life of traffic jams – a life of line-ups at the checkout stand in the grocery store. I wish that I could have travelled with John Rae to the Arctic coast.

Like many other readers of Canadian history, I also admire John Hornby, a more recent adventurer of northern Canada, whose legend is due mostly to his feats of strength and endurance. Malcolm Waldron's book, *Snow Man – John Hornby in the Barren Lands*, describes a prototypical Hornby event on the edge of the Barren Grounds in 1924. Susie Benjamin, a 22-year-old son of an Indian friend of Hornby's, arrived at the Lockhart River just as Hornby and six other men were moving across Pike's Portage out of Great Slave Lake. After talking to Susie for a few minutes, the 44-year-old Hornby rejoined his crew and said, "Susie and I are going to show you boys how to pack."

Five canoes still lay at the south end of the portage. The two men shouldered the first canoe and started off at a sprint across the uneven terrain. The second soon followed the first. Hornby's face apparently showed a little discomfort with the third canoe. Nevertheless, all five canoes were run across the portage without a break. At the finish, Susie was breathing more heavily than Hornby, whose shirt was stained red from where the canoes had rested on his shoulder. One of Hornby's companions asked, "Are you hurt?"

Hornby scornfully replied, "No, nothing can hurt you if you don't think about it."

Hornby lived like a man should live. Such a contrast to the modern world – a world where television commercials feature 'men' rejoicing over having purchased a new dust mop.

During the winter of 1924–25, Hornby and James C. Critchfield-Bullock lived out on the Barren Grounds in a small cave dug into the side of an esker. Both men nearly died before reaching the relative comfort at Baker Lake the following spring. At a feast that very first night, according to Waldron, Hornby told Critchfield-Bullock:

> *A week of this, Bullock, and we'll wish we were back in the Barrens. [Men] live by routine at these posts. We can go back*

*to the Barrens again next year. We can profit by the mistakes
we made this time.*

After Critchfield-Bullock observed that they had no money left, Hornby
continued:

*We don't need money. The caribou and the white wolves and
foxes and the fish are free. Free, that is, to men who know
how to get them. Men like you and me. You're going back to
civilization where every man is your enemy, because he is in
competition with you. Back where the man with the cleanest
shirt is the most respected. And what'll you do? You've built
a fine body for yourself up here. You will weigh close to two
hundred pounds in a couple of weeks, and all of it solid bone
and muscle. Try to sell that in a city. It may get you a day
laborer's job or a third assistant's birth in some gymnasium.
That's not for you, is it? Money! It isn't in the Barrens that you
need money, but in the cities.*

It's perhaps fortunate for me, though, that I did not have the opportunity
to travel with John Hornby back to the Barren Grounds. For in the winter
of 1927 he starved to death, with his companions Christian and Adlard, in
a small cabin on the banks of the Thelon River. Waldron says that Hornby
"loved the rugged, desolate, heroically beautiful part of the North known as
the Barren Grounds. He loved them more than women. He loved them more
that his cushy, privileged background in England. He loved them more than
his own life."

I love Canada's North, and I particularly love the Barren Grounds. I
don't know, though, whether I love the Barren Grounds more than my own
life. And I certainly don't love them more than I love my wife Kathleen!
Nevertheless, I empathize with the following quote from Hornby, found in
George Whalley's *The Legend of John Hornby*:

*In civilization there is no peace. Here in the North, in my
country, there is peace. No past, no future, no regret, no
anticipation; just doing. That is peace.*

While Kathleen and I lived in the cabin I played at being like Rae and

Hornby. I exalted in the beauty of winter as I dragged my sled, loaded with wall tent and portable wood stove through the Arctic forest. I thrilled at camping out at minus 30 degrees. I revelled in physical adversity, and came back to Vancouver very lean, and as strong as I have ever been in my entire life. I lived fully and completely, and, as Hornby predicted, I needed very little money. Except for the cabin rental, we spent only $150.00 in six months, and only then because we went to town twice. Most importantly, those 141 days in the cabin remain, nearly 10 years later, the most enjoyable period of my life. Like Hornby, and many others like him, Kathleen and I had both found peace.

Kathleen and I have told our story, through slide shows and conversations with friends and family many times since 1999. People often remark how 'adventurous' or 'brave' we are. These accolades are unwarranted, however. We did nothing special. Many people live in small, isolated communities and remote cabins all across northern Canada. Our experiences presented in this book are common, everyday occurrences to them.

Our experiences are 'unique' only to those people who have always lived in urban centres. Indeed, Grey Owl dedicated his marvellous book, *Tales of an Empty Cabin,* to 'those whose souls are longing for the freedom of the open road, but who are prevented by the invincible decrees of Fate from ever seeing the wonders of the Wilderness save in the pages of a book.' I could easily and logically adopt the same dedication. I also write this book, though, for all of you who dream of stepping beyond the end of your road, no matter what physical, fanciful or philosophical form it might take.

CHAPTER 1

Planning Our Escape

To pursue our dream, Kathleen and I both applied for one-year leaves of absence from our positions at the University of British Columbia. Leaves of absence at the University of British Columbia normally coincide with the academic year. Accordingly, our leaves had been granted from July 1, 1998 to June 30, 1999. This would certainly give us plenty of time in the summer of 1998 to find some unknown cabin, on a river still to be determined. It would also give us time to paddle to that cabin, and to arrange the logistics of shipping our winter food and gear to that cabin.

This plan, however, contained a major flaw. Break-up north of the Arctic Circle in western Canada generally occurs in early to mid-June. Even if we set off downriver from our cabin at the first signs of break-up, we likely wouldn't reach the Arctic coast by canoe until early to mid-July. We would then need a minimum of seven days to drive back to Vancouver. All this meant that we couldn't possibly be back on campus until at least three weeks after our leaves of absence had ended and the new academic year had begun. Our plan required tweaking. Damn that academic year! So very restrictive.

So, let's review the original plan – the ideal plan – which was to paddle, stay in a cabin, and then paddle some more. What if, though, we paddled the entire river first, and then went back to stay in the cabin? This strategy included several benefits. We could paddle the river in summer, when the Arctic would be filled with migratory birds and drenched with 24-hour sunlight. We could use the summer, and our trip north, to find a suitable cabin. In fact, with this revised plan, the cabin no longer even had to be on the same river that we paddled. It could be on any Arctic river. This new approach provided much more flexibility and opportunity.

We also realized that being away for the entire year was not entirely feasible. We could, perhaps should, use part of our leave to visit family and friends. I certainly should also use part of my leave to write and submit research grants. My career would certainly suffer if I abandoned it for an entire year. We would also likely need significant time to arrange for food and gear to be purchased and shipped to our remote, winter accommodation, wherever it might be.

So, while celebrating my 50th birthday in September of 1997, Kathleen and I agreed that the best plan would be to paddle an Arctic river in the summer of 1998. We would visit family and friends that fall. We would share Christmas at home with family, and then depart immediately for the cabin, where we could still enjoy more than five months of winter. After break-up in June 1999 we would return directly to Vancouver, rested and ready to resume work on the first of July.

Selecting the river to paddle that next summer was actually very easy. For several years I had wanted to descend the Anderson River, the headwaters of which rise north of the Arctic Circle. The Anderson then flows nearly 600 km north to Liverpool Bay on the Arctic coast. To access the river we planned to drive 3800 km to Inuvik, on the east channel of the Mackenzie River delta. From there we would charter a float plane to the small community of Colville Lake, where most people begin trips down the Anderson River. After reaching the coast we would be picked up by float plane, at a specified date, to be flown back to Inuvik.

While in Inuvik we could also visit and stay with our friends Marilyn and Alan Fehr. Alan, a former graduate student of mine, now worked for Parks Canada, and had extensive knowledge of the western Arctic. Both he and Marilyn could give us much needed advice on potential cabins, as well as proper clothing and equipment for enjoying an Arctic winter. They would also likely know whom we should contact regarding getting our food and supplies to an isolated cabin.

On 29 October 1997, I ordered topographic maps from Natural Resources Canada for our trip down the Anderson River. Five of the maps, at the scale of 1:250,000, covered our entire route. The town of Colville Lake actually sits on a tributary of the Anderson River, which the canoeist eventually reaches along a very circuitous route extending nearly 150 km through Ketaniatue, Legetentue, Sakatue, Niwelin and Gassend Lakes. Narrow outlets of lakes, with little change in elevation, can sometimes be difficult to find. For this stretch of the journey I ordered six maps at the scale of 1:50,000.

By mid-November I had applied waterproofing map seal to all 11 maps, and had finalized a tentative 30-day itinerary. I could already visualize our campsites, where we might have to portage around rapids, and where we might spend our rest days hiking, fishing, birding and botanizing. At this stage of planning a river trip, my mind always becomes irreversibly fixed. I now HAD to paddle down the Anderson River. I had my maps, didn't I? I had my itinerary, didn't I? I HAD to go.

OK. So now the river portion of our adventure was in place. The priority for next year, though, was winter, not summer. We still needed a cabin. I called Alan, and told him about our plans.

"It's going to be hard to find a suitable cabin, Mike," he said. "First of all, very few communities, let alone cabins, even exist north of the Arctic Circle. Secondly, trappers use most of those cabins that do exist. And, since trapping occurs primarily in winter, the cabins aren't available then. And it's possible that many trappers wouldn't even want to rent their cabin to tourists from the South. And also, as you know, many bush cabins aren't all that great. I think it will be difficult to find what you want."

"I need only one cabin, Alan. If you don't mind just asking around, I would appreciate it."

"OK, I'll see what I can do."

I hung up the phone feeling pretty optimistic. Something would work out. It always does.

In addition to finding a cabin, another, more serious, and now quite nagging obstacle remained – our lack of winter experience. I grew up in Sacramento, in California's Great Central Valley. Only very rarely did ice form on our backyard fish pond. One winter, when I was about 10 years old, hail beat down on our house for about 10 minutes, piling up several centimetres against our garage door. A very memorable event for me. I also clearly remember the first time I actually saw snow falling. I was a 22-year-old graduate student, collecting data for a professor researching the accumulation and decay rates of leaves and twigs in Sequoia National Park. As I bent over the collection trays in late September, a white, ash-like substance began swirling around my head.

"Who would be starting fires way out here, and at this time of year?" I wondered. There were no buildings around, and I hadn't seen anyone on the road.

Yes, I am almost embarrassed to admit it, but for that first brief moment, I mistook snow for wood ash. Since moving to Vancouver in 1975, I had taken up cross-country and back-country skiing. Nevertheless, in 1998 I still had never lived with snow and ice, and had never endured a long, cold winter.

Kathleen's winter résumé was not much longer. From the age of two she had lived in Vancouver, where snow occasionally falls for a few days each winter. The nearly incessant rain, however, usually quickly follows, turning everything to dirty slush and mush. Kathleen and I both faced a steep learning curve before we headed north of the Arctic Circle for winter.

We needed to learn about walking on frozen lakes and rivers. We needed to learn about winter camping. We needed to acquire the most appropriate clothing and gear. To begin our education, we purchased a copy of *A Snow Walker's Companion*, by Garrett and Alexandra Conover, a truly excellent book that provided detailed advice and recommendations on clothing and gear. Chapters included *Snowshoes and Footwear; Toboggans; Tents and Trail Stoves; Clothing for the Elements; Tools of the Trail;* and *Provisioning*. Additional information included addresses and telephone numbers of suppliers of winter equipment, plus detailed plans for making clothing.

We were especially intrigued with the Conover's recommendation for footwear: 'The [traditional] sock-felt-moccasin system is entirely breathable, very lightweight, and magnificently functional in conditions ranging from twenty-five degrees Fahrenheit [minus 4 degrees C] to as cold as temperatures go on earth. [The system] is comfortable and light as can be. You feel as if you are prancing around in bedroom slippers.'

That was quite a testimonial. I emailed Alan to get his opinion. He agreed completely with the Conovers, and recommended that we make our own duffel-cloth liners for our mukluks: "They are simple to make. Since Kathleen sews she could easily make them to fit your mukluks. As you know, patterns are available in the Conover book."

The Conovers also advised that we would need different boots during the transition season, at temperatures warmer than minus 4 degrees, when one's body weight will supply enough compression to melt the snow, making our moccasins wet. In an email Alan wrote that he preferred, "the Sorel boot [which is] far more commonly used [here in Inuvik] than [other brands]. I find the Sorel is more versatile because the rubber bottom means it can be used in fairly wet conditions and still keep you warm and dry."

Alan also cautioned us that we would: "need heavy mitts, leather I would suggest, for working around the camp. Hauling wood and fixing the stove, for example, require material that will stand up to snags and heat."

It was good to have access to Alan's experience.

A couple of weeks later I sat in my living room leafing through *Up Here*, a magazine devoted to articles about Canada's Far North. This particular issue featured a story about a man named Bern Will Brown. It seems that Bern had cabins for rent at the north end of Colville Lake. Cabins that we would be paddling by next summer on our way to the Anderson River! Could this be true? If so, it seemed like fate, and I called Bern the next afternoon, on November 29.

"Hello, my name is Mike, and my wife Kathleen and I are planning to overwinter, in a small cabin, as a holiday, somewhere north of the Arctic Circle. I read in *Up Here* magazine that you have cabins to rent at the north end of Colville Lake."

"Yes, I have two cabins at North End, but one is for storage. I rent out only the smaller one."

"We'd prefer a smaller cabin anyway. It would be easier to heat than a larger cabin."

"I've never rented it out in the winter before. Mostly I rent to fishermen in the summer and hunters in the fall. It's not really a winter cabin."

"Would it be liveable in the winter though? We are going to paddle the Anderson River next July, and we could get a look at the cabin then."

"That sounds good. You would want to see it, before you committed to staying there in the winter. You say your name is Mike? Would you be coming for the entire winter?"

"Ideally, we would like to come from January to break-up. What kind of heat does the cabin have? We would prefer to have wood heat."

"Both cabins have wood-burning stoves. If you do come, I could make sure that firewood is cut and stacked for you. But I would have to charge for it."

"Sounds fair to me. What are the cabins like? Are they in good shape? I've seen a lot of bush cabins. Some are good. Many are not so good. What would it cost to rent your cabin?"

"I made the cabins myself, Mike. They're both in good shape. I can send you some brochures, and we can talk some more after you've read them. What's your address?"

I hung up the phone, very excited, and thoroughly pleased with myself. This seems to be working out quite well. We're learning about clothing and gear, and now I have a great lead on a cabin north of the Arctic Circle.

The brochures arrived a week later, and from the pictures, the cabins were excellent. They were fully furnished, and sat on a small knoll above the outlet of Colville Lake. Docks extended on both sides of a short, narrow point extending into the lake. This couldn't be any better. The only potential drawback was the listed rate of $100 per person per night. Two hundred dollars per night for Kathleen and me. Six thousand dollars per month. Break-up normally occurs in mid-June. So the total cost, for 5.5 months would be $33,000. Certainly much more than any reasonable person would expect to pay or to receive. Obviously Bern intended these prices for short-term sportsmen, not for long-term winter enthusiasts.

What would be a fair price to pay, though? Once again, I called Alan.

"You're lucky to find such a cabin, Mike. Price is hard to determine. So many variables, such as location, condition, furnishings. But bush cabins in the Inuvik area generally go from between $500 to $1,000 per month."

For the next few days I spent a lot of time looking at the brochures. The north end of Colville Lake, and its little collection of buildings and docks, seemed perfect for our winter adventure.

I called Bern again to find out what price he actually would charge for the winter.

"So, Bern, Kathleen and I are very interested in coming. You mentioned before that you could provide firewood for us. How much wood do you think we would need?" [I thought I would proceed cautiously to the question of rent. There was a very large spread between Alan's estimate and Bern's brochure.]

"I think you would need at least two cords."

"What would be the cost for that?"

"Two hundred and fifty dollars a cord – split and stacked."

I didn't know if that was a fair price, but it was about the same that I pay for cordwood in Vancouver. The price certainly seemed acceptable.

Bern continued. "There's also two propane tanks on the porch. They're for the propane cook stove and for lights. There's also a generator that you're welcome to use."

"We're not really interested in a generator. They make too much noise. One of the reasons we're coming is for the quiet."

"I see. Do you know how to drive a ski-doo? It's a long way to town. About 40 km. I can rent you a ski-doo."

"I don't think we need a ski-doo. We want to do a lot of snowshoeing. Snow mobiles make a lot of noise."

"I see. Can you use a chain saw? There's one in the storage shed."

"If we pay to have firewood already there when we arrive, then I don't think we will need a chain saw. Besides, they make a lot of noise. We will bring a bow saw and axe. I like physical work. I think we'll be fine without the chain saw. But it's good to know that it's there if we need it.

"I see."

And now for the big question – "We're very interested, Bern. What is the monthly rent?"

"Did you get my brochures?"

"Yes, we did. So is the price in the brochure what you would expect for renting during the winter?"

"Yes."

"But," I countered, "the price seemed to be for people who are staying for only a few days. Or maybe a week. On a monthly basis, that would be $6,000. We can't afford that."

"What can you afford?"

"I don't think it's a question of what we can afford, Bern. I think it's a question of what it's worth. I have a friend in Inuvik who says that bush cabins generally go for about $500 to $1,000 per month."

Bern, after a short pause, offered a few more comments regarding the amenities of the Anderson River and Colville Lake: "As I mentioned in my letter, I do have a printed résumé of a canoe trip down the Anderson River, which I sell for $25.00. My wife Margaret and I have paddled down the Anderson River to the Arctic coast, so have first-hand knowledge of the trip. Pretty much everyone who goes down the Anderson River stays a few days here in town, at my compound and lodge. The town here is quite nice. You'll probably want to visit before you go down the Anderson."

Bern paused again, and then said, "You know, I'd be happier with the higher price mentioned by your friend."

"That sounds fair to me, Bern."

So it was all set. We were going to live at the north end of Colville Lake, a full 100 km north of the Arctic Circle, from January 1999 to break-up in June. The next day I ordered six more topographic maps at the 1:50,000 scale for the area surrounding the cabin.

Most of our friends thought that $1,000 per month was an exorbitant price. "Hey, you could get a pretty nice apartment in Vancouver for that amount of money. Why would you pay that much for just a cabin in the bush?"

They implied that Kathleen and I were getting ripped off. But I disagree. It's a question of value, and of supply and demand. Bern's is the only cabin available at the north end of Colville Lake, a perfect place for us to over-winter. And it seems that the cabin's well made and maintained. I actually preferred to pay the upper end of the range mentioned by Alan. Bern would be my primary contact for any emergencies and help throughout the winter. I wanted to begin with a good relationship. I certainly didn't want Bern to feel that I was taking advantage of him.

On March First, 1998, I prepared the following purchase order to send to Craig MacDonald, in Dwight, Ontario. Of all the suppliers listed in the Conover book, Craig provided the most complete selection of both clothing and equipment. He also included detailed instructions on techniques for hauling sleds, for travelling safely during winter, for erecting tents, and for avoiding tent fires. In fact, Craig would sell his winter wall tents and stoves only to those people who also purchased his use-and-safety guide. We appreciated Craig's prudent and careful approach.

Egyptian Cotton Tent	$1,199.00
Tent Fly (12 x 12 feet)	149.00
Tent Stove (3900 cubic inches)	239.00
Stove Heat Shield	9.00
Stove Pipe Thimble (4-inch pipe)	19.00
Stainless Steel Baking Trivets	4.00
Flat-faced Ice Chisel	59.00
Chrome-plated Iron Tent Poles	109.00
Ten-oz Duck Canvas Wind Suits (2)	338.00

Snowshoe Moccasins (4 pairs)	316.00
One Roll Lamp Wick (for snowshoe bindings)	24.00
Snowshoes (2 pairs)	258.00
Tent Candles (2 boxes)	38.00
Candle Holders (4)	1.00
8-foot Standard Trail Sled (45 pounds)	399.00
Tumpline	59.00
Shipping Deposit	100.00
Total	$3,320.00

In 1998, Craig manufactured and listed all his items in Imperial units. The tent measured 8 feet by 10 feet, with a 3-foot wall and a 6.5-foot ridge height, yet weighed only 16 pounds (7.25 kg). Very light considering that the tent's fairly roomy size could easily accommodate Kathleen and me, the stove, and much of our gear. Yet the tent was small enough to be set up quickly using metal tent poles, without needing to spend time cutting larger poles from the forest.

Before sending the order to Craig, I shared this list by email with Alan, who wrote that, "If you pull a toboggan [while snowshoeing], I would suggest a light plastic kids-type sled. These are cheap and slide very easily. You may want to have two – either two light ones, or one light one and a heavier-style (wood perhaps). We use these little sleds at camp for hauling ice, wood and fish. They are like winter wheelbarrows."

This recommendation seemed inappropriate to me. We planned to be hauling our gear over long distances and perhaps difficult terrain. A plastic 'kids-type sled' would certainly be too flimsy to endure six months of heavy winter use. I would go with Craig's sturdy, heavy (20 kg) sled. I sent the order off the next day. Craig called a week later to say that everything except the sled had been shipped by Canada Post. The bulky, heavy sled would be delivered by a small shipping company sometime in mid-July.

The Conover book advised that fur ruffs, which are much warmer than synthetic materials, should always be added to wind suits. Based on Alan's suggestion, we called the Winnipeg Fur Exchange to order two coyote ruffs. As soon as they arrived, Kathleen easily sewed both onto our canvas wind suits. Based on the patterns in the Conover book, Kathleen also made duffel-cloth inserts for all four pairs of our new moccasins. These moccasins, also known as mukluks, with their light canvas uppers and tanned moosehide bottoms, did appear very much like cosy bedroom slippers.

Duffel cloth is normally very expensive, around $50.00 per metre, but the pre-eminent fabric store in Vancouver offered remnants marked down to only $5.00 per metre. In fact, we obtained most of our winter clothing quite inexpensively, primarily because, like the Conovers, we prefer wool. Like many modern synthetic materials, wool breathes well and retains heat, even when wet. Unlike synthetics such as fleece, however, wool is easily repaired in the field, and does not 'melt' when contacted by heat or campfire embers. Several trips to the various thrift and army surplus stores provided all we needed in the way of wool pants, wool shirts and wool sweaters. We purchased medium and heavy sets of wool long underwear, both top and bottom, at the Army & Navy, Vancouver's most 'blue collar' department store.

Periodically I practiced setting up the wall tent. Most nights I studied my maps, or leafed through the Conover book, or reread Craig MacDonald's instructions – on some nights I did all three.

By late April, everything was set. We had our cabin. We had most of our equipment. We had most of our clothing. Our leaves of absence would begin in just over two months, when we would drive to Inuvik, and from there fly to Colville Lake to meet Bern, to see the cabin, and to canoe down the Anderson River. After returning home, we would make plans for shipping six months of food, equipment, supplies and ourselves to the north end of Colville Lake, where we would immerse ourselves in the cold and isolation of a true Canadian winter.

CHAPTER 2

A Bump in the Road

My appointment as Associate Dean in the Faculty of Agricultural Sciences at the University of British Columbia included secretarial support. I considered myself very fortunate that Lynn brought such skill and enthusiasm to her position and responsibilities. I therefore felt privileged in May when she asked me to serve as emcee at her wedding. And, to be honest, I also enjoy the microphone. I love the stage. I welcomed the opportunity to at least try to entertain her guests. On the afternoon of Lynn's wedding I reached into the closet for my most formal clothing, including some black dress slacks that I had not worn for more than two years. The slacks fit very snugly on my right thigh. In fact, I could barely get them on. The left leg was loose. The waist was loose. But the right pant leg fit extremely tightly.

Like most men, I immediately asked my wife to explain my predicament. "Kathleen, I can't seem to get these slacks over my right leg. Why would that be?"

As is her style, Kathleen answered honestly and candidly. "Why would I know why your slacks don't fit anymore? Clothes don't fit forever." See. I told you Kathleen would know the answer.

"Let me see, though. Turn around. Let me have a look. You're right, Michael. They are very tight. You know, for a while now, your right thigh muscle seems to have been getting bigger. You look almost lopsided."

"I do?"

"Haven't you noticed?" Kathleen asked.

"No. Why would I notice? I never look at myself from behind. These pants sure don't fit though. We both need to go to the dentist and the doctor for checkups before we head north, anyway. Maybe my thigh muscle has been strained or something. Maybe the doctor can recommend some physio-therapy. I'll make an appointment for next week. It's less than two months before we go now, but there's still time to do something, if something needs to be done."

A week later I sat in the doctor's tiny, cramped examination room reading decades-old *Canadian Geographic* magazines and daydreaming about the first of July, when Kathleen and I would head north into our year of freedom. The doctor entered, peered into my eyes and ears, took my blood pressure and tapped on my knees.

"Everything looks OK," he said. "Is there anything else?"

"Yes, there is," I began, as I hopped down from the table. "Some of my slacks no longer fit over my right leg. My thigh muscle seems to have gotten larger. Maybe I should see a physiotherapist," I suggested.

"Turn around. Let's have a look."

I'm not making this next part up. It happened exactly like this. I turned around, and my doctor yelled out, "Oh my God!" as he more or less fell backwards out through the door of the examination room. I generally try not to read too much extra into what people say or do. But I definitely interpreted a falling-backward, Oh-my-God to be a bad sign.

The doctor recovered from his initial reaction, and came back into the room.

"So do you think I need to see a physiotherapist?" I asked.

"No. I'm going to send you for some tests, starting with an ultrasound, and then, if necessary, an MRI."

"Does it take long to get those tests scheduled?" I asked. "I have to go away for a couple of months on July First. I need to get those tests done before then."

"You won't be going anywhere this summer," he replied.

Once again, I generally try not to read too much extra into what people say or do. But I definitely interpreted 'You won't be going anywhere this summer' to be a bad sign. Oh well, there's almost two months before we leave. Still plenty of time. And besides, I HAD to paddle down the Anderson River. I had my waterproofed maps, didn't I? I had my itinerary, didn't I? I HAD to go.

I went for the ultrasound test three days later. The technician told me that a cyst, which the ultrasound would detect, could be the cause my swollen thigh. Cysts are usually not serious, I thought. Besides, according to Kathleen, I seem to have had this cyst for at least a couple of years, and the only problem I've had is that my dress slacks didn't fit any more. Who cares about my dress slacks, anyway? I don't. I certainly won't be taking dress slacks north with me.

After the ultrasound I chatted briefly with the technician. "So, is it a cyst?"

"I don't think so," she replied.

"What is it then?"

"You should ask your doctor. Here's the phone number to schedule an MRI."

Damn! I hate going for all these tests.

I drove back to my office and called the number on the card. "I have been asked to schedule an MRI."

"Our first available slot is early July. Is that OK?"

"No. That doesn't work for me. I'm going away for a couple of months on July First. Are there any other MRI facilities around that might have earlier dates?"

"I'll check and get back to you."

Thirty minutes later the receptionist called back to say that they could take me tomorrow, at 1:30.

"Great! Thanks very much for your help."

The next day, at Vancouver General Hospital, I filled out all the forms, and checked the 'No' box to the question 'Are you claustrophobic?' The technician strapped me to the table, and slid me into the narrow tube where I spent the next 45 minutes listening to a series of loud, jackhammer-like noises. Afterwards, I took the rest of the day off, went home, sat in my garden, and wondered what all these tests would reveal.

Three days later my falling-backward, Oh-my-God doctor called me at work. "I'm afraid that the MRI results indicate that you have a tumour in your thigh – a liposarcoma. I can't tell you how serious it might be. I have forwarded your test results to the oncologist, and have made an appointment for you at the cancer clinic. You should be there next Tuesday, at 10:30 in the morning."

As I've said twice before, I generally try not to read too much extra into what people say or do. But I absolutely interpreted 'I've scheduled an appointment for you at the cancer clinic' to be a very bad sign. I had gotten quite a few laughs during the last week telling the story of my falling-backward, Oh-my-God doctor. It was good material. But this cancer clinic appointment didn't sound funny at all. For the first time, I began to worry.

"So what is a liposarcoma? I've never heard of it before."

"It's a cancer of the fat cells. If you want, I can send you some information, and I can give you some website addresses."

"Yes, please. I would like to have the website addresses and the brochures."

How could this be happening? Oh well, I might not actually have this cancer. The MRI test might be only suggestive, and not conclusive. And even if I do have cancer, many cancers are easily treated. And besides, there's more than a month left before we head north. Still plenty of time.

Despite what kind of cancer I might have, or how treatable it might be, just hearing the word 'cancer' applied to yourself is frightening enough. I don't feel ashamed telling you that when I called my father that afternoon, I had difficulty even saying, "I have cancer, Dad."

I didn't actually cry, but I wasn't entirely composed either.

On the Internet, Kathleen and I read that:

> *A liposarcoma is a malignant tumour that arises in fat cells in deep soft tissue, such as that inside the thigh. They are typically large bulky tumours, which tend to have multiple smaller satellites extending beyond the main confines of the tumour. Only when the tumour is very large do symptoms of pain or functional disturbances occur. The prognosis varies depending on the site of origin, the tumour size, the depth, and proximity to lymph nodes. In advanced cases, amputation is sometimes necessary. Metastases are common. The 5-year survival rate for a high-grade liposarcoma is less than 50%.*

Amputation? Damn. I felt real bad. And not just because I had cancer. I felt sorrow and wrenching disappointment that this liposarcoma, this bulging thigh, might keep me from pursuing my dream of spending an isolated winter in the Far North – a dream that was supposed to begin in only a month from now. I spent the next several days feeling quite morose.

Next Tuesday Kathleen took the day off, and we both went down to the cancer clinic, where we sat waiting with scores of other sombre, worried-looking people. Not a very happy place at all. When my turn came, Kathleen joined me, as together we walked into the small meeting room, where we met with Dr. Masri, the oncologist. He was smiling, and seemed happy. How could he possibly have bad news?

"As you probably know," he began, "cancers are generally rated in four stages, with stage one being the least advanced, and stage four being the most advanced. Your tumour is very large, one of the largest liposarcomas I have ever seen. Even so, it is still confined within the fat cells, and has not moved. It is not likely to metastasize, as it is not in contact with any organs. It's big, but it is still stage one. I am confident that surgery will be completely successful in removing all of it."

I didn't know what to think. I should have been pleased. And I suppose I was. But my first reaction was almost one of shame. For the past week I had been feeling very sorry for myself, fearing the worst. And now he tells me that my self-pity was entirely unwarranted and undeserved? I simply go into the hospital, he cuts the cancer out, and I go on with my life. I regretted that I ever even mentioned my cancer to anybody. My health problem didn't seem to be any worse than swollen tonsils or an enlarged appendix. What a baby I was.

Dr. Masri outlined two possible scenarios for me: "I know that you were planning to go on a canoe trip in July. You can still do that, and we can operate when you get back. Or we can operate now, say early next month."

What, I thought, the surgery is not even urgent? What a wuss I have been.

"Well, I'm sort of geared up to dealing with this. The sooner the better. Let's get it over with. Let's have the surgery now." I forgot all about my waterproofed maps and my itinerary for the Anderson River.

Kathleen and I left Dr. Masri's office, and walked past the waiting room filled with scores of sombre, worried-looking people. My week of anxiety now seemed quite trivial compared to the uncertainty and peril that surely awaited many of them. I slinked past, hoping they wouldn't notice the spring in my step and the relief in my heart.

Back at work the next day I relayed the good news to my colleagues, who suggested that I should take sick leave while I recovered from surgery. "No need to waste your leave on being sick. Why don't you begin your administrative leave of absence when you're better? Take as much time as you need."

This had never occurred to me. I always had believed that my bad luck is just that. My bad luck. I should have to deal with my bad luck. Other people should not have to make adjustments to accommodate me. Postponing my leave by just one month, though, to end July 31, created a tremendous opportunity. Kathleen and I could now go to the cabin and canoe out to the Arctic coast after break-up. This approach provided a more natural flow of events, compared to canoeing by the cabin in summer, and then returning in winter. I called Kathleen to see if she could change the terms of her leave. As it turns out, her Computing Services unit gladly supported her request to extend her leave of absence. Kathleen's leave was without pay, and Computing Services, which had been suffering financial cutbacks, welcomed the opportunity to save additional salary.

So one never knows about life. Because of my cancer, our original, ideal plan for how we would spend our year of freedom had been restored.

That evening, over a relaxing dinner, we discussed our new situation, particularly the greater challenge of getting food and gear to the cabin. The logistics were more difficult now that the canoeing and overwintering both had to be outfitted at the same time. A month-long canoe trip requires its own, unique set of gear (canoe, paddles, PFDs, canoe packs, small camp stove, food buckets) and dried food. These items fill most of our van. There would not be enough room left for the nearly six months of food and gear that we would need for our winter adventure. Somehow, we needed to get most of our winter and summer gear to a staging area close to Colville Lake this summer. [Note: PFD stands for 'personal flotation device' which is worn by most canoeists and kayakers. PFDs are less bulky than lifejackets but will not keep the head of an unconscious person above water.]

I should remind you that no roads go to Colville Lake. No roads went anywhere near Colville Lake. That's one of the main reasons we were so excited about spending the winter there. We would be truly and very isolated.

Colville Lake lies east of the Mackenzie River, which stretches more than 1500 km from its source at Great Slave Lake in the Northwest Territories to its vast delta at Inuvik. In 1998 most of this great river corridor contained no roads, and the few towns spread along its length were supplied in summer primarily by barges operated by the Northern Transportation Company

Limited [NTCL]. Norman Wells (often called 'The Wells'), the closest town with air service to Colville Lake, lies 195 km to the southeast. The last shipment downriver before winter was early September. So we could drive to the NTCL terminus in the town of Hay River on the south shore of Great Slave Lake in late August, loaded with as much gear and supplies as possible, and send everything by barge approximately 900 km to 'The Wells.'

We could then drive after Christmas to Inuvik with the rest of our gear, and leave our van with Alan and Marilyn. Our van would then be available to drive home to Vancouver when we came off the Anderson River in July of 1999. This approach would be less expensive than shipping our gear an additional 650 km to Inuvik, from where there was no scheduled air service to Colville Lake. Instead, when we reached Inuvik after Christmas, we would take a scheduled flight with North-Wright Airways to Norman Wells, where we would collect our supplies. We could then take our gear on a scheduled flight to Colville Lake. Once in town we could hire someone to take us and our supplies by snow machine to our cabin at the north end of Colville Lake. Although complex, we liked this plan very much. We just needed to find somebody to look after our supplies once they reached Norman Wells.

The next day I called North-Wright Airways, and talked to a pleasant lady who agreed to store our supplies in their compound when the NTCL barge arrived. I also sent Bern a letter, telling him of my impending surgery, and that we wouldn't be passing through Colville Lake in July. I assured him, though, that we still planned to fly in to the cabin in January.

On July 4, our wedding anniversary, Kathleen and I drove to Vancouver General Hospital, where I immediately entered the preparation room. Next to my gurney stood an intern and Dr. Masri, who still seemed happy as he patted my liposarcoma. "See, it's massive." The intern nodded in agreement.

Across the room, in a corner, a man about my age whimpered that he was going to die. I wasn't worried about dying. I just hoped that when I woke up my leg would still be attached to my body.

My gurney rolled out the door and down the hallway, beneath glaring lights, into the operating room. The anesthetist instructed me to count backwards from ten. I assumed he meant that I should stop at zero, and not enter negative territory. I think I made it to plus seven. I woke groggily and felt for my leg. It seemed to still be there; but I have heard that sometimes people continue to 'sense' hands, feet and legs that have been blown off or amputated. The next time I woke, Kathleen stood next to my bed. I had to ask her, "Is my leg still there?"

"Yes," she replied. "I checked. It's still there. Dr. Masri said that everything went very well. He believes that he got all the cancer."

I spent the next four days in a room that I shared with three other patients. I could have opted for a private room, at $4.00 per day, but I thought it would be more entertaining to have company. The man immediately opposite me rarely ate his food. He just moaned and slept. I mentioned to the nurse that he didn't seem to be eating. "I'm a bit worried about him," I said.

"Don't worry. That's our problem. We'll take care of him."

But he's not eating, I thought. How can he get better if he doesn't eat?

Several tubes ran into and out of my body. I won't go into too much detail except to say that one of them delivered doses of morphine, which I was supposed to administer myself.

"You should not allow the pain to build before squeezing the button," the nurse cautioned. "It's better to prevent pain before it begins."

On the second day of my stay the nurse asked, "How are you feeling?"

"OK, except that my hands are always tingling, and feel kind of numb."

"That's just the morphine taking effect."

To my way of thinking, hands should not tingle and feel numb. I didn't want my hands to tingle and feel numb. I never squeezed the button again. Even without morphine, I didn't experience much pain. I slept most of the time, but when awake, I spent most of my time daydreaming of Colville Lake, while listening to a cassette tape of a musical stream flowing through a mountain meadow – a special gift from Kathleen.

On the third day, a young woman came to teach me how to use crutches, with particular emphasis on going up and down stairs. Everyone should try this sometime. Going up and down stairs on crutches is very challenging, particularly for those who actually need crutches. The experience was humbling. I would need to regain strength quickly so that we could get our food and gear to Hay River by late August.

Dr. Masri stopped by to see me during dinner. "How are you feeling?"

"OK, but my leg is pretty weak. Maybe you can recommend some physiotherapy. We have to get to Hay River by August 25. I need to be stronger by then."

Dr. Masri just chuckled. He still seemed happy. "We generally recommend physiotherapy to those people who need a kick in the butt. I don't think you're going to need physiotherapy."

I generally try not to read too much extra into what people say or do, but I took his words as a good sign.

On my last day, a few hours before checkout, the nurse came by to ask if I wanted to rent the crutches.

"No, thanks," I said.

Now I don't intend this next comment to sound overly dramatic or macho, but I didn't want to use any crutches. Four days ago I walked into this hospital, and I wanted to leave the same way.

The nurse continued. "Well, I can make sure a wheelchair is here to take you down to the parking lot.

"No, thanks," I said. "I'm going to try to walk."

I could mostly dress myself, but couldn't bend over, so Kathleen put my shoes on and tied the laces. We walked slowly down the corridor, toward the elevator and stairwell. "You know, Kathleen. I always take the stairs. I want to take the stairs now, just to see if I can do it."

"There's no need to rush things, Michael. It's three flights down. Besides, you don't want to tear your staples or open your wound."

"That won't happen. I'll be going real slow. Believe me. And at least I'll be going down. Besides, we have stairs at home, and no elevator. I have to be able to go up and down stairs."

Kathleen opened the door for me, and I shuffled through, leaning up against the wall. I reached the stairs, and grabbed the right-hand rail. I felt nauseous. I slid my right foot forward until it dropped over the edge onto the step below. While supporting my weight on the rail, I stepped down with my left foot. I glanced at Kathleen, who looked worried. "I think I can do this, Kathleen. It's going to take a while, though, one step at a time."

I eventually reached the bottom floor, and walked outside into glorious sunshine. "I'm glad that's over, Kathleen. Let's go home. I don't feel so well."

Kathleen opened the middle door of our van, and I crawled onto the seat.

"I can't sit up, Kathleen. I feel sick. I'm gonna lie down on the floor. Don't go too fast, or make any sudden stops."

Thirty minutes later I climbed the stairs up to our bedroom. Kathleen untied my shoelaces and took my shoes off. I finished undressing and struggled into bed. I felt pretty satisfied. I was out of the hospital, and the cancer was allegedly gone. It was still only July 8. We didn't need to get our supplies and gear up to Hay River until August 25. Plenty of time to recover by then.

I spent the next two weeks mostly sleeping late, watching reruns of *Columbo* episodes, eating grilled cheese sandwiches, and dozing on the deck in the afternoon sun. Every two days a young home-care nurse came to my bedroom to change my bandages and to assess my wound, which continued to bleed. The nurse instructed Kathleen and me to empty my hemovac of blood and record the amount of accumulation three times per day. We continued monitoring until July 13, when the bleeding more or less stopped. We also measured the circumference of my swollen leg two times per day, until it reached the size of my healthy leg on July 31.

We had picked up our sled in an industrial area of nearby Burnaby on July 16. My leg was still quite weak, and although the crate and sled weighed only about 34 kg, we had a great deal of difficulty getting it up onto the racks of the van. Despite my frustration, though, we now had all of our winter gear.

Things were going very well, and I appreciated the genuine concern of friends and family. I still have all their get-well cards and letters. I also still have all the correspondence with Bern Will Brown, including the following letter of July 26:

> *Dear Friends;*
>
> *Sorry to hear about your recent illness, Mike, which might influence your winter trip here. I feel that it would be essential for you both to see our Outpost setup before committing yourselves to a winter stay there.*
>
> *Although I did take 200 lbs of propane down by ski-doo in May (for your light & stove), without any means of transportation yourselves I would be obliged to bring in a couple of cords of firewood before freeze-up for your fuel. Otherwise you would be faced with the task using a hand sled. And are you used to using a chain saw?*
>
> *These considerations lead me to discourage you making this sojourn this winter. What do you think?*
>
> *Regards,*
>
> *Bern Will Brown*

What do I think? I'll tell you what I think. I think that I'm going to the cabin in January. I don't really need to see the cabin first. And we have already talked about bringing in firewood before freeze-up anyway. Nothing has really changed. I'll have to get back to Bern about this. But right now I still needed to convince Dr. Masri, whom I visited once a week.

It was now August 10, and we planned to leave for Hay River, three days driving, on August 22. My wound was still bleeding. I still walked with a lot of pain, and a severe limp. Although I was now driving again, I had to lift my right leg up with my hands to get it into the driver's seat of our van. Dr. Masri consistently indicated that he did not support my going to Hay River, and advised against even going to Colville Lake this winter.

Those words depressed me almost as much as the initial news of my cancer. I HAD to go to Colville Lake. I HAD to get my gear to Hay River by August 25. I wasn't sick – just a little weak. No reason to abandon my plans and dreams.

My next meeting with Dr. Masri was scheduled for Wednesday, August 12. That gave me two days to practice walking without limping. I could show Dr. Masri that I was indeed getting better. I made four daily circuits around the backyard, and soon could walk 20 to 30 m, more or less normally, before the pain became too great. This ruse should work.

Kathleen and I arrived at the hospital, and quite coincidentally, saw Dr. Masri at the far end of the hall. It was as though Providence had intervened on my behalf. I went into my practiced walk. Dr. Masri seemed impressed. "You're walking pretty well."

"That's because I am pretty much better. I should have no problem driving to Hay River," I said, planting the idea in his mind.

"Well, come on in, and let's have a look at your leg."

Dr. Masri poked at the back of my thigh, and said, "You know, the swelling has disappeared, but your wound is still bleeding. You're not ready to drive to Hay River, and you're not ready to spend a winter so isolated from medical care. Your leg is still weak. There might be complications. Your liposarcoma was massive – 2.0 kg. We'll have to do more tests to determine if the cancer reappears. I'll need to see you every month for at least a year. You'll need another MRI in six months. I'll ask the nurse to come in and change your bandages."

The nurse came in, and I pleaded my case with her. "I have to go to.

Colville Lake this winter. I might never get another chance. My leg is bleeding less every day, and Kathleen and I change the bandages ourselves anyway. We can do that in Colville Lake. I can get an MRI in December, and then another one in July when we get back. That's not much more than a six-month interval. I'll be fine. I'll come in for tests and checkups when I get back next year. And you know, I don't think Dr. Masri really has the power to prevent me from going, does he?"

The nurse seemed sympathetic to my argument and plight. "I'll talk to Dr. Masri."

She returned a few minutes later and reported that, "Dr. Masri says to enjoy your trip."

We spent the next week busily buying the food that we would need for approximately five-and-one-half months at the cabin, plus one more month on the river. There would be no re-supply once we reached the north end of Colville Lake. Kathleen said that it wasn't difficult to prepare a list of supplies: "I just figured out how much we would need for a week, and then multiplied by the number of weeks we would be away."

It did sound easy. And besides, she knows what she's doing when it comes to food. I'm sure, though, that these few paragraphs don't adequately convey the effort, care and concern expended by Kathleen to ensure that we would remain healthy, that we would be well fed, and that we would enjoy a variety of meals. The potential success of our adventure depended a great deal on Kathleen.

By August 20 we had finally completed most of our shopping. We were still three cans short, though, of crushed and whole tomatoes. Three major grocery suppliers, including Costco and Safeway, had only 37 cans among them. Despite this minor shortfall, we began packing the van. I called North-Wright Airways one more time, and the same pleasant lady assured me that they could store and look after our supplies when the barge arrived. We were ready.

FOOD SUPPLIES FOR COLVILLE LAKE

Item	Amount
Sugar	20 kg
Maple Syrup	5 litres
Crushed & Whole Tomatoes	40 large cans
Scalloped Potatoes	20 packages

Soups	120 packages
Vegetable Oil	4 litres
Margarine	10 kg
Shortening	20 kg
Cheese	10 kg
Dried Fruit	20 kg
Spaghetti, Gravy & Chili Spice	60 packages
Pudding	50 packages
Spaghetti, Macaroni & Pastas	20 kg
Prem & Ham	40 cans
Chicken, Turkey & Corned Beef	60 cans
Salami	5 kg
Sardines, Tuna & Salmon	60 cans
Tea	600 bags
Ground Coffee	4 kg
Chocolate Drink Mix	9 kg
Dried Milk	5 kg
Jam	10 jars
Honey	5 kg
Flour	45 kg
Pancake Mix	10 kg
Corn Meal	6 kg
Oatmeal	8 kg
Granola	3 kg
Peanut Butter	8 kg
Various Dried Beans	9 kg
Assorted Crackers	10 kg
Yeast	2 canisters
Baking Powder	3 kg
Pepper	0.5 kg
Salt	1 kg
Assorted Spices	15 jars

CHAPTER 3

Barging North

On Saturday morning, August 22, Kathleen and I prepared to head up the road to Hay River. Kathleen's brother Frank, and his wife Patricia joined us for our adventure, and they looked forward to their first-ever visit to the Northwest Territories. They had also generously offered to take turns driving. By 9:00 am the four of us had loaded the van with 25 plastic bins, gear and supplies, which filled the back of our vehicle from floor to ceiling. We tied the canoe and sled onto the roof rack, and checked in the house one more time for anything that we might have left behind. Frank and Patricia stuffed themselves into the middle seat, surrounded by bins, blankets, pillows, luggage, sleeping bags and summer tent. I backed the van out of the driveway, and headed east, in the morning sunshine, toward the Trans-Canada Highway.

We planned to spend three days on the road to reach Hay River, a distance of about 2,000 km. On the first night we rented an A-frame cabin in a private campground just north of the British Columbia interior town of Quesnel. I sat before our campfire feeling very contented. On the second day, as we neared Dawson Creek in eastern British Columbia, we approached a highway sign that read 1,400 km to Whitehorse. Damn. Fourteen hundred km to Whitehorse, which Kathleen and I would pass through on our way to Inuvik this winter. That's a heck of a long way! After only two days on the road, I'm already a little tired of driving, and it's still 1,400 km more just to reach Whitehorse. Even in summer, it takes me three days after Whitehorse to reach Inuvik. In winter it would take us even longer.

I am not comfortable or confident driving in snow. My only real experience with winter driving is in Vancouver, where snow and freezing rain often occur together. To me, snow means ice, slippery roads and imminent danger. When I see snow, I immediately slow down to the point where elderly women whiz on by me. I'm not making any statements about elderly women. I'm just saying that I drive painfully slowly in snow. We'll never get to Inuvik in winter.

I was particularly worried about driving the Dempster Highway, which begins at the Klondike Corners in the Yukon, 40 km east of Dawson City. The gravel road then extends north to Inuvik 737 km through very isolated country and over several windswept passes. Services are available only at the Eagle Plains Motel 372 km north of the 'Corners' and at the small community of Fort McPherson, another 180 km farther north. During winter, this would be a very difficult and perhaps dangerous drive for me. Maybe Kathleen and I should take a bus, or maybe hook up with a truck driver. Perhaps a truck driver would like to have company. Kathleen and I would be very happy to share expenses. I made a mental note to call Alan, and ask his advice.

We stopped at the tourist information centre in Dawson Creek to pick up information on accommodation, and read about a bed & breakfast in Peace River, Alberta, only 44 km out of our way. We were all intrigued by the description of an early 1900s, three-storey house originally built for the Northwest Mounted Police. We knocked on the door of *Kozy Quarters*, and were greeted warmly by our host, Irene Kelly, who showed us the available rooms. The frilly, pink-walled room on the third floor, filled with antiques, was by far the most charming. Kathleen and I won the coin toss, and we carried our luggage upstairs to the pink room.

I sat in a soft, comfy chair, enjoying the evening light streaming through the window. We would be in Hay River tomorrow night, and I called North-Wright Airways just to confirm one more time that they could store and look after our supplies when the barge arrived in Norman Wells. A pleasant man answered the telephone. I explained my situation and mentioned my previous two conversations with his female colleague.

"What was her name?" he asked.

"I don't know. She never gave me her name."

"Well, we can't store your gear inside our hangar. We don't have enough space as it is. We would have to leave it outside, in our fenced compound. But we couldn't guarantee its safety, particularly for four months. I can't even guarantee you that we could be there to unload the barge when it arrives. I don't know why anyone here would have told you otherwise."

I thanked the man and hung up. This certainly put a bit of a crimp in our plans. What would we do now? We certainly weren't going to take six months of supplies back home to Vancouver. We would be in Hay River tomorrow. We had to ship our stuff somewhere down the Mackenzie River.

Obviously, our only other choice was to barge our goods all the way to Inuvik, where Alan and Marilyn might be willing to unload and find a place to store 25 plastic bins, one canoe and one sled. This scenario meant an additional 650 km of shipping cost. More importantly, it meant that we would need to charter a plane from Inuvik to Colville Lake, a distance of approximately 350 km. Chartered air service is expensive. At this point, though, we didn't have any other feasible alternatives. On the positive side of the financial ledger, if we barged everything to Inuvik, we would no longer have to fly back to Norman Wells next winter. We could fly, with our supplies, directly to Colville Lake. In fact, with a chartered flight, we could probably land on the frozen lake right in front of our cabin. We would then avoid the cost of hiring someone to transport our supplies and gear from the town of Colville Lake out to the cabin. Kathleen and I liked this plan. In fact, we loved this new plan! By comparison, our old plan appeared needlessly cumbersome. Almost stupid one might say.

I immediately called Alan, who said he would be happy to pick up our gear. "Thanks very much, Alan. Would it be possible to store our stuff in a heated place?"

"Heated space in the winter is very expensive, Mike. I don't think that such a space is even available. Besides, your stuff will be fine."

"Are you sure? We've heard stories that canned goods explode when it gets too cold."

"I've not really heard of that, Mike. People up here store canned goods in the cold all the time. The only problem I've ever heard about is canned milk. Those cans sometimes explode. Juice cartons would also explode. Everything else, which doesn't have so much water in the can, should be fine."

"OK, when we get to Hay River, we'll put everything on the barge for Inuvik."

"I think this is a good idea, Mike. Best to have all of your gear with us, here in Inuvik when you arrive. In fact, I think it would also be best for you to stay with us for the month of January. You could then practice winter camping, and try out all your gear. Marilyn and I agree that this would be better than flying directly to Colville Lake as soon as you get here. You don't really have any previous experience in very cold temperatures. It would be good to get some experience before you go to the cabin."

Of course Alan was right, and I immediately accepted his very generous offer. "Thanks, Alan, we'll do that. We look forward to visiting with you, and in spending some time in Inuvik, which should be very interesting. An adventure in itself! I have to tell you, though, that I'm not looking forward to driving up to Inuvik in the winter, particularly along the Dempster Highway. I'm not very good with snow, and our van, with its long wheel base, fishtails and slides out quite easily. Do you know if truckers coming up to Inuvik might we willing to bring us and our van?"

Alan hesitated for a moment, and then said, "You know Mike, pregnant women here in Inuvik drive down the Dempster all alone in winter, on their way to see doctors in Whitehorse. You say you want to spend the winter out at Colville Lake, but you're worried about driving up?"

"I accept your point Alan, although it's not entirely fair. I'm not worried about myself in the winter. I'm worried about my van. I won't be driving when we're out at Colville. I'll be on snowshoes. I won't be fishtailing or skidding on ice over cliffs."

"All the same, Mike, I think you ought to drive up yourself."

"OK," I replied, "I'll talk to Kathleen about it. Thanks, again, Alan."

After hanging up, Kathleen and I agreed that we would still inquire about the possibility of hiring a trucker to take us up to Inuvik. Neither one of us was happy driving on snow and ice, particularly on the Dempster Highway.

I was on a telephoning roll. I next called Bern, to let him know that we were now planning to arrive on February 1 rather than in early January.

"Good to hear from you, Mike," he said. "But did you get my letter of July 26? I think it's essential that you see the cabin before staying there."

"We have seen the brochures, Bern, and the cabin looks great. We're happy with it."

"But you need to know how to work the wood stove."

"I've used wood stoves before. What's there to know? Don't you just put the wood in and adjust the damper?"

Bern thought for a moment. "That's right, but I still think you shouldn't come until you've seen the cabin."

In fairness to Bern, he knew nothing about me, other than I was some guy from Vancouver. An urbanite. Perhaps I was simply a romantic, and unaware of the very real rigours and challenges of living so isolated and so rustic. He could be thinking that Kathleen and I might give up after the first week. He would then have gone to a great deal of effort for no reason. Worse yet, from his perspective, an inexperienced couple might find themselves in trouble, and needing rescue. Or, Bern simply might have wanted us to be absolutely sure that the cabin met our expectations and comfort levels.

These reasons were all valid, but none of them applied to Kathleen and me. I quickly played my strongest cards. "I appreciate your concern, Bern, but we're going to be putting our gear and supplies on the barge in Hay River on Tuesday to ship them to Inuvik. We're going to spend the winter in some cabin, and if we have to, we'll find another one. We much prefer to stay in your cabin, though. It's at the headwaters of the Anderson River, which we want to paddle. Your brochures looked very nice. I'm sure we'll be happy with the cabin."

"OK, Mike. I'll need to get some cordwood for you. How many cords do you want?"

"How many do you think we'll need?"

"I think two should do it."

"That sounds good."

With today's business now complete, Frank, Patricia, Kathleen and I walked into town for dinner. Things certainly seem to be coming together.

The next morning, after a fantastic breakfast that included fresh home-made biscuits, we drove to Hay River, nearly 600 km north. We arrived in the late afternoon, planning to stay at a bed & breakfast that Irene had recommended. We had thoroughly enjoyed staying at *Kozy Quarters*, arguably the best B&B we had ever visited. We called the number given to us by Irene, and were told to go downtown, to a bar, to pick up the key. Although surprised to be picking up a B&B key at a bar, we drove off as instructed. Inside, the man behind the bar indicated that he didn't know anything about a key. We persevered though, and pointed to the information written down by Irene. The name seemed familiar to him.

"Just a minute," he said, "I'll be right back." Moments later he handed us a small piece of paper, on which were written an address and directions. "You can get the key there."

"Is this the address for the B&B?"

"No, it's where you can get the key."

We climbed back into the van, rolled off to a suburban street, and parked in front of the house indicated by our instructions. This certainly didn't seem like a B&B. Patricia and I knocked on the door, while Frank and Kathleen waited in the van.

A young woman greeted us, and thrust a key at Patricia. "There's no one at the bed & breakfast," she said. "Let yourself in, and pick any room you like."

"Will someone be coming by in the morning to cook breakfast? What time would that be?"

"There's no one there," she repeated. "Here's a loaf of bread for toast. There's butter and jam in the refrigerator."

After that, we always referred to our Hay River accommodation as a 'bed & bread.' The building was essentially a two-storey dormitory, with a kitchen in the centre of the first floor. Partial loaves of bread filled the refrigerator. Perhaps the worst B&B we had ever visited. On the plus side though, the shores of Great Slave Lake beckoned from just across the road. We collected driftwood for a fire, cooked hotdogs on the beach, and watched the Northern Lights flicker above us when darkness finally arrived.

The next morning we drove out to the Northern Transportation Company dock, and began unloading our supplies and gear onto pallets. I much appreciated Frank's skill at organizing and marking everything for shipment down the Mackenzie River. His management background in the helicopter industry shone through. With Frank at the helm, we completed our task efficiently, and were done before noon.

Our 25 plastic bins, plus one canoe and one sled would soon be heading down river toward Inuvik, over 1,550 km away. The total cost to barge 585 kg of groceries and gear was only $225.00 – a fantastic price, I thought. Our supplies would enjoy a leisurely journey on the river, with the expected arrival date sometime in late September or early October. Before heading back south, we spent a comfortable afternoon driving to and visiting Fort Providence, west of Great Slave Lake, on the Mackenzie River. We ended our very successful day in the Lady Evelyn Falls campground, high above the Kakisa

River. Frank and Patricia set up house in the back of the empty van. I lay in our tent, next to Kathleen, snug in my sleeping bag, relishing my now inevitable winter escape.

The next morning we headed south, back into northern Alberta. We intended to camp again that evening, as the weather remained warm and dry. Approximately 100 km north of the turnoff to Peace River, the van began to act strangely. During acceleration it no longer seemed to shift easily into the next higher gear, particularly when going uphill. I wasn't really sure, but something certainly did seem amiss. When I stopped at a small restaurant-gas station for our afternoon coffee break, I asked Frank, who knows about engines, if he noticed anything unusual.

"I think there's something wrong with the transmission, Mike. The shifting seems very sluggish."

"That's what I think too. It's still a long way to Vancouver. I hope we can make it."

Back in the van, the problem became much worse. The automatic transmission no longer shifted into fourth gear. This was not good, as we were still about 50 km from Peace River, the nearest community that would likely have a mechanic. If we could get to Peace River, either on our own or by calling a tow truck, we could spend another night at Irene's bed & breakfast. That wouldn't be so bad.

We limped into Peace River, and stopped at the first service station we could find, the *All-Rite Transmission* shop on 102nd Avenue. We explained our story, and the mechanic drove our van away for a test drive. He returned to confirm that "your transmission is toast."

"How long will it take to fix it?"

"Well, first of all, you need to decide if you want a new transmission, which is pretty expensive, or a rebuilt transmission."

"How long does a rebuilt transmission last?"

"Hard to say. Depending on how you treat it. Rebuilts can last as long as a new one."

I looked over at Frank, who nodded in agreement.

"I'm happy with a rebuilt transmission. How long will it take to put it in?" I asked.

"Well, that's the problem. I don't have one. It's already late Wednesday afternoon. I can order one right away, but it might not get here until

Saturday, and I don't work on Sundays, so I might not be able to get to it until Monday."

Every day seemed to be bringing a new adventure. Frank and Patricia didn't seem too worried by this news, though, and we all looked forward, with genuine eagerness, to another few nights at Irene's bed & breakfast. Besides, this would give us time to explore the town of Peace River, an agreeable community of approximately 6,000 people.

"Can we drive the van to Irene's, to unload all our luggage, and then come back in the morning, or should we leave the van here?"

"You can drive. You will just be stuck in first gear."

By now we all felt pretty relaxed. Patricia had already confirmed with Irene that our rooms were available. We motored on over, almost stately, to find Irene and her daughter preparing a backyard BBQ for us.

The next morning we slept late, and straggled downstairs, more or less one at a time, for breakfast. While I sat sipping my third cup of coffee, a knock came at the back porch. Irene swung the door open to reveal a man with a very broad smile on his face.

"Irene, I was walking down the alley, and smelled fresh-baked muffins through your open window. Do you have any left?"

"Come on in, there's plenty for everyone. I'd like you to meet my guests."

It was just like being in Aunt Bee's kitchen on the old *Andy Griffith of Mayberry* television show. The down-home charm continued as we strolled down the street for lunch later that afternoon. I kid you not when I say that three people – strangers to us – actually crossed the street to say hello, knowing that we were visitors in town. Yes, spending a few days in Peace River was going to be very enjoyable.

After lunch we headed home to relax in Irene's backyard. We decided to cross the street, to walk in the shade on the other side. Kathleen stepped off the uneven curb awkwardly, and slipped to the pavement. She stood up, hands on hip, arching her back.

"Are you all right?"

"I think so. I've wrenched my back just a little. But I'll be fine."

We continued slowly back toward our *Kozy Quarters*. All the while, Kathleen's face showed signs of increasing pain. By the time we reached home she could barely walk. She struggled upstairs and lay down on the bed. "I should be OK after I rest, but it hurts just lying down."

While cooking another BBQ for us that evening, Irene fretted over Kathleen, who sat stretched out on the lawn chair, barely moving. Later that night, in bed, Kathleen lay wide awake, stiff with pain, staring up at the ceiling. She tried to get up, to go to the bathroom, one flight down from our bedroom. She could barely move, so I carried her down, and then back up the stairs. Here we were – the pair of us – leaning up against the wall for support. Me with one good leg, only recently able to walk without a limp. Kathleen with a very bad back, unable to walk at all. Our gear was on the barge, headed down to Inuvik for our winter escape only four months away. Four months is a long time, and we would certainly be better by then. Nevertheless, as we struggled, somewhat heroically, I might say, just to reach an indoor toilet, our current weakness contrasted ironically with our future life of physical challenges at Colville Lake.

I'm an early riser, and went downstairs at 6:30, to chat with Irene as she prepared breakfast.

"How's Kathleen this morning?" she asked.

"She's getting worse," I said. "I don't think she'll be coming down for breakfast."

"Does she have any medication?"

"No," I replied. "She's never had this kind of problem before. I don't really know what she should do."

"Well, I do," Irene said. "Robaxacet is what she should get. The pharmacy doesn't open until 9:30, but I know the pharmacist is there at 8:00 am, working in the back. I'll call him then, and tell him that you'll be coming down right away to pick up your medicine. I'll write down what you need. Just give him my instructions."

At 7:50 am, Frank and I drove to the drugstore in Irene's car. At 8:05 the pharmacist handed us a small bag of the requested medicine. Almost like making a clandestine drug deal. Almost, but not quite. Or so I assume.

On Friday afternoon the mechanic called to say that, "the rebuilt transmission arrived yesterday afternoon, and your van is ready. You can pick it up anytime."

We decided to wait until Saturday morning, when we could get a full day's travel behind us.

Frank and I were up early. At the breakfast table, Irene insisted that we take her car to the transmission shop to pick up our van: "It'll be easier for me than driving you myself." You gotta love Irene.

Two hours later we were packed, and had lifted Kathleen into her seat.

Irene wished us well, and handed Kathleen a soft but firm back support. "You'll need this for the ride home," she said.

We thanked Irene for taking such good care of us, and then headed south toward Vancouver. We stopped in Mackenzie, a small logging town, to inspect a vacant rental apartment owned by Frank and Patricia.

Kathleen spent the night stretched out on the hard, bare floor. "I feel more comfortable than lying on a mattress or a couch," she said. You gotta admire Kathleen's stoic determination and perseverance.

We reached our Vancouver home the following night, a little tired, a little broken, but content that our gear and supplies were heading north to Inuvik. Only four months now before we head north ourselves.

CHAPTER 4

And Now We Wait

We spent the time before Christmas dealing with a few remaining and important items. In a letter of September 5, Bern wrote that he:

> *flew three local natives down to the Outpost [which is what Bern called our cabin] this week, and spent two days there getting your two cords of dry wood, which I will cut up into stove-lengths when I am there over freeze-up.... Yesterday, I had Margaret buy you ten, 1-gallon tins of naptha for use in Coleman lamps & stove, both of which will be available... I want to send you by mail the duplicate front door key so you can get another made. The bill for the naptha is enclosed = $48.79. Being there for six weeks this fall will give me a chance to do routine maintenance work.*

On September 16, I sent Bern five post-dated cheques in the amount of $1,000 each for rental of the cabin for the months of February, March, April, May and June of 1999. In the covering letter I reported that our supplies barged to Inuvik "already include naptha for Coleman lamps and stoves. I appreciate, however, your additional supplies of naptha left at the cabin. We will certainly reimburse you for all of your naptha that we may use."

The next day I received another letter from Bern, dated September 12, in which he indicated that he and Margaret were leaving by boat for the 'outpost' in a day or two, and would be staying there until the new lake ice could support their sled, dogs and ski-doo. His letter also stated that he had enclosed:

one of our two keys for the front door of the outpost cabin.
Kindly have it duplicated and return (the) original. I will also
screw plywood over the front door of the cabin so you will
have to carry a Phillips screwdriver with you. I'll cut up all the
firewood while there.

Bern was certainly efficient and business-like. This was good, and another reason why I was happy to pay $1,000 per month. We took the key down to the mall and into the small store that made duplicates. We handed the key to the man behind the counter, who studied it rather intently. A little too intently for my liking. His interest made me feel a tad uncomfortable.

The man rotated the key in his hand and said, "This is an unusual size – very short. I haven't seen anything like this for quite a while. Don't know if I have any blanks that can duplicate this."

I wasn't feeling any better. But at least I had the original. That was something.

"I'll see what I can do," the man said. He searched through his rows of blank keys and finally selected one to place on the grinder. A few minutes later he handed the original and a pair of duplicate keys back to me. "Here. I made two. I'm not sure that either will work. If they don't, just bring them all back, and I'll try again."

"OK," I replied.

I didn't bother trying to explain that it would be impossible to bring the keys back from the north end of Colville Lake. I wasn't too worried, though. As I said, I had the original key.

On September 24 I sent a letter to Bern that included the two new duplicate keys. I also explained why I had kept the original key, and thanked him for his advice about the Phillips screwdriver. I concluded by saying, "Whenever I travel in the bush I always carry a variety of tools, including a Phillips screwdriver, a Robertson screwdriver and a slot screwdriver. You never know when you will need one." I intended this factual statement to help convince Bern that we knew what we were doing, and that he didn't need to worry about us.

We heard from Marilyn Fehr on October 1 that she had picked up our supplies in Inuvik. She and Alan stored the 25 plastic bins in an unheated shed at a Parks Canada compound, and took the sled and canoe back to their house. All goods looked to be in good order, except that they "seemed to be missing number 9, 18 and 26."

On the phone, I told Alan that number 26 was the sled, and that number 9 was a green plastic bin. Number 18 was a large plastic container, about twice as large as the others. "I hope it's there, Alan, as it had our axe, saws, sacks of flour, and other larger items. It was on pallet number two, probably near the bottom."

"We'll look again, Mike."

On October 23 we ordered two muskrat RCMP-style hats from the Winnipeg Fur Exchange. That day we also went shopping for Sorel boots, looking particularly for the *Glacier* model rated to minus 73 degrees. Not as cold as it gets on earth, but pretty close. Kathleen and I both tried on a pair of the black versions. Very bulky at nearly 2.5 kg per pair.

"I don't like these," Kathleen said. "I look like Frankenstein's monster."

"So what? Who will see?"

"I will, and I don't like them."

We trundled over to the next outdoor store on our list, where Kathleen tried on a pair of white *Glacier* Sorels. She grinned, obviously pleased. Now she looked like the wife of Frankenstein's monster. Much better, apparently. We bought them.

On December 2, Bern called to say that, "We need to have daily contact when you're at the cabin, Mike, and the SSBx radio isn't working. I need to get it fixed."

"Don't worry about it, Bern. I don't feel that we need to have daily contact. I think we'll be fine without the radio. Kathleen and I have often spent 4 to 6 weeks on isolated northern canoe trips. We are used to living on our own."

"No, Mike. We need to have daily contact. I need to know that everything is all right. I have checked, and there is a place in Victoria that can fix the radio. I will send it down to them. You can pick it up when it's ready. Since the radio is for your safety, you can pay half the cost, which should be about $500.00. What do you think?"

I didn't really think I had a choice. Bern demanded that we have a radio, essentially as a condition for renting the cabin. He also thought that I should pay half. So be it. Because I wanted to start out on a good footing with Bern, I should obviously pay my share of the repair bill.

"Sure, Bern, that sounds fair to me. Send the radio down. We'll see that it gets fixed."

On December 3, Bern wrote the following letter:

Dear Michael;

Following our telephone conversation today, I phoned RACAL CANADA INC., and they will try to make all the repairs I've indicated, but will not accept VISA. Therefore, if you will kindly pay them, I could reimburse you. Let me know when the SSB radio is repaired and if not hold it until I locate an alternate radio repair shop.

Best Regards,

Bern

Kathleen and I took the ferry to Victoria on December 15 and picked up the radio. The guy behind the counter said, "I'm sure it's working, but you will need to get it tested."

"Can't you test it?"

"No. We're not licensed or set up to use the frequencies that your radio sends and receives. You have to get it tested by someone in the region where you will be using the radio."

"Oh. I didn't know that. Thanks." The radio continued to be a nuisance, despite its new $500.00 clean bill of health.

Our health had also improved substantially since returning from Hay River. Kathleen's back seemed completely cured, while my leg continued to make progress. My wound no longer bled, and I could step up into the driver's seat without lifting my leg with my hands. It was good that Dr. Masri didn't live next door, however. I walked with a distinct limp, with some pain and obvious weakness.

We now had only one more major item to address before leaving – how to avoid driving up the Dempster Highway. We quickly learned that no buses went to Inuvik, so that left finding a trucker as the only possibility remaining to us. I called a casual acquaintance, a member of our canoe club, who ran a trucking business. I think he had two small trucks that operated in southern British Columbia and Alberta. He gave us his opinion that most truckers normally don't go up the Dempster in the week or two after Christmas. Moreover, no truck goes up empty.

"What would be the point of that?" he asked.

I had to agree. There would be no point in going up empty. No buses. No trucks. It looks like Kathleen and I would be driving ourselves up the Dempster Highway to Inuvik.

When we had ordered our new van in 1990, I requested that it be shipped with a block heater. The salesman said that he never brings vehicles to Vancouver with block heaters. "You won't need a block heater, here. Why do you want one?"

Even then I knew that someday I would be going north for the winter. I knew that I would need a block heater. Now was my first opportunity to use it. The next day I took our van in for snow tires, servicing and general maintenance.

"Please check all the fluids and hoses. We're going to Inuvik on January First. The antifreeze should be good to minus 40 degrees, and I need winter oil."

I also asked the mechanic to confirm that the block heater actually worked. His answer of, "I don't know how," surprised me. I guess he doesn't come across many block heaters. Problem was, I didn't know how either.

I called Alan, who said, "Just plug it in. You can usually hear it. Or, you can place your hand on the block and feel some warmth."

Alan says he shares that story with his northern friends to this very day. Apparently he was amused about how little his Southern friends actually knew about winter.

We were about to find out. On December 31 we packed the van with axe, wall tent, sleeping bags, candles, wood stove, winter clothing, food, snow shovel, chains and other survival equipment that we might need should we break down on the Dempster Highway. For additional weight over the rear axle I also added two large bags of cat litter for Alan's friend in Inuvik. I was not looking forward to the drive.

CHAPTER 5

To the End of the Road

We left Vancouver, heading north, into the first dawn of 1999. Kathleen and I drove silently, beneath clear skies. The Trans-Canada Highway through the Fraser Canyon was bare and only slightly wet from last night's rain – a good start for us. The first snow patches on the road appeared just north of Quesnel. From there we travelled on packed snow all the way to Prince George, which we reached just as night fell. We're doing very well. In fact, even in summer, we usually do not travel as far as Prince George on the first day.

We stayed that night at the *Chalet Sans Souci* Bed & Breakfast – a very cute residence, known locally as 'The Gingerbread House,' built and operated by our very hospitable hosts, Jacqueline and Lutz Klaar. After settling in, we drove a few kilometres north into town for dinner at *Earl's Restaurant*. Snow began to fall halfway through our meal. As Vancouverites, Kathleen and I began to fret. Everyone else in the restaurant, however, seemed oblivious to the impending disaster outside. As calmly as we could, we finished both our entrée and dessert and drove back to our B&B without incident.

At breakfast the next morning I talked with Lutz about the recent servicing of our vehicle. "Say, Lutz, maybe you can answer a question for me. When picking up our van, I noticed on the invoice that 10–30 oil had been put in, the same oil weight that we always use in summer. This didn't seem right to me. What kind of oil do people use here in the winter?"

Lutz replied that "Where you're going, with very cold temperatures, you should have a lighter winter oil. If I were you, I would stop at a service station and change the oil."

We took his advice before heading up the road in mid-morning. We expected to reach Fort St. John by early evening. First though, we would need to cross the Rocky Mountains through the Pine Pass, at an elevation of 935 m. Later on, just west of Fort St. John, we would climb up and out of the Peace River Valley on a narrow, steep and winding road. Both of these obstacles were much less fearsome than the ominous Dempster Highway. Nevertheless, I began to worry.

We travelled on packed snow with more snow falling until mid-afternoon. Pine Pass had been plowed and cleared. Very nice. The rise up to the pass was much shorter than I had remembered. Certainly much shorter than I had visualized all morning. The climb out of the Peace River proved equally uneventful. The van performed very well, with no fishtailing. All that worry for nothing. Maybe winter driving isn't all that bad after all.

We stayed in an old, somewhat tired motel right along the highway in Fort St. John. The evening temperature had dipped to -19 degrees, and we decided to wear our new mukluks for our short walk to the adjacent fast-food restaurant. Although Kathleen and I both felt very self-conscious, no one stared or even seemed to notice our traditional, northern footwear.

We left Fort St. John on January 3 at 7:15 am beneath a lightly overcast sky. Still dark, and -18 degrees. The sky soon cleared to reveal a full moon. The pre-dawn twilight bathed the snow-covered trees in a slightly golden luminescence. As the sun rose, the entire horizon glowed pink. A very enchanting start to our third day of travel.

We had covered 1,320 km on our first two days of travel, which put us on the Alaska Highway. We would now be driving through a much more isolated, often mountainous landscape, but expected to reach Toad River, 565 km away, in northern British Columbia, before nightfall.

Unfortunately, we drove all day in snowstorms – and on roads covered in snow. If there had been any elderly women drivers on the highways, they would certainly have whizzed right on by me. Mostly, though, we encountered 18-wheelers, travelling fast, creating whiteout conditions for us whenever they passed. Our first hard day of winter driving.

Finally, more than an hour after dark, we approached the bridge leading into Toad River, which consisted primarily of a rustic motel/restaurant/gas station, plus a few scattered outbuildings. From previous trips I knew that the road made a sharp right turn as it climbed up onto the metal-surfaced bridge. I suddenly had those old visions. Those recurring visions of our van fishtailing out of control. Just like in Vancouver, I slowed way down. To this day, Kathleen said that at times it seemed like we were standing still or actually going backwards. What can I say? I was tired. It had been a difficult day for me.

We eventually crossed the bridge and drove up to the lodge, where we booked a tiny, clean and comfortable room. We rested a bit, and then walked out in our stocking feet to the small dining area. In the booth next to us sat a mother and her two young children. It was Sunday, the end of the weekend. They were on their way to the Liard River Hot Springs, for an evening soak, after which they would return home. What makes this anecdote interesting is that they lived in Fort Nelson. What makes this story even more interesting is that the Liard River Hot Springs lie slightly more than 300 km west of Fort Nelson.

So I think you get the picture. I had struggled mightily all day to cover 565 km. I am beat. This family beside us, though, would travel more than 600 km round trip, in the middle of winter, just for an hour's soak. Probably laughing, joking and singing all along the way. Snow doesn't bother this young woman. At least she's not pregnant, though. That would be even more humbling for me.

Just as our dinner arrived, a young couple, also staying at the Toad River Lodge, sat down at the booth recently vacated by the Fort Nelson family. They were restless, agitated, and immediately began telling their story. The United States military had transferred him from his base in Florida to a new assignment in Anchorage, Alaska. As an adventure they decided to drive, rather than to fly. Before leaving they had been told, by Floridians (probably by people who didn't know how to tell whether or not a block heater worked), that snow tires weren't necessary. "The roads will be fine," they were told. [I don't know how Floridians would know about winter road conditions in northern British Columbia. I'm just telling you this story as it was told to me.]

Just about an hour ago, 24 km south of Toad River, the young couple were passing an 18-wheeler on a narrow, uphill climb above a river. They hit a patch of ice and tumbled over the side, apparently severely damaging the passenger side of their vehicle. Tomorrow they would return with their towed vehicle to Fort Nelson. Tonight they were blaming everyone but themselves.

"The government shouldn't have let us drive here in the winter. Those people in Florida should have known better about the roads. Some of these roads aren't even paved. It's dangerous."

Yeah, I thought. It can be dangerous. It can be very dangerous to pass 18-wheelers on dark, narrow, windy, icy mountain roads. It can be very hazardous to drive in northern British Columbia during winter as though you were in southern Florida in summer. Why did you do that? Perhaps you should have been more patient, and not have tried to pass the truck.

I tried to cheer them up – to get them to relax. "You know, you're actually pretty lucky. Your dog is not hurt. Neither of you is hurt. Your car will be fixed in a few days, and you will eventually get to Anchorage. Not so bad, you know."

They remained undeterred, though. "The government shouldn't have let us drive to Alaska in winter. They need to get us back to Florida, to see our families, and then fly us to Anchorage."

The next morning after breakfast we rolled away from Toad River at about 9:00 am. Not an early start, but sunrise was at about 9:30, and I preferred to drive during daylight. A little bit warmer than yesterday morning, at -14 degrees. Just north of the Liard River Hot Springs, seven bison stood next to the highway, grazing placidly in the snow, which continued to fall all day long.

We were making very slow progress, and tentatively decided to stop in Watson Lake, in the Yukon, a distance of only 320 km from Toad River. With 1500 people, Watson Lake was the only 'large' community between us and Whitehorse, which lay another 430 km beyond Watson Lake.

After lunch I told Kathleen that I felt pretty good about the driving conditions. "I know we're not going very fast, but we're making progress. I'm not too tired. Maybe we can go a little farther than Watson Lake."

Kathleen looked skeptical. "There's no reason to push it, Michael. Watson Lake is a good place to stop. We know there are several hotels and restaurants. There's also grocery stores where we can get more food for lunches. We need to shop, which will take some time. We might as well stay."

She made good points, but I offered a compromise. "Well, if we get there soon enough to shop, that's just like a rest. We can then go on if we agree."

Kathleen still looked skeptical. "Well, OK, but only if we agree. OK?"

"OK."

We reached Watson Lake at about 3:45. I still felt good, and apparently had forgotten about the pact that I had struck with Kathleen less than two hours ago. Without saying anything, I surreptitiously continued driving west, out of town.

My ruse hadn't worked, though. "What are you doing, Michael? I thought we were going to stop in Watson Lake!"

She sounded somewhat agitated, perhaps even irritated.

"I'm not tired, Kathleen. I think we can easily get to that little motel that we read about in the accommodation guide."

"But we agreed to talk about it first."

"It's less than an hour away. It would be good to get there. It would be good to put in some more distance."

Sunset in early January at 60 degrees north latitude occurs just after 4:00 pm. Night was beginning and the snow continued to fall. Poor visibility, but I pressed on. Seconds later an on-coming 18-wheeler showered us with swirling snow. Poor visibility became no visibility. I couldn't see the road. I couldn't see the side of the road. This is not good. A second on-coming 18-wheeler continued our whiteout conditions. I couldn't see to go forward, yet I dare not go too slowly in case more 18-wheelers were coming up from behind. They might not see me until too late to stop. This is very bad.

"We have to turn around, Michael!" Yes, she definitely sounded agitated and irritated.

But there was nowhere to turn around. No exits. No pullouts. I drove on, very much wishing that I had stopped. Very much regretting that I had 'forgotten' about my pact with Kathleen. Finally there appeared a gated road to the right. Just enough room for me to nose in, back out on to the highway, and head back to Watson Lake. I was a very happy and appropriately apologetic person when we checked into the hotel room.

We agreed to get an early start, and left Watson Lake on January 5 at 7:00 am. The small, roadside motel I had been headed for the previous night was closed for the winter. Kathleen didn't say anything as we passed by. The first light appeared at 8:15, and the sky turned pink-purple at 9:40. The sun rose above the mountains at 10:15, as we moved easily along a plowed highway beneath brilliantly blue sky. Easy driving. It felt good to be on the road.

We stopped for gas at one of the very few, small communities along this section of the Alaska Highway. We enjoyed a cup of coffee, paid our bill and returned to the van. My stomach sank when I noticed green fluid leaking from our radiator onto the snow. Damn! I just had the van serviced. Why is this happening to me? We trudged back inside and asked if there was a mechanic available.

"Not in the winter. There's no mechanic anywhere around here."

"But my radiator is leaking. Is there anybody that might have a look at it for me?"

"There is a guy renting that cabin down the hill. He's good with cars. He might be able to help you. But I don't think he's around right now. He sort of comes and goes. Besides, we don't have any radiators here. You probably can't get a new radiator until you get to Whitehorse. You could go back to Watson Lake. It's closer."

I didn't like either of these two alternatives. Certainly I wouldn't want to give up the valuable ground I've gained by going back to Watson Lake. And besides, I might not make it to either Whitehorse or Watson Lake with a leaking radiator. I'd rather stay here than break down along the highway.

"I've had leaking radiators before. I used to pour in that grayish kind of powder that comes in small cans. I don't know what it's called. It seems to work, though. Do you have anything like that?"

"Yeah, I have one can left. Two bucks."

I poured it in, headed northwest to Whitehorse, and hoped for the best.

We reached Whitehorse in the early afternoon, where we again stopped for coffee and gas. The radiator seemed to be working fine. We had not overheated at all. We agreed (yes, we agreed) to press on, rather than looking for a mechanic, or inquiring about new radiators. The weather had been getting colder all day. The thermometer at the gas station read -31 degrees.

We intended to stay that night at the Braeburn Lodge. This iconic institution of rustic cabins and café – well known for its cinnamon buns – lay approximately halfway between Whitehorse and Carmacks, a distance of about 85 km. We arrived about 3:30, just after the sun dropped below the mountains. Perfect timing. We walked inside to the warmth of a wood fire and the delicious aroma of fresh baking. Very inviting. We were looking forward to this.

"So would you like a menu?" the man behind the counter asked.

"Not right now. We'd like to get a room first, and then come back for dinner."

"I can't rent you a room. I've got no running water in the cabins."

"Do you have an outhouse? We'd be happy with that. We don't have to have running water."

"No. I can sell you food, but I can't rent you a room."

I was a little surprised by the unyielding attitude, which I suppose had something to do with government health regulations. But it was cold outside, nearly dark, and still almost 75 km to Carmacks. I was more than a little surprised and disappointed to be turned away.

We continued on slowly in the dark toward Carmacks, a town of about 400 people. The only hotel, with its downstairs smoke-filled bar, was noisy and uninviting. On the foyer bulletin board we read a flyer advertising the *Mukluk Manor Bed & Breakfast*. You gotta like a bed & breakfast called mukluk. I called the number and asked if they had any rooms.

"We're not really open this time of year. You can stay, but we're not set up to serve breakfast."

"We'll be right over!"

Our hosts, whose names I cannot remember, led us downstairs to a self-contained suite. Very luxurious, comfortable and roomy. Like having our own apartment. We turned on the TV to the weather channel, which forecast increasing cold for the Whitehorse-Carmacks-Dawson City area.

We spent Wednesday, January Sixth in Carmacks. Not because we decided to take a break from the road, but because our key would not turn in the van's ignition. Overnight the temperature had dropped to -46 degrees, and the van completely froze up. Perhaps the van still had residual moisture in the ignition from its normal life on the coast. Our *Mukluk Manor* host draped a tarp over our vehicle, and placed a small electrical heater inside the tent-like structure. "Maybe this will thaw your ignition. I've seen it work before," he said.

Carmacks sits at the junction of the North Klondike and Robert Campbell Highways, where the Nordenskiold River joins the Yukon River. We viewed our predicament as an opportunity to try out our winter gear, and to explore walking on ice. We donned our mukluks, layers of wool, canvas wind suits and Mountie-style fur hats and strolled about one km down the Nordenskiold River to where it joins the Yukon. Along the way we investigated cracks and odd-looking, yellowish discolourations in the ice. At the confluence we stared, somewhat in wonder, at the large ridges and hummocks created by differential freezing rates and overflow between the two rivers.

We strolled back along the road, toward the Mukluk Manor, very pleased with how warm we actually felt, even at -50 degrees Fahrenheit [I switched from Celsius to Fahrenheit here because -50 F sounds so much more impressive than a mere -46 C.] We particularly loved our mukluks. We were two happy people with warm feet, prancing along as though in bedroom slippers, just like the Conovers promised.

As we neared home, a passing car slowed, and the driver rolled down the window. "Do you need a ride?" he asked.

"No, thank you. We're just out for a walk."

We weren't trying to be flippant. We were indeed out for a walk.

The driver, however, seemed put off by our response. While rolling up his window he replied, rather disdainfully as he enunciated each word, "It – is – minus – forty – five – you – know."

We know. That's why we're out walking.

Back at the *Mukluk Manor*, the key still refused to turn in the ignition.

"I don't think it's going to work," our hosts reported. "I think you should call the garage, and have the tow truck come out. His garage is heated, and your van can thaw out overnight."

So we called the tow truck, and happily prepared for another night in our suite. Our hosts, ever gracious, said, "We won't charge you as much for the second night, as you didn't really intend to stay."

Now that is Northern Hospitality.

It turns out that several vehicles had been towed in for thawing before ours, which wasn't ready until 2:00 pm the next day. Even at this relatively late hour for us, we decided to head for Dawson City, 350 km away. We had always enjoyed our summer visits to Dawson City, and wanted to experience its winter ambience. We would have nearly two hours of sunlight for driving, and I was well rested.

Our hosts made us promise to call when we reached Pelly Crossing, about one third of the way to Dawson City, just to let them know that we were OK. I think they said something like, "no one goes out on the roads in this kind of weather." Kathleen and I were both eager to get going, though. We had been stopped too long.

Twenty km before reaching Pelly Crossing we started to experience the unwelcome effects of severe cold. Even with the heater at full strength, no heat seemed to be entering the cab. The *inside* of the windshield began icing over from the condensation of our own breath, and I had difficulty seeing the road even only a few metres ahead.

I had heard about this possibility, and had brought some cardboard to use as a homemade 'winter front,' a remedy about which I had read. All I needed to do was jam the cardboard in between the grill and the radiator. I had never done this before, nor had I ever seen it done before. I had only read about it. With our windshield rapidly becoming opaque, the job had to be done right.

So when we pulled into the combination gas station/grocery store/cafe/video game parlour at Pelly Crossing, which claims to be the coldest place in the Yukon Territory, I walked toward the large building to seek help. The thermometer on the wall registered exactly -50 degrees Celsius. Just inside the front door I encountered an elderly man sitting at a table, grinning at me.

"Pretty cold today," he said. "Minus 60."

I'm pretty sure he meant Fahrenheit, still clinging to those old Imperial units. Minus 50 C equals minus 58 F. So one might as well round up to minus 60. It sounds mighty impressive. Even to this day, that remains the coldest temperature I have ever experienced.

At the counter stood an RCMP officer paying for his purchases. A man of experience. A public servant. Here I stood. A man of inexperience. A member of the public. A match, as they say, made in heaven. Certainly he would like to assist me with my piece of cardboard. I walked up, said hello, told him about my windshield icing over on the inside, and asked, "Do you think it would help if I stuffed a piece of cardboard between the grill and the radiator?" I had posed my question in a sort of pathetic, helpless kind of way – thinking – even hoping – that he would do it for me.

He looked at me with an unconcerned expression, and said, "It might. You can always try."

Kathleen wasn't having any better success with making a phone call to our *Mukluk Manor* hosts in Carmacks. There was no indoor pay phone, and while I had been bantering with the Mountie she had tried using the outside pay phone. She now stood beside me to report, "The phone didn't work. The keys were frozen. I couldn't press individual keys anyway with my big mitts on. I even took my mitts off, and tried poking the keys with my wool gloves, but then my fingers didn't work."

The girl behind the counter said, "It's way too cold out there. Here, use the store's phone."

So, while Kathleen made the promised phone call, I crawled under the van and jockeyed the cardboard in between the grill and radiator. I seemed to get it positioned and secured reasonably well after only three attempts. The important lesson learned was that I could be reasonably functional at -50 degrees if properly dressed. Vehicles and other kinds of modern, mechanical conveniences such as telephones give up long before that. We drove away and the windshield eventually did defrost, more or less. The interior of the van remained very cold, however, and we rode fully dressed in our long underwear, parkas, mitts and Mountie hats.

It was now dark, and four o'clock. We agreed to abandon our plan to stay in Dawson City, and would instead get a room at the Klondike Corners, the beginning of the Dempster Highway. Dawson would take us 40 km each way out of our way. And, at my current speed of 20 km/hour [I was still having difficulty seeing, and with driving on snow], the trip to Dawson would add two additional hours of driving tonight.

Finally, at 8:00 pm, after having seen no other vehicles on the road since Pelly Crossing, a tall, beautiful, brilliantly-lighted outdoor Christmas tree, like a welcoming beacon, emerged from the darkness. We were at the Klondike Corners.

The motel/restaurant/gas station was just now closing, but the owner welcomed us inside. "I would have left the door unlocked, even after closing up. You could have let yourself in. I can't cook any more meals, but I can heat up some leftover chicken. Show yourself into any of the rooms."

The temperature had 'warmed' to -47 degrees. I remained worried, though, about my van. I asked the owner if his garage were heated. "Can I keep my van in there, so the ignition doesn't freeze up again?"

"I'm afraid I don't have enough room. I have to keep my tow trucks warm in case there's an emergency out on the highway. Sorry."

"That's OK. It will probably be fine."

Kathleen and I carried our suitcases inside, and a few minutes later I began uncoiling my frozen extension cord to plug in the block heater. The owner came up to me to say, "I've rearranged my trucks. There's room in the garage now."

"Thanks very much. I really appreciate it. I'm happy to pay for the heated parking. Can you add it to my room bill?"

"Just park on the far right-hand side," he said. "Good thing you didn't go into Dawson. There's no garage open in the winter in Dawson. If you had frozen, you would have stayed frozen. No charge for parking in my garage."

Now that is Northern Hospitality.

Back inside I waited at the counter while the owner filled out the paper work for our room. He looked up and said, "You know, at these temperatures I don't feel right charging normal rates for rooms. You get my 'minus 40 rate,' which is $40.00."

Need I say it again? Yes. Now that is Northern Hospitality.

The dining room was now closed, so I carried our re-heated chicken dinner to our room, where Kathleen had been organizing our stuff, including our gift of two bottles of wine for Marilyn and Alan. We brought them inside every night so that they wouldn't freeze. During today's cold journey Kathleen had kept them under her front passenger seat, nearest to the heat.

"Guess what, Michael," she said. Both bottles of wine were frozen solid. The corks had nearly popped right out. Good thing we didn't buy twist-top-lid wine.

Now that was cold. Obviously there are good reasons why 'no one goes out on the roads in this kind of weather.'

We woke early the next morning, Friday, January 8. Today we would begin the long-dreaded trip up the Dempster Highway. Two stretches worried me most: (1) the steep, winding climb up to the Ogilvie/Peel River viewpoint south of Eagle Plains, and (2) the Richardson Mountains north of Eagle Plains. I expected the climb to be icy, while the open, tundra-like 'Richardsons' are prone to blizzards and whiteout conditions. Our drive had been going pretty well so far, though, and Kathleen and I both felt confident.

At breakfast, the owner and staff advised us on winter travel. "You say you have sleeping bags. That's good. Do you have matches? Here, take this pile of newspapers. You might need them to start a fire. In an emergency you can always burn your spare tire for heat."

While I chatted and drank coffee, Kathleen called the Eagle Plains motel to make a reservation. From what I remember, the motel has at least a couple of dozen rooms, but we wanted to make sure. The Dempster is very isolated. We couldn't take a chance. We had to get a room at Eagle Plains.

"What did they say?" I asked, when Kathleen returned.

"The girl just laughed. She said we could pretty much have any room we wanted."

We packed up and headed out in complete darkness, up the Dempster Highway, to Eagle Plains, beyond which lay Inuvik, our final destination. We're getting close now.

After less than one km Kathleen said, "I think we're going the wrong way, Michael. I think we're on the way to Dawson City."

Like most men, I instinctively disagreed completely with my wife's sense of direction. I had been to Dawson City several times. I had been up the Dempster Highway several times. I knew what I was doing. "No we're not. We're going the right way."

Kathleen persisted. "I don't think so. There's a bridge just north of the Klondike Corners that crosses the Klondike River. If we were going north, up the Dempster, we should have crossed the bridge by now."

Uh oh. Kathleen made a strong point. I began to waver. "Maybe we haven't reached the bridge yet."

"No, Michael. We should have reached the bridge by now. Let's stop at the next one of those little distance markers along the side of the road. They have them every five kilometres. If we're going up the Dempster, it should say only 5 or 10. If it's a big number, we're still on the North Klondike Highway, going to Dawson City."

"Good idea."

A couple of kilometres later, Kathleen hopped out of the van to brush the snow away from the marker. I turned the van to shine the headlights on the number, which turned out to be 'big.' I don't remember exactly what number, but big, certainly more than 5 or 10. We headed back and turned left just after the Klondike Corners. Seconds later we crossed the bridge over the frozen Klondike River and headed up the actual Dempster Highway. Now you know why I married Kathleen. No telling why she married me. I don't even know where I'm going.

About 80 km later we reached the North Fork Pass, where the protracted dawn turned the northern horizon a deep purple. The land lay empty and still. Later, with mist rising all around, caribou wandered along the banks of the Ogilvie River. We reached the viewpoint above the river without incident, and eventually parked in front of the Eagle Plains Hotel just as darkness fell.

Staff outnumbered the guests, which included Kathleen and me, plus one highway worker. We saw just two other vehicles all day long. Only one day to go.

We left Eagle Plains on Saturday, January 9, at a balmy -32 degrees – we actually felt a bit of heat blowing in from the engine. We crossed the Arctic Circle at 9:30 am. A pink glow along the southeastern horizon promised another beautiful day. At 11:35 am, the crimson sun rose above the Richardson Mountains foothills. We climbed up to the Wright Pass and crept down to the Mackenzie River lowlands in first or second gear much of the way. I mistrust these snow-covered descents. I constantly worry that our van would suddenly begin a sickening slide that would end only when we plunged off the road. We drove down very slowly indeed. No elderly women whizzed by me, though. No surprise there. Since leaving Eagle Plains we had seen only one other car, and that one was heading south, toward us.

The sun slipped below the horizon just after we crossed the Mackenzie River ice bridge a little before 2:00 pm. We stopped for gas in Fort McPherson. Only a couple of hours to go now. We reached Marilyn and Alan's house in Inuvik in the early evening, after nine days on the winter road.

As we sat chatting over a glass of wine, the drive up didn't seem so difficult. Despite driving on snow since the end of the first day, I never once had to put on the snow chains.

"How did it go on the Dempster?" Alan asked.

"Somewhat anti-climatic," I replied. "Entirely uneventful. It surprised me, though, that we saw only four cars in two days between here and the Klondike Corners."

"What do you expect?" he answered. "No one drives the Dempster at -40 degrees."

I didn't ask him about all those lonesome, pregnant women on their way to Whitehorse. I was just glad to finally be in Inuvik. Kathleen and I went to bed early, and slept very well. The most worrisome part of our winter escape was over. After more than a year of planning and nearly a lifetime of dreaming, I had reached not only the end of pavement, but also *the end of the road*. I step *beyond* in only three more weeks.

CHAPTER 6

Acclimation

O n our first morning in town, January 10, Kathleen and I walked to the
iconic Igloo Church for the 11:00 am service. Minus 26 degrees, with
only a hint of light reaching up from the southern horizon. The sun finally
appeared eight minutes after one in the afternoon, and set less than two hours
later, at 2:57 pm. This means that the sun reached its zenith at around two
minutes after 2:00 pm, not at noon, as I intuitively expect.

Officially, Inuvik resides in the Mountain Time Zone, and although many
time zones have been adjusted for administrative, economic, or political convenience, Inuvik's time zone is particularly misaligned. The central merid-
ian for the Mountain Time Zone is 105 degrees west longitude. This means
that only those locations between 97.5 and 112.5 degrees west should be in
the Mountain Time Zone. The central meridians for the Pacific and Alaskan
Time Zones are 120 and 135 degrees west, respectively. Inuvik, at 133.5
degrees west, should technically be in the Alaskan Time Zone. Two in the
afternoon in the Mountain Time Zone occurs at noon in the Alaskan Time
Zone. This means that the sun in Inuvik on January 10 did actually reach its
zenith around noon, Alaskan Standard Time, not at two minutes after two in
the afternoon. This took me quite a while to figure out, but I felt much better
afterward. The sun is supposed to reach its zenith at 'high noon.' That's why
they call it 'high noon.'

The closing hymn at church that day, *Morning Has Broken*, celebrated the
first sun rise of the year, four days ago on January 6, which lasted 37 minutes.
The last sunrise before then had occurred one month earlier on December 6.
This lack of sun, however, does not mean that the citizens of Inuvik spent
those 30 days stumbling around in total darkness. Civil twilight, when the

centre of the sun is between zero and 6 degrees below the horizon, produces enough light to read a book outdoors and for pilots to fly using visual flight rules. In Inuvik, even on the shortest day of the year on December 21, civil twilight lasted 5 hours and 9 minutes. Therefore, even when the sun remains below the horizon for an entire month in Inuvik, no day is 'completely' dark for more than 18 hours and 51 minutes. Based on 24 years of personal experience, I can tell you that there are many dreary, rainy, sunless days in Vancouver during the winter that seem as dark as the darkest day in Inuvik.

Civil twilight also produces a beautiful, protracted morning sky. On some or our walks that first week along the frozen east channel of the Mackenzie River, Kathleen and I simultaneously witnessed a brilliant red sky to the rising sun, an indigo sky 180 degrees opposite, and a pink-and-blue sky sandwiched in between.

Kathleen and I thoroughly enjoyed our three weeks with Alan and Marilyn, and their four boys, Daniel, Andrew, Mike and Matthew. We spent most of our time getting to know Inuvik, and generally trying to be useful around the house. On most mornings I wandered into town for coffee at the Sunriser Café at the Mackenzie Hotel. Along the way I passed school children laughing and playing under the lights at morning recess. Kathleen usually stayed home, chatting with Marilyn, and helping out with shopping and household chores. In the afternoon I joined Marilyn at the dog yard to feed and clean up after her 15 sled dogs. We would then saw up frozen fish to bring home to thaw for the next afternoon's meal. After these chores, Kathleen and I often strolled to town for coffee at the Café Gallery. In the evening, after dinner, we occasionally saw Northern Lights flickering through the front room window.

Nearly everyday we also visited the computers at the public library to answer and send emails. Afterwards, I usually mentioned to Kathleen that I looked forward to when we reached the cabin. I looked forward to the time when we would not have electricity or access to the Internet. I looked forward to the time when we would no longer be subservient to this technology.

I suppose I could have chosen not to go to the library. In fact, though, I could not resist. I might have email, you know. I had to go. Even though I often didn't have any email, there I was, the next day, at the library, checking for email. I had ensnared myself in a repetitive daily routine. I very much looked forward to when we didn't have access to the Internet.

On one afternoon a man named Robert Lyslo came by the library looking for us. We didn't know Robert, but he recognized us from the descriptions given to him by Marilyn. She undoubtedly also told him that we would be at the computers playing with our emails. He walked over and held out his hand.

"Hello. My name is Robert. My wife Jo-Ellen and I are the new school-teachers in Colville Lake. I'm here in Inuvik for a couple of days for meetings. Bern Will Brown said I should look you up."

We chatted a bit, and Robert said that we were welcome to stay with him whenever we were in Colville Lake. "I'd also like to come out to the cabin to visit you, if that's all right," he continued.

"We'd love some visitors," I said. "Come out any time."

Truthfully though, I didn't expect to go to town. Moreover, I had planned our adventure at the north end of Colville Lake to be a winter of isolation. That dream did not include a steady stream of visitors.

In addition to drinking coffee and strolling about town, Kathleen and I also spent our time in Inuvik learning about northern winter life. During that first week we rode and drove a snowmobile for the very first time. Neither Kathleen nor I like snowmobiles, as they make way too much noise for us. Alan though, insisted that we practice driving them before going to the cabin. "You have to know how to drive a ski-doo. You might have to drive one when you're at Colville Lake. There might be a medical emergency or some other kind of situation where you need to drive the ski-doo. You have to be ready. You have to know what you're doing."

So out we roared one afternoon, astride one of Alan's snowmobiles, up the frozen Mackenzie River to Ron and Suzanne's tent camp about eight km south of town. Many families in the Inuvik area have these 'weekend' winter camps, which consist of a wooden platform raised above the level of the snow, about which is hung a canvas wall tent heated with a wood-burning stove. Kathleen noted that Ron and Suzanne's 12 by 14 foot tent seemed small. "You know Michael, according to Bern's brochure, our cabin is only a little bit bigger than this tent. We're not going to have a lot of room."

A small space has its benefits though, as the tent warmed up quickly after Alan started the fire. We spent a very comfortable afternoon drinking tea, enveloped in heat, despite the outside temperature of -30 degrees.

For the first half of our return trip to town, Kathleen stood on the back of a toboggan being towed behind Alan's snowmobile. "You should know what it's like to be standing on a toboggan being towed," Alan said. We were travelling at approximately 20 km/hour, with the temperature at -28 or -29 degrees.

Afterwards Kathleen reported that, "Basically it's quite a lot colder standing in the wind on the toboggan than riding on the ski-doo." Not a particularly insightful lesson I suppose, but we would certainly have empathy for anyone in the future that we might be towing behind our snowmobile.

I should point out that many Northerners refer to snowmobiles as 'ski-doos,' which is actually the brand of snowmobile made by Bombardier. This brand became so ubiquitous that the name stuck, much like hand and facial tissues are often called Kleenex. Even the very common *Bravo* made by Yamaha is called a ski-doo. So, with apologies to all the other manufacturers of snowmobiles, from now on I will refer to all such machines as ski-doos. I need to fit in.

For the rest of our return trip to town Kathleen had rejoined me on the back of my ski-doo. For some reason – I don't remember why – we had separated from Alan. By now Kathleen and I both felt reasonably confident on the ski-doo as we clamoured alone across Boot Lake toward the hill rising up to Inuvik. Many ski-doos had obviously come this way before, as indicated by the well-packed trail. We stopped at the edge of the lake and then proceeded cautiously and slowly up the bank. Big mistake. The ski-doo quickly slid backwards and sideways before sinking into the soft snow at the edge of the trail. I opened the throttle, which only caused the ski-doo to dig itself deeper into the snow. We were stuck.

We both climbed off to ponder our predicament. This was embarrassing.

"You know, Kathleen. I hope we can get unstuck before anyone notices. And by 'anyone,' I mean Alan."

I grabbed the ski-doo's tow bar and yanked backwards. It didn't budge at all. This wasn't going to be easy. I crouched, set myself, and pulled hard backwards with all my weight. The heavy ski-doo still refused to move. This was going to be difficult.

"I think I need your help, Kathleen."

"What do you want me to?"

"I'll count to three, and we'll both pull back together. One-two-three."

Kathleen and I are small people, and we don't expect to yank heavy stuff around easily. But the ski-doo didn't move at all, except to settle deeper into the snow. I'm sure I could hear it laughing. A smug, satisfied laugh. I told you before that Kathleen and I don't like ski-doos. They make way too much noise, except of course, when they refuse to move.

Eventually, by accident, we discovered that we could move the machine by pulling diagonally – a little bit sideways and a little bit backwards. First we heaved together in one direction, and then the other. Slowly we 'walked' the ski-doo back and forth out of its crater until we once again had it back down on the lake. This time we headed up the hill like we had seen other riders approach inclines, with the throttle nearly wide open. Our ski-doo leaped forward and climbed rapidly. Another lesson learned – better to be aggressive than timid. I vowed never again to become stuck in deep snow, which is way too much unnecessary work.

The following Saturday Kathleen and I ski-dooed [yes, Bombardier's brand name can also be a verb] with Alan and his sons, Daniel, Andrew and Mike, 42 km round trip to visit Marilyn's brother Graham and his future wife Amy at their tent camp west of town. Ten-year-old Daniel drove his own ski-doo, while Alan towed eight-year-old Andrew on a toboggan loaded with gear. This was no mere social visit, however. Alan had planned more lessons regarding winter travel. About halfway to the camp Alan stopped, and we all clustered around to hear him say, "Time to get off and run around. We need to get our circulation going."

Turning to Kathleen and me he continued, "Feet get particularly cold on the ski-doo. It's easy to get frostbittten if you don't stop every 30 minutes or so to warm up." We appreciated his continuing advice.

After enjoying tea and snacks with Graham and Amy, we headed east back to Inuvik. Dan, with Mike, led the way, followed by Kathleen and Alan, who alternated driving and being passenger on his ski-doo. I trailed behind, with Andrew riding on the toboggan behind my ski-doo. Just as I had nearly completed crossing a fairly large, windswept lake I thought perhaps Andrew might be feeling cold. Maybe it would be a good time to stop to run around and warm up. I turned around to see only an empty toboggan following merrily behind me. No Andrew! It was late in the day, -18 degrees, and I had lost Alan and Marilyn's second-born son!

This was not good. However, only seconds later, far back, nearly in the middle of the lake, Andrew emerged from the swirling snow, running quickly along the ski-doo track [yes, Bombardier's brand name can also be an adjective]. I turned around, headed back, and soon rejoined Andrew who said that he had fallen off a few minutes ago.

"Were you worried? I asked.

"No. You were bound to come back."

He didn't seem concerned at all. I had to admire his confidence and self-reliance.

By now our group had all gathered together, in their original travelling positions, and we once again headed east toward Inuvik. As we drove between small islands in a narrow side channel of the river, Alan halted the group, and dismounted his ski-doo.

"I just want to walk ahead a little by myself. Sometimes this area can have overflow. I want to check it out."

Alan certainly intended that his son Mike would wait while he determined that our route was safe. Mike was only four years old, and like all four-year-old boys he wanted to be part of the action. He wanted to check things out with his dad. As soon as Alan turned his back, Mike bounded ahead and only three steps later broke through the ice into wet slush. Alan quickly grabbed him by the collar and lifted him back onto firm ice. He then instructed Mike to shove his feet into dry snow to wick away as much moisture as possible.

For situations just like this all of us carried extra clothing, particularly socks and footwear. We were only ten minutes from home though, and Mike wasn't all that wet or cold. So we quickly started up our ski-doos and headed up the hill into town.

We sat around the kitchen table that evening, discussing the day's excitement.

"It was a good lesson out there today," Alan said. "I've seen overflow in that area only once before in all the times I've passed through there. You always need to be careful, Mike, even in areas that you think you know."

Marilyn suggested, in a thoughtful and considerate way, that Alan should have been watching Mike more carefully. Perhaps so. It's not for me to say.

That night Kathleen and I decided that we would drag our sled and gear to Ron and Suzanne's tent camp some time next week. This would provide a necessary orientation to what we might expect when we establish our winter camps around Colville Lake. So on Monday morning we drove down to the Parks Canada storage shed to retrieve some of our camping gear. The morning temperature stood at -21 degrees, but we both felt warm as we opened the door of the shed. We took off our mitts and began hunting through the plastic bins.

I have to say, with a little embarrassment, that we were both surprised at how cold it was inside the unheated shed. Our exposed hands and fingers numbed almost immediately. Damn, it was cold. We put our mitts back on, and worked quickly as we fumbled for the various items on our list. Although we had been living with cold for nearly three weeks, Kathleen and I still retained some innate, southern notions. We still subconsciously assumed that buildings are warm. Silly, I know. But we were surprised, nevertheless. We have a long way to go before we are fully acclimated.

That afternoon Kathleen and I drove a few kilometres back down the Dempster Highway to the Arctic Chalet Resort, where Carl Falsnes tested and confirmed that Bern's SSBx radio did indeed work. We would now have daily communication at the cabin. Oh, boy.

On Wednesday morning, January 20, Kathleen and I set off for Ron and Suzanne's camp at -34 degrees. Kathleen led the way while I pulled the sled. I had read in Craig MacDonald's instructions that dragging sleds becomes very difficult at extremely cold temperatures: "frost will often build up even while travelling to create running surfaces with the smoothness of fine sand paper." I don't know if Craig would have considered minus 34 to be 'extremely cold,' but it seemed as though I were dragging the sled across concrete. I began to tire after only 30 minutes.

Kathleen offered to spell me off. "I'm just standing here doing nothing, Michael. Let me pull for a while."

"I don't see how you can pull the sled if I can't, Kathleen. I'll just set small goals for myself. I'll go 100 steps and then rest."

Sometimes I could actually make 100 steps. Often though, I needed to rest after only 65 or 70 steps. This was not working. I was becoming fatigued and overheated, while Kathleen grew cold as she mostly just stood around feeling useless. I think she also felt a little sorry for me.

"Maybe we can pull together," she said.

"There's not enough room in the tow lines. We'd just be in each other's way. I'm not being stubborn. I just don't think there's anything you can do. We'll get there eventually."

We finally reached the tent camp early in the evening, having averaged only slightly more than one km per hour. The thermometer hanging on a tree outside the tent read -38 degrees, and we quickly started a fire in the wood stove. Kathleen noted in her diary that: "almost nothing works at -38 degrees. Even this pen had to be warmed up before it would write."

Ron and Suzanne's wood supply had dwindled quite a bit since we were here last week. We appreciated their invitation to use their tent, and didn't want to burn the rest of their best wood, so I stoked the fire mostly with 'punky' wood. Such half-rotten wood does not produce a lot of heat.

After dinner Kathleen rinsed the plates, and placed them on the floor behind the wood stove while she waited for more hot water to boil. She retrieved the plates 45 minutes later, and noted, with some alarm in her voice that, "the rinse water has turned to ice, Michael. It's frozen right on the plates!"

"Well, Kathleen. That punky wood's not very good. It doesn't make much heat."

I spoke somewhat patronizingly, I suppose, with the authority of a seasoned woodsman. Kathleen scowled just a little, perhaps intimating that if I were so darn knowledgeable, then why hadn't I used better wood. She did have a reasonable point.

Still concerned about Ron and Suzanne's wood supply, we intended to let the fire go out overnight. We crawled into our sleeping bags fully clothed. We woke the next morning, at around 5:00 am, to a temperature of -34 degrees inside the tent. Not too bad, considering that the outside temperature had dropped to -40 degrees. Still though, it was a cold start to the day. We needed heat. We also needed light.

We turned our attention first to the wood stove. The punky wood proved more intractable than even last night, and required over an hour of fits and starts before producing much consistent warmth.

We next focused on the Coleman lantern, which resented being so cold, and only stubbornly sent forth light after 45 minutes of frustrating struggle. I have learned since then that I should have pre-heated the lantern's fuel tube with a match or lighter. I have to admit though, that I felt somewhat pleased. Kathleen and I had endured and survived the cold, and ultimately enjoyed a hot breakfast in a relatively warm and well-lit tent.

The morning broke beautifully sunny, with the temperature warming to -31 degrees by mid-afternoon. We spent most of the day hunting for seasoned wood, which we cut with our bow saw, and then dragged back to camp on the sled. We felt comfortable travelling on the ice. We felt satisfied providing for our needs. That evening we enjoyed a much warmer tent, although we did let the fire go out again overnight.

We set out for home on Friday morning at a relatively warm -27 degrees. Children were out bicycling along the Mackenzie River, and the sled dragged a little easier. About an hour into our trek, a vehicle approached, heading upriver from town. It was Marilyn [the driver, not the vehicle], coming out to see how we were doing.

"I have to admit, Marilyn, I'm a little bit tired."

"I can load all your stuff into the van, and drive you home."

"That does sound tempting," I replied. "But I can't give up completely. Maybe you can take these two heaviest packs. I can drag the rest of the gear from here. I need the conditioning. Thanks very much for coming out, Marilyn. We appreciate it."

By the time Kathleen and I reached home in the late afternoon I really was very tired, and thoroughly enjoyed the glass of wine that Marilyn poured for me. During dinner I told Alan of the difficult dragging conditions, and of how Kathleen had nothing to do while I struggled with the load.

"You know, Mike, you really ought to get a second sled, preferably a kids plastic sled. That way Kathleen could share some of the load. You wouldn't have to drag as much weight, and she wouldn't be getting so cold."

"I accept your point, Alan. But Kathleen will be breaking trail ahead of me when we get to Colville Lake. She really couldn't be dragging too much weight and break trail at the same time. Besides, I wonder if a plastic kids sled would really stand up to the wear and tear over winter. Next time we go dragging, we're not going to take so much gear. For example, Kathleen and I both took our overnight cases, which means I was dragging two cans of shaving cream and two tubes of toothpaste. That's just one example. We could do a lot more economizing on what we take, which would make my load a lot lighter."

Alan seemed unconvinced. "Still, two sleds would be good. Also, most people don't let the fire go out overnight. A major reason I like to go to the wall tent on the weekends is to be warm. Most people get their tents very warm. There's no need to wake up to -34 degrees. It would have been easy for us to replace all the wood you used with a chain saw. We could have gone back to the camp and put up several days' supply in less than an hour."

"Of course you're right, Alan. But I wanted to experience the cold, and I was happy with how we could still function and work at such temperatures without feeling anxious or under pressure."

Alan remained unconvinced. "Most people don't like to suffer like you do, Mike."

Sunday was a warm and beautiful day. Minus six degrees, and already light as Kathleen and I strolled toward the Igloo Church at 10:30 am. After the service we hosted the Fehr family for brunch at the Finto Hotel. That afternoon we loaded our wall tent, portable wood stove, sled and other camping supplies into our van and drove five km out to the dog yard, where we stored all of our equipment in Marilyn and Alan's wall tent. Then, based on Alan's recommendation, we snowshoed about two km northeast from the yard, up on to a small knoll where we planned to set up our wall tent the next day. The site seemed perfect – private but open. I would need to clear only a few trees, which I required for fuel anyway. That night I reread, for what seemed like the 100th time, Craig MacDonald's instructions for erecting the tent and for building a sunken, stable platform for the stove and stove pipe.

We walked out to the dog yard immediately after breakfast on Monday morning. We wanted to get an early start. We loaded up the sled and headed toward the knoll. Kathleen led the way, making yesterday's trail even more compact as she stomped along on her snowshoes. At -25 degrees, the sled pulled fairly easily. I felt relaxed and strong. Kathleen noted in her diary that: "minus 25 degrees is a very nice temperature to work in. You can take off your gloves to tie tent ropes for short periods without feeling cold." We seem to be getting used to the cold.

In less than three hours we had reached camp, set up the tent, and cut 12 trees for firewood. Alan didn't say that he definitely would come out tonight to check up on us, but we assumed he would. We wanted the tent to be hot when he arrived. We wanted to show him that we could camp like true Northerners. All 12 trees were small though – maybe 20 cm in diameter at the most. We hoped we had enough. I filled the stove with kindling and rounds, and hung a thermometer from a clothesline strung below the ridge of the tent. Fifteen minutes later the temperature reached +35 degrees. Wow! This does feel good. We had to start taking clothes off. Double Wow!! I hope this is hot enough for Alan.

Alan finally arrived during dessert. We could hear him coming up the trail by ski-doo. He stayed for cookies and tea, and congratulated us for having the tent warm. He did say though, that perhaps we should have cut larger trees. Maybe so, but I didn't want to cut large trees. I wanted to thin out the small trees, and save the large trees. Alan replied that there were unlimited trees in the region. "No one else uses or has any interest in these trees, Mike. You should cut what you need. Larger trees make more efficient heat."

Kathleen and I agreed that we enjoyed the warmth, and during the night I refilled the stove twice, with the second refilling at 3:45 am. By 8:30, when we awoke, the temperature in the tent had fallen to -26 degrees. Perhaps I should have gotten up to fill the stove a third time. At least that's what Kathleen suggested. Nevertheless, it took only about 10 minutes once I started the fire to get the temperature back up to +27 degrees. I love this wall tent.

After breakfast we snowshoed into town for coffee and snacks at the Café Gallery. Our canvas wind suits, with their bold red-and-blue rickrack and voyageur-type sashes drew a lot of attention. We looked extraordinarily jaunty, and felt only slightly self-conscious. The canvas wind suits are light and breathe very well – much more useful than heavy parkas when hauling a sled or otherwise working hard.

While in town we stopped by the Northern Store where we had previously seen plastic kids toboggans. They were now on sale at half price for only ten dollars. I remained skeptical of the plastic toboggan's usefulness, but I bought one anyway, because of Alan's insistence. Later that night he did seem happy. Well worth the $10.00, even if we never use the toboggan.

The next morning we returned to the knoll to dismantle our camp. Since arriving in Inuvik we have learned to drive a ski-doo. We have practiced snowshoeing. We have stayed in permanent tent camps. We have set up and slept in our own portable wall tent. And, perhaps most importantly, we have actually come to enjoy cold weather. We seem to be ready.

We spent our last day in Inuvik, on January 30, packing up and driving our canoe, sled and 25 plastic bins of supplies out to the hanger of Aklak Air, who we have chartered to take us to the cabin at the north end of Colville Lake. After dinner Dave Jones, who rented the upstairs suite at Marilyn and Alan's, came by to give us a going-away present of caribou and homemade bread. Yes – a going-away present! Kathleen and I are going away. We are going *beyond the end of the road*. After more than 18 months of dreaming, planning and preparing, our adventure truly begins less than 12 hours from now.

Sunday, January 31. At 9:30 am, Kathleen and I sat in the upstairs office overlooking the centre of Aklak Air's large hangar. Our pilot Bob and co-pilot Bob [yes, they were both named Bob] sat behind a cluttered desk smoking cigarettes while they completed the paper work for our flight. Bern had sent us a hand-drawn map depicting a horseshoe-shaped bay east of the cabin. Bern said that this was the best place to land a plane. I showed Bern's map to our flight crew, and passed on his warning not to land too near the cabin because of thin ice at the lake's outlet. I don't know if they welcomed this advice, but they did look at the map before handing it back to me.

We were only moments away. The flight crew rolled open the hangar doors at 10:15 am, and we looked out onto a gray and snowy morning of -40 degrees. We walked, as though in a dream, toward the white plane in the all white pre-dawn light, led by pilots in their fur-trimmed, hooded parkas. Kathleen said she felt like she was in one of those grainy 1950s newsreels of adventurers who are about to board a plane on their final leg to the South Pole.

We loaded six months of food and gear into the belly of the Twin Otter, and buckled ourselves into the two rearward seats. Co-pilot Bob pointed out safety features, and told us what our responsibilities would be during any unexpected crash landings. I have to admit that we weren't paying very close attention. We were way too excited. The co-pilot helped us into our headphones. The propellers began to whine. The plane taxied down the runway, lifted up, and carried us away toward our quest for winter solitude, self-discovery, and freedom from the constraints of urban existence.

The Twin Otter crossed low over treeless plains crisscrossed by frozen, sinuous rivers. The land glowed amber golden, like autumn wheat, beneath a sun now just barely above the southern horizon. We stared downward, not daring to blink, as we flew in ecstasy over endless lakes and rivers laced with icy, angular, pressure ridges.

Two hours after taking flight, the Twin Otter descended toward the carpet of snow that adorned Colville Lake. We were flying north, down the lake,

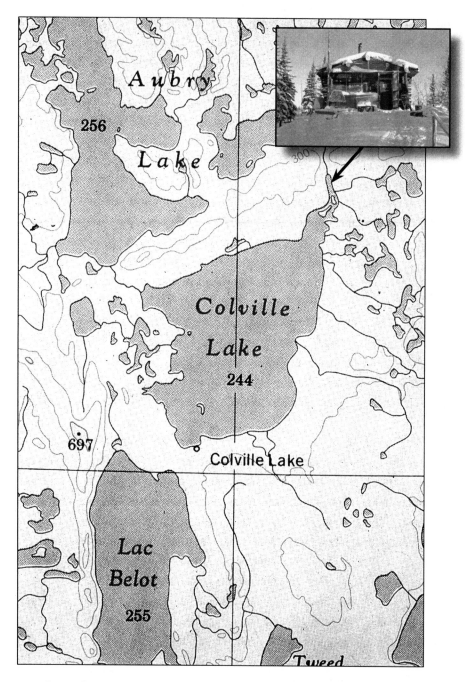

Our cabin was located on a point overlooking the lake's outlet,
approximately 40 km north of the town of Colville Lake.

and could see the cabin sitting on a low ridge at the lake's outlet. Kathleen and I looked at each other and smiled. It was a beautiful sight. We have not yet seen any pictures of the cabin's interior. We just hope that it's clean and liveable. You never know for sure what bush cabins will be like. Too late now, anyway.

Bob flew low over the cabin, banked sharply, then turned back south, descending slowly toward the surface of the horseshoe-shaped bay illustrated on Bern's map. Bob had never landed at Colville Lake in the winter, and despite Bern's map, was unsure of how thick the ice might be. Bob's voice crackled through the headphones: "I'm going to just skim the surface of the snow with the landing skis, and take off again. Then I can circle back to see if any water has wicked up into our tracks. If I see wicking, the ice will be too thin to land."

The plane's skis knifed two parallel tracks into the newly fallen snow. After maybe 300 metres the pilot opened the throttle, and the Twin Otter gained altitude toward the south. After banking east, and then circling back north, all of us could see that the plane's tracks shone pure white in the early afternoon sun. No evidence of wicking. The ice was probably thick enough to land our heavily-laden plane.

We circled once more, and approached from the south, again descending slowly until we finally touched down on the snow-covered ice. The Twin Otter skied north, along the east shore of the horseshoe-shaped bay, until it stopped 200 metres away from our cabin at the lake's outlet. Kathleen and I had finally arrived!

Co-pilot Bob lowered the stairs and he, Kathleen and I stepped down onto the snow. Seconds later, pilot Bob started handing out storage bins, packs, canoe, sled and the rest of the supplies we would need for the next six months.

"Make sure you spread this stuff around. I don't want all this weight concentrated around the plane." He seemed anxious to get away again.

"Before going, can you wait to see if our key to the cabin actually works? We want to make sure we can get in."

"Don't worry. I'm not leaving you out here until I know you can get in the cabin, and that you can make a fire. Do you have any matches?"

"Yeah, I have a lot of matches."

"Show them to me. I want to make sure that they're handy."

I reached into my shirt pocket and held out two boxes of strike-anywhere wooden kitchen matches. I always carry plenty of matches. I always keep them handy. It was good to know, though, that the pilot was concerned about our safety – very professional and reassuring.

Kathleen said that she wanted to try the key right away, and reached inside her parka to check yet one more time that the cabin key was still dangling from a cord around her neck. She then headed off through the snow, sinking in up to her knees. After only a few steps she returned to search in the growing pile of gear for her snowshoes. She laced the lamp wick bindings around her mukluks and strode easily across the lake, looking very much like she belonged.

By the time Kathleen came back, all the gear had been unloaded, and our pilot and co-pilot were sitting on a storage bin, smoking a final cigarette before departure.

"So the key worked?" I asked.

"Yeah. The lock turned easily. No problem at all."

I could tell from the satisfied look on Kathleen's face that she was happy with what she had seen so far. The cabin must have appeared clean and liveable.

The Bobs finished smoking their cigarettes, shook our hands, and said, "See you later. Have a great winter. Hope everything goes well."

They climbed back into the Twin Otter as Kathleen and I moved to one side to avoid the backdraft of the propeller.

The plane burst to life, roared across the surface of the lake amid billows of white, and lightly lifted above Colville Lake. Four minutes later Kathleen and I stood all alone, surrounded by a silent world of snow, ice and cold. I checked the thermometer clipped to my daypack. Minus 19 degrees. I stepped into the bindings of my snowshoes, and contentedly followed Kathleen toward our cabin.

Our freshly-minted snow trail led to the south side of the point where our cabin sat about 10 m above the level of the lake. As we approached the cabin, I was happy to see wood, stacked neatly about 2 m high, on the porch next to the door. I pushed the wooden door inward, and a small shaft of light penetrated the otherwise dusky cabin interior.

An oval, wood-burning stove rested on a 25-cm platform in the centre of the cabin, next to a wooden box already filled with newspaper, kindling and

The first view of our new home. The cabin's interior was much more comfortable than we had ever imagined it could be.

split lengths of wood. The stove seemed kind of small for winter, though, and wasn't much over 40 cm tall, and not much bigger around. Bern had told us that the cabin was not intended for winter use. I took the box of matches from my pocket, and quickly and easily started the fire.

In a few minutes our new home began to warm, and I filled the stove with more wood. Kathleen scooped some snow into a pot and set it on the stove to make tea. We sat at the table, just resting and contemplating. There was a lot to do to prepare for the night. First of all, I wanted to move all of our gear and supplies off the lake, and up to the cabin. Kathleen suggested that we didn't have to move everything today. "We need only to bring the essentials, Michael. The rest can wait until tomorrow."

She was right, of course, but I'm always worried about leaving supplies out in the open. I was particularly worried about leaving supplies so far away, out on the ice. What if the ice was thin, and opened up during the night? What if wolves or wolverines came during the night, and made off with our supplies? All of our supplies are essential. We need every item in every one of those bins sitting out on the lake.

So we spent the next 3 to 4 hours sledding and tobogganing all of our gear 200 metres from the landing spot up the hill to the cabin. We left much of it outside, as there was not nearly enough room inside the cabin, which Bern told us measured 14 by 14 feet from outside wall to outside wall. Most of that small space was already filled with tables, chairs, bunk beds and counters. At least our supplies are nearby, though. They can't slip through thin ice now, and I should be able to hear any marauding wolves or thieving wolverines. Like most suburbanites, I am not a hunter. I have come to see wildlife, not to kill wildlife. But I did bring my rifle, and I am ready, as I must be, to protect what is mine.

It was now about 6:00 o'clock. We were both a little tired after so much physical work. We were also experiencing the natural unwinding that always occurs when a much-anticipated event has finally happened. The southern horizon glowed with a protracted sunset. Kathleen and I were ready to call it a day.

Kathleen lit some candles, sliced several pieces from Dave's homemade bread, and set out a plate of cheese and dried caribou. We ate our sandwiches and sipped tea, enjoying the warmth of our fire. We stepped outside to check the thermometer that we had hung on the northwest corner of the cabin – still -19 degrees. A rising blue moon began to brighten the night sky. A beautiful way to end our first day at Colville Lake. At 8:30 we spread our sleeping bags out on the lower level of bunk beds. I filled the stove with 25-cm long spruce logs, blew out the candles, and quickly fell asleep.

CHAPTER 7

Akaradetsisa

[*Author's Note: By* now you will have noticed the somewhat unusual title for the current chapter. During the summer of 1998 I came across a book *Trail of the Hare: Life and Stress in an Arctic Community*, by Joel Savishinsky. The basis for this book came from Savishinsky's anthropological treatise of the native people living in Colville Lake during the 1970s. Savishinsky wrote that: "the people's calendar is a description rather than simply a demarcation of time [that] reflects their concern with the natural world."

During the rest of this book, you will see that Kathleen and I also became deeply concerned with the natural world, particularly weather and temperature. I thought it fitting, therefore, that the titles of all my monthly chapters should reflect local terminology, the meanings of which will be revealed to you during the following pages.

You should also know that the native people of Colville Lake belong to the K'ahshotine group, which means Big Rabbits' People, or Hareskins because they relied so heavily on snowshoe hares for food, blankets and clothing. These people were also among the most northerly communities of the Dene, who apparently referred to the Hare Indians as 'people at the edge of the world.'

And now, finally, after all these pages, I begin the story of our life at the north end of Colville Lake!]

Monday, February 1. I woke at 10:15 to pure blackness rimmed with dim light filtering past the shuttered windows. I climbed out of my bunk, lit the candles, and peered at our indoor thermometer, which read +8 degrees. Not too bad, I thought. Still fairly warm. I stepped over to the wood stove, which was nearly out, and stuffed in some kindling. I opened the circular air intake, and placed a lighted match to the newspaper. The kindling ignited, the stove sputtered, and the heat radiated outward in concentric circles. Only our first morning and yet lighting the fire already seems like a very comfortable routine.

There's a lot of work that needs doing today. We have to finish organizing all our food and supplies. We want to chop a hole in the ice so that we can get water, and we need to make the cabin fully functional.

I walked over to the propane stove and turned the left knob. The automatic ignition clicked, but no flame appeared. I checked the connections, and tried several more times. Lots of clicking, but still no flame. I couldn't smell propane, so maybe something's wrong with the tank. Maybe the tank's empty! That would be very disappointing.

I stepped outside into the screened porch to check whether the propane cylinder release valve was open or closed. Damn. Someone's locked the cylinder cap on the propane tank. Bern never said anything about the propane cylinder being locked. There better be a key around here somewhere. I don't want to be the one to tell Kathleen that we don't have fuel to operate her kitchen stove. She's not going to like that. I don't like that prospect very much myself. The surface of the wood stove is small, and not useful for much more than boiling tea water.

I searched through the 10 or so keys hanging just inside the door, suspended from nails on well-marked, 15-cm-long wooden key chains. 'Boathouse.' 'Tool Shed.' 'Cabin.' 'Upper Cabin.' Nothing identified itself as 'Propane Cylinder.' One key, though, dangling from a small wire loop, was unlabelled.

I hope to hell that this is it. Strange phrase, 'hope to hell.' Out of context, standing all by itself, the phrase doesn't really mean anything. Nevertheless, I sure hope to hell that this key opens the propane cylinder.

I felt a great deal of relief when the key fit, and smoothly turned in the padlock. I unscrewed the cap, opened the valve, and walked back inside to the stove. I smiled smugly as the ignition produced an instant flame. One unexpected challenge already dealt with successfully. At least now we can have some hot oatmeal for breakfast.

I found a screwdriver on the oval table next to the south wall – just where Bern promised it would be – and removed the eight Phillips screws that fastened each of the plywood shutters to the outside of the cabin's two windows. Sunlight streamed into the room, illuminating the space that would be our home until mid-June.

Kathleen was now up, and we closely assessed our new home. The cabin was better than we ever imagined it could be. A picture window faced up Colville Lake, south toward the winter sun. A reading and writing table sat below the window. On the corner of the table was a spot for the SSBx-11A radio, where we could attach it to the antenna and ground wire protruding through the south wall. A double row of bookshelves hung above the window.

The west wall featured the door and a semi-circular dining table, above which a nine-pane window would admit views of the setting sun in spring. Open shelving, supported by angled struts, provided storage for pots, pans and skillets above the window. Other domestic paraphernalia such as brooms, dustpans and two white-gas Coleman lanterns hung from various hooks and nails. The cabin was completely stocked with cutlery, dishes, linens, canisters and other household necessities. Curtains framed the windows.

Cupboards, breadbox, counter space, a propane refrigerator and the two-burner propane stove graced the north wall. A wash basin and mirrored medicine cabinet fit snugly and neatly into the northwest corner. A pair of three-tiered bunk beds lined the east wall.

A drying rack for parkas, boot liners and other winter clothes hung above the stove, suspended from crossbeams. The entire interior, logs and furniture, had been richly varnished.

"Pretty darn, cozy, Kathleen! I think we're gonna be very comfortable here. A great place to spend winter."

The cabin was also very well constructed. The spruce logs had all been professionally notched and fitted, and were tightly chinked with pink insulation. Framing above the wood-burning stove guided the smokestack through the ceiling, and guarded against accidental bumping or dislodging. We nodded appreciatively, and remembered Bern's admonition that "a cabin fire in winter is a man's worst enemy in the bush."

Time for breakfast. Kathleen retrieved another bucket of snow, and melted it quickly on the propane stove. Soon we sat at our kitchen table, eating oatmeal, sipping tea, and toasting the last slices of Dave's homemade bread on top of the wood stove – very comfortable. Getting a little too comfortable. We have work to do. Today's next priority is to establish camp procedures for getting water that's already in liquid form, as melting snow takes too much time and too many refills of the bucket.

A long-handled broom with a hole already drilled through the wooden end hung on the cabin wall. Perfect. I rummaged through a green storage bin looking for woven nylon rope. I'm very fond of saying, "You can't have too much rope on a wilderness trip." I cut out a 30-cm length, and burned both ends with a match to prevent unravelling. I then looped one end through the handle of our metal bucket, and poked the other end through the broom-handle hole. I now tied the two ends together with a sheet bend, an easy knot that, according to my old Boy Scout handbook, can be trusted to never work itself loose.

After grabbing an axe hanging on the outside wall in the enclosed porch, I strolled out into the crisp morning (still -19 degrees) down to the frozen edge of the outlet of Colville Lake. Bern had said that the ice was thin here, and often remained open for long periods during the winter. Standing at the outlet's margin, I eyed the ice cautiously. I slowly stepped out a few paces from shore, testing the surface before me by striking it with the wooden axe handle. I repeatedly glanced behind to confirm that no water was wicking up into my tracks. The ice seemed firm and solid. I dropped to my knees, to distribute my weight more evenly, and to protect my feet against a possible glancing blow of steel axe on slick ice.

I reached out as far as I could, and banged the axe on the ice. Within five minutes, liquid water gushed upward and slid across the ice, appearing almost black against the wonderfully pure white background. I extended the broom handle, and lowered the dangling bucket into the 'well.' Once again I felt smugly satisfied, as I lifted the bucket back out onto the ice – a bucket heavy with slush and ice chips floating in immaculate, clean water. Another challenge dealt with successfully.

I carried the water back up the hill, where Kathleen was already going through the bins scattered outside our cabin. Snow, wafting in from the south on a gentle breeze, swirled about her face as she studied and rearranged the contents of each bin. Periodically Kathleen would look up and say, "OK, this one is ready, Michael," and I would sled the repackaged bin or pack along the ridge to the second cabin.

By mid-afternoon, all the food that we would need for the next few weeks, plus the clothes and equipment that we would be wearing and using on a daily basis, was organized in our cabin. Everything else had been put in storage in the second cabin.

This second cabin would also serve as our emergency accommodation. Bern had left seven pages of instructions, in which he said, "speaking of emergencies, I have put enough firewood in Cabin II for one day in case Cabin I (our cabin) got burned out." Burning ourselves out would certainly be an emergency. We added some more wood to Bern's pile, put some newspaper and kindling in the stove, and left Cabin II unlocked.

Light snow continued to fall throughout the day and evening, accumulating perhaps as much as 2.5 cm. Inside the cabin we easily maintained the temperature at a very cozy +18 degrees. After a dinner of spaghetti and tea, we turned our attention to the SSBx-11A radio, and the instructions for contacting Bern Will Brown. Bern's notes indicted the following four frequencies:

> *2220 for Local Trappers;*
> *3360 (unused);*
> *4441 for the Yukon Trappers and Outfitters; and*
> *5730 a seldom-used frequency that would be for Bern and me.*

Bern's instructions said that we should call at 7:00 pm. If we failed to make contact, we should then call every hour on the hour until we reached him. At 7:00 pm precisely, I set the frequency dial to 5730, pushed the transmission button, and called out my first message of the winter: "Hello, Colville Lake Lodge. This is Mike calling from the outpost. Are you there, Colville Lake Lodge?"

I released the button, waited for the response, but heard nothing but static. I repeated the process: "Hello, Colville Lake Lodge. This is Mike calling from the outpost. Are you there, Colville Lake Lodge?" Again, nothing but static. I tried three more times before giving up.

At 8:00 pm I tried five more times: "Hello, Colville Lake Lodge. This is Mike calling from the outpost. Are you there, Colville Lake Lodge?" Once again, static mocked our ears as we strained to hear a response from Bern.

I paced around the cabin's interior. And pacing wasn't easy. Our cabin is small. I could pace only 2 to 3 steps before having to turn around. I was agitated though, and pacing seemed to help. I hate relying on technology that doesn't work. "I wonder if there's something wrong with the radio or antenna, Kathleen? Bern knows that we will be calling. We should hear something."

I turned the dial to 4441, the frequency of the Yukon Trappers, who just happened to be going through their daily 'winter sched' to make sure everyone living out in the bush was OK. It seemed there were about a dozen people giving each other updates on winter travel conditions, trapping success, the low price of fur, and their general well-being.

"At least we know that our radio can receive messages, Kathleen. It's getting kind of late. I don't really want to wait around until 9:00 pm to call again. Let's go to bed and try tomorrow."

Tuesday, February 2. I woke at 7:15 am, perhaps because of the cold. The fire had gone out, and the cabin was only +3 degrees. I restarted the fire and slumbered until after 10 o'clock. During breakfast Kathleen spotted several hundred caribou, approximately one km up the lake, travelling in loose lines toward the west. The herd rounded a ridge protruding into the lake and lay down on the snow-covered ice where they were partially protected from the strong south wind.

The caribou remained bedded down together on the lake all day, sharing their warmth, and apparently oblivious to the swirling snow and the gusting wind that occasionally must have reached 50 km per hour. A few adult females could be identified by their racks, which are normally not shed until just after calving.

The temperature, after 48 hours, remained unchanged at -19 degrees. Snow and ice, driven before the strong south wind, bit into any exposed skin. Blowing snow had drifted into all of our previous tracks. I could barely find yesterday's water hole, which showed slightly gray through the glazed surface of thin ice that had re-formed overnight. I approached carefully, still worried about breaking through. Again on my knees, I hacked at the ice until water gushed upward through the opening. I axed out a wider hole, and easily dipped the entire bucket into our winter well.

The 7:00 pm attempt at radio contact with Bern again produced nothing but static riding in upon the southern winds. I felt quite frustrated. To be regimented by a daily and then an hourly schedule made me feel as though we were under house arrest. I didn't come to Colville Lake to be monitored. I came to Colville Lake to escape regimentation.

The 8:00 pm contact also failed, although I again easily eavesdropped on the Yukon trappers, as they complained about low fur prices. I don't know why Bern doesn't try the 4441 frequency. The radio is producing the opposite effect for which it was intended. Instead of Bern knowing that we are fine, he will now be needlessly worried that something might have gone wrong. I very much resent this radio, and wish we didn't have it.

The Yukon trappers had said that the Northern Lights were causing transmission problems. Maybe our signal is too weak for Bern to hear us. Maybe the batteries are too cold. I ran my fingers across the back of the radio, which did feel quite cold. The radio is a long way from the fire. Maybe it needs to be warmed up.

I retrieved a roll of aluminum foil from the cupboard. I then fastened a rectangular covering, open at the front, which looked just like a Baker tent. I placed a lighted candle inside, at the back of the radio, and waited for the results. By 8:45 the radio compartment housing the nine 'D' batteries felt warm to my touch. At 8:58 pm I sat before the radio, holding the transmitter hopefully, even expectantly, in my left hand.

Two minutes later I pushed the transmitter button and yelled out my tiresome phrase, "Hello, Colville Lake Lodge. This is Mike calling from the outpost. Are you there, Colville Lake Lodge?" I released the button, but heard nothing but a monotonic, irritating stream of static.

I stared disdainfully at the silent, metal box. I felt quite annoyed with the radio's inanimate, malevolent stubbornness.

Wednesday, February 3. Last fall, we paid Bern to leave two cords of wood at the cabin for us. He told us that this should be plenty for the winter. Just before we drove up in January, however, he told us by telephone that two cords wouldn't be nearly enough. I think his revised assessment was based on his experience of living in the cabin during the month of September, just to try it out. I don't think he had ever lived there for such an extended period of time, particularly in the winter. The cabin was made primarily to rent to fishing parties in the summer. Bern also infrequently rented to hunters in the fall. He says Kathleen and I are the very first people to ever rent during winter. The cabin has not actually been winterized, and had no flooring

We were neophytes at walking on water. After every few steps we stopped to probe for overflow and thin ice.

insulation. Moreover, the stove is quite small, and certainly not intended for the depths of an Arctic winter when temperatures can remain at minus 30 and minus 40 for weeks at a time.

We began to worry about the two cords of wood that Bern collected for us last September. We have a stack of wood on the porch that stands about 2 m high, 1 m wide and 50 cm deep. We also have some 'extra' wood that Bern left for us on top of the snow behind the cabin. This is all the wood we can see. Bern says that the two cords of wood that he cut last fall are beneath a tarp, just below the cabin, next to the picnic table. The deep snow has buried the alleged picnic table, as well as our supply of wood beneath the tarp. How much wood is buried there? Is any wood buried there? How much wood will we need? Neither Kathleen nor I have ever lived in the bush. We have never lived where real winter occurs. We have never depended only on wood for heat. We have no idea how much wood we will actually need for the next four to five months, all alone here, at the north end of Colville Lake.

We decided that we need to conserve wood. Only three days into our stay, and we are already conserving wood. Conservation actually becomes quite easy when all one's resources depend on your own immediate personal, physical, and technical ability to acquire resources. If we run out of wood, then we must either get more wood, or risk freezing to death. Well, perhaps freezing to death is a little too dramatic. We likely won't freeze to death. People don't freeze to death any more, do they? Perhaps we would freeze only to uncomfortable. We don't look forward to either prospect, however – or anything in between, for that matter.

After a brief discussion, we decided to let the fire go out overnight. We loaded the stove at 9:30 pm. The temperature at our middle bunk height, where we are now sleeping to take advantage of heat pooling up against the ceiling, quickly rose to +36 degrees. Way too hot for comfortable sleeping, particularly for Kathleen, who hates heat.

I got up at 3:45 am to go outside to the outhouse. Back in the cabin, I opened the stove door, shined the flashlight inside, and saw that a few charred embers remained – glowing softly – sending out heat. The thermometer at middle bunk height read +10 degrees. This is very reassuring. Even without reloading our small stove, we can easily stay warm for most of the night.

I next woke at 9:15 am. Again I opened the stove door and peered inside. The fire had gone out completely – only -2 degrees at sleeping height. Nevertheless, I felt warm enough. Again I stepped outside for another trip to the outhouse (it doesn't take long to understand, or conclude, that indoor plumbing must certainly be one of the most spectacular human developments of all time!). I was greeted by a full moon, hanging low in the west, nearly resting upon the snow-covered, silent trees below. The morning was very calm. I looked at the thermometer hanging on the northwest corner of our cabin. The temperature had plummeted overnight to -35 degrees. I now felt more confident about our supply of wood, and our ability to remain unfrozen, or at least somewhat comfortable during the winter. Minus 35 is cold. Certainly -50, which we might still experience, is even colder; but -35 is cold. We had loaded the stove only once last evening, just before climbing into our bunks, and yet we remained warm enough throughout the night.

Just before noon, we loaded our plastic toboggan with supplies and gear for our first trip out onto Colville Lake. To be safe we packed heavy down parkas for when we rested; spare woollen mitts and gauntlets in case the ones we wore became wet or lost; and spare mukluks and duffel socks should we happen to go through the ice or step into overflow. We laced up the lamp wick on our snowshoes and headed south, along the east shore, into a persistent, chilling wind. My forehead began to numb. I pulled the fur ruff of my canvas wind suit over my head, and immediately felt my face begin to warm. Traditional, simple, and highly effective technology.

We continued up Colville Lake, accompanied by the musical 'swoosh, swoosh, swoosh' of our snowshoes. We rounded several points into our new, everlasting, grayish-white, frozen landscape. We poked at the ice almost constantly with a wooden broom handle, checking for overflow, and trying to determine if the ice was thick or thin. We have very limited experience walking on water, and Kathleen and I both felt uneasy. We were so all alone. What would we do if we actually broke through the ice?

After several km of very slow travel through our unexplored world, Kathleen spotted cabins on a ridge on the far western bank.

"Shall we go see?" I asked.

"I don't know, Michael. Do you think it's safe to cross over in the middle of the lake?"

"I don't know. How would I know?"

We stood and fidgeted, cooling off rapidly in the cold wind swirling over and around us.

"The caribou have crossed right near here. Their trail goes almost right to the cabins. If they can cross, the ice must be thick enough."

This certainly made sense to us. Moreover, just a month ago, we had driven our 2200 kg van, loaded with gear, across the ice on the Peel and Mackenzie Rivers. Two weeks ago we had been hauling our sled down the Mackenzie at Inuvik. We should, by now, know logically that the ice must be thick enough. Nevertheless, we remained uneasy. We stepped out gingerly toward the centre of Colville Lake. We poked at the ice, veered toward the caribou trail, and headed toward the three cabins.

Just before reaching the western shore we noticed the telltale "stained" colour of water that had flowed over thin ice, where the lake's current squeezed between shore and an island. Until now we had seen overflow only once before, in Inuvik. We congratulated ourselves for our caution, as we jabbed at the overflow. The broom handle easily – way too easily – penetrated and disappeared below the ice. We circled around the island, far away from the overflow, and struggled up a steep embankment. With every step we sank into deep drifts. Laboriously we lifted a snowshoe weighted down with snow, and then placed the next snowshoe forward and up the slope, only to sink again. This is not exactly what we had in mind.

Just as we reached the clearing at the top of the esker ridge, the winter sun burst gloriously from the clouds, and bathed the three log cabins in a soft, golden glow. This place had not been used for many years, as all three cabins were now disintegrating in the sub-Arctic stillness. I wondered who had lived here. Why had they come? Three cabins are more than a simple homestead for a trapping line or a seeker of gold. Three cabins are almost a community. How long had the residents lived here? Why had the cabins been abandoned? The North is filled with many of these untold stories of human hope, aspiration, disappointment and disappearance. Somebody must know the story of these cabins. I would love to hear it.

After a few minutes we felt the necessity to begin moving. Our bodies, without the mechanical heat of exertion, were once again beginning to cool. We quickly heated up as we struggled to follow our deep-snow path back down to Colville Lake. Feeling thirsty, we stopped for a drink of water. I took off my daypack, and pulled out the nalgene water bottle, only to find that the water had frozen solid! We were surprised, much like we had been surprised by the cold that day when we searched through the bins in the Parks Canada storage shed. We still have a lot to learn. During our return trip along the lake we stopped every few minutes to absorb the winter stillness, illuminated by the bright, heatless, February sun.

Back at the cabin, we busied ourselves with the daily chores that were necessary to maintain our life. We needed water for dinner. I sauntered down the hill to the south side of the spit, and reopened the water hole with my axe. I filled the bucket and stood up to enjoy the evening stillness, and to watch the sun sink below the southern horizon. The northern sky immediately turned a deep indigo. To the west, toward the ridge, the soft green of spruce trees reached elegantly and symmetrically upward from a snowy floor of purest white.

I returned to the cabin with my bucket of clear water. I mentioned to Kathleen how the sun had just set in the south. Many of the truisms of southern latitudes have no applicability here. (OK, perhaps some of the truisms of southern latitudes have limited applicability here.) For example, I have always 'known' that the sun rises in the east and sets in the west. All Southerners know this 'fact.' Here at Colville Lake, at 67° 32' north, however, in early February, the sun does not rise in the east. Nor does it set in the west. Rather the sun rises above the southern horizon in late morning, and settles again a few hours later below that same southern horizon.

In mid-summer, on our canoeing expeditions out onto the Barren Grounds, we have experienced the joy of a sun that never sets below any horizon. The sun simply circles above our heads in a wide ellipse, flying high in the south at mid-day – dipping low to the north at midnight. Actually, this statement is also somewhat inaccurate. In reality, the northern summer has no mid-day and no midnight. Day is perpetual, without middle – without night. There can be no midnight when day is perpetual. Mid-day can not exist without night. Although I would not call myself a moral relativist, 'known' facts and truths often depend on time and place.

After dinner, at 7:00 pm, we again failed to make contact with Bern on the SSBx-11A radio. We tried for nearly 30 minutes, but heard only the perpetual, irksome, high-pitched static. In disgust, I stepped outside to check the temperature, which read -43 degrees. Yowee! Above me spread a white mantle of Northern Lights, arching in wispy layers toward the northern horizon. Kathleen joined me on the south-facing knoll beneath the flagpole. The aurora borealis soared above our upturned heads. Rising like great columns of smoke from infinite campfires blazing below the southern horizon, the lights twirled, furled, folded and then fanned outward, until the eternal solar winds eventually hurled them beyond the northern limits of our vision. We stood transfixed for five minutes, until the penetrating cold drove us back to the warmth of our cabin.

At the next appointed hour of 8:00 o'clock I again dutifully tried to contact Bern. "Hello, Colville Lake Lodge. This is Mike calling from the outpost. Are you there, Colville Lake Lodge?"

I'm getting real tired of saying that. I tried for five minutes, with no response, other than the familiar static. I switched over to frequency 4441, and listened to each of the trappers recite in sequence their particular concerns and comments to their colleagues spread across the southern and central Yukon. Finally, Frank, coordinator of the nightly event, gave the usual invitation that I was waiting for: "Any other station wishing to call this winter sched can do so now."

I quickly depressed the transmitting button, and shouted at the radio. "Colville Lake calling. Can you hear me?"

"I copy you loud and clear, Colville Lake," Frank said. "What can I do for you?"

"I just wanted to see if anyone could hear me. I just wanted to confirm that my radio is working. I've been trying to contact Bern Will Brown at the south end of Colville Lake on 5730, with no success."

"Well, Colville Lake. I hear you fine. I can't help you with your party or that channel, though. Good luck."

"Thanks," I replied, only a little relieved. I turned off the radio. Where the heck is Bern, anyway? It was his idea to institute this daily schedule.

At 9:00 pm, I again tried the SSBx-11A radio, a stubborn and apparently useless piece of technology for which I was developing a very strong dislike. No response.

And then, at 10:00 pm, *blammo!* Like magic, Bern's voice came floating out of the radio. "This is Colville Lake, go ahead, Mike."

I have to give Bern credit for his patience and perseverance – sitting silently by his radio, 40 km to the south, waiting four days for our message that he knew must surely come eventually. I asked him why it took four days. Had there been some problem?

"Well, Mike, I've been calling on the hour every night since you arrived, with no luck. These radios can be quite temperamental. Sometimes you can't hear someone just across the street. Sometimes you can talk to a friend half way around the world using nothing more than a wet noodle for an antenna. It all depends on atmospheric conditions, the temperature, or even the Northern Lights. You never know, and there's not much you can do about it."

At least, for now, this source of communications turmoil has been resolved.

Thursday, February 4. I awoke at 4:15 am. Minus four degrees at sleeping height. I needed to scurry to the outhouse, but my bladder had given me too little warning, and there was not enough time for me to dress quickly. The chamber pot, which had originally belonged to Kathleen's grandmother, seemed an obvious alternative. I woke again at 9:15, rose up on my left elbow, and reached for the thermometer hanging on a nail approximately 1.5 m above the cabin floor. Minus 12 degrees. I crawled out of my mummy bag, slid down the varnished ladder, and set the thermometer on the floor, next to the water bucket. The mercury quickly slid down to -22 degrees. I suppose that explains why the contents of the water bucket and the chamber pot had frozen solid. At least our cabin had retained some heat overnight, particularly compared to the outside, where the thermometer indicated only -38 degrees.

Perhaps I should stop saying 'minus' when referring to the temperature. When we were staying with Alan and Marilyn in Inuvik, I would often report the temperature as 'minus this' or 'minus that.' I was enthralled with the very low temperatures. One day Alan posed a rhetorical question, "So, Mike, in Vancouver in the summer, when it's say 22 degrees, do you say that it's plus 22?"

I immediately understood his point. It's another one of those Southern attitudes that might not be so relevant in the North. We don't say it's 'plus this' or 'plus that' in the South during summer because it's obvious to everyone that the temperature is above freezing. Similarly, in the North during winter, it's obvious to everyone that the temperature is below freezing. One doesn't need to say 'minus.' So all I needed to report in the last sentence of the earlier paragraph, was that: "the thermometer indicated only 38 degrees!"

I don't think I can do it, though, and will continue to indicate explicit 'minus' temperatures during the rest of this winter narrative. 'Minus' 38 sounds exciting to this Southerner. Hopefully Alan will never find out.

I started the morning fire and boiled water for tea. Kathleen now began to stir in her bunk. She poked the upper half of her head out of her sleeping bag and said, "Let me know when the temperature reaches plus 18 degrees. I'll get up then."

I don't know why she picked 18 degrees, but 18 degrees is what she declared. Our first winter tradition was born.

Our small cabin reached this nearly tropical and very comfortable temperature in only a few minutes. "Eighteen," I called out.

"I'm ready," she replied. "Can you lift me down to the floor? It's too hard to get over to the ladder." Our second winter tradition took root. While I then toasted bread on the wood stove, Kathleen turned on the propane stove to prepare our oatmeal breakfast.

It's very interesting how quickly our bodies and biorhythms have adjusted to the short days and long, cold nights. We go to bed early, and sleep 12 to 13 hours each night. Our bodies have automatically adapted to the available light, as though we were hibernating half of the 24-hour day. We sleep easily

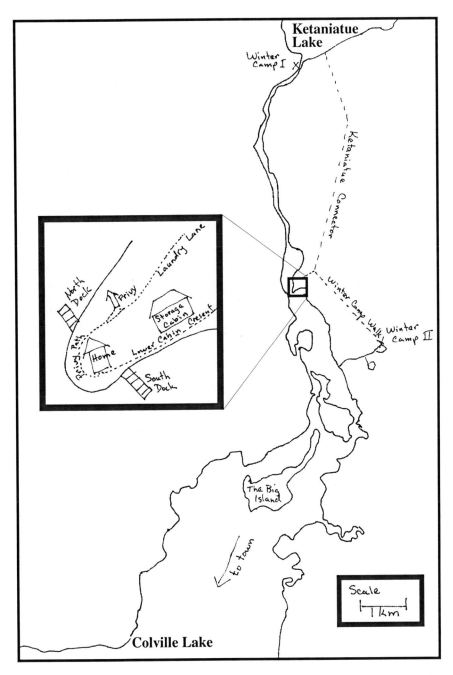

During the winter we put in over 20 km of snowshoe trails around our cabin, north to Ketaniatue Lake, and south to the Big Island.

and long. We awake refreshed and very ready for our new day on the north shore of Colville Lake.

And there is plenty that needs doing on the north shore of Colville Lake just to maintain our comfort and to enjoy life. There is water to chop out of the river and carry up the hill to the cabin. There are meals to make. There is gray water to carry back down the hill after dishes and washing. There are photographs to take, to document our stay here. There is writing to be done in our journals. And there are all those books we have brought, some of which we have been intending to read for several years. We should have time to read them this winter.

We also want to put in snowshoe trails along which we can more easily enjoy our new landscape. Ketaniatue Lake lies six km to the north, and the topographic map indicates a seismic cut line extending south from Ketaniatue Lake, up over Colville Ridge, to within less than 500 m from the bay in which we landed five days ago. This seismic cut line was put in decades ago by the oil and gas industry, during their insatiable hunt for new energy resources, but it still might provide a fairly open and easy route through the forest.

Moreover, this cut line could likely be easily accessed along the ski-doo trail that Bern had used last fall as he travelled back and forth between the cabin and where he had been cutting our wood. His map indicated where he had flagged a tree at the edge of Colville Lake to mark the beginning of his route, which should still be fairly obvious. Bern told us that we needed only to work our way north a few hundred metres uphill, until we came to two downed trees that he had left for us last fall. This few hundred metres would not only lead us to our wood, but would also take us nearly to the southern end of the cut line.

After brunch Kathleen and I set out east across Colville Lake, and easily found Bern's flagged tree. We turned north into the forest, which stood beautifully stark in the lightly drifting snow. Only a few animal tracks appeared sporadically to indicate that any other life existed in this winter palace. We continued uphill, and soon passed the two trees on our left, now nearly completely buried beneath the still accumulating snow. We eventually reached the cut line, which was still very open – like a highway through the forest.

It turns out that putting in new trail through soft, deep snow is strenuous work, particularly for the lead person, who sinks in deeply with every step. The trailing person fares only a little better. We frequently switched positions to spell each other off. After two km of hard labour bordering on drudgery, we decided to head back. By now the lead person was the third pass over the trail, which was becoming much better packed. The trailing person, now representing the fourth pass over the trail, essentially completed the job. The trail could now be used comfortably, without sinking in.

As city people, or perhaps as all people, we needed to name the places that we would commonly use during the winter. We christened the trail from Colville Lake to the cut line as Woodlot Way, while the cut line to Ketaniatue Lake became known as the Ketaniatue Connector.

We returned to the cabin at 2:30. The afternoon temperature had risen to -30 degrees. I moved our canoe to a grove of trees, where it would be more protected from accumulating snow. I then stacked some wood and chopped water from the ice for dinner. With all this mechanical heat, I felt very warm. In fact, I'm feeling very smug about my ability to stay warm. Layering is truly the key. All I'm wearing is light woollen long underwear – top and bottom – then a heavy wool shirt, wool pants and a canvas windbreaker. I'm almost stunned by how warm I feel at -30 degrees. No need to worry about maintaining a fire overnight tonight – not at these comfortable temperatures.

I'm particularly happy with our mukluks. In fact, I truly love wearing my mukluks, and am disappointed that I can't wear mukluks in Vancouver. First of all, it seldom snows in Vancouver. Secondly, any snowfall is usually quickly washed away by unceasing rain. Even if the snow remains for as long as a week, the weather is generally too warm or wet to wear mukluks. Vancouver is a poor place to live for people who like winter and winter clothes.

I could be quite tempted to move to a colder climate just so that I can wear mukluks. Don't laugh. Many people move to warm, sunny climates so that they can wear shorts and bathing suits, and go barefoot. The same principle applies to those who love winter clothes. I could easily be enticed to live permanently in the North just to cinch the fur ruff on my parka tightly around my face. To feel warm despite the cold is so reassuring and comforting.

Friday, February 5. I stood outside briefly at 6:15 am. Minus 42 degrees, but still -4 degrees at sleeping height in the cabin. I next woke just after 9:00. Minus 8 degrees at sleeping height and -43 degrees outside. The cabin retains heat so very well. I made the morning fire leisurely and comfortably. A few minutes later I lifted Kathleen to the floor.

During breakfast we decided to spend the day snowshoeing north, down the small river below Colville Lake, toward Ketaniatue Lake, 6 km away. Our topographic map shows an obvious constriction in the middle of Ketaniatue Lake. We later learned that in the Slavey language, *Ketania* means 'narrows,' and *tue* means 'lake.' I like this. Narrows Lake: a traditional, descriptive name that still remains on modern maps, albeit in a language that must be interpreted for me by the original people of Colville Lake.

Stepping outside, we were greeted by a spectacular pair of orange sun dogs resting low on the southern horizon. These circular images, appearing like two additional suns on a horizontal line with the real sun, actually sit on the more common parhelion, or 22° halo around the sun. The parhelion occurs because of refraction in tiny hexagonal ice crystals floating in the air. Sun dogs appear when light passes through horizontally-oriented ice crystals, compared to more randomly oriented crystals. The refracted light of sun dogs is so much more intense than the remainder of the 22° halo that they are often seen when the rest of the arc is not visible. Arctic people often referred to these images as the 'sun's dogs,' while the parhelion, or halo around the sun, was the ruff from the 'sun putting on its parka.' Indeed, because of the presence of ice crystals floating in cirrus clouds, sun dogs and parhelia often warn the winter traveller that snow is approaching.

For now, though, blue skies greeted our northward advance as we cut across the outlet of Colville Lake to skirt a small island. Out in the open, away from the forest of spruce, the wind had sculpted the soft snow into small, rigid furrows, like the uniform ridges on a sandy beach swept by a gentle ocean. Jamie Bastedo, in his book *Going North*, presents an essay about the research of Bill Pruitt, a renowned snow scientist. Pruitt reports that the Forest Eskimo of Northwest Alaska refer to these hardened snow formations as *upsik*.

The 'clack, clack, clack' from our wooden snowshoes clicking across the furrowed *upsik* was the only sound to disturb the frozen silence. No Ravens calling to each other across the valley – no Gray Jays whistling for hand outs. Silence dominated our physical world. Silence permeated our very existence. We followed a caribou trail down the centre of the river, trusting in the animals' inherent ability to find ice strong enough to support their weight. Tracks of snowshoe hare and a pursuing predator crossed our trail. Both sets of tracks led east, and then disappeared into the willows along the river's margin.

Half-a-kilometre ahead, the caribou trail veered right, along the edge of a light, yellow-gray discolouration. Water must be wicking into the snow from overflow. I poked at the overflow with my stick. An oily, black liquid oozed upward, and slid ominously across the ice toward our snowshoes. Kathleen and I both immediately jumped back, like cats startled by a bug in the grass. We were still very cautious in our new experience of walking on water. I would really hate to fall through the ice. I know that sounds obvious, but I would really hate it. I would like it even less if Kathleen fell through the ice. I worry most of the time about falling through the ice. Perhaps we will eventually become more confident.

In the afternoon the wind shifted to blow from the northwest, pulling a blanket of gray from the horizon down to the very tips of the spruce forest. Snow soon followed, and we returned to the cabin.

For the past three nights, after dinner, Kathleen and I have been playing cribbage, with the first person to win three games declared the winner. The two propane lights attached to the wall above our table and chairs were convenient to use, but they provided only a dusky atmosphere – poor lighting for counting the points in our cribbage hands. A Coleman lantern, which burns white gas and produces a very bright light, sat on top of the kitchen cabinets.

We had been reluctant to use the lantern, however, despite its superior lighting. First of all, Bern's instructions said that the lantern was finicky, and sometimes difficult to use. Secondly, the lantern was old. In fact the lantern could be considered an antique, as it was pressurized with a tube, like a bicycle pump, that was inserted into a hole in the lantern's base. I had never encountered such a lantern. All Coleman lanterns I had ever seen in my life were pressurized with a pump built directly into the base. Moreover, Bern had made it clear that we were responsible for replacing or paying for all broken or lost equipment. How could I replace an antique lantern?

Nevertheless, we needed to see our cards. I reached up and lifted down the lantern, opened the fuel reservoir, and poured in some white gas. Bern's instructions indicated that I should pump 30 times. The lantern quickly built up pressure as I pumped. This seemed good – the old lantern seemed to be working well – not so finicky or difficult. I turned the knob that released the pressurized fuel into the top of the lantern while also touching a lighted match to the lantern mantles.

"Holy Yikes [or something like that]!" I yelled.

The mantles instantly burst into flame, sending fuel outward and cascading down the lantern, where the wooden base, filled with fuel, became enveloped in fire. Our worst fears – a cabin fire – seemed imminent. I stuffed my hands into my leather gauntlets, which were always handy by the wood stove, grabbed the flaming lantern, and rushed outside, where the flames obligingly extinguished themselves.

Perhaps the lantern would not have actually exploded. Perhaps this 'fiery' adventure was how the lantern expressed its finicky personality. Or perhaps the old lantern was just feeling cranky. We decided that I should try again. After all, we needed to see our cards. This time, though, I pumped the lantern outside the cabin. After 25 pumps, five less than the recommended 30, I released the pressurized fuel, lit a match, and tentatively touched it to the lantern mantles. This time the mantles glowed, as they are supposed to do. Only a little fuel escaped, and the small, blue rivulets of flame quickly went out.

The last five minutes had been entirely too exciting. We believe that we are prepared to survive a cabin fire, as we have left the second cabin unlocked, with food, blankets and matches. We have carefully piled wood and kindling next to the second cabin's wood stove. Yes, we could likely survive a fire in our current cabin. That's not the problem. It would be much more difficult to report the news to Bern.

It might go something like this. "Say, Bern. Remember that small cabin on the point above the outlet of the lake. The one that you rented to us? Well, how can I put this? We accidentally burned it down. Nothing's left. It was quite a sight. The flames seemed to reach up all the way to the Northern Lights. You should have been there. It's a real shame, though. We have been here less than a week, and already we've burned down one of your cabins. It seems your old Coleman lantern was more finicky than even you suspected. We'll try to be more careful with your second cabin. After all, it's the only one you've got left." I have the feeling that Bern would not be amused by my cavalier slant to the story.

By early evening the temperature had risen to -23 degrees. And, even though our cabin was substantially warmer, the lower half of our legs felt somewhat cool while playing cribbage. The cabin door, less than one metre from where we sat at the table, did not close completely tight, which allowed a draft to creep across the floor through a small crack between the door and doorframe. "We gotta do something about that."

We searched through our packs to find our supply of woven nylon rope. I cut an appropriate length, and tied one end with a slipknot to a nail already partially embedded above and to the right of the doorframe. Using a taut-line hitch, I tied the other end of the rope to a companion nail on the left side of the doorframe. Then, from an upper bunk, Kathleen retrieved a thick, woollen blanket, which she hung from the rope with safety pins. Adjusting the taut-line hitch, Kathleen positioned the blanket so that it hung slightly beyond the floor, but could still be easily slid back-and-forth to allow entry and exit. Satisfied, we turned off the Coleman lamp, and climbed up the varnished wooden ladders to our respective bunks.

The only real downside of our cabin is that Kathleen and I can't sleep together. We enjoy sleeping together. We're married, and ought to be able to sleep together. By sleeping together we could also share body warmth, much as the Inuit did in their igloos. We reached out our hands to each other through the slats separating our bunks.

"Good night, Michael."

"Good night, Kathleen."

John Hornby had told Critchfield-Bullock that 'turtling down' in the sleeping bag was vital to keeping warm during the long Arctic nights. Like a turtle, Hornby would pull his head deep into the shell of his sleeping bag, leaving a gap at the top just large enough to breath through. I turtled down for the night. I could hear Kathleen doing the same on her side of the tier of bunks.

Saturday, February 6. I slipped down the ladder to the floor, stepped over to the wood stove, and opened the door. Only one charred half log remained from last night's fire. I turned it over, and felt just a hint of warmth beneath its blackened, corrugated surface. I stuffed a handful of paper shreds and small kindling inside the stove, directly behind the air intake. Over this kindling I placed the charred log, angled slightly upward to receive the draft of air flowing into the stove. I shut the door and opened up the damper. A few minutes later the paper shreds and kindling burst into flame. I added more kindling, put the tea kettle on the propane stove, and sat down at the table. Soon the wood stove began to crackle, like soft static, as the metal heated up. I love that sound – a fire well made – warmth and comfort would follow shortly. With real satisfaction I waited for the tea water to boil, and for the cabin to warm to +18 degrees. I would then lift Kathleen down to the floor, hand her a cup of hot tea, and read my book while she made our breakfast.

We've been here almost a week, and are starting to feel quite settled in – like this is our home – like we actually live here. Nevertheless, Kathleen says she's worried about conserving our supply of wood. I am also worried. At temperatures at or below minus 40, the landscape brings no heat. The only heat comes from that which we provide in the stove. The stove needs wood. Everywhere else beyond our stove is very cold. The corners of the cabin – our trails across the lake – the boreal forest that stretches infinitely away from our tiny spot of warmth in the cabin – all remain placidly cold and frozen. Our stove must have wood.

We agreed that we needed to increase our little cabin's ability to retain the heat that we create. After breakfast, I retrieved a shovel from the warehouse down by the lake. We dragged our plastic toboggan to areas with deeper drifts of snow. We took turns filling the toboggan with snow and hauling this insulating material back to the cabin. We considered it kind of ironic that snow – the iconic symbol of the frozen North – would provide our insulating material. On the other hand, the native peoples had been using snow and ice for insulation for millennia. Not really all that ironic.

We banked the snow nearly 1 metre high all around the base of the cabin, except for the screened porch. The entire task took less than 60 minutes. We stood back with a flourish to admire our completed project. We felt quite triumphant. We're confident that our morning's work would add a few more degrees of warmth to our home, and would help us conserve our precious supply of wood.

On our day trips outside the cabin, away from our stove, we generate mechanical heat, and feel quite warm. We also feel quite content to know that we are conserving wood by allowing the fire to go out during our absence. When we return, even after only a few hours, however, all of the cabin's heat has escaped. Our stove immediately demands more wood.

Today Kathleen decided that she would like to spend the afternoon in the cabin to make bread. This means keeping the fire going all day. It's my responsibility to get more wood. So, after lunch, I loaded my axe and 30-inch bow saw into the plastic toboggan, and headed out at -27 degrees, alone, to bring back the two trees left along Woodlot Way. Bern had offered the use of his chain saw, which was locked in the shed, along with a plentiful supply of gas and oil. I had come to Colville Lake, however, to escape the aggressive noise and offensive fumes of machines and engines. I would use my bow saw and axe.

I headed east across Colville Lake. A peaceful breeze carrying a few snowflakes blew in from the south. "Whump, whump, whump" sang my snowshoes as I broke through the surface of the newly fallen snow, called *api*, by the Forest Eskimo of Northwest Alaska. I strode into the swirling white, breaking trail, and 'searching underfoot' for our previous hard-packed trail. 'Searching underfoot' becomes obvious as a temperate-latitude figure of speech. In reality I was 'searching under snowshoe' for our hard-packed trails of the past few outings. We had read that when a man is lost in a white-out, that if he is careful, that if he remains patient, then he can always find his way back by searching for the packed snow of his outbound trail. It is said that these hardened trails, covered beneath successive layers of snow, will remain 'visible' to the experienced man from the beginning to the end of winter.

I crisscrossed the area where the trail should be. After searching for only a few minutes, I found what seemed to be our previous trail. Damn, if this doesn't work! I don't want to appear too boastful, though. I can't really claim to be wise in the ways of the northern snow trail. I was, after all, only 150 m from the cabin, searching in snow only 2 cm deep, in an area where I knew the trail unquestionably existed. Nevertheless, I felt good about having found a hidden trail during a snowstorm.

Moments later I reached the flagged tree, and climbed uphill, into the spruce forest. I stopped to rest, and immediately sensed something for which I had been searching for many years. I cocked my head in all directions, and listened intently. Could this be happening to me? Yes, I had found it! I had found perfect and absolute silence. I now stood enveloped by the silence of a world that had seemingly been created only moments before. The silence of a world that had not yet learned to speak. The silence before there were Ravens and jays. The silence before there were loons and wolves. The silence of a world before there were any people.

I remained motionless, transfixed by the utter tranquillity. No sirens screamed of emergency. No stereos blared unwanted music. No traffic intruded unceasingly in the background. I exhaled slowly, so as not to shatter the stillness. My breath condensed briefly, and then dissipated gently into the frigid, hushed air.

I stepped off Woodlot Way and cleared the snow from our future firewood. I limbed the butt end of the largest tree, and sawed out two 20-cm lengths for the stove. This new wood should provide enough heat for our cabin from bedtime to morning.

When I returned Kathleen seemed very happy. The cabin was warm, and she stood before the 2-burner propane stove waiting for her steam bread to rise. She smiled as I sat down at the semi-circular table below the west-facing window. Thirty minutes later Kathleen triumphantly produced our first bread of the winter. We both prodded and caressed the soft, resilient, white bread now cooling on the table. Our own bread! Created from simple basics. Sustenance created from ice and wood and flour. We look forward to tonight's dinner and tomorrow's breakfast. Our own bread. Man might not live by bread alone. But bread, where none existed before, is extraordinarily comforting.

Kathleen says she's very much enjoying having the area to ourselves. The purity of the new snow is broken by only a few animal tracks. In total we have seen about 300 caribou moving through our area. A large herd spent all day about 1 km up Colville Lake, clearly visible from our south-facing window.

After dinner with candlelight we prepared for another game of cribbage. First I pumped and lit the Coleman lantern (outside of course). I hung the lantern above the table, which glowed brightly beneath the light. Kathleen then popped the popcorn. Pump and Pop. Pump and Pop. We would repeat this procedure many times during the shortest days of winter.

After cribbage we heated water for hot chocolate, and finished the day by reading quietly by the purring wood stove. I then waited for Kathleen to climb up to her middle bunk before I turned off the lantern. As the mantles sputtered, I crawled up to my middle bunk and slipped into my sleeping bag.

We reached out our hands to touch each other through the slats separating our bunks.

"Good night, Michael."

"Good night, Kathleen."

We have settled into a comfortable routine. Our life is simple and basic. I'm very happy here.

Sunday, February 7. I rustled out of the mummy bag just after 7:00 am to answer nature's call. The temperature outside was -31 degrees, but a comparatively warm -1 degree at sleeping height inside. The bucket on the floor held water rather than ice. Banking the cabin walls with snow had apparently worked more successfully than we had hoped for. Even so, we decided that we should place the bucket on the counter overnight, where it would have access to more heat. Just like a few days ago when we had moved from the lower to the middle bunks. It took us only a week to hit upon this obvious bucket strategy. We learn slowly.

The pre-dawn light of the sun, still below the southern horizon, soon slipped past the drawn curtains of the south-facing window – the beginning of a new day at Colville Lake. The northern sky turned bluer than an alpine lake in summer. A thin layer of clouds shone from the golden reflection of the still hidden sun. The southern horizon immediately above the lake glowed deeply red, as though an unbroken arc of fiery embers stretched from east to west. At 10:05 the sun finally rose gently above the southeastern ridge, and the palette of colours immediately faded. The northern sky paled, and soon showed little more chroma than the ice-covered lake below. Only the dark, amorphous mass of spruce on the distant ridge provided any contrast to our winter world of gray and white.

We lingered over breakfast, reading, writing and sipping tea. The sun now poured directly through the south window, and the wood stove, like a satisfied house cat, purred contentedly at our feet.

I then slipped on my mukluks, grabbed the toboggan and axe, and headed back to the bush to limb the two trees next to Woodlot Way. Once limbed, I returned to the cabin, where Kathleen handed me a grilled cheese sandwich for lunch. Then back to the bush where I sawed seven, large-diameter, stove-length billets from one of the trees – another couple nights of heat. All together these two trees should give us about one week of nighttime stove loadings.

The weather remained clear and bright all day, with the temperature dipping to -38 degrees just before dinner at 5:30.

Monday, February 8. I sat at the evening table, savouring the memories of another very gratifying day. We woke late, at 9:00 am, when the morning light first crept quietly into our cabin. We then enjoyed a leisurely breakfast of fried Prem and pancakes, soaked in rich maple syrup. Although the syrup had frozen solid, Kathleen quickly resolved this problem by placing the syrup bottle in a bath of heated water. Even problems that initially seem frustrating and challenging usually have simple, obvious solutions. After breakfast we drank tea and read in the soft light pouring straight through the window, through which we could see the sun perched immediately above the southern horizon.

Just before noon, with my axe and bow saw stowed in the plastic toboggan, I once again headed out into the sunlight and snow. East across the frozen bay of Colville Lake, then north into the spruce forest to the downed trees lying next to Woodlot Way. I brushed off the new snow from the fallen spruce, and caressed the trunk that would provide the next billets of wood for our stove. I measured out an appropriate length, from wrist to elbow. There was no need to carry a tape measure – just one more unnecessary item that would undoubtedly break or go missing. After slowly inscribing the kerf, I methodically and rhythmically sawed through the 15-cm-diameter bole. I repeated this process up the trunk until all the pieces were ready for loading into the toboggan. I then hauled my wood back to the cabin, where Kathleen waited for me with dinner.

As darkness approached, we saw 16 caribou walking slowly down the centre of Colville Lake toward our cabin. The caribou moved purposefully, in single file, until they reached the narrows just opposite our west-facing window. Through this gap the water flowed beneath shallow snow and fragile ice only a few centimetres thick.

The advancing herd halted and assembled before the constriction, as though discussing strategy. After a few moments, three caribou suddenly burst through the narrows into a small embayment of firm ice on the west shore. The rest of the herd soon followed, in small groups of 2 to 5 animals.

As each group reached the other side, all the caribou looked back, seemingly to check on the safety and progress of their companions.

Did the caribou know that danger lay beneath thin ice? Did the caribou know that smaller groups could cross more safely than larger groups? Did the caribou know that speed could propel them across cracking ice? Did the caribou actually communicate their understanding of the challenge before them? I like to think that the answer to all four of these questions was yes. If the answer to all four these questions were no, then how could caribou possibly have survived for millennia in an environment where such challenges to life routinely existed?

Perhaps my wildlife biologist colleagues at the University of British Columbia would know the answer to these four questions. Likely not, though. These normative questions lie beyond the realm of hypothetico-deductive logic of cause and effect. There exists no feasible way to place groups of caribou in control and treatment groups to test these questions. I don't really care, though. It's not really necessary to know absolutely, and with quantitative data, the answer to all of life's questions. Test consequences, logic, predictability and rigid experimentation don't begin to address the true beauty, elegance and wonder of simply witnessing caribou safely cross thin ice. I am content to wonder.

I much prefer this life, with its simple, direct pleasures and challenges, compared to my recent life as scientist/administrator. In this previous existence I attended meaningless meetings, with vague agendas, that concluded only with a predictable recommendation to 'meet again sometime soon.' I often prepared rushed memos in response to University 'crises' that became immediately forgotten as tomorrow's 'crises' unfolded. I wrote endless applications for research funds followed periodically by jargon-infested publications that very few people ever read.

Ironically, the more scientific papers I might publish that very few people would read, the more complete and bright my academic reputation would become. Here in the boreal forest, however, living along the frozen, isolated banks of Colville Lake, neither academic fame nor the forgotten purpose of shredded memos provide any value whatsoever. Right now, all that matters, and matters very much, is that the stove required wood with which to heat our cabin.

Kathleen and I are like those caribou. We are two souls, all alone, who depend upon each other for our safety and security. I think I'll split some more logs before dinner, just to be ready in case it's a cold night.

Tuesday, February 9. Again, just before dusk, a group of caribou approached from the south, and stopped immediately before the thin-iced narrows opposite our cabin. The 12 animals assembled at the edge of the gap, seemingly uncertain about what to do next. They appeared relaxed. Then, without any apparent discussion, four caribou simply and slowly walked across. Standing on the other side, they looked back very nonchalantly toward their compatriots. These eight, however, were now walking very briskly back up the lake. The 'nonchalant four' burst back across the ice to reconvene the meeting. After much discussion, several vetoed motions and polite haranguing, all 12 eventually sauntered across the outlet together. Perhaps these were some of the same animals that we had seen last night, and maybe they had learned from previous experience that the ice was safe. I now have two nights of contradictory data regarding how caribou react when faced with potential danger. Back to the hypothesis drawing board.

After dinner, I pumped the Coleman lantern, Kathleen popped the popcorn, and we began our nightly cribbage games. About half way through the tournament, both of us commented that it seemed a bit chilly in the cabin. We checked the stove – it burned hot. The cribbage game continued.

"Fifteen-two, and a run of three makes five."

There was no doubt about it now, though. Our feet and lower legs definitely felt cold. We checked the indoor thermometer, which read +20 degrees. Everything was normal – no reason for us to feel any colder than usual. Maybe we just feel cold tonight. Kathleen counted her hand.

"Fifteen-two, fifteen-four, and two pairs make 8."

At the end of the last game, about 30 minutes later, we prepared to head for the outhouse one more time before going to bed. Kathleen pulled back the woollen blanket hanging across the doorsill and discovered that the door had been left partially open by the last person to use the outhouse! Minus 27 degrees outside, with a strong north wind blowing, and our door was open. At least now we know why we were feeling a little cold.

I can't tell you how many times my father told me when I was young not to leave the door open.

"Close that door, Mike. Do you want all the heat to get out? How many times do I have to tell you"?

It turns out that my father had been dispensing valuable advice. I should have paid more attention, or perhaps he should have told me just one more time. This is not an admission of guilt or fault on my part about leaving the door open. I'm just saying that I now realize that my father gave me good advice about how to make sure that all the heat doesn't escape through an open door.

Wednesday, February 10. In the early morning I sensed, rather than felt, that cold had intensified its assault on our cabin at the north end of Colville Lake. The thermometer remained below -40 degrees all day. Minus 43 degrees when I went to the outhouse at 8:10 am. I coughed involuntarily as the dry, frigid air rushed into my warm, moist lungs. Minus 42 degrees when Kathleen and I stirred from our bunks at 9:20.

For the first time, we believed the cold to be animate, insidious, powerful. We felt surrounded by its strength. Last night, as we returned from a short walk, cold peered down on us from beneath the Northern Lights that waltzed across the black sky. Cold lurked just beyond the rim of the ridge, up which we struggled, slowly and all alone. Cold concealed itself behind the trunks of spruce trees. Cold hid in the ground just below the depth to which our snowshoes sank in the soft, powdery snow.

Just before noon I loaded my axe and bow saw in the toboggan, and headed out to Woodlot Way to retrieve the last of the downed wood. The weather remained clear and bright, with the temperature rising two degrees to minus 41. The sun released no heat, and the open sky hungrily sucked all vestiges of warmth from the icebound domain of Colville Lake. Sparkling ice crystals floated and twirled through the clear, Arctic sky.

I worked quickly, and soon limbed and bucked up the trees into 2.5-m turns. I unzipped my parka, surprised at how fast I overheated when working, even at -41 degrees. I wore three layers of wool, including underwear, shirt and sweater beneath my parka, and felt very satisfied that I could remain warm so easily at temperatures below minus forty.

As I loaded the logs on to the sled, I allowed my hands to linger along the firm wood beneath the peeling, flaking bark. I love the feel of wood, the aroma of wood, the grain of wood. I love just being around wood. I particularly love bringing wood home when the temperature remains below minus forty.

After the 7:00 pm radio conversation with Bern, Kathleen and I both hunkered down in our chairs near the wood stove. The last time we looked, the outside thermometer quietly indicated a temperature of -39 degrees. For the first time, I began to empathize with the human vulnerability that even men like Rae and Hornby must certainly have felt at times like this – all alone, except for the pervasive, deepening cold.

We know full well that we can't survive without the heat flowing upward and outward from our 55-cm, airtight, wood-burning stove. We do not have the experience of Rae or Hornby to easily survive outside our heat-retaining walls of varnished spruce. Our cabin is like a nest to which we can safely return after each brief sojourn to gather wood or simply to enjoy the winter solitude.

Although we can always acquire more wood by falling, sawing and sledding trees back to camp, I worry about our fuel supply. The two trees I brought home today, both about 5 to 6 m long and 20 cm in diameter at the base, will last no more than 3 days. I hope that enough wood is buried beneath the snow so that we are not required to spend all or most of our time harvesting wood from the bush. I don't wish to live quite that close to the edge.

The wood stove seems the very centre of our universe. Like the sun, it pumps forth welcome, concentric bands of warmth. Within our small 14 by 14-foot cubicle of heat, life can be sustained. Outside, beyond the influence of this small stove, beyond the cabin walls, there lives a deadly, palpable cold. Only our stove, our pathetically small 55-cm stove, produces any heat at all in the empty, frozen landscape that stretches hundreds of kilometres away in all directions from this isolated cabin that sits 40 roadless km north of the nearest community. If for any reason we can no longer feed logs to our voracious stove, then the cold will quickly, silently and certainly overwhelm our haven of heat.

Tonight we feel acutely aware of the cold. Cold sits contentedly in the corners of our cabin. Cold squeezes into our cupboards. Cold rests in our storage bins. Cold smiles up at us from the black void beneath the bottom bunks. Although only 28 days, February seems such a very long month, as we sit quietly in our infinitesimally small cubicle of heat, surrounded by cold that seems to have neither boundary nor end.

Thursday, February 11. We began our morning at -45 degrees, the coldest temperature so far. I set a pot of tea water on the propane stove and turned the self-igniting knob to on. The stove clicked, but did not light. I turned the knob to off, waited a few moments, and tried again. Still no flame. Maybe it's too cold for propane to work. When we discussed our plans with friends and self-described experts last summer, we received a great deal of conflicting opinions regarding propane as a winter fuel. Some people said that propane does not work below freezing. Some opined that propane works fine until about -20 degrees. Others were adamant that propane gels at -40. Most everyone said that we would be foolish to rely solely on propane.

Our source of propane sits on the porch outside, completely exposed to the ambient temperature. Kathleen and I now have a grand total of 10 days of experience with propane. We know that it certainly flowed yesterday at -43 degrees. It seems that all of the advice we received last summer was from people who didn't truly understand what they were talking about. Certainly though, there must be some temperature below which propane does not flow. Perhaps that temperature is minus 45 degrees. Whatever the truth might be, the fact right now is that no propane is flowing into our stove. Bern had left a full 100-pound propane cylinder standing next to the cylinder currently in use. Maybe our cylinder is empty. I exchanged the two, and again tried the stove, which immediately produced a reassuring blue flame. Propane seems to work even at -45 degrees.

As we looked out our south-facing window in mid-morning, the scene seemed as inviting as August afternoons in Vancouver. Sun shone brilliantly above the lake. To the west and north, the green spruce forest glowed invitingly beneath the low rays of the golden sun. Long shadows of ridge-top trees slanted across the pure white of Colville Lake. Caribou trails zigzagged across its frozen surface. White puffs of cloud floated lazily through the sky. All looked so very enticing through the window.

We stepped outside, and were instantly numbed. Despite the pleasing scene through the window, the temperature was still only -40 degrees. We wandered down to the ice-covered lake, and peered across to the ridge still shrouded in shade. Without the sun, the forest appeared as patches of gray and black beneath a colourless sky. Kathleen tried to set up the tripod to take a few pictures, but complained that her hands and nose were beginning to freeze while composing the shot. Even only a few minutes at -40 degrees becomes uncomfortable when touching metal objects, which instantly suck all heat out of exposed fingers.

To me, minus 40 represents a magical, almost mystical term. At minus 40, Celsius and Fahrenheit are the same. In both measurement systems, people of the North talk about minus 40 like a threshold. Minus 39 might be cold, or at least somewhat cold-ish. But when the thermometer hits minus 40 – well then, now you've got something. Now it's starting to get really cold. Internal combustion engines often fail to start at minus 40. Propane often does not flow at minus 40 (or so I'm told). Most commercial airlines stop flying at minus 40. Explorers' journals speak to us respectfully of minus 40. Travellers need to pay attention – need to be cautious – at minus 40. Stepping in overflow at minus 40 – losing a parka at minus 40 – misplacing one's mitts at minus 40 – failing to start a fire quickly at minus 40 – breaking down at minus 40. All these misfortunes seem to be more serious at the minus 40 threshold.

The mere number itself evokes poetic parables and images: It rained for 40 days and 40 nights; Ali Baba and the 40 Thieves; the 'back 40'; minus 40. It's fun just to say minus 40. Try it. Say it out loud. Minus 40 means something.

We concluded that the best course of action on this winter day of minus 40 was to return to the cabin, brew some tea, read a book, and sit by the fire. There will be plenty of other times for exploration before break-up in mid-June.

Friday, February 12. Kathleen and I spent an exhilarating afternoon snowshoeing three km south, up Colville Lake, along the eastern shore. The sky hung so very heavenly blue above the spires of white spruce – its red inner bark fluorescing in the sun – its branches festooned with rows of sparkling snow. A lone Gray Jay twittered in the background, then glided across a clearing with a graceful, undulating flight. The temperature, at - 29 degrees, felt comfortably warm.

After dinner, in the early gloam of dusk, we saw two planets, very near each other, suspended low on the western horizon, just above the ridge across the narrows of Colville Lake. As the evening progressed, the lower planet,

Venus, rose up to meet its companion planet, which, based on reports on the CBC radio, is most likely Jupiter.

Today the sun remained above the high point of the ridge before setting, which gives promise of longer evenings soon to come. As is our routine on Fridays, we laundered and sponge-bathed. We filled the stove nearly to capacity before undressing, and then kept pushing in more wood until both of us had finished. A bit extravagant, all this heat and burning of wood. But we felt incredibly decadent and luxurious, as we sat naked beside our stove, basking in the warmth of our cabin.

Saturday, February 13. Cold continues to dominate the north end of Colville Lake. Minus 42 degrees this morning, although our sleeping bunks remained at a comfortable -8 degrees.

We lingered at the breakfast table, looking south, up the lake, through our picture window. Delicate ice crystals floated and twirled in the frigid air. A sun dog rose up from behind the distant ridge to follow the rising sun as it moved slowly west. Just before noon a second rainbow-coloured column appeared to the east of the sun, which spent the rest of its day flanked by both of its companion sun dogs.

We spent most of our day engaged in tasks around home – collecting water, stacking wood, writing letters, and organizing the storage cabin. A south wind blew unceasingly and bitterly. Although the temperature rose rapidly to -19 degrees by mid-afternoon, the wind quickly chilled our exposed faces.

As mentioned before, Kathleen and I highly appreciated and valued the Conover book, *A Snow Walker's Companion*, which provides excellent information for understanding the relationships among snow, ice and water. In summer, the coldest water in Colville Lake was at the bottom. As winter approached, the temperature of the surface water began to drop, eventually reaching +4 degrees, the point at which it reached maximum density. The lake now 'turned over,' as the surface water sank, and displaced the bottom water upward. This colder bottom water, now at the surface, quickly froze over, trapping the four-degree water at the bottom of the lake.

Water, even under pressure, does not compress. It must flow somewhere. As snow and ice accumulated during winter, the pressure increased on the water beneath, which continued to flow through the outlet. Much of this water flowing through the narrows is near +4 degrees, which helps to melt the ice and to keep the outlet open. The Conovers wrote that:

> *All winter this section of the lake will oscillate between open and ice covered, safe to cross or perilous to tread. At times, snow on top of thin ice shows discoloration from wicking up water, and this indicates danger. At other times, the ice may be thin, yet hold a dusting of snow so light that the ice is not depressed and overflow does not occur. The snow is not discolored, nor does it appear shallower than the snow over adjacent thicker ice. There are no signs of danger. If the open water of the outlet is nearby, you will need to test the ice before trusting it.*

This passage describes our situation perfectly. For the past week, 'The Narrows' below our home has been slumping in. By late afternoon, the wind had blown the snow free from The Narrows, revealing the dangerous, discoloured, green slush below. Our frozen world is not static or uniform. Rather, our frozen world is fluid and unpredictable. We are neophytes at winter travel, and need to be cautious.

Sunday, February 14; Valentine's Day. Finally, a day that began mild, at -20 degrees. We breakfasted quickly, stepped out into the pleasant warmth, put on our snowshoes, and broke more trail toward Ketaniatue Lake. Our snow trail now stretches 4.5 km, less than two km from Ketaniatue. By the time we returned to the cabin in early afternoon, the temperature had risen to a comparative blistering -14 degrees, the warmest day so far.

We hope eventually to snowshoe to town, camping in our wall tent along the way. If so, Kathleen says that we need to do a lot of toughening up, as our feet were quite sore after snowshoeing only 9 km today. The town of Colville Lake is 40 km away, and we would be breaking trail while pulling a sled and a toboggan filled with tent, stove, food and winter gear. In reality, we would be travelling farther than 40 km each way. The town of Colville Lake is 40 km away as the crow flies, straight across the lake. But we won't be going straight across the lake. We will need to drag our gear along the perimeter of Colville Lake, where we can cut wood to heat the wall tent at night. Yes, we certainly need to do a lot of toughening up before going to town.

The phrase 'as the crow flies' is actually not a very appropriate simile for the straight-line distance to Colville Lake. Crows are residents of more southern latitudes, particularly in winter, when they retreat southward in search of warmer weather. Ravens dominate our northern, winter skies, and seem to revel in the harsh climate. Like their southern counterparts though, our Ravens fly in very straight lines. Ravens seem to know exactly where they want to go, and fly there directly and quickly. The town of Colville Lake, therefore, is 40 km away 'as the Raven flies.' Whether the distance is measured by the flying habits of Ravens or Crows, however, Colville Lake is a long way away on snowshoes. Kathleen and I must toughen up our feet.

Most of what we have read about snowshoeing suggests that one needs time to become accustomed to this somewhat unusual way of walking. Alternatively, the Conovers wrote in their book, that "If you can walk, you can snowshoe (although) finesse comes with practice."

Maybe Kathleen and I just need a bit more finesse. I think though, that the design of our snowshoes is at least partially responsible for our weary feet. We purchased our shoes by mail order from Craig MacDonald, who supplied us with traditional wooden/babiche shoes made in the popular 'Michigan' or 'Maine' design. Compared to other snowshoe designs, they are of medium length (125 cm) and width (35 cm), and are suited to a wide variety of conditions, including pulling sleds and toboggans along frozen lakes and rivers.

Unfortunately, our snowshoes do not have an upturned toe, and the babiche weave is somewhat coarse. These last two attributes are poorly suited for breaking trail in fresh, deep snow. With each step, the coarse weave causes us to sink at least 10 to 25 cm into the snow. Then, when we lift out for the next step forward, snow covers the flat snowshoe from our foot to the tip. The snowshoe tilts downward, and often immediately re-buries itself in the snow after only a short step forward. Travelling all day under these conditions would make anyone's feet sore! A much better choice of snowshoe would have been the so-called 'Alaskan' design, which is longer and narrower, with a strongly upturned toe, and a fine weave. We had certainly read this recommendation in the Conover's book, but had no access to 'Alaskan' snowshoes. Oh well, we have what we have, and our 'Ontario' snowshoes are quite effective on flat, frozen surfaces. We have come here to learn about living and travelling in an Arctic Canadian winter. Lessons are learned best with personal experience.

For Valentine's Dinner, Kathleen made pizza, followed by butterscotch pudding for dessert. She was particularly proud of the pizza, which she said presented a great challenge because she had no oven. Kathleen is a resourceful, resilient person, and solved her pizza problem by using a heavy cast iron pan covered with tin foil. The pizza required only about 30 minutes to cook over a low heat. The bottom of the crust was crispy, but not burned. In addition to being a wonderful cook, Kathleen is also very modest. This time though, even she acknowledged that "the pizza was quite good!"

While Kathleen had been making the dinner, I strolled outside, telling her that I "just wanted to look around." I collected some dried grasses on the south-facing knoll below the flagpole. I then strolled down to a small depression to harvest a few fluffy heads from last season's cotton-grass. Returning along the snow trail, I picked up a few spruce cones. Back in the cabin I arranged them as a centrepiece for our Valentine's Day table. Kathleen's face beamed with surprise and happiness. I had to agree with her that I had indeed been very thoughtful.

Dining by candlelight, we planned our tasks and activities for the next day. Kathleen's current plan for tomorrow is to experiment with some of the suggestions in the landscape photography book that I gave her for Christmas. She points out, however, that if something else comes up – even if that something else is just sipping tea and reading by the fire – then that's what she'll do. Kathleen and I are both enjoying this stress-free environment.

Monday, February 15. Well, it turned out that something else did come up for Kathleen. Rather, I should say, something else went down – the temperature. We had been quite happy with the last 24 hours remaining above -20 degrees. We had even talked about how the coldest period of winter might now be over. Foolish Northern adventurers. Just before going to bed last night we stepped outside to check the thermometer, which read only -37 degrees. Winter definitely continues. We note, after all, that the calendar indicates mid-February. Very foolish Northern adventurers. Best not to hope for what might be. Much better to simply accept what is.

We accepted the colder temperature by spending the day close to home and our wood stove. After lunch I snowshoed up the lake to enjoy the silent, calm day. From a distance of about 0.5 km, our cabin looked so peaceful and inviting with the smoke from our wood stove rising up in to the clear, blue sky. I attempted to photograph the scene, but the camera battery failed, even though the temperature had warmed to -32 degrees.

I also failed in my attempt to catch a lake trout in the hole that I had chiselled through the ice in front of our cabin. Everyone back at home wanted us to do some ice fishing. I'm not all that interested in ice fishing, but I gave it my best try. Anyway, the water here at the outlet is likely less than one metre deep, perhaps too shallow to jig successfully for lake trout, which are more likely hunkered down in deeper water. I don't really want to chisel through a metre of ice out on the middle of the lake. I think I'm done with ice fishing for the winter.

The days are definitely becoming longer now. We no longer need to light the lantern in the morning, and the sun is rising much farther to the east than when we arrived two weeks ago.

Tuesday, February 16. As on all mornings, we lingered over breakfast, sitting close to each other and to the warmth of the wood stove – idly sipping hot tea – casually spreading jam on another slice of toast – savouring our panoramic view of Colville Lake. The morning sun slid softly west across the distant southern ridge, and eventually shone directly through the window, as though purposefully to bathe us in its brightness. The light sought out the cold corners of the cabin, and its varnished logs reflected the sun's warmth around the walls, and outward to the centre of the room. Within this brilliance we wrote in our journals and read from our favourite books. Sometimes we simply reflected – always without interruption. As never before, I felt completely content. These past two-and-a-half weeks have comprised the most rewarding and satisfying period of what has already been a very generous life.

Toward the end of breakfast a ground-level snowstorm raced toward us from the south, warming the land to -13 degrees, and shrouding our vista in fog, lightly suffused by the golden sun. We felt even more cozy and secure by the stove.

I stepped outside to split more kindling. The wind comforted me, caressed me, as I swung the axe, away from which flew beautiful, thin strips of wood. Two twittering Gray Jays alighted on the spire of a nearby spruce. Together, all three of us faced southeast into the wind, revelling in its tumult, and looking forward to the south wind's promise of eventual spring thaw.

Like many people, I originally knew the Gray Jay as 'whiskey jack,' a bird that definitely associates campers and hikers with food, even coming to the hand for bread, raisins or cheese. More often than not, they don't wait to be invited – I have seen whiskey jacks swoop in to take toast directly from our plates as Kathleen and I sat around the campfire. Their aggressiveness often frustrated trappers using baits to catch fur-bearing animals or early travellers trying to protect their winter food supplies. Such familiarity between bird and humans has inspired a long list of colloquial names for the Gray Jay. In addition to the once-official 'Canada Jay,' other names include meat-bird, camp robber, venison-hawk and moose-bird. The most familiar of all, 'whiskey jack,' is actually a corruption of aboriginal names, variously written aswiskedjak, whiskachon, wiskadjak and many other variants, of a mischievous prankster or trickster prominent in Algonquian mythology. I much prefer the name whiskey jack to Gray Jay. It sounds so much more romantic and fanciful. Despite the likely disapproval of taxonomic ornithologists I will call these playful birds Whiskey Jacks from now on.

The wind blew very strongly all day, with gusts up to 60 km per hour. Swirls of snow obscured our view of Colville Lake, and filled our carefully created snowshoe trails. Amorphous tones of white dominated the landscape, and we remained in the cabin all day, even though the temperature soared to -11 degrees. If the thermometer stays near this level at bedtime, we intend to let the fire die out, without adding one last full load before climbing up to our bunks. On many mornings the temperature has been only minus 8 or minus 12 degrees at sleeping height, yet we have still felt quite warm all night.

Wednesday, February 17. The temperature hovered all night between -14 and -16 degrees. Our home remained warm, though – plus 4 degrees at five o'clock and zero degrees when we rose at 9:00 am. We certainly don't need to keep the stove going at night when outside temperatures reach -15 degrees or higher.

The wind finally stopped at around 3:00 am, and the Arctic air regained control of Colville Lake. The temperature dropped six degrees, to minus 22 in less than 60 minutes. The new snow glistened in the morning light. The surface of the lake appeared like a sandy beach, as the strong winds of yesterday had carved and molded the formerly flat surface into multitudes of mounds, terraces and small dunes. Yet spring seems ever closer, as more

We welcomed four unexpected visitors on February 17, the only people we saw in our first seven weeks of isolation.

slumping has occurred in The Narrows, and the open lead flowing out of the lake extends for 100 m.

The south wind resumed at 9:45, and 15 minutes later the temperature had risen five degrees to minus 17. We watched the storm throughout the morning. Pencil-lead skies merged indistinctly with darker, spruce-covered ridges. Sand-like snow particles sped across the lake, and piled up in deep drifts against the lake's shoreline.

We decided to spend the afternoon in the cabin, as the poor visibility seemed very uninviting. While writing in her journal, Kathleen happened to glance up the lake. "Michael, I think I see a light."

"Where? Where would a light come from?"

"I don't know, but it looks like a light, way up the lake. I can't really tell with all that snow."

I peered into the drifting, swirling white. "I don't see anything."

"I can't see it now either. Must have just been an illusion."

We both stared through the window.

"No, I think I see it again," said Kathleen. "I'm going outside."

I followed her out, and we both stared up the lake. There was no doubt about it now. Not just one light, but two lights, side-by-side, flickered far out on the lake. They seemed to be getting closer. Moments later we heard the unmistakable sound of ski-doos. Someone is coming! Who could it be?

Five minutes later, two ski-doos roared to a fuming stop just outside our cabin door. A man took off one mitt, and held out his hand. "Hello, we've come to see how you are doing out here. I'm Ron. These are my two boys, and this is their friend."

Pretty darned exciting! For us, anyway, it was very darned exciting.

"Come in, come in. Have a chair by the fire. We don't have enough chairs, but I can move those books off the bed. Make yourselves comfortable. Would you like some tea?"

Ron introduced himself as the regional community constable from Fort Good Hope. Ron travels by ski-doo from Fort Good Hope to Colville Lake, about 165 km, once a month, checking up on people living in the bush. The role of a community constable, funded within the RCMP, is in the experimental stages. The premise is that a local person, who knows the people and problems of the community, would serve as a go-between with the regular RCMP officers. This would give a 'familiar face' to law enforcement, and soften the sometimes strained relationship between the community and the 'outsiders' within the RCMP. Sounds like a good idea, but Ron indicated that the community constable's role was often difficult. Ron is related to, or knows most of the people in Fort Good Hope. This makes it challenging for him, because of these personal relationships, to enforce the law, or to make arrests.

Ron said he had been in town, and Bern suggested that he check up on us. Apparently I hadn't completely convinced Bern during our radio conversations that things were going well. I can't blame him for perhaps doubting me, though. After all, I am a city person, without any previous experience of living so isolated during a northern Canadian winter. Ron also brought some provisions from Bern and Margaret – a huge box of frozen fish, and another box overflowing with frozen caribou. I don't know how we're going to eat it all.

Ron sat at the table, slowly looking around the cabin, cupping the hot mug of tea in his hands. "Nice fire," he said. "You got a lot of wood. I never been in here before." Ron sipped and looked around. "Not too big. Easy to heat. Where's all your food?"

"There's a second cabin about 100 yards farther up the hill. You want to see what it's like?" Ron nodded that he would.

"Well, we don't keep it locked when we're here, as we want it open in case our cabin catches fire. The second cabin gives us a place to survive. We also keep wood and kindling by the wood stove. Go have a look around."

Ron and the three boys set their tea mugs down, bundled up and trudged up the hill, disappearing quickly in the blowing snow. I immediately thought that maybe I should follow after them. Bern had told me not to let anyone snoop around. Bern had said several times that vandalism is a regular occurrence at his cabins during winter, and that he didn't want people to know that he kept guns at the north end of Colville Lake. I felt ashamed for feeling, even for a brief moment, that I should not trust Ron, the community constable who had ridden a ski-doo, through a blizzard, for 40 km, just to make sure I was all right.

A few minutes later Ron and the three boys sat down again, cradling tea mugs in their hands. "You seen any moose or caribou?" Ron asked.

"A lot of caribou. No moose though."

"You have a gun?"

"Yeah. Here it is." I handed Ron my Browning .308.

"Nice. Lever action."

"It's light. I can carry it easy."

Ron nodded, and looked around. "Bern said he was thinking that I should bring you one of his puppies. Said that you would probably like to have one. Didn't have enough room on the ski-doo, though."

I was glad about that. Kathleen and I had come to Colville Lake for selfish reasons. We wanted to follow our whims. We wanted to travel through the country spontaneously. A puppy would demand responsibility. We came to Colville Lake to live free from all responsibility.

Ron continued: "Bern says that you plan to go to town sometime. Maybe you can bring a puppy back then."

"Maybe," I replied.

"How you gonna get to town. Do you have a ski-doo?"

"No. We don't have a ski-doo. We had planned to go to town at the end of this month, with our wall tent and portable wood stove. But we're beginning to think that the trip would take too long. It would be pretty hard to break trail around the perimeter of the lake."

Ron again nodded and looked around. "Maybe you should wait until the weather gets a little warmer, and just go straight across the lake. You wouldn't need snowshoes on the lake. You could make it in two days. You could take a light tent and just sleep out on the ice."

"I like that idea, Ron. I think we might do that."

Ron finished his tea, and stood up. "I don't think I can tell you anything. You seem to be doing fine. Thanks for the tea. One of my boys lost his neck scarf. Pretty cold out there on the ski-doo. Do you have a spare scarf?"

Bern had told us not to loan anything to anybody. We should particularly not loan any gas. I felt I had to do Bern's bidding. I thought that perhaps I should say that we didn't have any spare scarves, which was actually true. My only neck scarf was one that Kathleen had given me for Christmas. I felt immediately ashamed. Only a bastard wouldn't loan his neck scarf to some-one about to head out into the cold and snow.

It reminded me of the time that Kathleen and I were staying at a chalet for back-country skiers at Diamond Head, in the Coast Mountains just north of Vancouver. A group of skiers arrived after dark, and asked the 20 or so people already there if anyone had seen a woman named Angela. No one had. The late-arriving group huddled among themselves, and then asked if anyone could loan them a headlamp.

"We have to go back down the mountain and look for her. We haven't seen her since the Red Heather Meadows, about 2 hours ago. We could use another headlamp."

"My friend has a good headlamp," said a man cooking dinner on his small, backpacking-sized white gas stove. "It's a really good headlamp."

"It cost a hundred bucks," said his friend. "I don't want to lose it."

"So, can we borrow it? We'll take good care of it."

"No. It cost a hundred bucks."

The friend refused to loan his headlamp to help find a skier missing at night. I always considered this guy to be a real bastard. And now, it seems, so was I.

"Sure, we have a spare scarf." I held out Kathleen's Christmas present. "You need a neck warmer out there tonight. Can you take our mail back to town for us too?"

Ron and the boys bundled up. "I'll be back next month. See you then." A few minutes later we could barely hear the sound of their engines, and then all went silent. Kathleen and I stepped back into the cabin, which now seemed very empty. I added more wood to the stove, while Kathleen prepared more tea.

Later that afternoon, feeling restless, I snowshoed east across the lake, toward our route up Woodlot Way. The wind tore at my body as I sank into loose drifts nearly one metre deep. It felt marvellous to be alive, wonderful to be able to stand in this boreal vastness, spectacular to be able to share the magnificent power and motion of the wind.

During our 7:00 pm radio conversation, Bern said that Margaret, Jo-Ellen Lyslo and Robert Lyslo would be visiting on Sunday. Great news. We very much enjoyed today's surprise visit by Ron, and look forward to receiving more visitors during the winter.

Thursday, February 18. There exists a saying in the North that in February the dry Arctic weather systems are at war with the moist, southern systems. Indeed, in his book *Trail of the Hare: Life and Stress in an Arctic Community*, Savishinsky reports that the local Hare Indian word for February, *Akaradetsisa*, means 'the month of the wind.' There seems to be wisdom in this traditional knowledge. The southern winds have blasted for two days, and have freed the trees from their covering of snow. Our environment now looks quite different, with the spires of green spruce trees reaching up darkly against the sky.

The snow swirled strongly all yesterday, and our paths along the lake are all drifted over. Even the much-used Privy Path to the outhouse was obliterated. The formerly smooth lake surface is now covered in rows of drifts, interspersed with patches of snow-free ice. The tops of the snow ridges are packed into a solid crust, strong enough to walk on in most places. Until yesterday, the tracks cut into the snow by our Twin Otter had remained perfectly intact. That evidence of our arrival has now disappeared.

We snowshoed up the seismic cut line toward Ketaniatue Lake. Although the deep snow made travel difficult on our open-weave snowshoes, we did extend the trail another 0.5 km, and nearly reached the top of Colville Ridge. As we returned home, a Raven greeted us with aerial dives and calls. Next to the loon, my favourite sound of the Canadian North is the Raven's throaty, visceral pronouncements, particularly during winter, when its voice floats eerily across the otherwise silent panorama of dense spruce forest and frozen muskeg. [*Author's Note:* I have been capitalizing the official names of birds, according to the style of the American Ornithologists' Union, so readers know 'Red-throated Loon' refers to a specific species of loon, rather than simply a loon that happens to have a red throat. Reference to a 'loon' means any one of five species of loons normally found in North America. This means I should not be capitalizing 'Raven' since the official name is 'Common Raven' which in North America distinguishes this bird from the 'Chihuahuan Raven.' This poses a minor dilemma for me. Like most people, I never say Common Raven, partly out of habit, and partly because this grand bird is never 'common.' In this book I will simply write 'Raven'.]

We dined on bannock and caribou for dinner, a truly Northern fare. We feel, however, somewhat pressured by the two gift boxes of fish and caribou. Even if we enjoy one fish and one caribou dinner each week, it will take literally months to finish them off. We appreciate the generosity, but not the largesse.

The day was dull and overcast, and nearly too warm at -6 degrees. My beloved mukluks were a bit wet after our outing. I hope that the sun, and moderately cold weather, say -15 to -25 degrees, return soon. Kathleen, happy in the kitchen, spent much of the day preparing a large pot of caribou stew. Nothing was too good for our guests coming on Sunday.

Friday, February 19. The day broke colder (-14), clearer and calmer. Just before noon we set off south up the lake to capture photographic images. The lake's surface was now a firm, supportive crust, and we travelled easily, as though on pavement, surrounded by a sea of whitecaps and swells that had been sculpted by the wind and frozen into place by the cold. Imbedded ice crystals sparkled like diamonds in an immense display case of exquisite jewellery. Winter has become even more exciting and variable than we ever imagined it would be.

Saturday, February 20. We spent most of the day preparing for tomorrow's visit by Margaret, Jo-Ellen and Robert. We rose early, finished our breakfast quickly, and then tidied the cabin. We swept the floors, put away pots and pans, organized our books, and made sitting space available on the lower bunks.

Of course, this 'housecleaning' did not take very long. Our cabin is small.

House chores are not so much chores, as mere afterthoughts. We completed our work in 30 minutes.

During the 7:00 pm radio conversation, Bern said that snow had been falling very heavily in town all day long. Poor visibility with near whiteout conditions. Without sun and shadows it is too difficult for people travelling on ski-doos to see undulations in the ice. Open leads of water and overflow become much more dangerous. Margaret, Jo-Ellen and Robert had to cancel the trip, and won't be coming until the first or second week of March at the earliest. We were very disappointed, particularly because our visitors were intending to bring two letters that had arrived for us.

My disappointment surprised me a little. I had come to Colville Lake to live my romanticized life of a hermit – a bush man. Ron had visited only three days ago, and yet I already yearned for more company. I don't think 'yearn' is too strong a word. I really wanted more guests tomorrow.

Nevertheless, the day had been relaxing and productive, as we completed all of our correspondence. We just need another mail carrier. For dinner, I prepared some of the fish, although Kathleen doesn't like the fish all that much. Maybe some unexpected visitor will drop by – a visitor on whom we can bestow a gift of fish.

During our meal, we heard scratching sounds just outside the cabin, on the porch. We opened the door to see a small, brown, weasel-like animal scurry away. We didn't get a good look at it – perhaps it's a marten, or maybe a mink. Kathleen says she thought she had seen it yesterday too. It seems to be living in the snow bank below the cabin. We have had our visitor after all. I bet it likes our fish, too. Certainly more than Kathleen likes our fish.

Sunday, February 21. The temperature has remained above -20 degrees, and what a difference that makes compared to -40. Kathleen notes that she can now visit the outhouse without first bundling up with parka, toque and warm gloves, particularly if the winds are calm. It could be that we are finally becoming acclimatized. Minus 20 degrees does feel warm.

Our 'visitor' returned this morning to peer at us through the window during breakfast. Its body is about 50 cm long, with a tail of 15 cm. It has a slender build, whiskers, dark eyes, a somewhat flattened nose and clawed fore feet. It's more likely a mink than a marten, which tends to be a shy animal, with much more pronounced ears. We should have brought a mammal identification book with us.

We spent the day collecting water, splitting and stacking wood, adjusting snowshoe bindings and writing in our journals. For dinner Kathleen prepared a sumptuous caribou soup. We are now starting to accumulate food scraps, particularly fish bones and skin. The weasel-family visitor provides an unexpected opportunity to 'take out the garbage,' a somewhat interesting task, as there is no garbage collection here at the north end of Colville Lake. After dinner I collected all our scraps and snowshoed about 0.5 km north down the river where I had seen what looked like a snow burrow in the bank. I emptied our small bag of food scraps at the burrow entrance and returned home, confident that our refuse would be much appreciated. Indeed, we used this place to dump our organic garbage for the rest of the winter. The food scraps were gone every time I returned.

Yesterday and today have been completely calm, with a gentle snow falling – the trees are again coated with white. The sky cleared tonight, and the temperature fell to -25 degrees by 8:00 pm.

During the 7:00 pm radio conversation, Bern confirmed that the animal was almost certainly a mink. "Don't let it live under the cabin," he said. "You ought to trap it. There's plenty of traps in the boat house."

I don't think we will trap it. It's not in our background or interest to trap animals. Besides, how could we possibly bring ourselves to harm our first return visitor of the winter?

Monday, February 22. It is definitely uncommonly beautiful here. This morning began with dense fog, which cleared around noon. Hoarfrost now coats everything – trees, axes and chopping blocks – the mosquito screens around the porch – the leafless branches of the Trembling Aspen and Balsam Poplars – even last year's grass stems on the sod roof of our cabin – everything is covered in glistening frost.

The sparkling white lake, the White Spruce spires reaching into the deep, blue sky, and the delicately white-covered branches of the deciduous trees make for a breathtaking scene. And all of it is ours to enjoy, simply by living and being here. We just step out of our cabin to become surrounded by purest beauty. How can Kathleen and I be so lucky?

Not all is beauty, however. There are more mundane aspects of being at the

It turns out that urinating in the outhouse was a very bad idea.

north end of Colville Lake, of living without electricity or indoor plumbing. We have spent a lot of time sitting by the fire, drinking tea, and then making the necessary trips to the outhouse. This, as it turns out, has been a serious mistake. For some reason, perhaps because the lighting is becoming better, I glanced down the hole. Not surprisingly, it turns out, at these temperatures urine freezes almost instantly, and doesn't drain away. Frozen urine had already nearly completely filled up our outhouse. And we have only just begun the fourth week of February! What are we going to do now?

When we describe this more 'human' aspect of life in the bush during our slide shows after we returned to Vancouver, the audiences always laugh. This anecdote is a surefire crowd-pleaser. Let me assure you, though, that this brought no laughter to us that cold February morning. We needed a functional outhouse, or so we thought. I happened to mention this 'mistake' to Bern during a radio conversation. I thought it was kind of amusing, even though problematical.

Bern said, "What did you do that for? No one urinates in the outhouse."

Well, maybe no one who knows about these things urinates in the outhouse. But we didn't know. From then on we never urinated in the outhouse. Instead, we extended Privy Path a little beyond, into the forest. A closer-in urination post for Kathleen, and a farther spot for me. We needed to reserve space in our outhouse for more 'significant' bodily functions. We could also save outhouse space by walking to the native tent camp, on an island, about six km south. We have been there twice already, and know about its brand new outhouse. The camp is vacant, and no one would mind. We enjoy taking snowshoe excursions, and the outhouse provides a useful destination for a three-hour round trip.

As a final solution to our predicament, I also began reading Horace Kephart's classic book *Camping and Woodcraft*, in which he explains how to build an outhouse. He makes it sound easy. Although I'm not very skilled at construction, necessity does provide a motivating imperative.

Despite our problems with the outhouse, the sun broke through shortly after lunch, producing a beautifully blue, clear afternoon. I sat at my writing table beneath the south-facing window, where the sun warmed my face through the glass. By early evening though, clouds again enveloped and shrouded our home at the north end of Colville Lake.

Tuesday, February 23. The day began overcast, as we headed down the river, to Ketaniatue Lake, shortly after 11:00 am. The sun emerged about 30 minutes later, bringing the snow-covered ridges into marvellous contrast with the dark sky above. Several sections of the river, up to 200 m long, now ran free and open. Areas that we had walked on only a few days ago were now flowing. Twice we had to leave the river corridor, and our previous path, to work our way through the bush. Twice my snowshoes became encased in ice because of wicking up from the slush below the snow. The lamp wick bindings had shredded apart by the time I returned from our 10 km, five-and-one-half hour trip. A successful day, as we finally reached Ketaniatue Lake via the river.

In addition to simply enjoying our stroll down and along the river, we had been scouting out potential spots for setting up our wall tent. We found several good camping spots, with standing dead wood on both banks, just before the river empties into Ketaniatue Lake. Depending on the weather, we plan to return in a couple of days.

Our little river that drains Colville Lake is unnamed on the topographic maps. Bern, however, refers to this river as the Ross River, which flows into the Anderson River, nearly 200 km north of our cabin. Our little river does eventually drain to the Ross River, and we are happy to adopt Bern's nomenclature.

Wednesday, February 24. We spent a relaxing morning watching the snow fall gently as it drifted in on a slight breeze from the north. In early afternoon the sun peeked through a partial cloud cover, and we snowshoed back down the river to assess the open leads of water. Three Whiskey Jacks cavorted back and froth across the river in advance of our route. Not much had changed since yesterday, but we were a bit worried about travelling on the river. We will need to move more of our previous trails up off the river and into the bush.

After dinner, I sat by the fire, enjoying the twilight descending around our cabin, and sipping at a full mug of hot orange juice. Back at home, in North Vancouver, I would most likely be sipping a glass of wine. In fact, Kathleen and I have wine with dinner virtually every night. We also often pour ourselves a glass of brandy before bed. It's just what we do. It is our habit – our lifestyle.

For our winter sojourn, however, we have brought no alcohol. None whatsoever. We have left our drinking habits back in the city for three reasons. First, it would be impossible to bring enough wine and brandy to last for six months, particularly if we were to continue drinking on a daily basis. Secondly, it's nice to break with old habits. We don't really need to drink every day. It's expensive and likely not good for our health. We likely drink every day at home simply because of routine. Here at our new Colville Lake home, we don't miss alcohol at all. Alcohol is no longer part of our lifestyle. When no alcohol is available, it is easy to resist the lure of alcohol. When no alcohol is available, it is very simple to give up alcohol.

The third reason we didn't bring any alcohol, and the most important reason for us, was that we didn't want any alcohol on site. We expect to eventually have visitors from town. Colville Lake lies a long way from easy access to alcohol, without any retail outlet. Nevertheless, we had heard that problem drinking does occur. When our town visitors ask us if we have any alcohol, we want to be able to honestly say, "No, we don't have any alcohol." We don't want to contribute to the problem or lie to people.

During our radio conversation, Bern informed us that the RCMP arrived in Colville Lake today to construct a jail. Bern believes that the jail is 'urgently needed.' I am disheartened that a jail would be needed in Colville Lake, a village of at most 90 people. This community, most of them related, should be small enough, supportive enough, and cohesive enough to not require a jail. The social structure, for whatever reasons though, does seem to be facing challenges. In his seven pages of notes that Bern left in the cabin for us, he mentioned that, "following nearly 30 vandalism-free years [at the cabin] we have recently experienced a rash of break-ins; hence the need for dead bolts [on the door] and plywood shutters [on the windows]."

We intend to drag our wall tent to Ketaniatue Lake on Friday, assuming that we have favourable weather. We also need to be sure that Bern is comfortable with us leaving the cabin vacant this weekend. Robert and Jo-Ellen went to Edmonton on Wednesday, and the school will be closed until next Monday. Bern might be worried that school kids with time on their hands during a long 'holiday weekend' might head out to the north end of Colville Lake for something to do.

The weather remains warm, between -10 and -20 degrees. The river continues to open up, and we wonder if this spring-like trend will continue. For entertainment, we switched on the SSBx-11A radio at 8:00 pm to listen to the winter sched of the Yukon trappers. Hey, we don't have a TV, and sometimes one needs a break from reading. This eavesdropping reminded me of the old days, way back in the 1950s, when our neighbourhood telephones were all on party lines. We were all connected to three other homes. As a boy, it was quite entertaining to listen in on other people's conversations. Apparently, this fascination with what other people are saying has stuck with me. Blame it on party lines. Anyway, the common wisdom of the Yukon trappers is that mid-March is the turning point. After then, deep winter is probably over.

Thursday, February 25. We spent the day organizing for our two-night camping trip at Ketaniatue Lake. There's a heck of a lot to take. There are obvious items such as tent and guy ropes, wood stove, food, sleeping gear and clothing, including spare mukluks in case we step into overflow. We will also require many tools. We must have a hammer and nails to make a platform for the wood stove. A bow saw is necessary to cut down trees for firewood. Taking a spare saw blade is only prudent. We gotta have a machete to collect spruce boughs to lay across the tent entryway and sleeping platform, which would otherwise become slick sheets of ice from the heat of the stove. And certainly we need a small axe to limb trees and to clear the tent site. This is only a partial list of tools. There are also many necessary incidental items including water buckets, candles, aluminum foil, headlamps, pots and pans and a tea thermos. Our sled and toboggan will be fully loaded and heavy.

We remember how hard it was for me to drag out to Ron and Suzanne's delta camp when we were in Inuvik. We should leave all superfluous items behind. We can't afford to be fatigued when we reach camp, as much work will still need to be done. We need to travel as light as possible. The ice chisel is heavy at 1.5 kg. We probably won't need it, as we expect to find thin ice, or even open water. We decide to combine our overnight cases – we don't need to take two tubes of toothpaste. I don't really need my razor, as I doubt that I will be shaving. Hey, every bit helps. Certainly we don't need two cameras – shall we take my camera or Kathleen's? Better pack the tripod though, to compose that special shot. On the other hand, the tripod is a bit cumbersome, and takes up a lot of room. Maybe we won't need the tripod. Let's leave it aside for now, and see how the packing goes in the morning.

We reread our instructions for how to set the tent up, and for how to organize a winter camp. I would like to leave our cabin no later than 10:00 am. This gives us four hours to drag our gear down the river, to arrive at Ketaniatue Lake no later than 2:00 pm. We estimate it will take one hour to set the tent up, plus another 90 minutes to cut, haul, split and stack wood. This takes us to 4:30, leaving two more hours of daylight as a cushion should anything go wrong. We'll see how it goes.

During our nightly radio conversation, Bern gave the go-ahead to leave the cabin unattended for the weekend: "Just be sure you lock up both cabins and put the plywood shutters back on the windows." Too bad it's come to this.

Friday, February 26. We were ready to go at 11:00 am. Following Bern's instructions, we shuttered all the windows and ensured that the doors

Our first winter camp, at Ketaniatue Lake. After starting the fire, the temperature in the tent warmed to +25 degrees in only a few minutes.

to both cabins were locked before heading down the Ross River – into a northwest wind at -18 degrees. Kathleen was responsible for the lead toboggan loaded with sleeping bags, pillows, ground sheet, tarp, therm-a-rests and down booties. Her toboggan also contained the down parkas, axe, maps, a shovel and the machete. My sled was stacked with the wood stove, canvas tent, vinyl tent fly, aluminum poles, my camera, the tripod (it truly is essential to capture well-composed images), water bucket, first aid kit and two white, plastic buckets containing kitchen gear, ropes and assorted tools. Kathleen set off as I raised the continuous leather towline over my head, and snugged it around my shoulders. I double-looped both arms into the line, and strained forward against the weight. Our loads dragged us down to the bottom of the hill, where we turned toward Ketaniatue Lake, 6 km to the north.

The river had opened up even more since our trip out two days ago. Once, as we stood on an outside bank, an ice jam broke free just beneath our feet to muscle its way down river, shearing off snow and 15-cm thick ice as it eventually came to rest 200 m downstream.

In general, though, we pulled our loads easily and without worry along the edge of the frozen river, warmed by our own mechanical heat trapped by three layers of wool. Canvas wind suits, stitched with red and blue rickrack, prevented the wind from stealing our precious body heat. Coyote fur ruffs cinched tightly around our faces prevented the northwest wind from freezing exposed cheeks, noses and chins. Our feet, clothed in wool socks, duffel-cloth liners and moosehide mukluks, remained dry and warm.

We travelled mostly without speaking, lulled by the rhythmic 'whump, whump, whump' of our snowshoes sinking into soft, fluffy crystals. We walked in shared silence, heading down the frozen Ross River. The boreal forest stood passively, receptively, on both banks. No bird flew, no animal moved. Nothing disturbed our winter reverie. Only a few tracks appeared sporadically in the snow to suggest that any other life existed in our private, winter palace.

Through billowing snow we followed a caribou trail down the centre of the river, once again trusting the animals' innate sense of ice strong enough to support the herd's weight. Tracks of snowshoe hare – and its predator – crossed our route, leading to a clump of willows on the right bank. A blood-encrusted crater in the snow indicated the hare's death that had come so suddenly, and so irreversibly. Had the hare made the proverbial fatal mistake? Or had the hare simply been in the wrong place at the wrong time? Either way, the result was the same. Kathleen and I felt some of that same vulnerability. A careless mistake, at these temperatures, three days away from the nearest help, could also prove fatal to us. Nevertheless, we also felt confident and secure in our winter environment. We continued pulling our loads past the clump of willows that hid the blood-encrusted crater. We looked forward to our first winter camp.

Half-a-kilometre later, the caribou trail angled toward the left bank, and skirted along a margin of yellow-green overflow oozing out from the centre of the river. We moved forward a few steps, when Kathleen suddenly stepped into overflow. She quickly retreated to dry snow, into which she buried her feet to wick away the moisture from her mukluks and snowshoes, which momentarily froze into the dry snow.

As Kathleen knocked away the snow and frozen slush, she said her feet seemed dry. No need to change into the spare socks and mukluks that we had packed on top of the gear, where they would be easily and quickly available.

We now looked for another route around the overflow. We could see that the caribou tracks veered sharply toward the willows lining the left bank. Just at the river's edge, the ice sloped upward at an angle of 20 degrees. Below this ice ramp we clearly heard the sound of water rushing past the outside bend.

"I don't like this," Kathleen said. "If there's a gap between the ice and the river, then the ice might not be strong enough to support us."

I picked up a stick and poked several times at the angled ramp of ice. The entire sheet, perhaps only 4 to 5 cm thick, wavered, cracked and buckled. "This doesn't seem like a good way to go. Perhaps the caribou came this way before the river dropped so much."

"Well," Kathleen said, "we can't get to the right bank because of the overflow, and now we can't get up onto the left bank. We seem to be boxed in. Maybe we'll have to go back a ways."

"I don't know. Maybe we don't have to go back. Let's go have another look at the overflow. We might be able to get through there."

We walked back to the oozing overflow in the centre of the river, bringing my stick with me. "Just stand back a little bit, Kathleen, in case I need room to jump back quickly."

I jabbed at the overflow, and the stick effortlessly sliced through the newly-formed ice only 2 cm thick. Water bubbled up, and slid sickeningly and blackly across the previously hardened overflow. We calmly, but intently, backed up in our snowshoe tracks, which offered the only known route to safety.

We returned along our previous path 100 m back up the Ross River, where I again tested the ice. Although the stick easily pierced through the overflow, no water seeped upward. The gurgle of the river was barely audible, suggesting only a thin gap between thicker ice and flowing water.

"What do you think?" I asked.

"How would I know? You're out there poking with the stick. What do you think?"

"Well, I think we can cross over here. That would save us a lot of backtracking. But I can't get that image out of my mind of Charles Martin Smith falling through the ice in that movie *Never Cry Wolf.*

"Well, you know, if you're at all worried, Michael, we don't have to cross here. We can always head back even more upriver."

"Yeah, I know. But I think it is safe to cross here. Maybe though, we should cross one-at-a-time, so as not to concentrate our weight."

"OK. But we don't have to cross here, if you have any doubts."

It seemed that Kathleen had some doubts.

"I'm feeling pretty confident, Kathleen. I'll give it a try."

I moved cautiously, jabbing and poking at the ice every few steps. I soon stood on the right bank, the inside bend, where shallower water had frozen all the way to the riverbed. I looked back toward Kathleen, who stood calmly in the centre of the Ross River, nearly enveloped by drifting, blowing snow.

"Damn, you look beautiful out there, Kathleen. Just like Julie Christie in *Dr. Zhivago*. I think the ice is fine. Just go slowly. Make sure you don't jump up and down too much."

"Not funny. Here I come. Wait there for me." Moments later we stood side-by-side, and continued our journey down the frozen Ross River toward Ketaniatue Lake.

Suddenly the sun burst through the snowy mist. The amorphous, nearly featureless, seemingly lifeless river corridor instantly awakened, as though to spring. Small coveys of Willow Ptarmigan, pure white save for their black tails, exploded from riverside copses. Whiskey Jacks swooped coyly out from the forest, twittering pleasingly as they begged for handouts. A lone Boreal Chickadee performed acrobatically for us, flitting from tree-top to tree-top, searching for overwintering insects that slumbered, unsuspectingly, in their cocoons.

The Ross River now flowed between ridges that sheltered us from the persistent northwest wind. By mid-afternoon, the Ross River narrowed to 20 m, and ran nearly north/south, in a direct line with the prevailing winds. Winter gusts had sculpted and hardened the ice to create a surface as smooth and firm as a suburban sidewalk. Our snowshoes clattered happily as we pulled our loads easily on the frictionless crust.

We arrived at our intended camp at 2:45 pm, but needed nearly 4 hours to set up the tent, organize camp, and cut wood from two nearby dead spruce trees. We cleared an area of brush, and strung our tent between two live spruce trees. The sides of the tent were pulled taut with guy ropes tied to adjacent stumps, snags and saplings. I excavated a snow basin for the wood-burning stove while Kathleen used the machete to harvest spruce boughs for our floor of green.

I then placed some of the split wood around the stove, where it would dry during the night. This wood, which absorbs heat from the stove, will also help prevent melt-back of the cooking area that could cause the stove and stove pipes to shift or collapse. I stacked the rest of the split wood outside the tent door where it would be easily accessible during the night. Finally, I started the fire, and collected snow to melt for tea and drinking water. A difficult day for me physically, but thoroughly enjoyable. I'm finally experiencing what it means to camp in a frozen, winter, Northern forest.

The tent quickly warmed to +25 degrees. While I rested in the heat, Kathleen leisurely prepared chili and cornbread bannock for dinner on top of the wood stove. We have now been at the north end of Colville Lake for nearly one month, and have seen only the RCMP who came specifically to visit us. Kathleen remarked how fortunate we are to live and travel in a landscape that is essentially ours to enjoy in whatever way we wish.

I now write by candlelight with the stove purring and all the chores complete. I feel completely satiated with our chili dinner; but Kathleen is passing oatmeal chocolate chip cookies my way!

Saturday, February 27. The temperature remained at -16 degrees all last night. We allowed the fire to go out at 11:30 pm, partly out of concern about a tent fire, and partly because we had previously been warm in our wall tent in Inuvik, even when the temperature fell overnight to -26 degrees. Minus 16 degrees sounded downright toasty by comparison. Nevertheless, Kathleen said she felt cold, beginning about 2:00 or 3:00 am.

I went to bed last night only reluctantly, as our tent looked so cute and charming by candlelight, with our winter gear silhouetted in the corners, and the stove keeping us warm. Even after Kathleen blew out the candles at 11:45 pm. I lay awake, enjoying the moment for another hour. The white cotton walls of our tent pass a great deal of light, such that it was still easy to see by the moonlight that periodically broke through the partial overcast.

I plan to stay up as long as I can tonight, ideally all night. It's possible that mid-March could be our last winter camping trip. By late March, when we plan to go town, the weather could be warm enough to travel more lightly, with our summer gear. The temperature could be +10 degrees during the day, with zero or only slightly colder at night. This would be similar to many of the days on our Northern canoeing expeditions. Once we return to Vancouver, and become constrained by our careers, our winter camping days, where we can go when we please, and cut wood where we want, will likely be over. I need to stay up as long as possible, so that I can thoroughly enjoy what might be one of my last nights in the tent. By staying up all night, I can also keep the tent warm for Kathleen, and still be watchful for a possible tent fire.

More hours of heat in the tent will also give me a better chance to dry my mukluks, which were frozen stiff this morning from too many trips last night into and out of the tent. Snow on the moosehide soles instantly thaws when re-entering the tent. When the temperature fell back below zero in the tent, the moosehide soles froze solid.

We now wear our down booties in and out of the tent for simple tasks like eliminating the many cups of tea after dinner. We try to leave our mukluks hanging on the drying line inside the tent as much as possible.

Our short jaunt to Ketaniatue Lake today served two purposes, the first of which was to see some new country along the lake shore. Our second goal was to create a trail directly up against the right bank, just in case we can't retrace our original path back across the river and the overflow tomorrow. We don't want to take risks. If any doubt exists we'll drag our sled and toboggan 0.5 km down to Ketaniatue Lake, and then head over to the right bank on lake ice that we know to be thick, firm, and solid.

This afternoon we shored up the tent-stove platform with additional pieces of wood, and filled the melt-back area around the stove with more snow. Stove shifting that separates the sections of pipe is a common cause of tent fires. I then resumed the tasks necessary to live comfortably through the winter night. I crossed back over the river to the right bank where this morning we had seen two, dead 4-m-tall spruce trees. I felled both, and sawed one of them into stove-sized lengths. I filled the toboggan with firewood and kindling, and returned to camp.

Kathleen stood in front of the tent, holding up our water buckets. She suggested that we try to get liquid water, rather than melting snow and slush. "After all," she said, "there's plenty of thin sections out there that should be easy to break through."

Together we snowshoed happily 150 m along the edge of the river toward a narrow strip of discoloured snow. Here, on the outside bend, the water still ran quickly, and an insulating layer of snow kept the ice thin, even in very cold weather. Throughout the winter, the mass of ice developing in the centre of the river had been squeezing water up into this thin, weak zone of greyish slush. In a few minutes I axed a small hole, large enough for water to percolate up through the ice. We filled two water buckets with nearly 'pure' water that contained only a little slush.

Kathleen stayed in camp to prepare dinner and to boil some tea water while I returned to retrieve the rest of the firewood. Because so much wood still remained to be collected, I took the larger, heavier sled, rather than the smaller toboggan. I finished sawing up and splitting the second spruce tree, loaded the sled, and headed back across the river. We have enough wood now, even if we keep the stove stoked all night. I stopped to rest in the centre of the river by leaning slightly forward into the sled's leather towlines. Dusk was beginning to descend. I thought of our log cabin -- our home base -- which lay 4 to 5 hours back up the Ross River. The cabin's cozy charm far exceeded our expectations, and contained all we needed to live comfortably, until break-up in mid-June. We had a wood stove for heat, a propane stove for cooking, and all the necessary food and supplies. Two cords of firewood lay outside, beneath an orange tarp buried by snow.

I looked across the frozen river toward our tent. Through its diaphanous walls the flames from two candles shone so brightly that the small clearing glowed like a church alter at midnight Christmas services. The tent beckoned to me, and spoke of warmth and food. I could see and smell the satisfying essence of wood smoke wafting toward me on the now gentle breeze drifting languidly up from the south.

From up the Ross River, a lone, black Raven approached, flying strongly with deep beats of its powerful wings. The bird circled once, and then called out as it dove toward me: "Cronk. Cronk." Its resonant, guttural greeting echoed across the silent, narrow valley of the Ross River.

I wished that I could communicate with the Raven, to hear first-hand of its brash, bold wanderings. The Raven, ever resourceful, remains in the North when unbearable winter drives the mighty, majestic Bald Eagle southward. The Raven, ever confident, soars above the lifeless forest when brutal cold forces the Willow Ptarmigan to huddle headfirst in deep drifts of snow. The Raven, ever audacious, clothes itself in deepest black to contrast flamboyantly with its white, winter world of snow and ice. If reincarnation exists then I would like to return in my next life as a Raven – to venture dauntlessly and fearlessly throughout my frozen, Northern Kingdom.

I thought of our day, and of Kathleen, in the wall tent, likely stirring our pot of caribou stew simmering on the wood stove. Like me, I know that she also feels secure and safe in the isolated forest of our winter home. She also knows that wind and cold can be endured – even enjoyed. She knows that the vast, immeasurable solitude can be travelled easily, one km at a time, one day at a time. Yet, I also know that she still feels a little uneasy when I'm not with her. I know that she worries about me when I'm working all alone out in the bush. I can imagine her parting the tent flaps to peer anxiously into the developing darkness. The southeast wind would be lightly touching her cheek and caressing her hair. She would be wondering why I was taking so long to return with the wood.

I should be heading back, but I enjoyed standing in the middle of the river as darkness descended. I continued to think about all that had happened to us since arriving at the north end of Colville Lake four weeks ago. Like denning grizzly bears, our metabolism had slowed to accommodate the soft, subdued rhythms of the Northern winter.

As I rested on the ice in front of my sled-load of wood, I thought about my life in the suburban community of North Vancouver, now so very distant. In North Vancouver, the bedside alarm stridently terminated our sleep every weekday at precisely 5:58 am. This rigid, immutable insult repeated itself every morning, irrespective of the sun's position in the sky.

I would then rise to dress and eat breakfast alone at 6:20 am. Kathleen quickly gulped her breakfast at 6:42, and together we backed out of the driveway of our suburban home at 7:06. Waiting through three red lights that blocked access to the Iron Workers Memorial Bridge, we listened to the morning weather report, which usually only confirmed the obvious reality of what was taking place just outside our van.

At 7:41, I would say goodbye to Kathleen as she stepped out onto the curb in front of her office. Six minutes later I turned the key in one of the many doors facing a long, narrow corridor, and walked into a white-walled, rectangular cubicle, where I would spend the rest of my day.

In the evening, we climbed back into our van, and retraced our route back across Vancouver, over the Iron Workers Memorial Bridge, and into the driveway of our suburban North Vancouver home. After dinner and a few household chores, we would ascend the stairs to our bedroom, where we slept, and waited, for the bedside alarm to stridently announce the beginning of another day.

A comfortable life, I thought. Comfortable, successful, predictable, unchanging, confining, interminable.

I continued to rest in front of my sled-load of firewood. I wriggled my toes to generate warmth, feeling a little cold after standing still for so long. I stared at the beacons of twin candles flickering from within the wall tent straight across the Ross River.

I raised the continuous leather towline over my head, and snugged it around my shoulders. I double-looped both arms into the line, and strained forward against the load. The sled barely budged; the plastic shoes had bonded with the crystals of ice during the short time that I had rested to reflect.

I turned my body to face directly into the southeast wind. I could hear the wind singing out to me from the spires of the riverside spruce trees. The wind sang to me of ancient landscapes, and of all it had seen. The wind sang to me of vanished herds of buffalo thundering across the short-grass prairies of southern Alberta – of the snow-covered expanse of Great Slave Lake – of the caribou wintering in the trees north of Great Bear Lake – of the immaculate, circumpolar vastness of the boreal forest. I felt as though I could accompany the wind. I felt as though I could share its vision and its song as we travelled together down the Mackenzie River – past the great delta and across the Beaufort Sea before finally resting with the muskoxen pawing at the snow near the mouth of the Thomsen River on Banks Island.

At that moment, I recognized, consciously and undeniably, that my life-long dream had finally been fulfilled. I was now experiencing the purest, unadulterated joy of living confidently in an elemental, primeval world. A Raven had called out – to me. The wind had sung – for me. A willing, warm companion waited in the tent – for me. At that moment I lived and moved only in the present. The past did not exist and the future did not matter.

I was standing in a Perfect Moment. My life would never be any better than exactly at this moment. The thought pleased, yet sobered me. It reminded me of a time long ago, when I was 21 years old, in 1968, at a party in San Francisco's Haight-Ashbury district. A young woman, by the name of Kathy (no, not my Kathleen), for no apparent reason, suddenly blurted out that she believed that the best times in her life had already come and gone. I did not really know her – she had been a high-school classmate – a friend of a friend. So, like me she was young – only 21 years old. Kathy was a beautiful woman, and not just because she was young. She was truly beautiful. Kathy was also intelligent, and had graduated as part of a cohort of our high school's most gifted students, groomed academically to attend her choice of prestigious universities. Only 21 years old, physically attractive, and brimming with potential. And yet she believed that the most exciting, the most rewarding, the most fulfilling, the most intriguing days of her life had already passed. I asked her why. She only shrugged.

Her point, if she had one, made an impact on me. For certainly, there will come a day, for all of us, when we will indeed have experienced the best days of our lives. How will we recognize that day? Is it important to recognize that day? What criteria should we use to define our 'best' days? What are the implications of knowing, or not knowing that our 'best' days are behind us? Maybe it's better to always believe, no matter what, that our best days lie in the future. Kathy expressed despair for her future, and looked as Pandora might have looked if even Hope had flown from her opened box. What's worse, though? To believe at 21 that your best days are gone, or to realize on your deathbed that your hoped-for best days never came?

As I stood on the frozen Ross River that evening, I was convinced that my best day, my Perfect Moment was being offered up to me. I had come a long way for this Perfect Moment, and stood still, exhilarating in its purity.

I don't wish to sound trite, or melodramatic, but I believed then that I could accept death. If my cancer returned, I would certainly be unhappy; but I would neither despair nor cry for myself. At that moment, I had achieved all that I had ever wanted in my life.

With renewed energy, I leaned forward into my towlines. The sled broke free from the inertia of bonding between plastic shoes and ice crystals. I easily resumed my journey across the shallow embayment toward the warmth and security of the wall tent, my caribou stew, and Kathleen's smile. A few moments later I reached the centre of the embayment near its outlet, where I could barely hear the nearly inaudible current flowing beneath my snowshoes. Again with a stick, I probed through the newly-fallen snow. I struck firm ice. No sign of yellow-green slush. No sign of overflow wicking up into my snowshoe tracks. Only a barely-audible current below the ice. I shrugged and moved forward toward the beckoning wall tent.

What if I had made a mistake in judgement, though? What if, like the snowshoe hare, I was now striding toward the wrong place at the wrong time? What if the new snow had covered a small 1-m wide lead of open water flowing toward the outlet of the embayment? In the deepening dusk, I would not see that the new snow had covered the tracks of caribou that broke through the thin ice last night to drink from the Ross River. I would not know that this morning's new snow insulated the open water, and prevented new ice from re-forming during the day.

If so, then perhaps I was only seconds away from plunging, without a sound, into the frigid, black water below. Unlike Charles Martin Smith falling through the ice in *Never Cry Wolf*, however, I know that I would never survive such an accident. As a whitewater canoeist in British Columbia, who has capsized many times, I know that the numbing cold that lies just below the ice would instantly take my breath away. It would be as though a large, vindictive adversary had stomped on my chest. The current would instantly sweep me downstream, away from the opening in the ice. Blackness would envelop me as I feebly scratched, likely for only a few seconds, at the thick ice above me. Soon I would no longer be able to discern up from down, front from back. Perhaps I would gasp when a projecting branch of a submerged spruce tree punctured my shoulder. The air would rush from my lungs to be replaced by the unknowing, uncaring, unforgiving ice water that flowed beneath my isolated, winter wonderland 100 km beyond the Arctic Circle. Soon I would cease to struggle. I would close my eyes forever to the surrounding darkness and tumble away toward Ketaniatue Lake.

What then would happen to Kathleen? Up on the bank, in the tent, the caribou stew would still be simmering on the wood-burning stove. Two candles wired to spruce branches imbedded in the snow would still flicker brightly as Kathleen reached to stir the bubbling pot. She would wonder where I was, and why I was taking so long to return with the wood. She knows that I had already felled the trees, and that I would not have to spend much time cutting and splitting. She would remember that I had said I would be back soon – for a cup of tea before dinner. Where is he, she would think.

Perhaps after 5 or 10 or 30 minutes she would part the flaps of her wall tent and peer out upon an impassive, deepening stillness. Stars would now be filling Kathleen's universe. Perhaps she would glance quickly at the thermometer hanging from a tent guy rope, and note that the thermometer registered only -21 degrees. Where is he, she would think.

With increasing anxiety, Kathleen would walk down her packed snow trail to the edge of the embayment, and turn to face the southeast wind. If I were to have fallen through the ice, I hope that the wind would speak to Kathleen of memories and laughter, of the past and of the future. I hope that the trees would whisper to her of strength and stability, of life, and of moving forward. Standing there, all alone on the banks of the frozen Ross River, Kathleen would chew on her lower lip, as she always does when she begins to truly worry.

At some point, 60 minutes from now, 2 hours from now, or maybe even just before dawn, Kathleen would realize that I was not coming back. She would likely wait for daylight to look for me. She would certainly see my sled-load of wood, sitting next to the misting lead of open water. She would certainly cry, and retreat to the tent. Eventually, out of necessity, she would begin to think of her log cabin, her home base, four hours away, back up the frozen Ross River, on the north shore of Colville Lake.

I don't think I'm being macabre as I write this. In reality, virtually all couples end their lives together in one way or another. At one moment, they are together. In the next second one of them is gone. It makes no difference whether death comes in a hospital bed after a struggle with cancer, in an automobile crash out on the highway, from a heart attack on the living room sofa, or from falling through the ice. The remaining member of the couple must move on.

John Hornby died by starving to death on the banks of the Thelon River. All the books say that he died a tragic, untimely, death. Perhaps so, but I'm not convinced. In my opinion, he died as his own man, in the Barren Grounds, living his life in a landscape where he found peace, contentment and joy. I don't wish to die in a hospital bed, with my body poisoned by chemicals and violated with tubes. I remember my mother lying in a hospital bed in 1964, with her body poisoned by chemicals and violated with tubes. She couldn't talk, with that tube rammed down her throat, but she had a slate and chalk. She scribbled, as best that she could: "I want to go home." But she never came home. She died in that hospital bed.

Maybe I won't die in a hospital bed. Maybe I will die in an automobile crash. But I don't wish to die in an automobile crash, either, sitting in Vancouver's traffic and rain, rammed from behind by an uncaring drunken driver. I don't wish to die from a heart attack on my living room sofa, wishing seconds before that I were somewhere out in the bush – somewhere out on the trail. Falling through the ice pulling my sled-load of wood seems a better way to go.

Kathleen would cry for a long time. She would repeatedly run down to the river, and call out my name. Before noon, Kathleen would realize that she needed to return to the cabin. She is resourceful and resilient. She would arrive in only a few hours. No need to drag all the gear. At 7:00 pm she would tell Bern what had happened, and a ski-doo would come for her, either that night, or more likely the next morning. Would Kathleen eventually realize that I had died while experiencing my Perfect Moment? I hope so. She certainly knows that I truly love this life out here. She certainly knows that I have been seeking just such a life for a very long time. I hope she always will remember that we enjoyed a beautiful life together.

None of this happened, though. I was on the same trail that I had followed out and back for the first toboggan load of wood. There was no open lead. I didn't plunge through the ice. Minutes later I sat cross-legged on the spruce boughs spread out on the sleeping area of our tent, sipping tea, and relishing the warmth of the wood-burning stove.

"What took you so long, Michael?"

"I don't know. I was just standing out there, looking at the candlelight shining through the tent, and thinking about you. You know, I'm pretty happy here. Probably happier than I have ever been in my entire life. I don't think I could be any happier."

Later that night, while Kathleen slept, I tended the fire and savoured tea. Periodically I stepped outside to a nearly completely cloudless sky. Stars filled our universe. Snow, two metres deep, reflected and diffused the pale light of the full moon throughout the surrounding, silent forest of spruce trees, which, like sentinels, stood guard over my winter sanctuary. A slight, gentle breeze wafted our smoke to the northwest. Maybe this southeast wind will bring warmer temperatures.

The night grew quickly clearer, losing its insulating cover of cloud. By 10:45 the temperature had dropped to -26 degrees, dropping even lower to -29 degrees at midnight. I became too sleepy to stay up any longer. I placed a pot of water on the stove, damped down the air intake, crawled into my sleeping bag next to Kathleen's, and quickly fell asleep. The stove continued to purr until the few remaining coals flickered out. The last vestige of heat

Our breath condensed into frost as we travelled. We stopped often to rest, and to admire ice crystals as they floated and glistened in the sunlight.

then filtered through the canvas roof to disappear, wraith-like, into the Arctic night. Cold encircled our tent, where Kathleen and I were turtled down, Hornby-like, very deep inside our sleeping bags.

Sunday, February 28. I got up for a bathroom break around 2:00 am. Stars filled the sky, and the moon shone brightly. The thermometer read -30 degrees. Back in my sleeping bag I was pleased, and a little surprised at how warm I felt, even though the temperature in the tent was certainly no warmer than minus 25 degrees. Of course, I was fully clothed in long underwear, wearing fleece mitts on my hands and a muskrat Mountie hat on my head.

Shortly after 8:00 am, a Raven sounded the wake-up alarm. Time to get going. The smouldering logs in the stove had kept the pot of water on top in liquid form, even though another pot only 50 cm away on the ground had frozen solidly to the bottom. Outside, the slightly overcast morning had warmed to -19 degrees. Kathleen happily reported that she had slept comfortably all night.

The return trip to our cabin home was gloriously beautiful, with the sun shining brightly for the first time in many days. A light mist of ice crystals fell through the clear, clean air. As the crystals settled on the surface of the snow, they sparkled like millions of individual stars. We often stopped, not only to rest, but also to enjoy and to admire the spectacle at our feet, glistening in the sunlight.

When we first travelled along this river two weeks ago, very little open water existed. We had snowshoed easily, and without concern. Now, however, the river had carved out long stretches of open water, even more than had existed only two days ago. Everything seemed to be in transition and unstable. We no longer trusted our original route, and often left the river completely to break new trail along the edge of the bank. Once, just as Kathleen had stepped off an ice shelf into the trees, the ledge gave way beneath her toboggan, and fell away into the river. Fortunately we didn't lose any gear. Even more fortunately, we didn't lose Kathleen. I also was fortunate to have been trailing behind Kathleen far enough that the bank gave way before I started to cross. How ironic it would have been for me to fall into the icy river when I wasn't even having a perfect moment.

The sun was actually warming my face when we reached the cabin in mid-afternoon, somewhat tired, but very satisfied. It felt like coming home. It also seemed as though a new portion of the winter had begun. The outside thermometer read -11 degrees. I hesitate to say that spring was near, but icicles hung and dripped from the south-facing eaves, and the ice in The Narrows lay decaying before us. Maybe warm weather is not too distant into our future.

We unlocked the door and removed the window shutters. Sunlight streamed and sparkled throughout the cabin as never before. We started the fire and settled into a tranquil evening of reading, writing, sipping tea, pumping the Coleman lantern, popping a bowl of popcorn, and playing cribbage.

CHAPTER 8

Raxo^{n}raselsa

Monday, March 1. The first day of March, and still cold at -33 degrees when we rose this morning. Nevertheless, the days are noticeably longer. The sun climbs higher in the sky each day, bringing encouragement and warmth to the frozen landscape. By late afternoon the thermometer registered -15 degrees.

As presented by Savishinsky, the Hare Indians referred to March as *Raxo^{n}raselsa,* which means 'the month of a slight touch of snow blindness.' This sounds promising to me. The past two weeks have been mostly overcast. A touch of snow blindness must mean that the sun will become more dominant. Brilliant, light-filled days must be on their way. Today remains cloudy, though. I suppose I need to be more patient. Today is only the first day of March, as measured by the Gregorian Calendar. The first day of Raxo^{n}raselsa, as measured by the Hare Indian Calendar, might not be here yet. Indeed, the Hare Indian calendar likely, indeed certainly, did not correspond exactly to the 12 months of the Gregorian Calendar.

We have comfortably survived February, which next to January, is the coldest month of the year. The nearest weather station with long-term records is at Norman Wells, with a mean daily temperature in January of -26.5 degrees, compared to -24.7 in February. March warms to -18.4 degrees. This is good news for our woodpile. We have not yet even started using the two cords of wood buried beneath the snow under the orange tarp. So far we have heated ourselves entirely with the 'extra' wood piled in back of the cabin and stacked on the porch, supplemented with what I have been able to provide. We still have nearly a three-day supply left from the wood that I have brought back. Wood should not be a problem for us. I anticipate that we will need, on average, half-a-cord per month from now until break-up in mid- to late June. This projected use totals less than the two cords hidden beneath the snow. We should be fine. I hope so.

During our seven o'clock radio conversation I told Bern how well the winter camping had gone, and how much we enjoyed it. I also mentioned that we had not talked to him for three nights, since February 25, and nothing had gone wrong. "You know Bern, it might not be necessary for us to talk every night. We've been here for a month now, and are quite settled in. Maybe we don't need to talk every night. Maybe we can talk every other night." I really wanted to reduce some of the daily regimentation. I wanted more freedom.

"Well, I think we should continue our nightly sched."

"You know, Bern, some nights when we don't make contact you can't know for sure if something's gone wrong, or if it's just poor atmospheric conditions. You haven't assumed that something is wrong just because you don't hear from us. You don't send out a rescue team. So maybe a nightly schedule isn't all that useful. I'm sure you would like to do other things sometimes rather than wait around to talk to us."

"Well," replied Bern, "I prefer to contact you every night at seven. That way I'll know if anything's gone wrong."

I can't blame him too much. I'm sure he feels at least partially responsible for our well being. I would like to make contact less often, though.

Tuesday, March 2. Last night we added only one medium-sized log to the stove before going to bed. Despite lows last night of -31 degrees, the cabin temperature fell to only +1 degree at sleeping height. Both Kathleen and I remained warm all night. We're becoming even more confident about our woodpile. On the other hand, we have never actually seen the two cords of wood that is supposed to be buried beneath the snow. What if it's actually not as much as two cords? What if the extra wood out back was actually some of the original two cords? Either of these possibilities would mean that our wood supply is insufficient to carry us through the winter.

After watching the snow drift and fall until mid-morning, I began shovelling away the snow where I suspected the tarp and wood must be. After a few minutes I found the orange tarp, and continued shovelling around its perimeter. It was a very large tarp. This is good. A large tarp likely means a large pile of wood. The tarp seemed to spread downhill, where the snow became even deeper. I decided to work at one shallow corner, and in about 40 minutes had exposed a good supply of wood. I carried the wood up to the cabin and piled a stack 2 m high, 1 m wide and 50 cm deep, the same amount that was on the porch when we arrived on January 31. It will be interesting to monitor how long this 'standard' stack of 1 cubic metre lasts. I still don't know how much wood is buried beneath the tarp, though. Probably won't ever know until the snow is gone and winter is over. Even if we don't already have enough wood, I can always get more.

We haven't seen caribou for a week, and we've been wondering if the herds have already started their migration north. During our nightly radio conversation, Bern said that the people of Colville Lake have recently shot a lot of caribou, and that the town's meat supply should now last the winter. Wood and caribou. Heat and food. Essentials of human life. Perhaps our caribou have all gone into the bush to escape being ambushed by the citizens of Colville Lake. I like to visualize these elegant animals filtering through the forest, hiding from town, escaping the bullet.

What if I needed meat to survive the winter, though? What would I do? It's much too easy for a suburbanite like me to cheer for the animal at the expense of the hunter. I have a lot of food in the storage cabin, food that I brought with me from the grocery stores in Vancouver. My situation is some-what artificial, and totally removed from the lives of the people in Colville Lake. If I needed meat, if I were hungry, if I had no other easy or inexpensive source of food, then I would certainly shoot a caribou. Hornby died because the caribou didn't pass by his cabin on the Thelon River. He and Christian and Adler had a lot of wood. But they couldn't get any more caribou.

We modern suburbanites can be very judgmental. Our biases often stem from ignorance and privilege. We should not be so quick to condemn those who hunt or trap out of necessity or tradition. The tradition of suburbanites is to eat cultivated grains and domesticated meats. Wheat and barley and corn all grow on land that once was habitat for wildlife – wildlife that has been extirpated to produce food for those who condemn killing of wildlife. Ham and beef and chicken come from animals that have been killed for our con-sumption – animals that likely wished and deserved to live just as much as the caribou of Colville Lake now wish and deserve to live. It is inconsistent for me to want life for the caribou, but to accept death for the pig.

I'm glad, though, that I don't have to shoot caribou to supply meat for the rest of the winter. I wouldn't enjoy killing one, and we haven't seen any caribou for a week. No telling when they will pass by this way again. I do have plenty of wood, however, and that makes me very happy.

Wednesday, March 3. After breakfast we headed back up Ketaniatue Connector to break more snow trail to Ketaniatue Lake. Above Colville Lake, to our south, a spectacular parhelion encircled the sun. Bright sunlight shone down upon us as we snowshoed through open stands of spruce draped with sparkling mounds of snow. In slightly less than two hours we had packed an additional 1.5 km of trail, and finally stood on Colville Ridge, at the height of land, gazing down upon Ketaniatue Lake 120 m below us and 2 km north. The hardest, uphill section of our trail has now been completed.

Kathleen and I stood together, content with our work. We silently faced into the cold wind that streamed toward us from somewhere out over the Arctic Ocean, 500 km to the north. At that moment, during the depth of winter, it is very likely that Kathleen and I were the last two people on the North American continent. In a 350-km-wide swath between Tuktoyaktuk and Paulatuk, we were likely the only two people in all of that isolated vastness north to the polar sea. Behind us, 45 km to the south, fewer than 100 people lived in Colville Lake. Only 640 people lived in Fort Good Hope, the next closest community, 160 km to the southwest, as the Raven flies. The nearest paved road, the end of the Dempster Highway at Inuvik, was 350 km to the northwest. The next closest all-weather road, at Wrigley on the Mackenzie River, ended 500 km due south.

We were truly alone – alone as we can be in today's modern world. I thought about Radisson, and how he must have felt more than 300 years ago when he wrote: 'We were as Caesars of the Wilderness – there being no one to contradict us.'

Pierre-Esprit Radisson and his partner Médard Chouart Des Groseilliers were iconic, independent 17th century explorers who personified the image of a *coureur des bois*, a title given to an individual who engaged in the fur trade without permission from the French authorities in Montreal. The term *coureur des bois* literally means 'runner of the woods.' The Montreal officials disapproved of the *coureurs des bois,* who were leaving the developing agricultural areas to seek their fortune trading. The French authorities preferred

It was likely that Kathleen and I were the last two people on the continent in a 350-km-wide swath that stretched 500 km north to the Arctic Ocean.

that the transportation of furs continued to be handled by the native peoples rather than independent, unregulated colonial traders, who were bringing in so many furs that the market became oversupplied.

I wonder what Radisson meant when he referred to himself as a caesar of the wilderness. Radisson and Groseilliers tried to interest the French in trading furs out of Hudson's Bay, where New France could avoid both the Iroquois attacks in the south and the direct competition with the Dutch traders. Radisson and Groseilliers were unsuccessful with their proposal, perhaps because of their reputation for not showing proper deference to authority. So they became caesars unto themselves, travelling where they wished and trading with whom they pleased. Perhaps, then, when he titled himself a caesar of the wilderness, Radisson simply meant that he answered to no European or colonial authority in the fur trade. It is not likely that he viewed himself as a caesar that ruled the native people who inhabited the extraordinarily vast Canadian landscape. It is more likely that Radisson simply preferred 'running in the woods' so that he could escape being ruled by the true caesars of the world.

If so, then I am very like Radisson. I also rebel at authority. I distrust power. I rankle at being told what to do. I object to people and to governments who try to impose upon me their rules and philosophies of how life should be lived, and of how society should be organized. I suppose one could more accurately label me a Libertarian rather than a 'Caesar of the Wilderness.'

Thoreau wrote that, 'In Wilderness is the Preservation of the World.' For me, the phrase might better be written 'In Wilderness is the Pursuit of Libertarian Ideals.' In wilderness there are few rules. In wilderness there is sufficient space for me to live my life while you live yours. When I am out 'running in the woods' I answer to no authority. Well, that's not exactly true. On canoe trips Kathleen usually decides where and when we will camp. I answer directly to her authority as the chef who has specific campsite requirements for preparing dinner.

I also need wilderness for what it is not. I crave wilderness to escape from the concrete and roads and constant noise that continue to consume North America – a North America that was essentially pristine only 300 years ago. I need to escape strip malls, box stores, line-ups, garbage dumps, land fills, forest clear-cuts, open pit mines, stop lights, used car lots, decaying tenement houses, eight-lane freeways and airports. I could go on for many pages.

Please don't accuse me of over-romanticizing about the past. I know the past was not perfect. People suffered tyranny. Native people starved to death when game became scarce. People died in wars. People succumbed to sicknesses and diseases that are now curable. On the other hand, in today's world, people still suffer tyranny and people in developing countries still starve to death. Even in the wealthy, privileged world of North America, people still die in wars and people still succumb to incurable sicknesses and diseases. No, the world has really not changed all that much. If one must endure the hardships and struggles that always accompany life, then one might as well have the opportunity to be surrounded by beauty. For me, the supreme beauty lies in the natural world. Yes, I was born into the wrong century. I was born much too late to have travelled with Radisson and Groseilliers – much too late to have enjoyed first-hand the pristine 'New World' that was once North America.

Kathleen and I continued to gaze toward the north. From that ridge I could see to the end of Ketaniatue Lake. After break-up in mid-June, we will launch our canoe down the Ross River and drift into Ketaniatue Lake. From there the water will carry us north through Lugetentue (Frozen Fish) Lake, and then on to Niwelin and Gassend Lakes. Soon after Gassend Lake we will reach the Anderson River. By mid-July, a month after leaving Colville Lake, we will eventually arrive at Liverpool Bay on the Arctic coast, a journey of 550 km. Kathleen and I should be the first people down the Anderson River this year, and it is likely that we will not see another human being the entire time. We will be as Caesars of our Wilderness.

Very content, Kathleen and I returned to the cabin. Only a few embers from this morning's fire remained in the stove, and the cabin temperature had fallen to a chilly +4 degrees. Although today's temperature had held steady at about -25 degrees, a persistent, strong wind from the north made the day seem much colder. I quickly started a new fire, and we spent the rest of our day by the stove, snacking and sipping hot drinks. We sat cozily in our chairs, enjoying that comfortable feeling of relaxation after vigorous exercise. Our feet seem to be more accustomed to snowshoes, as we no longer have any soreness. Perhaps we are finally toughening up.

During the radio conversation that evening, Bern said that Margaret, Jo-Ellen and Robert plan to ski-doo out to see us after school on Friday, two days from now. They plan to stay for the weekend! I hope they make it this time. Even a caesar in his wilderness enjoys company once in a while. Maybe they will bring mail.

Thursday, March 4. Our most important task for the day was to make three additional bunks available for sleeping. Kathleen and I are sleeping in the middle two bunks. We are storing items such as maps, tripod, wash basin and tools – things that we use on only a periodic or irregular basis – on the upper two bunks. The left-side lower bunk serves as our 'library,' while two suitcases acting as 'drawers' for clothing occupied the right-side lower bunk. Margaret, Jo-Ellen and Robert had nowhere to sleep.

I climbed up the ladder and shifted everything from the left-side upper bunk to the right-side upper bunk. One extra bed was now available. Kathleen then handed the books up to me to pile on the right-side upper bunk. With the library now empty, a second extra bed became available. We shouldn't need to change clothes during the visit, so we sledded our two suitcases up to the storage cabin. The third extra bed was now available.

While Kathleen added bedding and pillows to the new sleeping areas, I re-banked the walls of our home with snow, and added more wood to the stack outside the door to make sure that it reached the porch ceiling. Even though we had not used very much wood during the last two days, I wanted our visitors to know that we are organized and comfortable. Bern will undoubtedly be asking for a report when they return to town. Kathleen, anticipating mail pickup, wrote four more letters to family and friends.

Last night the outside temperature held steady at -26 degrees. The inside temperature this morning, at the middle-bunk level, was +4 degrees. This temperature suits Kathleen and me, and we both slept warmly all night. We don't know, however, what sleeping temperatures our guests might prefer. To maintain moderate temperatures at the middle bunks means that sleepers in the lower bunks might be too cold, while sleepers in the upper bunks might be too hot. I suppose we'll have to allocate bunks based on what is most comfortable for our guests. Many people in the North keep their houses very warm, so it might be that Kathleen and I will move to the colder, lower-level bunks. On the other hand, Margaret, Jo-Ellen or Robert might not want to be climbing up and down ladders, and would prefer to sleep in the lower bunks, with the wood stove stoked all night. I hadn't anticipated how complicated this 'sleepover' could become.

In the late afternoon we saw a red fox out on the lake, circling and turning as it apparently hunted for prey. After a few minutes, the fox quickly turned west, headed directly to shore, and disappeared into the forest. Perhaps the fox was now looking for a place to spend the night, or perhaps it was already bedded down in its own cozy burrow. The fox looked pretty content when it trotted off the lake. Probably wasn't expecting any guests tomorrow. Certainly wasn't thinking about sleeping arrangements, or how to keep his visitors optimally warm.

Friday, March 5. We woke to a beautiful, sunny morning. Although crisp at a -32 degrees, there was no wind, and the day was much more pleasant than the past few very blustery days. We sponge-bathed, and then tidied the cabin. Kathleen cooked a caribou stew, steamed some fresh bread, and made a chocolate pudding for dessert. We were ready and eager for guests.

Last night Bern had asked us to call in at 4:00 pm, so that he could confirm whether or not the visit was still happening. Sure enough, our three weekenders had roared off on their ski-doos 30 minutes ago. I changed into a fresh shirt, grabbed my binoculars, and sat down at the south-facing window. Kathleen placed three table settings on our main dining room table for Margaret, Jo-Ellen and Robert, who should arrive sometime between 5:00 and 6:00 pm, depending on travelling conditions. We were getting real excited!

At 5:30 we became even more eager. At 6:00 we became somewhat anxious. By 6:30 we began to feel despondent. At 7:00 pm, during our normal radio conversation, Bern reported that Margaret, Jo-Ellen and Robert had turned back after only 15 km because of rough ice and cold weather. I turned off the SSBx radio and looked at our tables set for five. There would be no visitors tonight. There would be no mail to read. There would be no one to take our mail back to town.

Kathleen cleared away the place settings for Margaret, Jo-Ellen and Robert. She ladled some caribou stew into our two bowls, and we ate our dinner and chocolate pudding mostly in silence. Kathleen and I had come to Colville Lake hoping for isolation. In five weeks, our only visitor has been Ron, the community constable, with his sons. Darn.

The weather has certainly turned decidedly cold again. It's now -34 degrees at 9:00 pm. Indeed, the thermometer has registered -30 degrees or below all but one day this month. When we had returned to the cabin from our camping trip last Sunday, the day had seemed so spring-like. We thought that temperatures might actually begin to warm in March. It seems though, that winter will be with us for a while yet.

Saturday, March 6. At 8:00 am this morning, the temperature had fallen to the magical -40 degrees. Kathleen decided that minus 40 was a perfect day to make the bannock breakfasts for our canoe trip down the Anderson River. We pretty much have bannock for breakfast every day on canoe trips. Bannock provides carbohydrates and energy for the canoeing day, particularly when we smother them in margarine and jam. Regardless of their nutritive qualities though, we just love bannock. We like everything about bannock. We like sitting in front of the fire cooking the bannock. We like flipping the bannock over in the pan. We like seeing the bannock turning a golden brown. We like sliding the bannock out of the skillet and onto our plates. We plan to be on the Anderson River for 28 days. We must have 28 bannocks.

Twenty-eight bannocks required more flour than we had stored in the kitchen, so Kathleen put on her parka, toque, mitts and boots, and trudged up the ridge, along Lower Cabin Crescent, toward the storage cabin, which was still shuttered for the winter. She switched on her headlamp and began to search through the 15 or so plastic bins stacked in the frozen darkness. Perhaps it was good memory, or perhaps just good luck that Kathleen found the two 10-kg bags of all-purpose flour in the very first plastic storage bin that she opened. One of the bags would be more than enough. She loaded it into the toboggan, and returned back down the ridge.

Kathleen has made literally hundreds of bannocks for our canoe trips, beginning in 1990. She's a machine when it comes to making bannock. She's focused. She's intent. She cranks them out. Settled comfortably in her warm kitchen, Kathleen set our largest mixing bowl on the table, and added four cups of flour, two tablespoons of baking powder, one teaspoon of salt, four tablespoons of dry milk powder and two tablespoons of sugar. She was on a roll. There was no stopping her now. Next she cut in one cup of shortening and mixed thoroughly. The first batch was now done. Kathleen measured out a cup-and-a-quarter of the bannock mixture into each of 5 individual freezer bags, and tied them off with twist ties. I watched the pile of breakfast bannock bags grow as Kathleen filled the bowl five more times. In about two hours Kathleen had made 28 bannocks for the canoe trip, with quite a few extras for our breakfasts at Colville Lake.

Kathleen's morning work was now done, and she sledded the remaining flour and the 28 breakfast bannock bags back up to the very cold and very dark storage cabin. Kathleen had already dried most of the food for the Anderson River canoe trip back at home. We always pack canoe trip food in the large, green, canvas canoe pack, to which Kathleen added the 28 breakfast bannocks. In terms of meals, we are now ready for our month-long paddle to the Arctic Ocean. All we need is break-up and flowing water.

By late afternoon, the temperature had risen to -26 degrees, but has remained below -25 degrees for three consecutive days. The large area of open water in The Narrows opposite our cabin has frozen over again.

Sunday, March 7. I stepped outside at 6:30 am to walk along Privy Path, and knew instantly that the temperature must have fallen back below -35 degrees, which is the temperature at which my nostrils begin to stick together. I shone the flashlight on the thermometer. Minus forty-three degrees. Apparently there is still no warming trend.

After breakfast of pancakes and fried Prem, all smothered in syrup and accompanied by three heaping cups of steaming tea, I set out up the cut line looking for more trees to cut down. At -40 degrees, I usually start thinking that we need more wood. At -40 degrees our stove consumes about one tree per 24-hour day. I know these Colville Lake trees are small, but the need to have one tree per day seemed a bit alarming.

On all our trips out now, I am constantly assessing the forest for standing dead trees. Standing dead trees make great firewood as they have already seasoned without being in contact with the ground. Very little rot – just exquisite, dry wood. I have made mental notes of the locations of all the best standing dead trees within about two km from our cabin. The optimal tree is between 30 and 45 cm in diameter at the base. Smaller trees don't provide enough wood to make the effort worthwhile. Larger-diameter trees are too big for my bow saw. The trees should also have minimum taper. There's no sense working hard to cut down a tree that tapers quickly to a diameter of only 10 to 15 cm. Trees with my preferred dimensions and attributes were usually between 6 and 10 metres tall. At -40 degrees, a smaller tree lasts about one day. A tree-a-day is a lot of trees, but plenty of trees are available. Kathleen and I are the last two people on the continent. We are as caesar, and all the trees belong unto us.

Along Woodlot Way I found two trees very near to those Bern had left us last fall. Both of those trees from Bern had already gone into our stove. I stomped out a snow path to my newly-found standing dead trees, which were about 30 cm in diameter at the snowline – small enough to be easily felled with my bow saw, yet large enough to burn hot and steady without constant refuelling of the stove.

The trees were already leaning over, perhaps because they were growing on permafrost. This was good for me, as I wouldn't need to make an undercut. I simply sawed toward the direction of lean, about 80% of the way through the trunk. I then shoved from behind until the tree fell lightly, showering me with a cascade of fluffy, dry snow.

I preferred to push the tree over. A tree sawn all the way through, even with an undercut, can sometimes bind, and break the saw blade. I have only two spare blades. Worse, the tree might stand on end, and rotate on the stump. It would then fall unpredictably in any direction, perhaps snapping my leg, or crushing me to death as it toppled over, or pinning me in the snow. At -40 degrees I might slowly freeze to death before Kathleen came looking for me. I'm very cautious though, and bad things, like careless accidents, usually don't happen to me. After felling both trees, I limbed each with the axe, sawed one of them into 25-cm rounds for the stove, and dragged the first load back to camp.

After my work and lunch, Kathleen and I snowshoed back down the Ross River, about 2 km, toward Ketaniatue Lake. The temperature had finally struggled back up above -25, to reach -23 degrees. Many of the previous open spots on the river were now refrozen, although one stretch still ran swiftly for about 300 m. The afternoon mist rose lightly from this open lead, and the riverside willows lay covered with a fine, fragile dusting of hoarfrost, which contrasted delicately and beautifully with the blue sky above.

For dinner Kathleen fried up one of the fish that Ron had brought from Bern and Margaret. We think it's a lake trout, but we're not sure. Next to the trout, and taking up most of the room on my plate, sat a golden bannock. Lake trout and bannock, a perfect Northern winter meal to end the first week of March. We were both stuffed, and couldn't even eat our pudding dessert. We still 'pumped and popped' for our cribbage game, though. No matter how full our stomachs might be, popcorn goes with cribbage. Popping always follows pumping. That's just the way it is.

Monday, March 8. The day again began sunny and clear, at -42 degrees. After breakfast I returned to the woodlot to saw the second tree into stove-sized lengths. I thoroughly enjoy working alone, in silence, surrounded by the silent, frozen forest. The snow trail beckons to me. The wood waits patiently for me. Ravens and Whiskey Jacks welcome me. The sun seems to bless, smile upon, and approve of my work. I spent all day at this satisfying, pleasant task, and by late afternoon I had sledded most of the wood back to the cabin.

The large pile of limbs and twigs left over from my work provided an unanticipated and valuable benefit. The spruce branches were covered with a short, densely-clumped, black lichen known as 'horsehair.' This lichen/dead twig combination, when dried overnight in the cabin, made a highly flammable kindling that never needed more than a single match. I loaded several piles into the toboggan, and headed back down the snow trail toward home. In the late afternoon, I split the wood that was too large for the stove into medium-sized pieces. During dinner, I often turned to admire my box full of horsehair lichen kindling sitting next to my box full of split, 'bridging' pieces of wood.

As twilight approached, clouds drifted down Colville Lake, and a light snow began to fall. Perhaps this means the end, even if only temporarily, of very cold temperatures. If not though, with my increased supply of wood stacked from floor to ceiling just outside the door on the screened porch, I feel much more prepared for cold weather.

Tuesday, March 9. After breakfast, Kathleen and I snowshoed out at -27 degrees, into a steady wind blowing in from the northwest. It was a fine and beautiful day, as we finally finished packing our snow trail over the Connector to Ketaniatue Lake. The last two km of new trail passed through very deep snow, particularly as we neared the lake. Even so, the entire 11-km round trip took only 4.5 hours. Now we can easily visit Ketaniatue Lake on day outings. True 'picnics' at the lake, though, will likely have to wait for warmer weather. Although we're quite comfortable when moving, we cool off very quickly – in only a few minutes – when we stop for lunch or snacks.

[*Author's note:* When we returned to Inuvik in July, I mentioned to Alan how we cooled off so quickly when stopping. His response was "Why didn't you make a fire? Making a fire and boiling up some tea water is the main reason we go on winter walks. In fact, if we're getting home too soon, we stop on purpose just to make a fire." I can't really say why Kathleen and I didn't make fires when on the trail. I suppose we were just too focused on our work.]

Wednesday, March 10. This book is based primarily on my diary. I occasionally insert information that comes from Kathleen's diary. So far, I have used her words as though they were my own. This 'plagiarism by consent' has worked well to avoid redundancy or duplication, particularly when discussing events or facts. When Kathleen writes about her feelings, though, I think those perceptions are better presented in her own words. The following description is based on her diary.

> *The last week has been truly cold! We've experienced*
> *-40 degrees nearly every night. Even the afternoon high*
> *temperatures reach only into the upper minus twenties. We are*
> *becoming impatient for warmer weather. I would like to be*
> *able to go to the outhouse without having to put on my parka*
> *and mitts. I look forward to such a simple pleasure. I hope that*
> *today is a foretaste of warmer weather – it is now -18 degrees*
> *at 2:00 pm. The sun is shining brightly, and I can actually*
> *feel its warmth when I'm outside. Michael and I are from the*
> *South, from Vancouver. When we see the sun, we automatically*
> *expect warmth. Here at Colville Lake though, north of the*
> *Arctic Circle during winter, a bright sun implies nothing about*
> *warmth. But today is different. I feel warmth when the sun*
> *strikes my face. I also feel a biting wind as I stand outside*
> *looking up Colville Lake. The wind is from the south, so*
> *hopefully it's bringing a warming trend our way.*
>
> *We finished breaking the overland trail to Ketaniatue*
> *Lake yesterday. The route, about 5 km long, runs mostly along*
> *a seismic line extending over Colville Ridge. The height of*
> *land occurs conveniently about halfway between Colville*
> *Lake and Ketaniatue Lake. The ascent on both sides is quite*
> *gradual, which makes for an easy climb. The surrounding*
> *forest, particularly at the crest, is very open, with scenic vistas*
> *in all four directions. As we snowshoed along, my mind often*
> *conjured up the proverbial but descriptive phrase of a winter*
> *wonderland.*

[Kathleen, I already wrote about completing the trail to Ketaniatue yesterday. I already said that it was a fine and beautiful day. You don't need to say that again. It's redundant. Oops, sorry to interrupt.]

Kathleen continues:

As I was saying, Michael... The day was much more than 'fine' – it was a winter wonderland. As we neared Ketaniatue Lake, breaking trail became more difficult because of the deep, soft snow, and we often sank in up to our knees, despite being on snowshoes. Sinking in, though, provides a benefit, as the trail becomes well defined. It remains open, and easy to travel over, even after a new snowfall. [In contrast,] our trails over the ice on Colville Lake and the Ross River are continually being covered by newly-fallen or drifting snow

Since arriving here on January 31st we have seen only four people – Community Constable Ron and his three young companions. And they visited for only a couple of hours. For all practical purposes, Michael and I are the only people in the country and we go at will or by whim wherever and whenever we want. We have explored our country north along the Ross River. We have provided access to Ketaniatue Lake via the overland route, and we have ventured south up Colville Lake. Our trails in the snow mark our passing. We see no one. This is truly our place. There aren't many places in the world two people can have such freedom.

We have diligently been writing letters to family and friends. However, because Ron has been our only visitor, most of the letters simply sit in the 'outbox' waiting to be taken to Colville Lake. Margaret, Jo-Ellen and Robert started out for here last Friday, but were turned back by the cold. Bern says they are busy on the weekends for the rest of the month, so likely won't be visiting very soon. Last night Bern told us that the program that funded Ron had been cancelled due to lack of funds – so potential visits by the RCMP or by Ron seem very unlikely. It seems that if we want to mail or receive letters that we will just have to go to town ourselves.

Indeed, we are responsible for all aspects of our life out here. Most importantly, we are responsible for our own heat and light. In the city we take heat and light for granted. At temperatures of 20 or 40 degrees below zero, one needs a lot of wood to heat even a small space. Michael cut down two fairly large trees this week – that wood lasted about three days. There are three major reasons we spend so much time travelling outside. First, we enjoy exploring our new home. Second, we actually like being outside, and experiencing the cold. And third, we conserve wood by being away from the cabin. We heat the cabin only when absolutely necessary. It's not necessary to heat the cabin when we're away.

We are storing most of our food and gear in the larger storage cabin, which we never heat. It still surprises me when I retrieve a can of tomatoes or a tin of tuna to use in a meal, and find it frozen solid. The food and water that we take with us when travelling outside freezes in only a few hours. I have become very focused on conserving all sources of fuel. Wood is our only source of heat. Propane is our only source of fuel for the two-burner stove. White gas is our only source of fuel for the Coleman lantern. We can physically see all that we have of these three sources of fuel. Other than the propane, we can physically see them diminish each day. When one sees your sources of fuel diminishing every day, it becomes easier, even imperative, to conserve and to use wisely.

We are fortunate that the ice just outside the cabin is thin, and that Michael can bring buckets of water up to the cabin. We would need a great deal more fuel to melt ice or snow.

Thursday, March 11. [*Author's Note:* As I write this book it has been very interesting to return to my diary ten years after leaving Colville Lake. Some of the entries actually stun me. Now that I have been back in the South for so long, some of the entries seem unbelievable. For example, my diary entry on March 11 begins: "Another day of increasingly spring-like conditions. Minus 37 degrees at 7:00 am, warming rapidly to -23 when we departed on our snowshoeing outing at 10:45."

Spring-like at -37 degrees? Did I really think that -23 was warm? Well, I have no choice but to take my own words at face value. There would have been no reason to lie to myself. For whatever reason, I apparently felt warm and spring-like on a day that began at -37 degrees.]

*The teepee site marked the mouth of a frozen stream
leading to our second winter camp.*

We spent much of today searching for a suitable location for our next wall tent camping site. We struck out south, along the east shore of Colville Lake, two km to where a frozen stream entered Colville Lake on a rounded point extending into the lake. For the past month Kathleen and I had been referring to this cleared area as the 'Teepee Site' because of the poles standing on end in the shape of a teepee. The people of Colville Lake must use this place as a more-or-less permanent summer fishing, hunting or trapping camp.

For the first time this winter, Kathleen and I turned east onto the streambed, between two ridges that sheltered us from the quickening southwest wind. Again I felt so very lucky to be walking through a scene that, to me, cannot be surpassed in beauty, tranquillity and allure. The winding stream covered in pure white snow beckoned us ever onward to reveal its secrets hidden around each bend. Clumps of Red-osier Dogwood. Mature White Spruce with its red inner bark glowing in the afternoon sun. Green and black spires of the noble forest reaching upward into an azure sky, all bathed in sunlight, silence and the sublime cold that now seemed soothing, invigorating and inviting. We snowshoed up the river until we eventually reached a small lake, where we found an idyllic spot to establish our second winter camp. Definitely the most beautiful place we have seen so far. We look forward to dragging out, probably late next week.

Winter is such a glorious season, and northern Canada is blessed with a winter that lasts 6 to 7 months. It is unfortunate that Canadians expend so much time complaining about winter. I am somewhat perplexed that Canadians spend so much money avoiding winter at southern resorts. It seems to me that Canadians should embrace a time of year that is so pure, so clean, and so crisp. I have come to thoroughly enjoy the cold and the bright sun glistening on the perpetual snow. Canada is a nation blessed by winter. We should receive and enjoy that blessing.

Other people share my opinion. One of the books we brought with us to Colville Lake is Grey Owl's *Tales of an Empty Cabin*. This book is an extraordinary collection of essays and short stories about Canada and the author's life as a trapper (and ultimately a conservationist) during the first four decades of the 20th century. Grey Owl (whose true name was Archie Belaney) also loved Canada's winter. In his essay entitled *Canadiana*, Grey Owl wrote that Canada's North has:

> *a climate consisting of a short Spring, a warm but bracing sunshiny Summer, a very wonderful Autumn such as I think few other countries in the world are favoured with, and a bright, clear, cold, snappy invigorating and healthful winter.... Winter in Canada is in many ways the best time of the year, and we have no reason to deny it.*

I'm glad to know that I'm not the only one that believes in, and extols the Canadian climate, particularly its winter. Probably the only exception to this climate is where I live, on the southwest coast of British Columbia. I find this climate to be generally depressing. From mid-October to mid-February rain dominates the gray sky. The sun remains elusive and the ground oozes dampness and moss. Temperatures near zero, combined with the moisture-filled air, bites into the body's core temperature. Summer brings drier weather and warmer days. But the evenings quickly turn cool – no lounging outside for languorous and extended summer evenings. In fall, the dense forest stands dark, impassive and sombre as it towers into the overcast heavens. No magnificent fall colours enjoyed by most Canadians.

People in Vancouver who say they can't live in the cold always frustrate me. These same people also claim, and rightfully so, that they love Canada. They are proud to be Canadians, and would live in no other country. I sometimes think I should carry with me a folding pocket map of Canada. I could then invite the cold-haters to study the map.

"Look at this map," I would say. "Virtually all of mainland Canada, the world's second largest country, enjoys a long winter. Only this tiny little spot centred on Vancouver and Victoria remains unfrozen. You tell me you love Canada, but you also tell me that nearly 100% of the country is unliveable for you. Don't you see the irony? How can you love Canada and also hate the cold?"

The day at Colville Lake continued to be warm, and Kathleen and I sat down for lunch in the shallow snow at the head of a frozen lake, out of the wind, where we enjoyed the heat of the sun shining upon our faces. Throughout the winter, we had always felt warm outside, as long as we were moving, dressed in our layers of wool and canvas wind suits. Now, for the first time since arriving on January 31 we were able to sit outside, comfortably, without becoming chilled when resting, without needing mechanical heat to produce warmth.

When I ask cold-haters what it is about the Canadian winter that they don't like, the first response is either (1) that they don't like scraping car windows, or (2) that they don't like shovelling snow. Fine. Cars and roads and sidewalks are made for summer. They become less convenient in winter. But this inconvenience is no reason to summarily hate or flee winter.

Those who escape winter, or who dislike the cold, often express envy for people who live in places like Florida, or Arizona, or California. I grew up in California, and I can speak (or write) with personal knowledge that Californians spend a lot of time and money protecting themselves from their climate. Cars sitting in the sun become unbearably hot. Air conditioning is essential. Indeed, without air conditioning, homes become sweltering hothouses. For most Californians, air conditioning is an absolute necessity to protect themselves from the overwhelming heat. Drive down a suburban street in California during summer and note that most people close their curtains during the day to keep the sun from fading their furniture and from overheating their homes. Sure, it's sunny all day, but many Californians hide from the sun behind closed doors and curtained windows. Many Californians insulate themselves during the long, unending summer – the very climatic attributes that Canadians envy during winter.

Yes, I agree with Grey Owl. Give me dry cold, with the sun shining brilliantly on a snow-covered landscape. Northern Canada offers unlimited opportunities for that landscape, and for experiencing the changing of seasons.

But I have to be honest with you. Although Kathleen and I are enjoying winter, we are also looking forward to spring. At lunch today we had been able to stop and sit in the snow for about 30 minutes without feeling cold. This is a major change. We can definitely feel the sun's warmth. Kathleen commented that for the first time this winter, frost no longer accumulated on our fur ruffs and neck warmers. On all previous trips they had become covered in frost when our breath condensed on their surfaces. Today, the fur on the front of Kathleen's hat actually felt warm to her touch. Now that the days are becoming increasingly longer, the temperature will certainly continue to trend upward.

When we returned to the cabin, the afternoon temperature had soared to -5 degrees. While eating dinner we watched water drip from the western eaves of our cabin roof. The snow is wilting beneath the heat of the magnificent sun. Overflow has reappeared near the lake's margin. No matter what the temperature does now, we know that spring is on its way.

During our radio conversation with Bern, his main comment was that: "today it dripped – the first time this year we've seen it drip." There was excitement in his voice. A man who has witnessed a half-century of Northern winters was excited by water dripping from his roof. And why should he not be thrilled by dripping water? It is precisely because the Canadian Northern winter is so powerful, that its end becomes truly magnificent and exciting.

Friday, March 12. The morning temperature remained in single digits, at -8 degrees. By mid-afternoon the mercury registered -1 degree, but never reached the zero mark. Our cabin is now very easy to heat, and we are comfortably warm, even when seated as much as one metre from the stove. For the first time, even the side of our face away from the stove feels warm.

Also for the first time we lounge in stocking feet, as the cold air that used to pool on the floor has fled before the onslaught of warming temperatures.

We still expect more cold weather, though. According to one of the participants on the Yukon trappers winter sched last night, "March is a joker. There's always one more cold snap after the initial warming." We actually hope so, as we're not quite ready for the lakes and rivers to thaw.

The winter sched will end in a few days. Too bad, as we've enjoyed listening to their stories and perspectives. We share many of their experiences. Just as I always feel the need for more wood when the temperature falls to -40 degrees, one of the trappers mentioned that, "When the mercury hits -30, I'm always out checking the woodpile."

A couple of days ago, the temperature in the southern Yukon hit +8 degrees. Even so, Don said, "You can't count your chickens in February, and you aren't out of the woods (in terms of cold weather) until March 15."

I've never heard that saying before. I don't know why people would even be tempted to count chickens in February. I have a lot to learn.

The southeast wind blew very strongly all day, and most of the trees were bared of their burden of snow. Other than for the forest floor, the scene imparts a summer-like quality, particularly in combination with the washed-out, faded blue of the sky at mid-day. Now that the sun no longer remains low on the horizon, we have lost the deep azure horizon that we so thoroughly enjoyed until a few weeks ago.

Out on the lake, approximately a dozen spots of various sizes and shapes have been blown free of snow, and now lie in greenish-black contrast against the surrounding snow-covered surface – like cut-blocks carved out of a virgin forest. Slumping and overflow also seem to have accelerated in the last 24 hours. As of yet, however, no sections of the lake or its outlet are running free.

Saturday, March 13. The day broke warm again, at -6 degrees. For the first time this winter, I was able to dip my water bucket into the lake without first needing to chop through the ice.

Our primary task today was doing laundry. Doing laundry without power differs considerably from doing laundry at home. Doing laundry in Vancouver is almost like an afterthought. Put the clothes in the washer, and then go away to do some gardening for half an hour or so. When the washer stops, transfer the clothes to the dryer. Turn on the dryer and then go away to enjoy a toasted bagel for lunch. Come back in half an hour or so to put away clean, fresh clothes. Get on with the rest of your day.

Here at the cabin, without electricity or running water, laundry is the rest of our day – laundry is our whole day. And it's not because we have so many clothes to wash. In fact, we have very few clothes to wash, as we often wear the same clothes throughout the week. The laundry usually includes only two pairs of long wool underwear, two pairs of wool socks, plus 3 to 5 pairs of 'regular' underwear. Without power, however, laundry poses a formidable challenge to those of us accustomed to the comforts of city life.

To begin the process, I need to bring up eight buckets of water from the lake, two at a time. Kathleen heats the buckets on the propane stove and dumps the hot water into a larger metal basin. The clothes then soak for a while, until Kathleen washes them the very old-fashioned way, by rubbing and agitating them with her hands. We don't even have a rock to pound them with. In Vancouver, we often go to antique and second-hand stores looking for interesting furnishings. We commonly have seen old washboards sitting idly on corner shelves. We then remark, with respect, how hard it must have been to wash clothes using just a washboard. How much we wish we had a washboard now. In all the readings we have done about the 'how-to' and romance of isolated cabin life in the bush, no one ever mentions the mundane task of doing laundry. No one ever mentions how useful it would be to take a simple item like a washboard. No one ever mentions how much this simple washboard could improve one's life.

After the washing is done, I need to take out eight buckets of gray water, two at a time, and dump them, about 20 m behind the cabin, over the hillside. I can't just toss the used water outside the door, which would be much easier for me. Water is heavy, and difficult to carry very far. Water chucked outside the door, though, would instantly turn our pathway into a winter-long sheet of ice. The pathway to the outhouse, compact and slick from constant use, is already far too slippery. The path takes us over a little rise at the corner of the cabin, where we can read the thermometer hanging on the outside wall. Heading back down the slope has been particularly risky. Kathleen and I have fallen many times – probably twenty times each. Like a gunslinger's belt, we should be carving notches into the wall to record the carnage. It's getting to the point where we expect to careen down the hill, and we are becoming skilled at falling gracefully. Perhaps we should have planned a better route to the outhouse, or perhaps we should line the path with spruce boughs.

After dumping the gray water, I then need to bring eight more buckets up the hill, two at time. Kathleen heats the buckets on the propane stove and dumps the hot water into the metal basin. The clothes then soak for a while, until Kathleen wrings them out the very old-fashioned way, by twisting them with her hands. Kathleen says that the item she misses most from our home in Vancouver is the washing machine. More specifically, she misses the spin cycle of the washing machine. It takes a very long time of twisting and resting, and re-twisting, and flexing of tired wrists, and twisting again to wring enough water out of the clothes so that they are ready to hang.

We remember those long ago days of the 1950s, when our parents and grandparents owned ringer-washers – washing machines with a mechanical

No one ever told us how difficult laundry day would be.
The 'wash and rinse cycles' both required eight buckets of water
brought up from the lake two at a time.

wringer mounted on the side. One still occasionally sees these machines at second-hand stores. How simple it would have been for us to have brought an old mechanical wringer. In all the readings we have done about the 'how-to' and romance of isolated cabin life in the bush, no one ever mentions the mundane task of doing laundry. No one ever mentions how useful it would be to take a simple item like a mechanical wringer. No one ever mentions how much this simple wringer could improve one's life.

After the rinsing and wringing, I take out eight buckets of gray water, two at a time, and dump them, about 20 m behind the cabin, over the hillside. We are now ready to hang the clothes. When we first did laundry at the cabin, we hung the clothes on drying racks strung from the ceiling. This seemed logical, but was very inconvenient. First, the racks were small, and sometimes could not accommodate all of our clothes at once. Secondly, we quickly grew tired of walking into and between wet clothes for the rest of the day. So last week I packed in a path called Laundry Lane, at the end of which I strung a clothesline between two trees so that we could dry the clothes outside.

Now I know that some of you may laugh, or might even be downright skeptical about hanging laundry out to dry in the middle of an Arctic winter. But we had read that even in the coldest temperatures, laundry would dry if the wind were blowing. The strong southeast wind from yesterday persisted, and we decided to hang our laundry outside, hoping for the magic of sublimation, whereby ice turns to a gas (vapour) without first passing through the liquid stage. Such a miracle would leave our dry clothes fluttering happily at the end of the day. I loaded up our laundry basket, grabbed my can of clothespins, and trudged out back to the clothesline. I picked up the first wool sock, which had frozen solid, and stood rigidly upright when I held it by the toe. I pinned it to the line, and reached for the next sock. It too was frozen solid. In fact, all the clothes had frozen solid.

Now, as you might suspect, pinning clothes to a line requires dexterity. Pinning clothes can not be done while wearing bulky mitts. Pinning clothes to a line requires fingers – fingers that quickly become numb and useless when exposed to wind and to frozen underwear, even at a relatively warm -6 degrees. After a few minutes I retreated to the cabin to thaw my fingers. Eventually though, after a few trips out to pin, and a few trips back to thaw, all the clothes were hanging from the line. I sat down at the table to enjoy a mug of tea. The laundry seems to be under control.

Unfortunately the wind died a few hours after pinning our clothes to the line. Even nine hours later, all laundry except the pillow cases remained stiff as that proverbial board. Maybe we'll have better success next time. Any way, laundry day was now over. In all the readings we had done about the "how to" and romance of isolated cabin life in the bush, no one ever mentioned how difficult laundry day would be. Then again, no one ever cautioned us against urinating in the outhouse, either.

Snow now falls gently, in large, moisture-laden flakes, obscuring the large patches of overflow and thin ice. Travel on the river under such conditions, particularly in poor light, would be dangerous.

A group of six to eight Whiskey Jacks flitted around the cabin throughout the day, attracted to and feeding at our 'kitchen gray water disposal site.' Presumably the small bits of food have become slightly less congealed during the warmth of the past few days.

Sunday, March 14. I rose at 8:30 am, started the fire, boiled water for tea, and lifted Kathleen down from her bunk just before 9:00 am. The wind was calm, with the temperature hovering at a warm -15 degrees. Nevertheless, the overcast morning seemed gloomy and uninviting. We decided to stay close to home. While Kathleen relaxed and read at the table, I spent nearly an hour baking a breakfast bannock on top of the wood stove.

Open water finally appeared at The Narrows in front of the cabin. Even more momentous, open water nearly appeared at the pier on the south side of the point. I easily broke through a thin skiff of ice, banging away at it with the water bucket. I can now get water simply by walking out on the dock, and dipping the bucket into the lake. No more extending a bucket dangling from the end of my broom handle. The vernal equinox is now only one week away. We both hope and expect to see temperatures above freezing before the end of March.

For dinner, Kathleen prepared a pizza. As I had done for the breakfast bannock, Kathleen cooked the pizza on top of the wood stove. This not only conserved propane, but was also very relaxing. The wood stove sits within reaching distance of the dinner table, where Kathleen sat drinking tea. She would occasionally set her tea mug down to reach out to investigate and poke at the pizza. Our small, 'open-plan' cabin provides a spatial convenience not available in more modern kitchens, which are much too large to provide the luxurious opportunity to prepare dinner while sitting at the table. The wood stove radiates heat and comfort and friendship. A banana crème pudding, intended for dessert during our evening cribbage match, sits on the counter next to the propane stove. Life is very simple. Life is very good.

Monday, March 15. We again awoke to dense fog and low, overcast skies, both of which persisted throughout the day. Yesterday Kathleen had wrenched her back slightly, when she reached to lift one of the storage bins while off-balance. A day or two of rest and stretching exercises seems to be the wisest choice. We decided to postpone our intended snowshoeing outing to a sunnier, more inviting day. Pending good weather, and Kathleen's back, we plan to drag our wall tent up Colville Lake on Thursday or Friday to set up camp along the banks of that picturesque little river that flows by the Teepee Site.

As you might suspect, we don't hear very many new jokes out here, all alone, at the outlet of Colville Lake. We do listen to the Canadian Broadcasting Corporation in the morning, primarily to hear the weather forecast. For true entertainment and information, we listen to the Yukon trappers winter sched at 8:00 pm. Tonight's best observation was: "These fur prices may not be high, but they sure beat a kick in the pants with a frozen moccasin."

We've repeated this line several times since returning to Vancouver. It never goes over very well, though. Maybe we don't tell it right, or maybe we haven't found the right context yet. Or maybe Kathleen and I, all alone at Colville Lake in mid-winter, were just a more receptive audience – a lot more ready to laugh.

Tuesday, March 16. The sun appeared only briefly during another cloudy, overcast day. A fair-sized pond has opened up in The Narrows, and Bern said that river otters can often be seen swimming in this early lead of open water. That would be great to see an otter, which is my favourite animal. The river otter always seems to be playing – always seems to be enjoying itself. It's also equally at home on either land or water, and seems completely unconcerned about potential predators. In fact, there is no reason for the otter to be concerned about becoming someone else's meal. The otter is at the top of the food chain in the river, and it is much too nimble and observant to be caught on land by bears, wolves or lynx. Life would be very good as a river otter.

Bern also reported that three female RCMP are in town. We extended our invitation for them to visit. We'd love to receive, and to send, our mail.

Wednesday, March 17. The 'pond' in The Narrows continued to expand rapidly, even though the temperature remained between -5 and -12 degrees. We snowshoed up Ketaniatue Connector, through the spruce forest, now muted with a layer of hoarfrost, beneath a low, sombre, gray sky. It's already mid-March, a month when we are supposed to experience 'a slight touch of snow blindness.' Yet we have seen very little sun, certainly not nearly enough to cause even a 'slight' touch of snow blindness.

We returned home across the horseshoe-shaped bay at the north end of Colville Lake. We have travelled across this bay many times before. We always cross this bay going to and from Woodlot Way and the Ketaniatue Connector. We moved in silence, enjoying the stillness, and thinking about dinner and the warmth of our cabin. Suddenly, out of nowhere, we heard a loud 'whump' and felt the snow vibrate beneath our feet.

"What the hell was that?"

"I don't know, but I didn't like it."

We stood still, wondering what had happened, reluctant to move. Was this some kind of danger? Should we be worried? Should we get off the ice? We pushed forward, somewhat gingerly, along our well-used snow trail. A few seconds later, the snow again collapsed around us with a loud, ominous 'whump.'

I really didn't like this now. Was our very movement causing the snow and ice to give way, to sink into the icy water below? Was there an unknown current in the lake eating away at the ice above? Were we now standing on only a thin layer of ice covered by snow too deep to show discoloured overflow? We could see no telltale cracks. We could see no indication that the snowpack had shifted beneath us. The snow on which we stood was seemingly at the same level as the rest of the snow for as far as we could see. Everything appeared normal, but we felt very uneasy, very threatened. Danger that can't be seen or assessed or guarded against is the most sinister kind of danger. We quickly headed straight to shore, and worked our way home through the bush. After dinner, I stomped in the first two passes of a short 'detour' snow trail around the curve of the bay, where perhaps there was a current striking shore before deflecting west to the outlet of Colville Lake.

Thursday, March 18. We woke to another fogbound morning. Before breakfast I climbed onto the cabin roof to clean the chimney of the wood stove. According to Bern's instructions, I lowered three animal traps tied to the end of a polypropylene rope into the Yukon chimney. I raised them up and down a few times, and the job was done – simple to do, but very necessary.

The view from the cabin roof, only a few metres higher than ground level, afforded a grand view of the lake and surrounding forest. Hoarfrost coated all the buildings and trees. The frost dangled perpendicularly to the underside of aspen branches, like individual miniature flags hung to mark the arrival of a visiting dignitary. A gentle breeze wafted in from the south, and freed the frost to swirl and dance like cottonwood fluff floating adrift on a fine spring day.

During lunch, we thought we saw an otter swimming in the growing pond of The Narrows – too far away to be certain, though. Through binoculars we saw pieces of ice, drifting slowing in the current, beginning their 550 km river journey to Liverpool Bay on the Arctic coast. We look forward to joining their adventure, in approximately three months from today.

During the nightly radio conversation, Bern reported that Margaret, Robert and Jo-Ellen might come to visit on Saturday. We were planning another winter campout this weekend, but will gladly change our plans. We would much rather receive visitors, and to receive and send mail. Word from the 'Outside' becomes increasingly important to us. We won't get our hopes up this time, though. We'll just see what happens.

Friday, March 19. Shortly after midnight, a strange noise outside woke me. I lay half-awake, listening to a strong, rhythmic, irritating tapping noise.

Whack. Whack. Whack. Whack.

What could be making that noise? Maybe it will go away. Kathleen was also awake now.

"What is that, Michael?"

"I don't know."

"Maybe you should go out and have a look."

"Maybe it will stop soon."

Whack. Whack. Whack. Whack.

She was right, of course. I should go out to have a look. Why would the sound stop all by itself? I was pretty warm turtled down in my sleeping bag though, and just before going to bed the temperature was -18 degrees. I didn't feel like going out into the cold, to poke around in the dark for a sound that I might not be able to find, much less do anything about.

"I'll look in the morning, Kathleen. It'll be easier then."

Whack. Whack. Whack. Whack.

After 30 minutes, the mysterious sound wasn't going away. And here I was, a would-be Northern adventurer hearkening after Hornby and Rae, hiding in my sleeping bag, whimpering that it was too cold and too dark to go outside. I climbed down the ladder, dressed by candlelight, and headed outside with my headlamp. Hoarfrost had been accumulating all night, and the light from my headlamp sparkled wherever it shone.

Whack. Whack. Whack. Whack.

I traced the noise to the upper right rear corner of the cabin, where the radio antennae wire first reached the cabin. The wire was vibrating in the wind, banging against the sides of the hole through which it entered the cabin. This hasn't happened before, even with strong winds. There's only a gentle breeze tonight. Why should this be happening now? I played a bit with the wire, pulled it tight, and lodged it more securely in the hole between the cabin's logs. The sound stopped. Good.

Back in the cabin, Kathleen asked what had been making the sound.

"Just the wind blowing the antennae wire," I said. "It's fixed now, at least temporarily. But I'll have a closer look in the morning."

An hour later the sound began again.

Whack. Whack. Whack. Whack.

Damn! What's making the antennae wire do that? It's really annoying. Here we are, 40 km from the nearest town, and I can't sleep because of all the noise outside. Darned ironic. Obviously though, I can't fix the problem until daylight, when I can see what is really happening. Maybe I can sleep through it.

Whack. Whack. Whack. Whack.

Sleeping wasn't going to be easy.

Whack. Whack. Whack. Whack

When I stepped outside at 7:00 am, I discovered that the entire antennae wire hung heavy with hoarfrost suspended below. The weight of the frost created a taut line, which vibrated, even in the gentle breeze. I grabbed the wire and shook until all the frost floated away, leaving the wire bare and quiet. Last night I had fixed the sound by unknowingly shaking the hoarfrost off when playing with the wire. The sound resumed when the hoarfrost had re-formed.

Hoarfrost is a winter cousin to summer's dew, and develops by similar processes, in that crystalline structures grow from water vapour evaporated from liquid droplets suspended in thin air. Hoarfrost accumulates on objects when there is more moisture in the air than the air can carry. If the air is sufficiently dry, the dew point, or completely saturated air, is reached below zero degrees. In fact, pure water suspended in clean air remains in liquid form down to temperatures near -40 degrees.

Or as Kathleen says, hoarfrost is like tiny, thin sections of broken glass, in delicate shapes that float like feathers in the wind – landing intact on objects to produce a thick layer of magical sparkles.

The morning sun suddenly and finally burst through the cloud cover, to create a stunning day of glittering white beneath deepest blue. Finally, a slight touch of snow blindness! I put on my snowshoes and headed up Colville Lake. The sun shone warmly at -11 degrees, and I travelled without hat or face warmer.

A Raven swooped down and called out to me, "Cronk."

I stood still to listen to his echo reverberate from the opposite shore. The Raven landed in a nearby spruce and called again, "Cronk."

We looked at each other. Hoarfrost crystals floated through the air.

"Cronk." He appeared to be waiting for a response.

Perhaps it was the same Raven that had been part of my Perfect Moment back in February.

I had been practicing my Raven sound, and gave my best imitation: "Cronk."

The Raven now stared intently at me, and said, "Cronk."

I answered again, and again the Raven replied. We exchanged guttural greetings for the next 15 minutes until the Raven tired of the conversation and flew off toward Colville Ridge. I hesitate to be too anthropomorphic, but

I am quite sure the Raven had wanted to communicate with me. He seemed to enjoy the contact. I know I did.

I returned home to re-stack wood on the porch to shoulder height. Based on last week's consumption rate, the stack should last about 17 days, to April 4. If we go winter camping the stack should last until April 7. If we go to Colville Lake the stack should last until April 13. Warmer weather should extend the stack until approximately April 17. If so, I think we have plenty of wood. These predictions are not much more than guesses. Nevertheless, Kathleen and I both feel the need to manage and monitor our dwindling supply of wood.

The evening weather on the CBC reported positive temperatures for many of the southern Northwest Territories communities such as Hay River and Fort Smith. Even the western Arctic coast temperatures are rising up into the minus teens. At 5:00 pm the sun remained high in the sky, and did not drop below the western ridge until 6:45. The days are becoming longer, and the sun brings warmth. A large patch of open water straddles The Narrows opposite our cabin.

Saturday, March 20. Last night Bern confirmed that Margaret, Robert and Jo-Ellen were still intending to visit today; but we didn't want to get too excited. We've been disappointed twice before. We ate a casual breakfast and cleaned the cabin. Only occasionally did we look out the window, up Colville Lake. If they come, they come. If they don't, so what? Our hopes have been dashed before. We were prepared to spend the day alone.

Despite our feigned nonchalance, however, Kathleen and I actually felt like two children eagerly waiting for Christmas morning. When will our parents come to call us to the tree? It seems like we've been waiting all day for that knock on the bedroom door. And then, just when we were starting to lose hope, the roar of ski-doos shattered the morning stillness. Our cabin instantly filled with guests and excitement. Santa Margaret handed Kathleen a gift box of bacon and eggs, bread, coffee, onions, apples and oranges. Wow! Fresh food! Just what we wanted! Santa Margaret then presented me my neck scarf that I had loaned to Ron in February – the neck scarf that Kathleen had given to me last Christmas. We sat down at the kitchen table to tea, while Kathleen served a first course of stir-fried caribou on rice that she had prepared last night. The aroma of percolating coffee and sizzling bacon filled the cabin.

Great food, fantastic company, and marvellous conversation. Without doubt the most enjoyable meal of the winter so far.

Eventually though, Kathleen and I began to think about our unopened letters still sitting on the counter, beneath the metaphorical Christmas tree. These were our best presents. We longed to rip them open, and to discover the surprises inside. We could hardly wait.

Margaret, Robert and Jo-Ellen left in mid-afternoon. We prepared a fresh pot of tea, and settled in to our chairs to open our letters. We tried to be calm and deliberate, but all the letters were read voraciously in a few minutes. After waiting nearly four weeks for Margaret, Robert and Jo-Ellen to visit, it was all over. Our house was empty and so very quiet. Just like Christmas night when all the presents have been opened and all the guests have gone home. Kathleen and I felt keyed up and deflated at the same time. It was a very unexpected emotion from two people who had been revelling in our isolation.

Today marked the first day of spring – the vernal equinox – and it actually felt like spring. Last night was clear, and the temperature this morning was a chilly -27 degrees. Yet the sun now has so much strength that the day quickly warmed, peaking at -5 degrees at 5:00 pm. From now on, the sun will spend most of its day above the horizon. The amount of 'daytime' will continue to increase quite noticeably, with almost an hour of additional daylight to enjoy each week. I doubt if we'll experience any temperatures colder than this morning's -27 degrees. Within a week, the mercury should not dip below -20 degrees. That's my prediction, based on no local experience or knowledge whatsoever.

Tomorrow we leave for our second winter camping trip. We plan to set up in that picturesque little river valley that enters Colville Lake at the Teepee Site.

Sunday, March 21. We are sitting in the wall tent, where I write in my journal by candlelight at 9:00 pm. The temperature remains at -7 degrees, after reaching zero at 4:00 pm. Such balmy weather creates problems for winter travellers. Soon after leaving the cabin, I quickly overheated, and had to remove my toque and face warmer, despite the strong head wind. More importantly and seriously, our mukluks, liners, mitts and gauntlets all became wet from perspiration and melting snow. Wet clothing means cold hands and feet. Everything is now hanging from a drying line stretched across the centre roof-line of the tent. It's a bit crowded, but our clothing will easily dry by morning. A very domestic, restful scene as I sit in front of the stove, with a plentiful supply of wood within an easy arm's reach.

I love the wall tent, and the process of selecting a site, setting up, and gathering wood and water for the evening. This process required nearly four hours though – much too demanding and time consuming to make any real distance during a day. Even taking down the tent, and packing the sled and toboggan, requires nearly three hours.

This means that we would spend almost 7 hours engaged in camp work every day, which has serious implications if we were to actually drag the tent to Colville Lake. If our morning were to start at 6:00 am, we wouldn't leave camp until 9:00 am. To be comfortably set up before dark means that we would need to reach our intended camp by 3:00 pm. This leaves only five hours of travel, with one hour for rest stops and lunch. I doubt that we could pull our gear through deep, unbroken snow any faster than 2 km/hour. This means that our maximum distance during a day would be 10 km.

The distance to town, around the perimeter of Colville Lake, is approximately 50 km, which would take us five days. It would also take us five days to return home. I assume we would spend at least four days in town, if for no other reason than to make the very difficult trip worthwhile. This means we would be away from our cabin for two weeks. I'm beginning to think that we should certainly abandon the idea of dragging our winter gear to town.

We travelled only about 3 km today, and I'm quite tired. Not worn out. Not fatigued. But quite tired. I worked very hard dragging the sled, and couldn't keep up with Kathleen, who easily sauntered along with the plastic toboggan. Sometimes the sled pulled very easily, as though it wasn't even there. At other times the sled seemed like it was stuck in sand – I could barely budge it, even when I leaned into the tow lines with all my weight. These Jekyll and Hyde episodes occurred in about equal proportions, and often lasted only 30 to 40 seconds. All so very frustrating, particularly when I had no idea when or where each of the sled's personalities would next appear. Today's dragging through snow was so much more difficult than last month's camping trip when we dragged on ice down the Ross River.

So it appears we will certainly take Ron's advice to travel to the town of Colville Lake 'light' with our backpacking tent and summer gear. Our current plans are to leave for town on March 31. If the weather remains this warm, we should have no trouble sleeping out for a night or two on the lake, even without a wood stove.

Monday, March 22. I woke late, at 9:00 am, feeling quite rested after yesterday's struggle with my recalcitrant sled. While Kathleen continued to dawdle in her sleeping bag, I slowly cooked our breakfast bannock on the wood stove. I am not too humble to report that it was one of my best bannocks ever. A beautiful golden brown. Crispy on the outside, and moist in the middle.

Although the temperature had fallen overnight to -17 degrees, our clothes had completely dried in the warmth of the tent. Our mukluks and mitts were once again supple and functional. For a day-trip, we headed farther up the frozen stream, not only to explore new territory, but also to find water, as we once again confirmed that melting snow is very unsatisfactory and inefficient. I don't know why we even bother with melting snow. Finding water should be one of our first tasks when reaching a new camp. We rounded a narrow bend where the stream coursed through a 1.5-m-wide channel. Like robins hunting for worms on a suburban lawn, we cocked our heads and could faintly hear the current flowing beneath the ice. I chopped away, and in a few minutes reached yellowish ice that indicated previous overflow. This was encouraging. I continued to flail away with my axe, and after 10 minutes had excavated a hole 15 cm deep and 25 cm wide. Still no sign of water, though, and the sound of the current remained faint. This was hard work, and not much better than melting snow. We needed to find an easier source of water.

We continued snowshoeing up the drainage, and in a few minutes reached the stream's headwater lake. Animal tracks led to an open section of water where the ice had slumped in as the water level had been dropping over winter. This was exactly the same situation that had been occurring at the outlet of Colville Lake, in The Narrows opposite our cabin. We were beginning to see patterns and predictability in our winter landscape. I carefully approached the slump hole, testing the ice with my axe handle as I went. I struck a hollow-sounding section two metres before the open water, and easily chopped through 2.5 cm of fragile ice. We filled our two water pails, capped them with snow to prevent spillage, loaded them into the toboggan, and dragged our precious liquid prize back to camp.

After lunch I bucked up two more trees, which would give us more than enough wood for tonight's fire and tomorrow morning's breakfast. I always tend to overestimate how much wood I will need at camp, even at summer camps. Better to have too much fuel than too little fuel, particularly in winter.

During the afternoon we explored a side creek entering our little river valley. As we poked our way up the creek, Ravens seemed to be taking heightened interest in what we were doing. Increasingly, one or two Ravens would swoop toward us, calling out repeatedly, as though extending a greeting. Eventually we stood at the base of a knoll at the head of the frozen creek. At the top of the knoll stood a single tree – the largest spruce tree we had yet seen. Old, gnarled and multi-forked, this ancient, venerable tree truly dominated its surroundings. Near the top of this tree perched the most impressive and grandest Ravens' nest I have ever seen. From this vantage the Ravens commanded the best view of the valley. Surely they had seen us coming. We now understood that the Ravens had not been greeting us – had not been welcoming us. Rather they had been trying to discourage our advance into their territory. The Ravens were now silent. We could see them in their nest, staring at us, wondering what we would do next. Perhaps they were getting ready to lay their eggs, or were even guarding their eggs. We left as unobtrusively as we could.

At 4:00 pm, for the first time since our arrival on January 31, the temperature reached slightly above zero – not quite to one degree, but certainly above freezing. These conditions were rather unpleasant, though. Not warm enough to sit outside soaking up the rays and lounging in our lawn chairs. Yet so wet that our mukluks froze into the snowshoe lamp wick bindings when the temperature dropped back below freezing.

Tuesday, March 23. It snowed overnight, but remained warm. Minus four degrees at 7:00 am. We relaxed throughout most of the morning – cooking bannock and sipping tea in the wall tent. We broke camp slowly, and started for home at 11:30, heading into a strong northeast wind beneath an overcast sky.

So far I had been dragging the sled with the two tails of the towlines attached directly to the tips of the sled's runners. This is known as the 'two-point-hitch.' The instructions that came with my sled suggested that a 'pack-eteers hitch' tied to the middle of the sled is less tiresome, and significantly reduces shoulder strain. I thought I would give it a try, and had re-tied the towlines before leaving camp. As also suggested in the instructions, however, this 'one-point-hitch' proved very troublesome on winding, uneven trails in the bush. At every turn, the sled merrily continued straight in its current direction to bury itself in the deep powder next to the trail. If the trail sloped slightly to one side or the other, the sled simply slipped off, once again to bury itself in deep powder. In my brief experience, attaching the tails directly to each runner provides vastly superior directional control. When we reached the straight pull on Colville Lake a little after one o'clock, I was again very tired. We're definitely not going to drag 50 km through unpacked snow to town.

Back at the cabin, Kathleen and I were stunned to see that the pond in The Narrows had grown into a veritable lake during our absence. The river flowed free for approximately 200 m, and much of the ice above the outlet was rotten. Snow dripped from trees to form large icicles. The water at the pier was completely open. I shouldn't ever have to axe through ice again before dipping my bucket. Spring seems to be approaching rapidly now.

Wednesday, March 24. Winter, or at least the extreme cold of winter, most certainly feels over. The afternoon temperature reached -3 degrees, and the 'lake' in The Narrows continues to expand.

Again today, as I headed east across the bay toward Woodlot Way, the snow around me settled in a stomach-churning 'whump.' I instantly skedaddled to shore. I don't know if one can truly skedaddle on snowshoes, but I unquestionably felt like I was skedaddling. In fact, it might be the first time in my life that I have skedaddled, which my dictionary defines as 'to flee in panic.' Yep, no doubt about it. Irrespective of footwear or relative speed, I was skedaddling the heck on outta there.

We don't really know what causes the snow to settle so quickly and uniformly, but we suspect that weaker layers beneath more recent snowfalls are simply giving way. Much like an avalanche in place. Mere settling of a snow layer does not necessarily imply danger or thin ice, but we now felt uncomfortable making this crossing. In the afternoon I completed the new snow trail, known as Upper Cabin Crescent, through the bush, from our cabin to Woodlot Way. If the warm weather continues, and if the ice comes away from the shore, our current route across the lake might become inaccessible.

By the time I returned to the cabin, my mukluks had once again iced up and frozen into the lamp wick bindings. I had to step out of my mukluks in my stocking feet. It's probably time to change footwear, so I spent the hour before dinner making new lamp wick bindings for our Sorel boots. I'm not looking forward to wearing them. They weigh a metric tonne compared to our moosehide-and-canvas mukluks. But at least they won't ice up or freeze into the bindings.

During our evening radio conversation Bern supported our opinion that the weather should only become warmer from now on. "The worst of winter is over." He likewise agreed that we should be warm enough if we have to camp out on Colville Lake when we go to town with our summer tent. "You won't need a wood stove."

Bern also extended an invitation from Jo-Ellen and Robert to join them for Easter dinner. School will be closed for Easter holidays, and they would love to entertain us. This sounds good.

Thursday, March 25. Early in the morning, I lay in bed, still groggy with sleep, trying to convince myself to get up to light the fire. Other than Kathleen's soft breathing on the other side of the partition separating our bunks, all was very still and quiet in the cabin. Outside, I could hear frogs croaking from somewhere down near The Narrows. Their calls were soothing, and a sure sign that spring was coming.

I wonder what kind of frogs they are. I strained my ears to hear them call again.

There can't be too many species of frogs this far north. The calls had stopped.

It would have to be one very tough amphibian to survive such long, cold winters and very short summers. Why would they call only a few times? That's not like frogs.

How could it be frogs, anyway? Snow and ice still cover most of the land. It's still quite cold. It can't be frogs. What was it, though? It sounded like frogs.

I lit the fire, put on the tea water, and lifted Kathleen down to the floor when the cabin warmed to +18 degrees.

"So, Kathleen, did you happen to hear any sounds this morning?"

"What do you mean? What kind of sounds?"

"You know, animal sounds, from outside." I purposefully phrased my question vaguely. I didn't want to lead Kathleen into any preconceived ideas that I might have. I wanted an independent opinion.

"Well, about an hour ago, I thought I heard frogs. But it can't be frogs. There can't be any frogs out now."

"That's exactly what I thought! I thought I heard frogs too. But you're right. It can't be frogs. I hope we hear that sound again. I'm very curious now."

Frogs or no frogs, though, we spent the day getting ready for spring. Our primary task was to create an alternative access to our winter camp of two days ago. We're worried that our usual route to this valley might soon become impassable. Our recent experiences with the snow settling on Colville Lake might mean that the ice is coming away from the shore. We're also concerned that warmer weather might thaw the frozen stream that leads to the camp. Either of these possibilities means that we can't reach the camp. And we must be able to reach the camp for two reasons. First of all, it's our favourite valley, and we hope to enjoy leisurely picnics, dinners and campfires there when the weather actually does become warmer. Secondly, and most importantly, we left a lot of wood there. No reason to let my wood go to waste. I worked hard for the wood. It's my wood. And I'm going to use it.

So, after breakfast we put in 3 km of new snow trail. We began from Woodlot Way, crossed over a low spot at the south end of Colville Ridge, and then followed a cut line that ran southeast almost directly to the camp. My wood was still neatly stacked, exactly where we had left it. I look forward to burning it.

As we turned to head home along our new snow trail, which we called Winter Camp Walk, a covey of Willow Ptarmigans burst from a willow thicket, clucking and croaking in alarm as they fled. Yes! That's it. The mystery is solved. The Willow Ptarmigan sounded very much like croaking frogs. We heard the sound several more times during the return trip. The ptarmigan were definitely excited about something. Perhaps they were preparing for spring.

Back at the cabin we continued our spring preparations. Bern's instructions indicated that periodically we needed to clean the wood-burning stove. We had been postponing this task, which seemed difficult. First we would have to remove the screws that connected the stove to the stovepipe. Then we would need to remove the leg screws and legs while I held the stove so that it wouldn't fall. Kathleen would then have to slide out the platform upon which the stove sat, while I lowered the stove carefully to the cabin floor. Then we would have to take the stove outside to brush and scrape out the creosote that had been accumulating all winter. Then we would have to put everything back together again. This seemed all so very challenging, particularly because we would have to go without heat for several hours before and during the procedure.

Today seemed like a good day, though. The fire had been out since morning, and the afternoon temperature was warm, at -6 degrees. It was time to clean the stove. Like many tasks in life, thinking about the job was much more difficult than the job itself, which took only about 30 minutes. We were both pleased that the smoke still went up the stovepipe when everything was back together again.

Today was mostly darkly overcast, with a constant, strong wind from the northwest. The wind battered the ice in The Narrows, and pushed warm water out and over the surface of the ice. Open water at the outlet of Colville Lake continued to grow as spring approaches.

Friday, March 26. The northwest wind has now dominated our home for 36 hours, keeping temperatures lower than those to which we had come to expect in the past four to five days. The -19 degrees last night was the lowest temperature since last Sunday. Today's high of -16 degrees was our lowest high since March 10. These temperatures, combined with the wind (30 km/hr according to the CBC), forced us back into our parkas and face warmers when outside for extended periods.

Nevertheless, we put in another 1 km of snow trail along Upper Cabin Crescent, from the cabin, northeast to the junction of Ketaniatue Connector and Winter Camp Walk. We now have a short circle route, out from the cabin and back along Woodlot Way and Lower Cabin Crescent. These trails take us through a variety of habitats, which should be great for birdwatching when the weather warms and clears. We have enjoyed only a few days of sunshine in the past two weeks. I am weary of cloudy days, no matter how warm they might be. I do hope though, that the weather remains mild, even if cloudy, for our trip to Colville Lake, now only five days away.

The open water at the outlet of Colville Lake continues to expand, primarily in response to buffeting by the wind. Ominously though, I needed to chop through thin ice below the pier to obtain drinking water. Maybe spring is not really coming yet.

Saturday, March 27. The wind continues, and the weather becomes increasingly colder. At 7:00 am, the temperature equalled only -25 degrees, the coldest morning temperature since last Saturday. On the positive side though, this temperature is not so cold considering that we've endured two days of wind surging down mostly from the north. A month ago, continuous north winds would have brought substantially colder temperatures. This suggests to us that we might be enduring the last hurrah of winter, which could be expelled altogether by the next weather system reaching up to us from the south. We hope so. It is now only four days before we intend to leave for town. We need warmer weather to make the journey comfortable.

Sunday, March 28. Winter seems to have returned. The temperature plunged to -32 degrees last night, and the predicted high for today is only -16. The thaw of the past week is now reversing. Bern had told us that Colville Lake would be passable by ski-doo until late May. Yesterday we were skeptical, but today we are believers. Approximately 1/3 of the open, flowing water in The Narrows has refrozen. The wind remained strong from the north today, and Kathleen and I no longer use words like 'spring approaches.' We hope for a south wind. We hope for warm weather for our trip to town in three days.

We spent the afternoon putting in a snow trail to Ketaniatue Lake along the right bank of the Ross River, which has become impassable in many places because of open water. Sections of this trail, which we call Riverside Drive, were already in place from previous times when we were forced to relocate from the river. We plan eventually to link up Riverside Drive with the Connector at Ketaniatue Lake, which will give us a 12-km circle route for warmer days that surely cannot be too far off.

Monday, March 29. I stepped outside at 7:00 am and my nostrils momentarily stuck together. Uh oh. Must be colder than -35 degrees. I walked to the corner of the cabin and peered at the thermometer. Double uh oh. Minus 41 degrees. I glanced toward The Narrows, where the 'lake' of two days ago had shrunk to the 'pond' that existed when we left for our winter camp on March 21. And we thought winter was over. Silly us.

After lunch we again snowshoed along the river toward Ketaniatue Lake. An island of ice surrounding a mid-channel rock had grown to three times its size of yesterday, and the 0.75-km open channel had narrowed to no more than 1 m wide. Winter has reasserted its grip; but I still believe that 'the season that follows winter' (I don't use words like 'spring') might be no more than one or two weeks away. We have decided to delay our trip to town by several days, as we wait for warmer weather.

We completed another 1 km of snow trail through the bush along Riverside Drive, but still have nearly 3 km to go before reaching Ketaniatue Lake.

Tuesday, March 30. Minus 43 degrees at 7:00 am. In the cabin, the temperature at sleeping height registered only -12 degrees. The open water in The Narrows has shrunk to a mere sliver only 50 m long, and the 'water hole' beneath the pier was covered in ice 2 cm thick. The north wind, however, has finally relented, and we welcomed the calm day. On our walk we were only mildly surprised to see that the 0.75-km open section of river had clogged with ice at the halfway point. The lower section of open water, however, still flowed very quickly towards its ice-covered terminus at the bottom of the drop.

Whenever it's -40 degrees or lower, I begin to feel as though I need more wood. Certainly we have been burning significantly more wood during the last few days of cold weather. Our current stack of wood on the porch will last only two more days, until April First. Back on March 19, I estimated that the stack would last at least 17 days, until April 4. I predicted the stack would last until April 7 if we were to have gone winter camping. This means that we will have consumed the current stack of wood six days faster than originally estimated. This is not good. We burned the wood six days faster

*Whenever it was -40 degrees or colder,
I began to feel as though I needed more firewood.*

than expected over only an 11-day period. This is definitely not good – it's definitely very bad. We'll be heading to the woodlot tomorrow.

We expect to begin our canoe descent down the Anderson River on approximately June 20. If we continue to burn wood at the rate of the last two weeks, we will need to re-stack seven more times. Even with our original estimate of 17 days to burn the stack, we would have needed to re-stack five more times. Perhaps the best we can hope for now is to re-stack only four more times, assuming the weather does eventually warm up. We still don't know how much wood actually lies buried beneath the snow under the orange tarp. One can't really tell when the wood is spread out and invisible. We won't know for sure until we actually stack and burn it. I doubt very much though, if more than four re-stacks are available. We need more wood.

Wednesday, March 31. I stepped outside to walk along Privy Path at 5:00 am. The light already showed faintly but unmistakably above the eastern horizon. The thermometer read -40 degrees. I rose for the day at 7:00 am, thinking only of wood, focusing only on my need for more wood. The thermometer still read -40 degrees, and the open water in The Narrows had shrunk to the size of a backyard fish pond. It was relatively large for a backyard fish pond, at 10 m by 50 m, but substantially reduced from the lake that existed only a few days ago. I gotta get more wood.

The morning was calm and very pleasant, with ideal working conditions. A man could work hard without sweating or overheating. I began by searching in the snow behind the cabin to see if there was any more 'extra' wood. During times of famine or shortage, a person naturally returns to where one last found precious commodities, whether those necessities are food or wood. After an hour of digging in the snow, I uncovered much more wood than I ever hoped would still be available – about 5 days' supply, even at the consumption rate of the last few days of very cold weather. This was a significant bonanza, as exciting as finding buried pirate treasure. We were both very happy about it.

While we worked away in the snow, we also saw a pair of Pine Grosbeaks extracting seeds from spruce cones. This was our first sighting of Pine Grosbeaks this winter, even though they are often residents, and migrate south primarily in years of low cone production. Perhaps they too were searching harder and wider for treasure hidden within the frozen forest. Or maybe, just maybe, they were returning from the South, anticipating the advance of warmer weather.

After lunch, Kathleen and I headed out to Woodlot Way, where I felled one tree, and bucked up about one third of it into 25-cm rounds approximately 15 to 20 cm in diameter. Just these seven rounds filled our toboggan. We now had enough wood to feed our stove at bedtime for two or three nights, which is necessary now that the temperatures are dropping to -40 degrees. While I worked, Kathleen packed snow trails to three more suitable trees.

I'm becoming optimistic that we might have enough wood now. One tree is already down waiting to be bucked up, with three more standing dead trees ready to be felled. Also, a strong southeast wind today produced afternoon temperatures all the way up to -12 degrees. We are comfortably warm in the cabin, even with the stove damped nearly completely down, and only two rounds of wood burning at any time.

At 9:00 pm, the outside temperature was still at -19 degrees, and the ice above The Narrows was rotting in a large semi-circle nearly from shore-to-shore. During our radio conversation, Bern said that the unusually cold weather of the past five days should not return. And Bern knows about these things. And finally, there was the sighting of the Pine Grosbeaks. Their appearance just might be more than mere coincidence. Warm weather might actually be on the way. Perhaps we'll go to town next week.

CHAPTER 9

Raxo[n]radesa

Thursday, April 1. The new month has ushered in a warmer weather system. Last night never turned any colder than the 10:00 pm temperature of -20 degrees. The southeast wind blew strongly all day, sweeping warmth up from the south, to raise the 4:00 pm temperature to -5 degrees. It's likely that tonight will remain warmer than -10 degrees. If so, we could have travelled to town. Nonetheless, we are happy with our decision to postpone the trip until the days are calmer, and the nights prove themselves to be consistently warmer.

We again snowshoed along the river, which looked so beautiful and felt so exhilarating. We stood on the bank where two broad bends swung first west and then back east, watching the river flowing swiftly between banks of ice, as it swept past us on its way to Liverpool Bay on the Arctic coast. I long to be on the river, paddling north. Now that the days are so long, with a hint of coming warmth, I'm beginning to feel a tad restless. I'm ready to wander, to saunter. I'm ready to stoop over a flower of spring, to feel the gentle summer sun on my face, to hear the midnight laughter of a yodelling loon. I long to be paddling on a wild river as it flows, week after week, toward a mystical world beyond the distant horizon. I'm ready for all these sensual pleasures for which I have journeyed so far – and for which I have waited so patiently.

The Hare Indians referred to April as *Raxo[n]radesa*, which means 'the month of very bad snow blindness.' I'm expecting a lot of sun in the coming days and weeks.

Friday, April 2. I was up at midnight and again at 7:00 am to walk down Privy Path. On both occasions the thermometer read -10 degrees, with absolutely no wind. Finally, I could just saunter along the trail, leisurely viewing the horizon and the nearby ridges. I stopped to gaze, unhurriedly, at the decaying ice in The Narrows. I felt warm without my parka, without woollen pants, without even mitts or gloves.

We pushed our snow trail along Riverside Drive to within 1.5 km of Ketaniatue Lake. Much of the lower stretch of river ran open, except for the large bays. The upper river was noticeably more open than yesterday, and the current has eroded much of the shoreline ice into attractive, scallop-shaped undulations.

While we snowshoed along the banks, we scouted potential routes and dangers for our descent by canoe in June. Although the river runs swiftly, it is broad, without sweepers or ledges or difficult rapids. It should be an exciting but easy reintroduction to moving water, even after more than seven months without paddling white water.

As we sat eating our oatmeal and toast this morning, the north wind rose rapidly, and blew unceasingly and briskly all day. The temperature, beneath a gray, cloudy sky, rose to a high of only -8 degrees at 4:00 pm. Still no sun, despite being two days into 'the month of very bad snow blindness.'

Saturday, April 3. After breakfast, we headed up Woodlot Way toward Ketaniatue Lake. It was a glorious morning, with only a slight breeze and a blazing sun. Perhaps the month of Raxo[n]radesa has finally arrived. We reached Ketaniatue Lake in late morning, and turned south, back up the Ross River, packing in a new snow trail along the right bank. We soon stood on the shore opposite our campsite of February 26 through 28. Even after five weeks, our old trails were still quite visible.

One-and-one-half km later we looked over the bank to see our tracks of yesterday heading north, down the Ross River. Our 12-km snowshoe loop was now complete. We felt like railroad tycoons of the 19th century, whose iron tracks reaching out from the east and west coasts had finally linked the continent together. It was all so very exciting. We sat down for lunch in a grove of trees that we christened as the Golden Spike Café. We 'ordered' a can of sardines, which had only partly refrozen since we left the cabin three hours ago.

Our two trails had joined on a low flat immediately adjacent to the river, which would obviously flood the Golden Spike Café in spring. Most of the trees were surrounded by ice that had formed from overflow during freeze-up last fall. Not a good place to locate either a café or a snowshoe trail. We re-routed the trail to the low ridge above the flat, and headed home. We felt very satisfied with our work, knowing that we now have nearly 20 km of snow trails that should keep us entertained on day trips for the duration of winter.

We also felt satisfied with our physical conditioning. We spent seven hours snowshoeing today, and travelled approximately 14 km. Five of them were uphill, and nearly two involved breaking and packing new trail. At no point did we ever feel tired – a pretty successful day for us. We feel ready to travel the 40 km to town. All we need is warm weather.

Today's highest temperature reached -8 degrees. Last night remained cold, however, dipping to -21 degrees. The mercury this evening at 9:00 pm has already fallen to -20 degrees. Not warm enough to go to town with our summer gear.

Sunday, April 4. A day spent mostly doing laundry, odds and ends, and writing. In the afternoon, I sipped tea, watched various-sized pieces of ice float down The Narrows, and studied my topographic maps of the Anderson River. All the maps of northern Canada suggest a land of broad, flowing rivers, azure lakes and innumerable ponds. A land of water. A land seemingly created primarily for the enjoyment of canoeists. All these maps though, are blatantly misleading. By the time we arrived at the cabin last January 31, all of Canada north of the Arctic Circle had already been resting beneath snow and ice for at least three months. During winter, rivers are no more common in northern Canada than in the thirsty, parched, sandy deserts of Arizona and New Mexico. For 7 to 9 months of every year, few places on earth provide as much 'land' as does northern Canada, where one may walk freely across 'lakes,' or wander equally easily up and down 'rivers.'

This simple fact eluded the British Royal Navy for centuries, as detailed in the stories and diaries of men like Captain John Ross, whose ship, the *Victory*, became entrapped by ice on the east coast of the Boothia Peninsula between 1829 and 1833. Like virtually all Western explorers of the 16th to

19th centuries, Ross mistakenly believed that the Arctic 'Ocean' provided a route upon which his ship would sail through the elusive Northwest Passage. For Captain Ross, though, the 'Ocean' remained an icy land for all but a few weeks during four successive, unending winters, which reduced his elegant sailing vessel to an irrelevant hodgepodge of canvas, timbers and nails.

Right now, outside isolated cabins all across the North, dormant canoes rest on log rails, useless in a solidly-frozen world of white. Their owners sit comfortably by the wood stove, surrounded by unbroken boreal forest, which stands serenely in the sublime silence of an enduring winter. The crusted surfaces of myriad frozen lakes sparkle beneath a sun rising ever higher above the land. Yet, like Ross more than 150 years before us, canoeists can only read or dream or write or just wait patiently for a spring that never seems willing to return.

Beyond the cabin walls, our world still slumbers silently. An Arctic high-pressure system has banished the wind. Spruce and willow branches sit motionless. No water spills or flows across the land. Deep snow muffles and absorbs the occasional croaking of a solitary Raven soaring far above a lonely valley. Even on the last day of March, 10 days after the official beginning of spring, the mercury in our thermometer sat near the bottom of its tube, at -40 degrees. Even on the last day of March we could still snowshoe nearly anywhere we pleased. We could only talk about the great Northern rivers that disappeared more than half-a-year ago. We could only ask ourselves, rhetorically, if the land would ever again become water.

Now, in early April, at the outlets of lakes and ponds, we finally hear the water stirring beneath snowy blankets. After dinner, we snowshoed along the river, to where it squeezed around narrow bends confined between steep ridges. Together, at 9:00 pm, we watched the water flowing swiftly between banks of chambered ice. Superlatives would only underestimate the beauty of the landscape. The sun hung low over the ridge, sending shimmering shafts of light skipping across the black, opaque water. The sun's oblique, alpenglow filtered through the open forest of White Spruce, whose red inner bark radiated warmly in the protracted evening twilight. Even the rickrack on Kathleen's wind suit glimmered with light as the subdued rays swirled around her face. Beside us, the black water welled up from beneath catacombs of ice, finally released into the evening sunlight. The current bubbled and rushed past us, laughing like exuberant school children just released for

With a high of minus three degrees on April 4,
the north bay began to open up.

their summer holidays. I wonder what it would be like to be the river itself. Northern rivers are always reborn – always young – always alive.

I felt both joy and depression. Joy with the beauty surrounding me – depression with the future before me. In terms of lifestyle, how can I willingly return to the congestion and traffic of Vancouver? In terms of spirituality, how can it possibly be fair to be offered such beauty, only to have it withdrawn by my own ultimate mortality? In terms of my very privileged time and place on this earth, what right do I have to experience any depression at all? For six months, I will have lived every minute exactly as I have fantasized since adolescence. Few people have such an opportunity. Nonetheless, I am not satisfied, and long for the fantasy to continue. Kathleen and I returned to our cabin in silence, as the sun slipped gently below the ridge.

Monday, April 5. We spent another relaxing day. We rose late, at 9:15, to lounge by the fire, lingering over a bannock breakfast while sipping tea. We puttered about the cabin and camp. I filled the Coleman lantern with white gas, and sawed slices of frozen caribou for Kathleen to prepare stew for dinner. After our 7:00 pm conversation with Bern, we again snowshoed out to the river, which was now running over and through parts of the bank ice. I don't mean to sound rash, but once again I believe that it was appropriate to use phrases like 'spring is approaching.'

Once again, we talked about going to town. This afternoon I cleared out a flat spot in the snow next to the storage cabin, and put up our summer tent. I want to test whether or not I can sleep comfortably at current temperatures. Last night's low was -24 degrees, and it's already -12 at 10:30 pm. In only a few minutes I will be leaving the warmth of the wood-burning stove to head out to the tent where I will spend the night. Kathleen says she prefers to stay in the cabin. She's happy enough for me to conduct the test by myself. She says she's willing to accept any test results that I report to her tomorrow morning.

"Do you want me to lock the door, Michael, so you can't get back in? You certainly want this to be a fair, complete and accurate test, don't you?"

I'm sure she was joking. At least I think she was joking. Even if the door were locked, Kathleen would certainly let me back in if I knocked on the door. She would, wouldn't she?

"Better leave the door unlocked, Kathleen, just in case. I wouldn't want you to have to get up just to let me in."

Tuesday, April 6. The temperature fell to only -14 degrees overnight, beneath a cloudy, snowy sky. It would have been a fairly warm night for sleeping out on the ice, on our way to Colville Lake. And although I slept well in the tent, I didn't feel as warm and toasty as I had expected. I woke at about 6:00 am, but forced myself to wait until a little after 8:00 before sneaking back into the cabin. I had to wait until the experiment was truly over. Also, no need to give the impression that I had been a little on the cold side of comfort. Back inside, I enjoyed lighting the stove, and lifting Kathleen down to the floor when the temperature reached +18 degrees.

I submitted my report during breakfast.

"When I first entered the tent, I lit the candle lantern, laid out my sleeping bag, blew up the therm-a-rest air mattress, and prepared myself for the evening. All this release of body heat, plus the heat of the candle, warmed the tent in only a few minutes to zero. That was a full 12 degrees warmer than the ambient temperature. I have to admit, though, Kathleen, that after only a few minutes in the bag, I was not all that warm, even though I was wearing my long underwear, and my fleece toque on my head. I spent much of the night buried way down in my bag, even though the temperature never got any colder than -10 degrees in the tent. I was a bit surprised. I think I felt just as cold as the night we spent out at Ron and Suzanne's when the temperature was -34 degrees in their wall tent. I think I was cold last night because of being so close to the chill coming up from the ground. At Ron and Suzanne's we were on a bunk, above a wood floor, probably one-and-a-half metres above the snow. It might be a little warmer, from additional body heat, when you join me in the tent, but it probably wouldn't make much difference if the cold is coming from below. I think that maybe we should take some wool blankets to put below our air mattresses. That would give us more insulation from the ice, and we should sleep more comfortably. So I learned something from spending last night outside. Still, I thought I would be warmer."

Kathleen just nodded, took a sip of tea, and said, "I was pretty warm in the cabin all night."

We spent the morning mostly reading and relaxing while the snow fell around us. In early afternoon though, the sky cleared and blue sky returned. Our faces warmed to the caress of the sun as we stood outside enjoying a temperature of -4 degrees. Snow now contracts everywhere. Snow retreats from the pier. Snow melts into bowl-shaped depressions at the base of trees. Snow has vanished from our doormat on the porch.

Just before afternoon tea we heard the sound of an approaching motor. We rushed outside, hoping for visitors. The motor belonged to a plane flying towards us, low over the lake. The plane dipped its wings as it passed over, obviously extending a greeting. We waved back. The plane belonged to Aklak Air. Perhaps it was Pilot Bob saying hello on his way back to Inuvik. It was nice to be remembered, but we would have much preferred a ski-doo, as opposed to a plane. Despite our love for this isolation, we would welcome visitors.

During dinner we heard, and then saw a lone ski-doo about 1.5 km to the south, near the Teepee Site. We grabbed our binoculars, and ran outside. The ski-doo headed west, across Colville Lake, toward the general area of the three deteriorating log cabins. Moments later the ski-doo raced behind a point, and vanished into silence. Again, no visitor for us. Our second disappointment in only one day.

We settled back into the cabin to finish dinner, and were startled by a loud commotion on the porch. Could it be visitors after all? Why didn't they knock, or say something? We opened the door, but no one was there. The commotion continued at the other end of the porch. As we turned to investigate, a Whiskey Jack fluttered out from behind the propane tanks and banged into the screen, knocking itself to the floor. It took us several minutes before we eventually herded it to the opening, through which if flew to freedom. Our only guest – our only visitor – and he couldn't wait to get away.

During our walk along Riverside Drive after dinner, we were excited to see the river running through, over and under the shore ice. With the sun above the horizon for approximately 14 hours/day (7:00 am to 9:00 pm), the ice must surely soon disappear entirely from The Narrows and from all running sections of the river.

The evening was warm, completely calm and absolutely clear. We lingered on the banks of the river until the twilight began to fade at 10:30 pm – a thoroughly satisfying evening. Rather than trying to describe the scene, I will resort to mere platitude and simple superlative.

"It is not possible for an evening, or a location, to be any more beautiful than that which we have experienced tonight."

We returned to the cabin very slowly. Both of us were wishing that this moment could continue forever.

Wednesday, April 7. The north wind has returned. After three successive days when the temperature soared above -5 degrees, today's high reached only -12 degrees. Although -12 degrees is substantially warmer than the -40 degrees we experienced only one week ago, we both felt like staying home, sitting near the heat of the fire. Now that spring seems so near, we long to ramble outside without parkas – without mitts. We grow a little weary of winter, but not because of winter itself. We are enjoying the winter, but right now the promise of spring offers so much more freedom and comfort.

Some might suggest that we were suffering from the malady popularly referred to as 'cabin fever.' I disagree, however. Personally, I think that cabin fever is a myth created and perpetuated by Hollywood's fanciful portrayals of miners, trappers and adventurers living all alone in their isolated cabins while searching for gold along the Yukon River – much like Kathleen and I are living all alone in our isolated cabin. In the movies, cabin fever usually results because the miner or trapper is confined to the small interior of his cabin. Brutal weather prevents him from going outside to escape the seemingly shrinking confines of his small room. The walls continue to close in until the occupant finally cracks, and runs off screaming into the snow and bush, never to be seen again. This situation becomes even worse if someone else also lives in that same small space, someone whose normally winsome personality becomes progressively more irritating and unacceptable. One of them (it doesn't make any difference which one) eventually murders the other, only to slowly starve to death because he has somehow lost the skill or will to prepare dinner. Cabin fever is a horrible disease.

This very premise of cabin fever strikes me as patently false. Kathleen and I are essentially suburbanites, and have had no previous experience with living comfortably in the bush during cold winters. Yet we go out everyday for wood, to collect water, to put in snow trails, or simply to enjoy our environment. We are not confined to the cabin. Miners of 19th century gold rushes would have had considerably more experience than either Kathleen or me, and would have been much busier going about their work of searching for gold, cleaning up the gold, trapping furs, or hunting for meat. They would not have been confined to their cabins.

Certainly one can argue that personalities confined to a small space could eventually grate on one another. This happens today, even in urban areas among couples who live in four-bedroom houses, where both husband and wife enjoy exclusive use of their own separate bathrooms. We don't call it 'mansion fever,' however. We simply say that the couple has irreconcilable differences.

In reality though, most people who lived with a partner or two out in the isolated bush would have been very much like Kathleen and me, in that they needed to rely on each other for their survival and comfort. There are many tasks to be done, and four hands are much better than two. I have read many diaries of just such situations, and none of them mentioned cabin fever or described a developing hatred for their companion in the opposite bunk. In fact, the reverse is true more often than not. Edgar Christian's diary *Unflinching* describes in wrenching detail his slow starvation shared by Harold Adler and John Hornby on the banks of the Thelon River during the winter of 1926–27. In one of his very last entries, Christian writes of Hornby to his father: "Jack alone was one man in this world who can let a young boy know what this world and the next are. I loved him and he loves me. Very seld(om) is there true love between two men." Christian never mentioned cabin fever or his companions' maddening idiosyncrasies. His diary speaks only of three men doing their very best to survive together.

I grant that the malady of cabin fever is certainly possible. I think though, that it is more likely to occur in people who are truly confined to small places, such as prison. For example, the phrase 'cabin fever' is speculated to have first been associated with ocean-crossing sailing ships in which passengers had to endure weeks and months of slow travel while living in cramped cabins below deck. Passengers would become restless and irritable from being in a confined space for an extended period.

Kathleen and I are neither confined nor irritable. Yet we are restless for spring. As prisoners become restless when the date of release approaches, and as a ship's passengers become restless when the distant shore finally appears on the horizon, so too are Kathleen and I becoming a bit restless now that spring seems so near. We love our cabin, though, and our life here. We have no desire to leave either our cabin or each other. Restless, yes; cabin fever, no.

Thursday, April 8. Today is Kathleen's birthday! When we left Vancouver last January 1, it never occurred to me that I should have brought a present with me. Now I have nothing to give her, and nowhere to purchase a gift. I should have done a better job of thinking ahead. Still, April 8 is Kathleen's special day, and I need to provide her with a special Northern celebration.

I began by pulling out her chair and seating her at the table for a bannock breakfast that I prepared while she sipped her tea. I then surprised her with a match box, inside of which was a folded piece of paper with the following words:

> *"I so very much treasure walking with you on our own*
> *snowshoe trails – through our own spruce forest. I'm fortunate*
> *to have the time, the health and the partner, all of which are*
> *necessary for me to enjoy this winter of solace and solitude.*
> *My only regret is that all I have to give to you on your 47th*
> *birthday is my gratitude for making this all possible."*

Kathleen read the improvised birthday card, and began to cry. So far I'm doing pretty well. But wait. There's more to come. Much more. We're going out for dinner at Winter Camp II. It's a lovely spot, and I have plenty of wood there for preparing the meal. As we won't be taking the wood stove or the wall tent, our loads will be comparatively light. Even so, we still required a lot of winter 'stuff,' as the temperature at mid-morning equalled only -16 degrees.

So just before noon we loaded up the toboggan and sled with parkas, water buckets, saw, axe, cameras, tarp, ropes, cooking utensils and food. We headed up Woodlot Way, turned right onto Winter Camp Walk, and reached the restaurant, 3 km away, in only 90 minutes. The sun was shining brightly, the temperature had risen to -10 degrees, and my wood was still neatly stacked.

For our 'outdoor terrace table' I made a lean-to shelter with the tarp tied between four trees. I attached two corners on one side of the tarp low to the snow surface, while the opposite side slanted upward to be tied at a height of approximately 1.5 m. I placed the sled in the rear of the shelter to serve as our condiment table, and dragged in a log for our chair. Kathleen sat down, and spotted a snowshoe hare hopping casually through the restaurant. Despite hare tracks appearing frequently and everywhere, this was the first one we had seen this winter. Wearing its winter coat of white, it looked very much like a small mound of snow with a pair of eyes and black-tipped ears. It momentarily stopped, frozen by our presence, and then silently bounded away.

I now began to prepare the fire, which I located directly in front of the tarp, hoping that the shelter would retain some of the fire's heat. It was, after all, still only -10 degrees, a little too chilly for just lounging about on one's birthday. The snow was more than a metre deep, and I didn't really feel like digging down to ground level. I had prepared a quick-cook meal of pasta and tea. I shouldn't need very much fire. I decided to make a wide platform of thick logs, crisscrossed to form a bottom layer 10 to 15 cm deep. I then made my cooking fire on top of this layer, added a grate, and put the pasta pot and tea kettle on top.

My plan contained two major assumptions: first, that the heat of the fire would go up, and quickly cook the pasta and boil the tea water; and second, that the thick, wide, bottom layer of wood would support the cooking fire, while also insulating the snow below. The dinner would be done before the snow began to melt.

This was an excellent plan, except for one minor drawback. The plan didn't work. Within minutes, perhaps even the very moment I started the fire, the entire structure began to settle into the snow. The hole quickly became deeper and wider. As I watched my pasta pot and tea kettle sink farther from reach, I wished that we had brought a long-handled stirring spoon. It was also now very difficult to add more wood to the fire, and the meal took much longer to prepare than I had planned. The fire did provide some heat in the tarp shelter though, and Kathleen enjoyed her birthday dinner. Or so she said. And I believe her. She did comment, however, that she had never before dragged food and pots 6 km round trip to her own birthday dinner. I took this as a hint that she would like to do it again some time.

In the late afternoon we returned home via the little frozen river that winds down to Colville Lake at the Teepee Site. Out on the lake, we came across a ski-doo trail, almost certainly made by the ski-doo that we had seen two days ago. We removed our snowshoes and easily pulled our loads along the nicely-packed trail. With the one-point packeteers hitch, my sled dragged very comfortably, with excellent control. We both hope that we're able to travel to town most of the way without using snowshoes.

Halfway between the Teepee Site and home, the sun burst upon us, and bathed Colville Lake in those oblique rays that occur only in the Far North. Although I look forward to summer, this simple beauty of winter, with its quiet, collage of sun-dazzled snow white, forest green and sky blue is unsurpassed. I am thrilled, on nearly a daily basis, to be surrounded by so much beauty.

Friday, April 9. Back on March 31 we had approximately eight days of wood on the porch, which is once again empty. I spent the morning restacking, and now have a porch supply that should last 15 days at recent consumption rates. I estimate that only two more full stacks are available beneath the tarp, which gives us an inventory of 45 days, not counting the two trees that we have already earmarked for falling. Assuming we leave the cabin on June 20, 72 days remain, for a shortfall of 27 days. If we go to Colville Lake for a total of 10 days, the shortfall decreases to only 17 days. And, as we repeatedly tell each other, our rate of wood consumption will certainly decrease as spring brings warmer temperatures. Last night, though, the mercury fell to -31 degrees.

Despite last night's very low temperatures, I do feel genuinely optimistic that warming trends are on their way. I collected today's stack of wood from around and beneath the picnic table, which is finally poking out from beneath the snow. I'm thinking barbecue, and I want to be ready!

The sun now spends most of its time above the horizon, and the snow is subsiding quickly beneath its lengthening influence. Harbingers of spring are certainly beginning to appear all across the Canadian North, from the shores of Great Slave Lake to the Mackenzie Delta, from Virginia Falls on the Nahanni River to Wardens Grove near the confluence of the Hanbury and Thelon Rivers. Along the margins of lakes and atop wind-exposed knolls, glacier-polished granite deflects the sun's heat outward, and in so doing, pushes the adjacent snow into retreat. Even dead twigs of Jack Pine, and droppings of snowshoe hare and Willow Ptarmigan reflect the heat, forcing the snow to shrink back from their surfaces. Deep in the awakening boreal forest, the bowl-shaped cavities that encircle the trunks of spruce and aspen are radiating outward, releasing the dark soil beneath the retreating snow-pack. The crowns of Northern Labrador Tea and Bog Birch are beginning to emerge to capture and eventually retain the sun's energy.

Ultimately the heat-retaining surfaces of soil, plants and open water will wrest control from the waning power of snow and ice. The reign of white will eventually end, even if only temporarily. No longer will all the day's heat be returned, extravagantly, back to the black void of empty space from which it had come. By late May the Coppermine, Back and Anderson Rivers will begin to rise. By mid-June the Kazan and Slave Rivers will rush up and over their banks, ripping away vegetation and glacial till with massive loads of decaying, careening ice.

By the end of June the tumult and carnage of renewal and birth will subside. The grand rivers will once again flow stately between majestic banks. Like the seductive siren of Greek mythology, the immortal Arctic Summer already calls out to me, and I am ready to answer that sweet summons.

From a more mundane and practical perspective, we also need heat to thaw the outhouse. You might remember that until late February we had been using the outhouse for all our elimination needs, not thinking ahead regarding the accumulating impact of frozen urine. We were essentially boiling tea, and then depositing it, frozen, into the outhouse. We literally pissed ourselves out of an outhouse. Since then we have been urinating in the bush, farther along

Privy Path. Our defecation deposits, however, are perilously close to filling the remaining outhouse capacity. We need warmth to melt the frozen urine. No one ever advised us about the importance of outhouse management.

For the first time this winter we didn't light the Coleman lantern, as we now have light, sufficient for reading and writing near the window, until 10:00 pm. We tentatively plan to go to town around April 20, but the nights remain cold. Minus 31 degrees last night. Kathleen hasn't written to her parents this week. She's discouraged when there's no way to send her letters. The nights have to warm up soon. We need to go to town.

Saturday, April 10. We seem to have reached a new phase of winter weather, as the sun now brings almost instant warmth. Beginning last Sunday, the daily afternoon high temperature, at approximately 5:00 pm, reached -3, -2, -4, -12, -10 and -4 degrees. Today's afternoon high also reached -4 degrees, and we strolled outside with our insulated tea mugs, excitedly pointing out new spots of bare ground and exposed rock, however small. We sat on the porch bench, facing the southwestern sun, feeling warm, even without moving. Kathleen fed a Whiskey Jack that swooped in to take bits of food directly from her hand.

During our radio conversation, Bern indicated that James and Sharon, a Dene couple from town, were camping on what he called the 'Big Island' 6 km to the south. "They plan to visit you sometime during the weekend."

They hadn't come yet, and we didn't think that they would come after 7:00 pm, so we went for our evening snowshoe stroll along Riverside Drive. As we were returning along Upper Cabin Crescent about 8:30 we heard the sound of a ski-doo. It must be James and Sharon! Running as best that we could on snowshoes, we arrived 10 minutes later. Ski-doo tracks ran up the bank, over to the storage cabin, and then back down to the lake. Exhaust still hung in the air. The camp was empty. Damn, we missed them. Both of us were very disappointed.

There is reason for optimism, though. Throughout the day we maintained the cabin at a comfortable +20 degrees, and barely dented our woodpile. And James and Sharon might come tomorrow. We might be able to mail our letters.

Sunday, April 11. A gloriously brisk (-24 degrees), sunny morning, with a persistent breeze from the southeast. Two otters, just downstream from the cabin, slid enthusiastically from a snow bank into the open water of The Narrows. They immediately clambered up the slope to tumble in again. I tell you with all honesty that if given a choice I would gladly be reincarnated as a river otter! No existence could possibly be better. Otters are always playing – always enjoying life. Otters are not immobilized by winter. Otters do not wait impatiently for spring. Yes. If only I had been born a river otter. Then, like otters, I could live – luxuriantly and easily – year-round – along any of Canada's isolated river sanctuaries.

In hope that James and Sharon would return today, we postponed our intended roundtrip to Ketaniatue Lake over the Connector and then back up Riverside Drive. Instead, we spent the morning doing laundry and writing letters. Around 4:00 pm we heard ski-doos, but no one came. For the second day in a row we were disappointed, not only because we wished to send our mail, but also because we would have enjoyed meeting local people.

The afternoon brought cloud, southeast winds and a high of -2 degrees. Out on the laundry line my heavy, wool undershirt flaps casually in the breeze, even though icicles hang from its waist and wrists. We look forward to seeing if the night remains warmer.

Monday, April 12. This morning we loaded the sled with spare clothes, lunches, water, mail, tripod and camera, and began dragging 6 km south to the Tent Camp on the Big Island. We had gone there several times before to use the outhouse, but had never dragged a full load, and had never expected to see people. This time we hoped to find James and Sharon, and we also wanted more practice at hauling our gear. The day was sunny, bright and -13 degrees. I felt euphoric, much as I imagine Victoria Jason must have felt as she was dragging her gear from Spence Bay to Gjoa Haven in June of 1992. Spence Bay is a small Inuit community at the southern tip of the Boothia Peninsula in the Arctic Ocean. Gjoa Haven is a similarly small community on the southeast side of King William Island, very near to where the sailing ships *Erebus* and *Terror*, under the command of Sir John Franklin, met their fatal end searching for the Northwest Passage. But that's another story.

Jason's book, *Kabloona in the Yellow Kayak*, is truly compelling and inspirational, at least for me. A grandmother, who took up kayaking at the age of 45, Jason spent four summers travelling through the Northwest Passage.

As the title of her book implies, much of the journey was by kayak. The 175-km stretch of the frozen Arctic Ocean from Spence Bay to Gjoa Haven, however, could be completed only on foot. The following passage is from the seventh of nine days during which she struggled across the ice with Don, her only other companion beneath the midnight sun:

> *At midnight, the glorious sun did a glancing bounce on the horizon and started rocketing upward. The snow crystals turned a trillion dancing, twinkling prisms. The wind gently caressed my face. The air was crisp and clean. I could contain myself no longer. I snapped my harness and danced in idiotic abandon on the ice. I love it! I love it! A claustrophobic's paradise!*

Jason's story, particularly this passage, instilled in me a desire to travel on the ice. Like Jason, I wanted to experience living out on the ice. I wanted to sleep out on the ice. I will likely never have the opportunity to live and camp on the Arctic Ocean, but I will soon be going across the ice to town – a distance of 40 km.

Kathleen and I reached the Tent Camp in one hour and 50 minutes, arriving just before noon. The camp, except for two wall tents, was empty. There will be no mail delivery today. We lingered for an hour, staring across Colville Lake, an ice-covered expanse up to 25 km wide, and 34 km across to town. Not exactly the Arctic Ocean, but impressive and challenging, nevertheless. We returned to the cabin in two hours and five minutes, for a total of nearly four hours to cover the 12-km roundtrip.

Today's outing proved to be very easy, as we simply followed a well-packed ski-doo trail, without any need for snowshoes. We are considering 'making a break' for town on Thursday, to be there in time to call Kathleen's mother Terry, whose birthday is on Saturday. Our pace today of approximately 3 km/hour suggests that we could reach Colville Lake in less than 14 hours. Even if we have to, or should I say get to, spend one night camping out on the lake, we should easily make town by Friday afternoon. We are willing to accept being cold in our tent in exchange for the adventure.

During our radio conversation I told Bern that we were planning to leave for town on Thursday, and should be there on Friday.

"It's a long way, Michael. Margaret would be happy to ski-doo out and give you a ride to town."

"I know she would, Bern, and I appreciate the offer. But we want to travel across the ice ourselves. It should be interesting."

Tuesday, April 13. We puttered about in the morning, preparing for our Thursday journey to town. We would need to take a stove of some sort, and fuel for cooking dinner and breakfast, and for melting snow, if we spend a night out on the ice. On our summer canoe trips we always take two small stoves that run on white gas. Our primary stove can burn at a very low flame, which is great for simmering. Our second stove does not have a simmer control. It is either on or off, but serves as a backup should the first stove fail. In fact, neither stove has ever failed. They are reliable and efficient in summer, but I have had no previous experience with using them in cold weather.

So after breakfast, I set both white gas stoves outside to let them cool down to the outside temperature of -10 degrees. Last night's low dipped only to -12 degrees. This is very encouraging for going to town. After 30 minutes I pumped the primary stove 20 times, which usually produces more than enough pressure. I lit a match and opened up the fuel jet, but no gas escaped. I closed the fuel jet and pumped 40 more times. Still no gas escaped. I then tried to pre-warm the stove by holding it in my hands. I again pumped 40 times and opened up the fuel jet. The stove simply sputtered weakly, but produced no flame. This was disappointing.

Perhaps my primary stove was just not working. Maybe it's broken. I took it inside to let it warm up. I pumped 20 times, lit a match, and opened the fuel jet. Gas sputtered upward and instantly burst into flame. Just like it always does. OK, maybe the stove was just rusty after sitting idle since last summer. Maybe it would work now. I took it back outside, and set it in the sun for 30 minutes. I pumped 40 times, lit a match, and opened the jets. No gas. No flame. Damn.

I then followed the same procedure with our backup stove, which worked inside the cabin, but not outside in the cold. Our only other choice was to use Bern's spare two-burner propane stove that we had seen in the storage cabin. First, though, we needed to determine if Bern's spare propane stove worked at the current outside temperature. I retrieved the stove, set it in the snow, and screwed in a small propane cylinder. Even after waiting 30 minutes the stove lighted instantly. I guess we'll be taking Bern's stove to town.

After lunch we snowshoed along Riverside Drive. The open water continues to expand rapidly beneath a sun that blazed high in the sky. It seemed like summer had arrived, completely bypassing spring. We were way too hot, even in our light layers of wool. My forehead began to sweat, and I removed my toque. The temperature must be close to zero. Maybe it's even above freezing. That would be exciting. We looked forward to getting back to the cabin, to read our thermometer. We arrived home just before 5:00 pm, almost racing against each other to be the first to read out the temperature. But no, how could this be? The temperature was still much below freezing, at -7 degrees. If minus seven feels so hot, then how would we deal with temperatures above freezing, particularly if we will be pulling heavy loads to town? Let's hope the temperature doesn't warm up too much in the next few days.

For the first time in weeks, we saw caribou. Approximately 10 were reclining right in the middle of the lake. They lay there in the wind, on the ice, cooling off in the afternoon heat. Or at least that's what we thought they were doing. It was darned hot outside.

Wednesday, April 14. It finally happened. A positive reading! Even though this morning's temperature was only -23 degrees, we reached +3 degrees at 5:00 pm. A strong wind blows from the southeast, bringing with it a thin cloud cover, which should help retain some of the heat overnight.

We are definitely heading to town tomorrow morning. To get an early start, we have set the alarm for 6:00 am, although I doubt I will need it. I'm quite excited, like a child on Christmas Eve. It's reassuring to know that I can still feel this kind of excitement at nearly 52 years of age. I'm not so old after all. Tomorrow evening we'll be camped, out on the ice, in the middle of the lake. If the afternoon sun makes mush of the snow, we might camp early, and then drag on the crust that should re-form overnight. Imagine the thrill of pulling my sled, in the twilight of an Arctic spring night, beneath the dancing Northern Lights! The Northern Lights have already danced for us five times this month – we see them on most clear nights.

Over and above the grand adventure of bivouacking on the frozen lake, I'm also eager to be in town, which is quite ironic. Usually Kathleen and I retreat to the wilderness to escape people and cities. Now we're leaving the wilderness for the sights, sounds and amenities of a town, albeit one of only 80 to 100 people. It should be interesting. We don't yet know where we'll be staying. That should also be interesting.

The afternoon sun has made slush of the snow in front of the cabin. The chips from the winter chopping and splitting of wood have emerged from hiding, and much of the ground in front of our cabin is now bare of snow. This means I'll have to load the sled and toboggan tomorrow morning about 20 m out along Lower Cabin Crescent, so that we have enough snow on which to drag our gear all the way down to the lake. This will add additional time to get everything organized and ready to go. But the melting snow also means that spring continues to advance.

During our radio conversation Bern repeated Margaret's invitation to take us to town by ski-doo.

"Thanks again, Bern, but I want to drag to town. I want to experience being out on the ice."

"OK, but it's a lot of work."

"Well, that's what I want."

"Go ahead, then. Just make sure you shutter the windows and lock the door before you come."

Just after midnight, the Northern Lights pulsed across the heavens, arching upward from the town of Colville Lake. This is a good omen – like the proverbial pot of gold at the end of the rainbow.

Thursday, April 15. I woke before the alarm sounded, and climbed down the ladder to start the morning fire and boil the tea water. The temperature outside was -20 degrees. Sleeping out on the lake would have been chilly, but not overly uncomfortable. During breakfast, the CBC news indicated that a warming trend was coming up from the south on the strong southeast winds that had been blowing constantly for the past 24 hours. Everything seems to be falling into place. This will be a fantastic trip.

Even though we weren't taking the wall tent or wood stove, we still needed a lot of gear, including food, water, summer tent, sleeping bags, spare clothes for travelling, clothes for town, propane stove, propane cylinders, wool blankets, cameras, tripod, toiletries, and of course, our mail. I even packed the heavy ice chisel, just in case we couldn't find enough snow to melt for drinking water and for cooking. We piled our snowshoes on top of the load, and were ready to head out.

"You know, Kathleen, I've been thinking about it. I think we should pack two of Bern's lawn chairs."

"Why the heck would you want to do that?"

I could tell from the tone of her voice that Kathleen didn't immediately embrace the suggestion.

"It will be a great picture, Kathleen, of us sitting in our lawn chairs, out in the middle of the lake, on the ice, beneath the late evening sun. I can't miss that opportunity. Besides, it would be nice to have a place to sit."

"We're probably going to be pretty tired at the end of the day, Michael. We've never dragged this long or this far before. I don't see us just sitting around. I think we'll be ready for bed soon after dinner. And why add extra weight for no reason?"

As usual, Kathleen was probably right. "But it would make a great picture. How about I take just one lawn chair. I'll put it on my sled. You won't have to drag it. I'll even let you sit in it."

"If that's what you want, go ahead."

I could tell that she still wasn't convinced. I placed one lawn chair on top of my load, and cinched it down with a bungee cord. It will be a great picture.

We lowered the sled and toboggan by rope down the hill below the storage cabin, and stood on the ice at 8:30 in beautiful conditions. The morning had turned calm and warm, at -16 degrees, a very good temperature for dragging heavy loads. We had decided not to wear our mukluks, as we were worried that they might not stand up to the strain, particularly because we would be dragging on ice, packed hard by the ski-doos, as opposed to dragging on soft snow. Instead, we wore our very heavy Sorels. They seemed huge, as I've said before, much like the footwear that Frankenstein's monster always wore in the old horror movies. But they should provide very good traction, and would provide excellent ankle support, much like hiking boots.

And so we were off to town! We leaned into our towlines, and reached the Tent Camp on the Big Island in only one hour and 40 minutes. A ski-doo was parked outside one of the wall tents, whose flap was tied shut.

We called out "Hello, is anyone there?"

"Just a minute," came the answer.

The flap opened, and a young native man, about 30 years old, peered out at us. We had apparently disturbed his sleep.

"I'm Mike, and this is my wife Kathleen. We've been staying at North End, and we're on our way to town. Should be good travelling conditions today."

"Yeah, should be pretty good."

We had obviously surprised him. He certainly hadn't been expecting company or visitors. Although he was friendly, he didn't invite us in for tea – a bit disappointing. It would have been nice to chat with our new neighbour, and to have an indoor tea break.

We said goodbye, and let our loads slide down the brow of the island, and stood before the great expanse of Colville Lake. It was like descending the east slope of the Rocky Mountains in southern Alberta to stare across the infinite Canadian Prairie. Only 34 km to go. We rested and snacked at the edge of the ice, and could feel the southeast wind rising from beyond the lake. Time to get going again. So far we have averaged more than 3 km/hr, and I still felt very strong. I began to think that we might even reach town today. Even if we didn't camp on the lake, I could still get a picture of Kathleen having dinner on the ice, seated in her lawn chair.

We stopped for lunch just under two hours later. We were still travelling at a good rate, and likely covered another 6 km. Only 28 km to go. We didn't feel tired yet. We leaned into our towlines and continued heading south, into a wind that was becoming increasingly stronger.

Over the next three hours we stopped to rest four times. We were beginning to tire, but were still moving at a good pace. We had probably covered 22 km, leaving only 18 km to town. Over half way there. We were beginning to have problems, though. The southeast wind had been building strength all afternoon. At our third rest stop, Kathleen pulled her parka out of its stuff sack, which the wind immediately ripped from her hands, and sent it sliding across the ice. We gave chase, but the stuff sack picked up speed, eventually took flight, and finally sailed away into the sunshine, far across the lake. Darn. Well, we always carry spare stuff sacks, but I hate to lose equipment because of inattention or carelessness.

We again headed up the ski-doo trail. The wind blew directly into our faces, and Kathleen was having difficulty controlling her toboggan, which was repeatedly blown off course by the strong gusts. Instead of sliding easily over packed snow along the ski-doo trail, we were now often dragging laboriously through and over deep drifts of snow flying in from the south. This was not going nearly so well.

We continued to struggle forward, hoping the wind would leave us alone. By 6:45 after 10 hours on the trail, we had finally had enough. We didn't feel like stopping to put up a tent in the wind, but we were quite tired, and needed to rest and to replenish our energy with a good meal. We stepped out of our towlines, and began to unload the sled and toboggan.

Kathleen stood up and said, "Oh no, Michael, I think I've lost my Watson gloves!"

"Are you sure? How could that be? Weren't you wearing them?"

"No, my hands were too hot. I was just wearing my knitted gloves. I had my Watson gloves pinned to my sash. The pin must have come loose. They're gone."

This was bad news. The Watson 'gloves' were, in fact, supple gauntlets, lined with thinsulate, that we had purchased from the Watson Glove Company in Vancouver. They were actually mitts, and were very warm and durable. We wore them constantly, except when working with our hands, or when we were too warm. Kathleen was wearing her 'spare' gauntlets, but they were not nearly as warm as the Watson gloves. We needed the Watson gloves in cold weather.

"When's the last time you saw them, Kathleen? Are you sure you didn't drop them just now around camp?"

"No, they're not here. I don't know for sure when I had them last. I might have put them on while we were resting at our last stop."

"I'll go back and look for them. They must be just right along the ski-doo trail."

"Don't go too far. The storm's starting to really pick up."

"I won't. I'll help you get the tent set up, and then I'll go back along the trail."

We piled our sled, toboggan and gear in a semi-circle, and set up the tent in the lee. We pounded the tent stakes into the ice, and they seemed to be holding against the wind. I wish this wind would leave us alone.

"OK, Kathleen, I'm gonna go look for the Watson gloves. I won't be gone too long. I'll go back along the ski-doo trail at most 15 minutes, so I'll be back in no more than 30 minutes."

"You don't need to go. I have spare gauntlets."

"But your Watson gloves are better. You need them."

I headed back up the trail, pushed along by the relentless wind. Five minutes and still no gloves. I hurried along as fast as I could. Ten minutes and still no gloves. The snow was now very thick and blowing hard across the surface of the lake. I turned to look back. Only an hour ago, we could see completely across the lake. Now I could see nothing but snow, which was settling into and filling the ski-doo trail. What the hell's the matter with me? What am I doing out here in a blizzard? I can't see the trail. I can't see the shore. I could easily become too disoriented to find Kathleen and our camp. I gotta get back. Victoria Jason 'danced in idiotic abandon on the ice.' I was just an idiot wandering all alone on the ice.

I hurried back, reminding myself to remain calm. Only stretches of the ski-doo trail remained, but they were enough for me to find my way, and I eventually saw the tent appear in the snowy gloom. I was happy, and somewhat fortunate, that my foolishness hadn't been more costly.

Kathleen sat hunched over the propane stove, and looked up as I came into camp, which she had completely organized in my absence. She had already inflated the therm-a-rest mattresses and laid out the sleeping bags in the tent. She had already melted snow for water, and was now ready to spoon out some stir-fried caribou for dinner. She looked completely content and in control, all alone, out on the ice, in the middle of the lake, with the wind and the snow blasting around her. She's quite a woman and a true adventurer. I'm very lucky to have her as my wife.

"I didn't find the gloves, Kathleen."

"That's OK. I don't have to have them. I have spare gauntlets, and it's not cold anyway. The temperature is +3 degrees."

The warm temperature was a mixed blessing, as all our clothing became instantly wet when the wind-driven snow melted. We quickly ate our dinner and crawled into the tent, feeling exhausted and worried. I wish the wind would leave us alone.

The wind did not grant my wish, but continued to assault our little tent. At 10:15 pm we peered out through the vestibule to a scene of driving, blinding white, which surrounded our exposed position. All of our gear had been buried beneath snow. We stepped outside to urinate, and could barely stand up. By midnight I truly feared for the stability of the tent, which shuddered,

We headed to town, 40 km away,
with our summer tent, on April 15, at -16 degrees.

and bowed inward with increasingly strong blasts of unrelenting wind that drove snow through the nylon fly and walls into our small, vulnerable haven. Every few minutes I had to kick away the snow that piled up against the tent door, which sagged heavily beneath the weight.

I sat upright until 2:00 am, just to be ready to grab the tent should it come apart. At 2:30 am the wind no longer hurled snow and I felt slightly more confident that the tent would survive the onslaught. By 3:00 am the wind stopped, and we were surrounded by beautiful silence, broken only by the soft, frog-like clucking of a Willow Ptarmigan that had sought refuge in the immediate lee of our tent. Truly extraordinary that the ptarmigan had found us way out here. I fell into a restless sleep.

Friday, April 16. I awoke at 8:00 am to a calm, but heavily overcast morning, warm at +3 degrees. On the windward side of the tent, snow that had been hardened by the gale had accumulated halfway up the tent, blocking our front door egress. We kicked our way out to a gloomy morning. All our gear, including the sled, lay buried beneath the snow. The packed ski-doo trail had been completely obliterated. We ate a quick breakfast of dry granola and packed up.

We still couldn't see any shoreline, and were not exactly sure of our position. Based on how long we had travelled yesterday, I estimated that we had covered 26 to 28 km, which put us 12 to 14 km from town. Assuming we could still travel at 3 km/hr, we should reach town in 4 to 5 hours, by early afternoon. I placed the lawn chair on top of my load, and cinched it down with a bungee cord. The lighting was too poor, and the snow too thick to take a good picture. It wasn't the kind of image I had wanted anyway. Kathleen was supposed to be relaxing in the sun and sipping tea. She was supposed to be enjoying life out on the ice.

We leaned into our towlines and headed down the ski-doo trail, which disappeared in only a few steps. We floundered about looking for it, continually breaking through the wind-hardened crust. After only a few frustrating minutes of unsuccessful searching we unpacked and put on our snowshoes. These conditions would certainly make for a longer day.

The wind resumed its attack at mid-morning, creating whiteout conditions. Our world had shrunk to a very small realm, often 200 m in diameter or less. We travelled by 'dead reckoning,' which is a navigational process of estimating one's current position based upon a previously determined position, and advancing that position based upon known speed, elapsed time and course. I was pretty sure of our position last night, and had set my compass to 208 degrees, to a point around which lay the town of Colville Lake, perhaps now only 10 to 12 km away. We just needed to be able to walk in a straight line at 2 km/hr for 5 to 6 hours, and we should be there by mid-afternoon. Of course, it's not possible to walk in a straight line for 10 km when one can't see fixed points up ahead. I hope that the term 'dead reckoning' didn't actually arise because people 'reckoned they were dead.' Just a joke. With patience I'm sure we'll make it. We're bound to touch shore somewhere, eventually. Even if we don't reach shore today, we can always spend another night out on the lake.

As the day wore on, the temperature remained above zero, which made the snow slushy, with poor dragging conditions. Our pace slowed. The slush froze to our lamp wick snowshoe bindings, which eventually frayed and tore away completely. We were forced to stop to make four new bindings. Weaving the new bindings into our snowshoes required that I remove my mitts to be able to use my fingers. I had to stop several times to re-warm my hands, and the process took over 30 minutes. Still, though, there's no deadline for when we have to reach town. We'll get there eventually. I held out the compass. We leaned into our towlines and continued heading 208 degrees into a wind that refused to leave us alone.

The ice now became quite jumbled, with large fields of blocks and pressure ridges more than a metre high. The Conover book had warned us about pressure ridges on large lakes. When the ice had formed last fall, it had also expanded. Since the edges of Colville Lake are immovable, the expanding ice developed stress cracks that rose up – just like mountains rise up above colliding tectonic plates. Sometimes, during very cold weather early in the winter, these stress cracks can separate and expose open water that might refreeze beneath thin ice intermixed with deeper ice. Within these jumbles of pressure ridges there is often no way to tell where the ice is thick, and where the ice is too thin to support a person's weight.

For an hour we worked our way cautiously through the maze, poking at and testing the ice as we pulled and pushed our loads up and down the ridges. This was very hard work. Not at all like the euphoria that we had hoped for. It was an adventure, though, and I was glad for the experience.

Finally we reached smooth ice, and stopped to rest. We hadn't covered much distance in the last hour or two, and we certainly hadn't been going in a straight line through the pressure ridges. No telling how far we were from town. No telling in what direction town lay. On the other hand, pressure ridges often form around islands that offer resistance to the expanding ice. The topographic map shows an island more than 1 km long only 2 to 3 km from the cape toward which we have been heading. Maybe we're near that island. Maybe it's not too far to go now. We'll just have to press ahead and hope for the best. We hope it's not too much farther. We're getting a bit tired.

Thirty minutes later the wind began to subside, the weather cleared a bit, and the shoreline came into view. Wow! We're almost there. We seem to be right on track.

In less than two hours of dragging our sleds,
we stood before the great expanse of Colville Lake.

The town of Colville Lake sits in a cove behind a cape, and can not be seen by travellers approaching from the north and east of the cape. Bern had mentioned that we would see no sign of Colville Lake until we were close enough to see the windsock at the airport, which sits on a hill above the town.

We stopped, and gazed toward the shore through our binoculars. Yes, there it was! The windsock, like a beacon, stretched out in a line directly toward us. With renewed energy we leaned into our towlines. We dragged on for what seemed like hours without getting any closer. We were obviously getting very tired and impatient now that the goal was so near. About 1 km from town we saw Margaret and Jo-Ellen, out running Margaret's dogs. They roared over on their ski-doos and offered to drag us and our loads up into town.

"No, thanks. I want to say I went all the way. It's not far now. We can make it."

Kathleen didn't look very happy with my pronouncement. Perhaps she thought I was being a tad stubborn. Margaret suggested that maybe she could take some of our gear, to lighten our loads.

We spent the night on the ice. When we reached town, people told us that we had been caught in the worst storm of the winter.

"No, thanks, it's not too heavy."

Kathleen had heard enough, and lifted her heaviest pack onto Margaret's ski-doo.

We continued to walk, but still had not reached town by the time Margaret and Jo-Ellen had finished running the dogs. Margaret once again asked if we wanted a ride. Town was only about 300 m away, but the ski-doo trail went up and over the hill. I was pretty close – close enough to say that I had done it. The hill looked steep. It would be a lot of work pulling up the slope. I wasn't that stubborn. We hitched our sled and toboggan to the ski-doos, and moments later, at 5:00 pm, after eight hours on the trail, we were shaking hands, for the first time, with Bern Will Brown himself.

By six o'clock we were enjoying the hospitality of Bern and Margaret's dinner table. We felt very comfortable. It was good to get off the ice. It was good to rest out of the wind. After dessert and coffee, Bern handed us our mail, and showed us to one of his guest cabins. We lay down on the bed to read our letters. I had received a small package from Bill Owens, a friend that I have known since childhood. I removed the screws from the homemade, plywood box, and pulled out the packing material, which consisted of recent sports sections dealing with the upcoming baseball season. Owens knows that we love baseball. Within the packing material was another, even more prized and unexpected gift: a 375-ml flask of brandy. What a friend that Bill is. I had not been thinking of brandy, but brandy is exactly what I wanted at that moment. Letters were good; but letters with baseball news and brandy were truly excellent. I thank you, Bill, with much gratitude.

I have enjoyed the last two days, as I wanted to experience winter travel in the North. I have now done so. Even if not matching the exploits of men like Hornby or Rae, or of women like Jason, I feel satisfied. This morning we dug ourselves out of the drifted, crusted snow, set off in a blizzard, repaired gear, crossed difficult pressure ridges, and still reached town somewhat according to plan. It's good to know that we can succeed, reasonably comfortably, in such challenging conditions. I felt very satisfied.

Saturday, April 17. Immediately after breakfast we headed off to the Co-op store to mail our letters. Then over to Robert and Jo-Ellen's to call Kathleen's mother on her birthday. Her parents had no idea that we would ever be coming to town. I'm sure that they sometimes felt they would never hear from us again. The call had to be very exciting. I'll let Kathleen describe the call in her own words:

> *The phone rang, and my father answered.*
> *"Hello, Dad, it's Kathleen."*
> *There followed just a little bit of silence, as he grappled with this unexpected information. "Kathleen! Where are you?"*
> *"I'm in town. We came across the lake. Took us two days, but here we are. Is Mom there?"*
> *"She's out at the store, she should be home soon. She will be so unhappy to miss this call. Tell me about your trip to town." I gave him the main details, all the while wishing Mom would come home.*
> *Suddenly my father said, "I hear the door, your Mom is home."*
> *"Don't tell her it's me."*
> *I could hear their conversation on the other side. "Here, dear, there's a call for you."*

"Who is it?"

"I don't know. They just asked for you."

"Hello?"

"Hi, Mom. Happy Birthday!"

Now there was a lot of stunned silence.

"Hi, Mom. It's Kathleen. Happy Birthday!"

"Kathleen! Kathleen! Where are you?"

I told her of our trip across the lake to town, but left out all the scary parts about wind and blizzards and pressure ridges and hard work. No need to worry her.

She was so excited and happy, and so was I, especially when she said, "You're the first of my eight children to call me today."

Today was the next to last day of the annual Spring Carnival, which began last Thursday. To us, people from the South, many of the competitive events were entirely new, including ice chiselling, snowshoe biathlon, tea boiling, bannock making, ski-doo races, dog team races, and caribou head skinning. There was approximately $40,000 in prize money available, which seemed pretty substantial for such a small town. Bern said that the Federal Government, with some corporate donations, was the primary source of the prize money, which was intended to support traditional customs and games. I think that an additional underlying goal was to provide cash to people living in small, Northern communities, most of which suffer high unemployment rates.

For example, most of the Colville Lake events were divided into age classes, and some were restricted to either male or female entrants. The top three finishers in each category won cash prizes, and very few categories had more than three entrants. Pretty much everyone who participated in any event finished in the money.

One elderly lady had entered the snowshoe biathlon, which required the participants to snowshoe around a fairly lengthy course on the lake, and to shoot at balloons hanging at various stations. She was an expert markswoman, and never missed a shot. It was painful, though, to watch her hobbling around the course, coughing and wheezing all the way. At the end of the race, in which she finished a very distant third, Jo-Ellen asked her if she felt OK.

Our gracious and hospitable landlords, Margaret and Bern Will Brown.

"No, I have a bad cold."

"Why did you enter, then?"

"Because I need the money."

I admired her determination and integrity. Despite her age, and despite her poor health, she asked for no special concessions. She competed according to the rules. She struggled to the first station, raised her gun, and hit all the balloons. She sheathed the rifle on her frail back and continued to each of the successive stations with equal success. She finished the race, and earned her prize money.

Spring Carnival in Colville Lake stretched over four days for several reasons, including snow conditions, and the need to share dog teams and equipment. Events rarely started on time. Most importantly, though, Spring Carnival in Colville Lake was truly a celebration – a time to share memories – a time to socialize. Because we were totally unexpected strangers in town, people were naturally curious about what Kathleen and I were up to. They were surprised, and a little concerned that we had crossed the lake, during what they said was the worst storm of the winter. "We're glad you made it. The houses here in town were shaking in the wind. We didn't know that you were coming to town across the lake. If something had happened to you on our land, we would have felt responsible."

A native man, Gene, volunteered to take us back to our cabin by ski-doo. We accepted his offer. I have already dragged to town, and am pleased to know that I can do it. At this point, neither Kathleen nor I really want to struggle back to the cabin, although I would enjoy camping on the ice, in good weather. And, I would like to get that picture of Kathleen sitting in the lawn chair. Even so, I asked Gene when it would be convenient for him to take us back, and he suggested early on Wednesday morning. That's a little bit longer than we had planned to stay, but we were glad for the ride.

The afternoon was clear, calm and warm at +11 degrees. The first Snow Bunting of the year arrived, which is the surest sign that spring is coming. We again appreciated the hospitality of Bern and Margaret, who hosted us for dinner, along with Robert, Jo-Ellen and Carroll McIntyre, the manager of the Co-op general store.

The spring carnival events included ice chiselling, snowshoe biathlon, tea boiling, bannock making, ski-doo races, dog team races and caribou head skinning.

I ended our first full day in town playing cribbage, for a nickel a point, with 'the boys' up at Carroll's house.

Sunday, April 18. Bern Will Brown is a true icon of the North, and in the popular press his name is often considered synonymous with that of Colville Lake. Bern was born in Rochester, N.Y. in 1920, and from a very young age became fascinated by the North. After becoming an Oblate of Mary Immaculate priest in 1948 he was sent to northern Canada. When Bern arrived in Colville Lake in 1962, only one other family remained in the traditional village. Most of the original inhabitants had moved to larger settlements, particularly Fort Good Hope. Bern envisioned a resurrected Colville Lake that would provide a refuge for native people to pursue traditional lifestyles of hunting and trapping, while also escaping the drawbacks of 'modern' city life such as alcohol and unemployment.

Indeed, after Bern built his log house in 1962, aboriginal people started to return. Bern eventually built a church called *Our Lady of the Snows*, a nursing station, a museum and a library, which contains approximately 700 books on the North.

In 1971 Bern received permission from the Vatican to be married, and is now considered by the church to be a lay leader. Bern's wife Margaret was born at Stanton, 18 km east of the mouth of the Anderson River on the Arctic coast. Margaret raises a pure-white strain of sled dogs, and comes from a trapping family whose Texas father married an Inuit woman.

Much has been written about Bern, and rightfully so. He is extraordinarily accomplished and talented, along the lines of a Renaissance Man. As a priest with a classical background, he is obviously broadly educated and well-read. He has written several books, is a gifted painter of Northern landscapes, is fluent in the local language, is skilled with an axe and a chainsaw, and is completely at home out on the snow trail and living in the bush. I envy his talents.

At the time of our visit, Colville Lake retained many of the qualities that Bern had hoped for. Most of the residents still pursued traditional activities such as hunting and trapping. The town itself was quite picturesque, consisting almost entirely of log houses. Electricity had arrived only very recently. No indoor plumbing existed, and residents were personally responsible for hauling their own drinking water in buckets from Colville Lake. A very rustic lifestyle, much like that which we were living at North End.

Kathleen began Sunday morning by attending church, after which we spent the day checking emails on the school computers, banking by telephone and making more phone calls to friends and family, all of whom seem to be well and healthy. We toured the museum, which housed a very interesting collection of historic artifacts of the North as well as exhibits of trapping gear and examples of native sewing. We witnessed the final events of the Spring Carnival, and I played a little more cribbage with Bern. Only the second full day in town, and already my life was shifting a trifle to the side of passivity, predictability and routine.

In the afternoon we moved from Bern's guest cottage to Robert and Jo-Ellen's house, where Kathleen helped Jo-Ellen tabulate and enter the results of the Spring Carnival into the computer. Just before 11:00 pm we walked over to the new gymnasium, where the Spring Carnival Dance was just beginning. It seemed that the entire town of Colville Lake was there to dance and jig to a guitarist and fiddler in from Fort Good Hope. Kathleen and I wore our comfortable mukluks, as did most of the older adults. Everyone else less than 45 years of age wore some variation of Nike tennis shoes, which suggested that at least some of the older traditions were passing away. Kathleen and I left at 1:30 am, with the festivities still going very strong, and everyone looking forward to the 2:00 am distribution of Spring Carnival prize money. School had been cancelled for Monday.

The day had been sunny, calm and warm, with lots of snowmelt. The sun didn't set until about 10:00 pm, and it was light until well beyond 11 o'clock. Before going to the dance, Kathleen and I stood quietly out at the edge of the lake to watch the glorious deep-crimson, everlasting sunset that filled the entire horizon. We read in the Norman Wells newspaper that on April 31 there will be 19 hours and 33 minutes of daylight in 'The Wells.' Our home at the north end of Colville Lake is more than one degree of latitude farther north than Norman Wells, which means that we should have close to 20 hours of visible light by the time we return to our cabin. Only three weeks after the vernal equinox, and already darkness is becoming a meaningless concept. We are free to travel, work, play and sleep whenever we want.

People often tell us that they wouldn't like the 24-hour daylight of the Arctic summer. They say they would have trouble sleeping. And maybe they would. In our experience on canoe trips in the Far North though, if we're tired, we sleep, even when the sun soars far above the horizon. And because the sun never sets, we are always at liberty to do whatever we want. We can start paddling whenever the urge strikes. We can paddle for as long as we wish. We can dawdle and stop to watch birds, or to identify plants. There is never any need to 'get to camp before it gets dark.' We can eat dinner at midnight. We can fish for breakfast at noon. In reality though, time becomes irrelevant, and we live only in the present. Tomorrow can never come if today never ends. Tomorrow never arrives when the sun never sets. On our summer canoe trips, just as for the old British Empire, the sun never sets on Kathleen and me.

I also believe that most people can very easily sleep when the sun is up, even if they're not sleepy or tired. I have often seen people head down to their favourite beach in summer, spread out their blankets, eat a sandwich for lunch, and then immediately fall asleep beneath the blazing sun. They weren't tired, and they weren't sleepy. Yet they easily slept while all around them children ran, jumped and screeched. (Nothing against children. I used the word 'screech' simply to indicate the joy of youth.)

I also contend that given a true choice, most people would select daylight over darkness. People turn on the lights in their houses to banish darkness. People often fear descending the stairs into a darkened basement. Dark forests in horror movies portray danger and lurking evil. Indeed, the very first four sentences of the Christian bible deal with the victory of light over darkness:

> In the beginning God created the heavens and the earth. The earth was without form and void, and darkness was upon the face of the deep; and the Spirit of God was moving over the face of the waters.
> And God said, 'Let there be light'; and there was light.
> And God saw that the light was good.

Suppose though, that the victory of light over darkness could have been complete, rather than partial. Suppose that God had not merely separated light from darkness, but had given human beings the choice of 24 hours of light with no darkness, compared to our 'norm' of 12 hours of light and 12 hours of darkness. (I'm assuming that no one would choose 24 hours of darkness with no light.) How many of us would have chosen to be afraid of the dark for 12 hours every day – to essentially live half of our lives hiding in the dark forest or stumbling around in our dark houses looking for the light switch? I know that I would have voted for light. I would have opted to never be afraid of the unseen threat prowling in the dark forest. I would have selected the freedom of movement and the far-reaching vistas provided by light.

At the north end of Colville Lake, we will be gaining close to one hour more of light per week. Light is good. More light is better. All light is best. I look forward to the constant daylight of mid-summer.

Monday, April 19. Another comfortable, but idle day in Colville Lake. In the morning we bathed in Robert and Jo-Ellen's living room while they prepared lessons at the school. Yes, you read correctly, we bathed in the living room – in a child's inflatable swimming pool that we filled with a hose that drained their indoor water tank. We cranked up the wood stove to heat the water, and also to create that extra-special spa feeling. We briefly considered buying a plastic pool to take back to our cabin until we thought about the difficulty of bringing all that water up the hill, only two buckets at a time.

After lunch we walked over to the Co-op general store to say hello to Carroll, and to just sort of hang around with everyone else in town who had nothing much to do. In only five minutes we exhausted the excitement of strolling through the four aisles. We bought a $5.00 box of stale potato chips (we didn't know they were stale when we bought them), took them outside, sat down in the sun, and consumed them all in about 30 minutes. We felt overly stuffed and slightly sick to our stomachs. Such is life at the 'mall.' Nothing much else to do except wander around and eat junk food.

I was beginning to suffer from that perfidious malady that commonly afflicts people who have left their isolated cabins in the bush. Yes, I was coming down with 'Town Fever.' I was restless, and eager to escape. That night we lay in our bedroom, rereading our letters and polishing off the bottle of brandy. No more chips. No more booze. Time to go home.

Tuesday, April 20. Another day hanging around town, mostly waiting to go home. Did some visiting and emailing, made some phone calls, and played a little cribbage with Bern. In the afternoon I helped Robert replenish his household water supply. We hitched a sled to his ski-doo, and dragged a plastic tank 200 m out from shore to where a hole had been chiselled through about 75 cm of ice. I kneeled over the hole, and lifted buckets of water up and over to Robert, who poured it into the plastic tank. I must have lifted a hundred buckets, all with my left arm. The repetitive lifting 'up and over' part was not a good idea, as I think I might have damaged my left elbow, which is quite sore.

A squadron of Bohemian Waxwings made their first appearance of the year, and the afternoon temperature rose to +10 degrees. The season is advancing rapidly, and we're curious to see what changes have been occurring at the cabin and along the Ross River. We confirmed with Gene that he still plans to take us home tomorrow. He suggested that we get all our gear together outside Robert and Jo-Ellen's house, and be ready to leave about noon. I'm more than ready to go home.

Wednesday, April 21. The day began calmly enough. We woke late, lingered over our breakfast, and wandered over to Bern's compound to retrieve our sled, tent, snowshoes, lawn chair and other camping gear that we had stored in his warehouse. We dragged it all back to Robert and Jo-Ellen's, and left it by the side of the road. We climbed up the stairs back into the house, boiled up some tea water, and began packing our clothes and bedding. Little by little, in between sips of tea, we had finally gathered all our possessions in one spot. At 11:30 we sat outside eating sandwiches. We were ready.

Noon came with no sign of Gene. We weren't worried, though. Things always happen according to their own time. About 12:30, someone sauntered by to say, "Gene says he might not be going today. Maybe tomorrow. He's not sure."

Oh well, he's probably just busy doing something right now. The days are long. Kathleen and I were both confident that we would actually be going today. We continued to sit outside, drinking tea, and enjoying the sunshine.

People began to cluster around, and were naturally interested in the kind of equipment that we had brought. A man picked up one of the snowshoes, and balanced it thoughtfully on his right hand. He turned it over, quietly assessing its shape. I knew that he must be thinking that our snowshoes were pretty heavy, that they tilted forward, and that they were poorly shaped for travel through deep, soft snow. I knew these things, even though I've been snowshoeing for only two-and-a-half months. Heck, I knew about the deficiencies of my snowshoes way back in mid-February, after using them for only two weeks.

He set the snowshoe back on the pile, looked up, and simply asked "How you chase moose through bush on these?" He didn't want to say that my snowshoes were poorly matched for local conditions. That would be undiplomatic. And it has been my experience that native people prefer diplomacy to confrontation. They tend to prefer rhetoric to direct criticism.

Another man picked up our ice chisel and asked, "What's this for?"

"I brought that just in case we couldn't find enough snow to melt when we were camping on the lake. I thought I might need to chisel through the ice to get water."

"Pretty heavy to carry all that way."

A simple comment that neatly summarized his true opinion, which was probably something like "there's always plenty of snow out on the lake, and besides, do you know how long it would take you to chisel through ice that's usually more than a metre thick? You'd die of thirst or exhaustion before you could chisel through with this." He didn't say it was a bad idea. He didn't say that bringing it just meant that I had to work harder. He didn't say that it's not a good idea to be dragging things I don't need. That would be undiplomatic, so he just said it was pretty heavy to carry all that way.

I was glad that no one ever mentioned the lawn chair. They probably didn't want to embarrass me. They knew there couldn't possibly be any good reason why someone would drag a lawn chair for two days and 40 km across a frozen lake to town. There could be no explanation other than I was just one more crazy city guy from the South. Best to not mention the lawn chair. That would be undiplomatic.

Just before four o'clock, Gene came down the hill, dragging a toboggan behind his ski-doo. "I've just gotta finish doing a few things at home. Load your stuff in the toboggan. I'll be ready to go at 4:30. It should be fun."

This news created a great deal of interest in our journey back to North End. School would be out for the day by the time we would leave. Robert and Jo-Ellen said they would like to come with us. Doug, an administrator with the Board of Education, was in town to review the school curriculum. He'd never been to Colville Lake before. He'd hardly ever been on a ski-doo before. It sounded like a grand adventure to him. He would like to come too.

An RCMP officer, Jean-Marc, was in town on his monthly visit from Fort Good Hope. He'd never been north of town before. "I'd love to come," he said.

And of course Margaret wanted to come. She's always ready for a ski-doo trip. "You can ride with me, Kathleen," she said. "I'll get some food together. We can have dinner out at the cabin. Just come by the lodge when you're ready."

It was a beautiful evening, and everyone wanted to go to North End.

At 4:30 we were mostly packed, so Kathleen started walking to the lodge to meet Margaret, who showed up a few minutes later on her ski-doo looking for Kathleen. "You just missed her, Margaret. She's probably waiting for you right now over at your place."

Margaret roared off and Gene arrived a few minutes later. Without saying a word, and without turning off his machine, he hurriedly threw the rest of our gear into his toboggan. Gene seemed to be in a rush for some reason. Without warning, he turned the throttle full open and sped away, without even folding and tying the toboggan wrap. Like catching a train leaving the station, I ran after Gene's accelerating ski-doo and just managed to jump on back of the toboggan.

Gene and I raced through town. The treads of the ski-doo kicked out mountains of snow, which filled the open toboggan and covered our gear in wet slush. As we sped onto the lake, we spotted Margaret up ahead, all alone on her ski-doo. Where was Kathleen? She's supposed to be riding with Margaret. Where was everybody else? They must all still be back at the loading site, waiting for us.

We roared back through town, up and down all the streets, without finding any of our entourage. We thundered back out through town and onto the lake, where a cluster of three ski-doos waited for us. Kathleen was riding with Jean-Marc, Doug with Margaret, and Jo-Ellen with Robert. We were all together and ready to go. Gene turned off the motor, and still without a word, threw all our stuff onto the ice, emptied the deep slush from his toboggan wrap, reloaded everything, and then wrapped and tied the tarp securely over the load. A little bit like closing the barn door after the proverbial horse has run away. It would take days for our soaking gear to dry out.

We now headed north, with Gene in the lead. The other three ski-doos quickly fell behind and dropped out of sight. Gene was definitely in a hurry.

After about 10 km Gene decided to stop and wait for the others. I think he really had no choice, as his ski-doo was overheating. Still without saying a word, he turned off the engine and lifted up the hood. The others arrived a few minutes later, and they likewise lifted the hoods on their ski-doos to cool them off. The evening was warm, and the snow was thick and slushy. The ski-doo engines were working hard, and being pushed to the limit.

A few minutes later, we blasted off again, even faster than before. We were going hell-bent for leather. I have no idea why that phrase means going fast. But I like the way it sounds. You just know that you're going fast when you're going hell-bent for leather. Gene and I sped past the Tent Camp on the Big Island. I looked back and could see only Jean-Marc and Kathleen, fairly close behind, and gaining. Jean-Marc eventually pulled up beside us, which seemed to surprise Gene, who I'm sure thought he could never be caught. And certainly he didn't like being caught. Jean-Marc presented too much of a challenge, and this could not be tolerated.

After the Big Island, the ski-doo route crossed two more islands where the 'portage trail' wound around and through the trees. The race now demanded not only speed, but also required skillful manoeuvring. And Gene was very skillful. We raced over the portages, barely slowing down, with Gene hanging off to one side or the other of his ski-doo as we rounded the turns. I was now being drenched in snow and slush, and could barely hang on as the toboggan swerved and careened through the trees. But I was determined not to fall off. I was determined not to be just one more crazy city guy from the South who couldn't handle a little ski-doo ride.

Finally, at 6:45, we reached the cabin, and came to a merciful stop. Without a word, Gene tossed all my gear out, sat down on his ski-doo, and began to eat a lard sandwich. A man needs a lot of calories when working so hard out in the bush. There was no sight or sound of any other ski-doos. I asked Gene if he wanted to come in. We could start a fire, and boil up some tea water. "No." Something seemed to be bothering Gene, but I had no idea what it was.

Last night I had asked Bern if I should offer to pay Gene for taking us back to the cabin. I didn't really know what to do. On the one hand, Gene might expect some payment for service. On the other hand, he might be insulted if I offered him money for a favour that he simply wanted to provide to visitors. Bern suggested that I offer to pay for the gas. This seemed like a very appropriate solution to me. It would only be considerate to offer to pay for gas.

I didn't know much about ski-doos, and had no understanding about how much gas would be involved in an 80-km round trip. I walked over to Gene and held out two twenty-dollar bills. "Can I help pay for the gas, Gene?" He could decide to accept one or both of the bills, or to say no thank you. Gene took both bills and said, "I'm going caribou hunting tonight."

He mounted his ski-doo, and rumbled back down to the lake at 6:55, after spending only 10 minutes in camp. Still no sight or sound of our travelling companions.

I unlocked the cabin door, removed the window shutters, started the fire, and began to unpack our gear. At 7:30 I heard the sound of an approaching ski-doo. It was Gene, with Kathleen on the back, and Jean-Marc riding in the toboggan. Just after Gene and I had pulled away from them on the Big Island, their ski-doo had begun to backfire, and finally broke down on the last portage trail. Jean-Marc had replaced the spark plugs, but still couldn't get his ski-doo to start. Gene dropped off Kathleen and Jean-Marc, and then left again 'to go caribou hunting.'

At 7:50 Robert and Jo-Ellen arrived with news that Margaret and Doug had broken down near the Tent Camp on the Big Island. Robert and Jo-Ellen had brought a full 100-pound propane cylinder, which Bern said we might need before the winter was over. Jean-Marc, Robert and I wrestled it into place on the porch. Kathleen invited everyone inside for tea, but our guests said they couldn't stay. "We have to get going to find Margaret and Doug."

We stood around outside chatting, and commenting how warm the weather had become. How the weather had become too hot for driving ski-doos at top speed. At 8:30 Jean-Marc, Robert and Jo-Ellen left to find Margaret and Doug. Kathleen and I were alone again at our cabin. We were disappointed that our guests couldn't stay for dinner, or even tea. Kathleen had also brought some coffee back, as a gift from Margaret for the party planned for tonight. There would be no dinner party now, though. What had started out as a calm morning ended up as a very rushed, chaotic and disappointing evening.

During our absence, a great deal of melt had occurred. The south-facing knoll near the flagpole now showed bare ground. The pier extended over open water. Our cabin roof was snow free. Our front yard was a morass of mud and wood chips. Open water extended along the shore south of the cabin. I felt restless, uneasy, and depressed. The winter I had come north to enjoy seemed over, yet canoeing season was likely still two months away.

Thursday, April 22. Once again I had rashly predicted the demise of winter, which seems to have returned. After five consecutive days of clear, calm skies in town, with temperatures near +10 degrees or higher, snow fell all day, drifting south before a strong north wind. We spent the day indoors, reacquainting ourselves with the comfortable routine of life in our cabin. A slow breakfast toasting bread and warming tea on the wood stove. Snacking on popcorn with our evening game of cribbage. Kathleen scored a 29-point hand tonight, the first time I have ever seen this maximum score in my entire life. And I've played a lot of cribbage since I was about eight years old.

The temperature remained between -8 and -4 degrees all day. Mild, but wet. I wish for either colder or warmer temperatures. This shoulder season is so uninteresting. This afternoon we saw a group of approximately 45 caribou standing and sitting on the ice 200 m from the cabin. They looked serenely ghostly as the misty snow swirled about them. After a few hours they drifted away to the northeast, toward Ketaniatue Lake. We had enjoyed going to town last week. At times we also enjoyed being in town. It's good to be home, though.

Before we left for town Kathleen had been feeding a Whiskey Jack that had become quite attached to her. The bird would follow her whenever she strolled down Privy Path, and would perch next to her as she settled in at the end of the trail. Kathleen said that the bird just seemed to like 'talking' to her. This morning he (or she) spotted Kathleen as she walked down the path, and swooped along beside her, chattering away. When Kathleen stopped to say hello, he (or she) flew right down to the branch by her face and, as Kathleen says, "went on and on, changing sounds and puffing himself up. He sure had a long story to tell! He must have missed me."

That's how Kathleen tells the story. I didn't actually see this myself, so can not verify its accuracy. I believe it happened though, just that way. Kathleen wouldn't make it up, and the Whiskey Jacks certainly do know us by now. It's good to be home, among friends.

Friday, April 23. The north wind continued to blow all day, and the ground is once again covered with snow. The temperature fell last night to

-12 degrees, and rose only to -6 today at 5:00 pm. Again we mostly stayed inside, resting and reading. Kathleen made fresh bread, and for lunch she prepared grilled cheese and bacon sandwiches. The Whiskey Jacks glided in for their afternoon visit, and eagerly dined on the leftover crumbs of cheese and bacon grease.

Saturday, April 24. A clear, cold morning, at -24 degrees. Our Sorel boots, sitting next to the door, froze to the cabin floor. Maybe we should go back to wearing mukluks. The northwest wind blew all night, and continued throughout the day, although it slackened somewhat toward evening. The open water below the pier turned back to ice. Nevertheless, we believe that spring approaches. Even though afternoon temperatures never exceeded -8 degrees, the heat of the sun melted the thin snow and ice at the base of nearby trees. We damped down the stove between 5:00 and 8:00 pm, as the cabin interior easily remained at +20 degrees because of the sun's heat slipping through the south-facing window.

We remained quite busy all day, mostly doing laundry. I also oiled our portable wood-burning stove, which we will not likely be using again this winter. Kathleen spent time up in the storage cabin inventorying our food. We had arrived with enough supplies to last six months, but Kathleen just wanted to check how well our reserves were holding up.

Before coming to Colville Lake, some of our friends and most of Kathleen's family expressed concern that we were living way too much beyond the edge of civilization. "Where," they asked, "would you get more food if you run out?"

I appreciated their worry about our welfare, but we feel completely comfortable and safe out here. We still have plenty of food left. We should have enough food to last another three months. And, if forced to, we could hunt caribou or catch fish or trap snowshoe hares. We have substantially more food available to us than people who dwell in cities, where grocery stores generally have no more than a three-day supply. I could just as easily have asked our friends, "What would you do if the roads were suddenly closed because of snow or floods, or if the trucks stopped rolling because of labour strikes or gas shortages? How long could you last without having to replenish your food supplies?"

I could make similar arguments about water and heat. Kathleen and I have unlimited water just by dipping a bucket in the lake. We have unlimited heat just by cutting down another tree. We have a generous supply of white gas and propane for lights, which we don't even need now, because daylight extends nearly 20 hours each day. Note that we have complete control over most of our resources, and depend on no one.

Not so in the city, where everyone is highly vulnerable because heat and light require an infrastructure that can, and occasionally does fail. For your consideration, I provide the following summary of the 1998 Ice Storm, which I have gleaned from the Internet site Wikipedia:

> *The North American Ice Storm of 1998 was a massive storm that struck a relatively narrow swath of land from Eastern Ontario to southern Quebec to Nova Scotia in Canada, and bordering areas from Northern New York to Southeast Maine in the United States, from 5 to 10 January 1998. It caused massive damage to trees and electrical infrastructure all over the area, leading to widespread long-term power outages.*
>
> *Many power lines broke and over 1,000 pylons collapsed in chain reactions under the weight of the ice, leaving more than 4 million people without electricity, most of them in southern Quebec, western New Brunswick and eastern Ontario, some of them for an entire month. At least twenty-five people died in the areas affected by the ice, primarily from hypothermia. Twelve more deaths and hundreds of millions of dollars in additional damage were caused by the flooding farther south from the same storm system.*
>
> *Critically, about 1,000 steel electrical pylons (said, in Quebec, to be the most solid in the world) and 35,000 wooden utility poles were brought down, further damaging power supply and hampering the return of electricity.*
>
> *Three weeks after the end of the ice storm, there were still thousands of people without electricity. In Quebec alone, 150,000 persons were without electricity as of January 28.*

People died during the ice storm in the presumed safety of their own homes. People died during the ice storm in the presumed security of their own beds. People died and suffered during the ice storm precisely because they depended entirely on an infrastructure that could not, indeed cannot ever, truly guarantee safety and security.

The aftermath of Hurricane Katrina in New Orleans in August of 2005 provides an even more glaring example of how vulnerable people actually are in the presumed safety of a modern city. I remember so clearly seeing those people on rooftops, holding up hand-drawn signs begging for help as the helicopter swooped in. We all saw them on TV. We all knew they needed help. Yet no one came to pluck them from their island roofs. No one came to save the huddled thousands in the Superdome. Society merely filmed and reported their plight and despair.

No, I do not feel vulnerable living all alone and isolated here at the north end of Colville Lake. My safety and comfort depend entirely on my own physical, mental and natural resources. I feel completely secure.

People also ask, "What if something bad happened when you were out there all alone? What if you had an accident? Who would help you?"

This is a legitimate question. Something could happen. We could have an accident. Help might not arrive in time. Even in the city though, people have accidents and die. People fall off roofs. People fall under the wheels of cars. People fall victim to random muggings.

There is no guarantee in life, no matter where or how carefully one lives. Helen Keller is quoted as saying, "Security is mostly superstition. It does not exist in nature. Life is either a daring adventure, or it is nothing at all."

I'm not suggesting that one must take endless or foolhardy risks to make life worthwhile. I am saying though, that to live one's life constantly trying to protect against accident or mishap or danger is inherently limiting and ultimately futile. I believe that one should at least try to live the life of one's dreams. All of us have these dreams. For many years I dreamed of living in an isolated cabin – of walking down the middle of frozen rivers – of meeting the kinds of physical challenges such as dragging my gear to town during the worst storm of the winter. I am so very fortunate to be living my dreams, even if only for six months. I encourage everyone to listen to your dreams – to try to bring your dreams to life. You might just have a grand adventure along the way.

Sunday, April 25. After a breakfast of bannock, we snowshoed up Woodlot Way and then turned southeast down Winter Camp Walk toward our campsite of last March. We hadn't travelled this way since Kathleen's birthday dinner more than two weeks ago. At that time, only we were using the trails. Since then, however, many caribou have passed along, across and over our carefully-made paths, which are no longer smooth, continuous and pristine. All seems in upheaval. At breakfast this morning we saw a herd of approximately 80 caribou filter down Colville Lake on the east shore. About half way between the cabin and the Teepee Site they turned east into the forest, travelling purposefully, in single file. The caribou around Colville Lake are part of a herd generally known as the Bluenose Caribou Herd, and have likely begun the spring migration to their calving grounds east of Bluenose Lake.

One of the books I have been reading is E.C. Pielou's excellent *A Naturalist's Guide to the Arctic*, which is well written and filled with interesting information. Pielou notes that caribou are superbly adapted to the rigours of the Arctic winter. The guard hairs of the winter coat are hollow, which provides excellent insulation. The hooves grow longer in the fall while the pads of the feet shrink. This raises the tender pads above the hard, frozen ground of winter, while the sharp edges of the hooves give traction on snow and ice. Also, like birds, the arteries and veins of the leg are close together; the heat of out-flowing arterial blood is exchanged with venous-blood heat, which conserves precious warmth. Caribou body temperatures in winter remain at +40 degrees, even though leg temperatures are only +10 degrees. Caribou survive the long winter primarily by eating lichens, which are normally indigestible to most ruminants. The caribou digestive system though, contains the enzyme lichenase, which allows the caribou to break down and subsist on these little packages of algae and fungus. Lichens are low in protein, which is useful for caribou in a frozen environment, because a low-protein diet requires comparatively little water for digestion.

Yes, the caribou is superbly adapted to winter. Nevertheless, caribou still face danger and death from wolves that commonly follow them on their spring migration. Wolves had also obviously been using our trail, and the frozen foot of an unfortunate or unwary caribou lay disconsolately at the edge of the path.

I've often seen images like this on television. More often than not the narrator intones in an unctuous baritone that nature is harsh, unforgiving and ruthless. When the program features Arctic landscapes, with intense cold added to death, the language becomes even more emotive. The Arctic landscape becomes brutal or cruel or vicious. This is usually when I turn the television off. Such terms are judgmental and have no applicability to natural ecosystems. The wolf was not vicious. It was simply hungry. The cold is not brutal. The cold simply exists. Caribou are not cold at temperatures of -40 degrees. Caribou do not believe that the Arctic winter is brutal. Only humans use such terms. In fact, it is generally humans of temperate climates who make these inane television comments about Arctic landscapes.

For at least 60 centuries Arctic Canada was home to 300 generations of men, women, children, grandfathers and grandmothers. They played, laughed, lived, worked and died in a quiet world that provided food, clothing, shelter, beauty, joy and pride. If these people could somehow be magically transported through time to stand on the streets of Vancouver or Toronto, then certainly they would declare our congested, noisy, polluted cities as harsh. Perhaps they would walk down our streets, and see for themselves that homeless people went hungry, or froze to death on the sidewalk during cold winter nights. Undoubtedly they would wonder how this could happen when only a few metres away other people sat satiated in warm, cozy restaurants before returning to expansive houses that far exceeded their need for shelter. Perhaps then these time travellers from Arctic Canada would declare our southern cities to be brutal, unforgiving landscapes.

We reached the little narrow valley that we call Winter Camp II. Again we delighted in its idyllic beauty. The configuration of small frozen lakes, streams and shoreline appealed to us greatly. We decided to sneak up on the Ravens that lived on top of that ancient, gnarled spruce at the head of the small side stream. We wanted to see what they were up to. We would sit, or so we plotted, concealed in some nearby shrubs, and just observe what they were doing. Right. Real good plan. Sneak up on Ravens.

As soon as we began ascending the small tributary, the Ravens became aware of our approach. In contrast to our last visit though, the Ravens did not remain silent. They did not simply stare at us from within their nest. This time they took immediate flight, and never stopped voicing their displeasure. Even after 30 minutes they remained agitated, swooping over and around their nest, but never landing – calling out to each other all the while. It is likely that they were protecting their eggs or young family.

We should have known better. Reverend Henry Ward Beecher has been quoted as saying that, "If men had wings and bore black feathers, few of them would be clever enough to be crows." And Ravens are smarter than crows. Kathleen and I were severely overmatched. We slinked away.

For lunch we stopped on the south-facing bank of the stream, where we sat on dry, bare ground; a small rectangular patch, about 1 by 2 m, but dry ground nonetheless! The sweet scent of crushed White Spruce boughs made me long for summer, which certainly looms nearer. All along the river, open patches of ground punctuated the south-facing hillsides. Throughout the valley, the snow was now crusted, and often not more than 0.3 m deep.

Just as we neared the mouth of the river, near Colville Lake, we found a 1-m-long, 25-cm-diameter log of sawn White Spruce. Someone must have dropped it here last fall. A great find! I loaded it into the toboggan, and cut, split and stacked it as soon as we returned to the cabin. The 'new' wood should provide two additional evenings of warmth, between cribbage and bedtime. One can never have too much wood.

There was no wind today, and we felt very warm and comfortable outside at -4 degrees. Kathleen is now wearing her light, silk long johns, and talks about putting her heavy wool underwear away for the winter.

In the evening, a river otter played on the snow on the west shore opposite our cabin. Caribou are heading to their calving grounds. Ravens are guarding their young. Snow Buntings and Bohemian Waxwings have arrived in town. Kathleen and I are warm outside the cabin. Otters, caribou, Ravens, Snow Buntings, Bohemian Waxwings, Kathleen and me. We all sense that spring approaches.

Monday, April 26. In the late afternoon, before dinner, we returned to the open river. We snowshoed through a land seemingly divided against itself – a land seemingly uncertain of its future. The continuous north wind of the last six days, with its accompanying cold temperatures had refrozen some previously open sections. Yet the ground surrounding the trees, particularly larger trees on the west-facing bank, continues to expand, revealing Northern Labrador Tea, blueberries and Kinnikinnick. Common Juniper lies exposed on south-facing knolls. Even the east-facing ridge of the Ross River, the side of the ridge that has not yet enjoyed the light of the afternoon sun, is pockmarked with bowl-shaped cavities. For two weeks now we have seen a Bald Eagle soaring overhead. Snow Buntings flew past the cabin this morning. If only a southeast wind would appear for a week, then spring would surely rush forth to reclaim the land.

Just before dinner, at about 7:30 pm, a ski-doo raced into camp carrying Gene's son George, and a young woman named Snowbird. Very exciting to have visitors! George said that we should have warm weather in another week, with only one more cold snap, of 2 to 3 days, in May. "Ducks should arrive in two weeks. One of the first places they come is here, because the outlet of the lake is the first open water. You'll have a lot more visitors then, as people will be out hunting. They want to get fresh meat."

He also said that, "the ice will start coming away from the shore of Colville Lake in early June." That would be great. That means we might be able to paddle to town in only another six weeks or so.

While sipping tea, George also indicated that he and Snowbird (that's a beautiful name – given because she was born in spring, when the Snow Buntings arrived), along with several other younger people in town, will be going to Calgary next weekend as guests of some oil and gas companies. Apparently the companies have discovered significant reserves of oil or gas on native land around Colville Lake. George says that the elders are generally opposed to allowing drilling and development, whereas the younger people are more interested in the economic implications and opportunities. My understanding from what George said is that there must be a favourable vote by the entire community before development can begin. The companies will be providing all travel expenses, accommodation, meals and spending money for the weekend junket to Calgary. I leave it to you to draw your own conclusions about the likelihood that this development will proceed.

We thanked George and Snowbird for their visit, and welcomed them to drop by again, anytime they were in the area. We also gave them a bag of brown sugar and three kg of shortening for Gene, as gratitude for bringing us back to the cabin last week.

Tuesday, April 27. We snowshoed to Ketaniatue Lake, over the Connector, and then back up the river along Riverside Drive – approximately 12 km. Minus 19 degrees when we left, with a persistent northwest wind, but a gloriously clear day. The lower third of the river is now running free, nearly to Ketaniatue Lake. Large blocks of ice, 0.5 to 1 m thick, lay slumped, broken and strewn about the banks. Small, gravelly rapids sang joyously with freedom and light. The steepest, west-facing banks were shedding their winter cloaks of snow. But the cold weather persists. Minus 29 degrees last night, our second coldest recording of the month. I expect tonight's temperature will fall nearly as low, perhaps even lower. We tire of cold weather, now that spring is apparently so near.

Wednesday, April 28. I firmly believe that yesterday morning's -29 degrees is the coldest temperature that we will see during the rest of our stay at North End. A 20-km/hour southeast wind has blown all day, bringing an afternoon high of -4 degrees. I anticipate that the thermometer will remain above -15 degrees tonight.

The previous week of north winds caused the ice to re-form on previously open sections of water on Colville Lake. With just this single day of wind from the south, however, the new ice has begun to rot, and could easily disappear by tomorrow afternoon.

The snow continues to contract from around and beneath the orange tarp. I briefly poked about looking for deposits of wood, like a miner inspecting new diggings along veins of gold. My 'claim' does not seem to be paying as well as it once did, and this morning I cut down another tree for firewood. I'll probably have to re-stack the porch with wood on Saturday, and will have a better idea then of our remaining wood supply.

The wind died in the evening, and I stood on the dock, listening to the sucking and creaking of weakening, shifting plates of ice. The sun slid quietly north along the western ridge above the Ross River.

Thursday, April 29. I felled another tree today, and now have two on the ground. Both were approximately 6 m tall, with very little taper, and a diameter at the base of 25 to 30 cm. This new infusion of fuel will last only four to five days, but every extra day now becomes increasingly significant. The temperature at 8:30 pm remained a blistering -1 degree. With the south wind, I expect the temperature tomorrow to rise above freezing. Bare ground is expanding rapidly everywhere, as the snow continues to retreat.

In the afternoon, a group of 40 to 50 caribou walked down the lake. After a great deal of hesitation, false starts, and temporary retreats, they eventually turned east into the forest, *en route* to their calving grounds. It seemed they weren't quite convinced that it was time to head north.

Friday, April 30. The last day of the month and the weather is definitely warming. Plus 2 degrees at 5:00 pm, and still zero at 9:30. The day brought many indicators of spring. Large, wet flakes of snow falling heavily to earth. Snow Buntings flying north past the cabin. A Bald Eagle soaring above the river. Caribou migrating to the northeast. The aroma of moist earth permeating the air. More water opening up beneath the pier. Oh, it's happening now! Spring rushes north as winter retreats.

Just after 10:00 pm, Tommy and another younger man staying at the Tent Camp on the Big Island stopped by to borrow some salt. Tommy reports that ducks have arrived in Fort Good Hope. He expects no more cold snaps, and I believe him.

CHAPTER 10

Liⁿyatisa

Saturday, May 1. Liⁿyatisa: 'The Month of the Barking Dog.' I suppose that even the dogs must now recognize that spring is inevitable. The temperature fell only to -6 degrees last night, and the cabin interior, at sleeping height, registered +8 degrees at 7:00 am! We need almost no wood, comparatively speaking, to maintain cabin temperatures of 18 to 21 degrees. We often damp the stove completely down.

I bucked up most of the two trees I felled last week, and again re-stacked the wood on the porch. I believe that we have enough wood to take us through to the end of our stay here, but will make a more definitive assessment tomorrow, when I've brought all the wood back to camp. While snowshoeing back from the woodlot, I actually 'felt' like spring, which is no longer just a prediction or a concept or a hope or my fantasy. The day was warm and sunny.

The open water under the pier expanded even overnight, and opened up considerably more during the day. I stood on the pier in the evening, gazing at the water, which appeared so fresh and new and enticing. Snow Buntings passed overhead on their journey north. Whiskey Jacks foraged at the edge of the retreating snowpack, snapping up food morsels that had remained hidden since the first permanent snow of last October.

Shortly before 10:00 pm we heard a motor approaching from the south. Moments later we spotted a lone ski-doo, driving hard directly toward the open water at the outlet of Colville Lake. What was he doing? No one ever comes directly to the outlet. Even Ron, way back in February, headed to the shore before reaching the outlet. Everyone knows that the ice remains thin and dangerous at the outlet, even in mid-winter. Everyone knows that the outlet is open by May!

We ran down to the pier, waving our arms, and gesturing to the rider to head to his right. The ski-doo continued onward, unwavering, toward the outlet. We started shouting, jumping up and down, and waving even more wildly. Still the rider continued straight ahead. We finally caught his attention, less than 50 m from the open water, when he quickly veered right and charged his ski-doo up the bank below the cabin.

It was a young man, someone we had not seen in town. He had been drinking, and was quite unsteady. "Would you like to come inside, and have some tea?"

"Yep."

We sat down at the table, where our visitor, I'll call him 'Young Man,' became quite talkative. YM was about 25 years old, tall, muscular, and in the prime of his physical life. Although his English was rudimentary, we gleaned that he had been drinking with friends at the camp on the Big Island, when the discussion had turned to ski-dooing prowess. YM apparently claimed that he knew everything about travelling through the bush on ski-doo. Boasted that he could ski-doo down the Ross River, beyond where the river knifed through Colville Ridge. He could then skirt west behind the ridge, cross back over the ridge by a route that only he knew, and be back to the Tent Camp, after 25 km, in a time so short as to be unbelievable. Or something like that.

Needless to say, his friends expressed skepticism, even outright doubt. So here he was, drinking tea at our table, and determined to go on.

"I think your friends are right," I said, "We walk along the river almost every day. There's a lot of open water. The banks are steep in many places. It would be difficult for a ski-doo. I don't know where you want to cross, but pretty much the entire lower third of the river is completely open."

"You got map? I can show."

I spread the map out on the table. YM bent over, tracing his finger along the contours. We stood behind him, bent over his shoulder, eager to see where this secret trail might exist. We love trails. YM turned his head toward us and said, "I'm afraid."

"Why?" I thought that maybe he had forgotten where the route was, or that he had realized that his adventure might actually be dangerous.

Instead, YM simply said, "Never been all alone with white people before."

That answer surprised us. We had actually been feeling a little afraid ourselves. Kathleen and I are both physically small and no longer young. We were now all alone with a young, strong man who was drunk. A man whom we did not know. A man who might be unpredictable. And he was afraid of us. It seems that all three of us had become victims of stereotypes. All three of us were afraid of our suddenly unfamiliar circumstances.

"No need to be afraid of us. Would you like some more tea?"

YM continued to look at the map, and then asked, "Why you here?"

We told him that we had come at the end of January to enjoy the winter, and then to paddle down the Ross River to the Anderson River, and eventually to the Arctic coast. Now he became very interested in our map, and began to point to places along the river between our cabin and Ketaniatue Lake. "Shallow here. Rapids here. This part easy." He was eager to help – eager to help visitors in his neighbourhood.

YM then stood up and pulled out a knife that had a blade approximately 25 cm long. It was a big knife, used for skinning caribou and moose.

What the hell was happening now? He held the knife out toward us, and said, "Here. Gift. My grandmother make handle. I give to you."

This took me aback. It also worried me, perhaps more than if he had meant to stab us with the knife. He was drunk, and still very unsteady. So maybe we could have taken the knife away. Instead of physical confrontation though, I faced an awkward social situation. Should I take the knife that his grandmother made? If so, how would YM feel tomorrow morning, when perhaps he would want his knife back? What if I didn't take the knife? Would YM feel insulted? Worse yet, would YM become angry?

"Thanks very much. But I can't take your grandmother's knife. She made it for you, not for me. You need to keep the knife. To remember her by."

YM sheathed the knife, and sat back down. Maybe he was happy with my answer. He had made the offer. He had done the right thing by offering a gift to his visitor. I only speculate though, as YM said nothing.

Just before 11:00 o'clock, three ski-doos arrived. The men had come to retrieve YM. They couldn't stay for tea, but Tommy said he would stop by tomorrow.

Sunday, May 2. I finished bucking up and dragging in the felled tree, and then re-stacked the wood on the porch. I believe that enough wood remains under the tarp to re-stack again. In fact, there's likely more than enough. I also believe, and I write conservatively here, that at current consumption rates, each stack should last 18 to 20 days, for a total wood supply of 36 to 40 days. Assuming that we spend seven days going to and returning from town, we have enough wood at the cabin for 43 to 47 days. Assuming we head down river for the Arctic coast on June 20, we need 48 days of wood, which leaves a shortfall of only 1 to 5 days. And certainly, by June, we will need to burn much less wood to keep warm. I am so confident that we have enough wood that I have mentally 'put away' my saw and axe.

Kathleen is also confident that winter is over. She reorganized and re-packed our winter clothes, which are now ready to send to town and then on-ward to Inuvik. We also moved our sleeping bags down to the bottom bunks, where the cooler temperature at night is more comfortable for sleeping. It's also a lot easier to get in and out of bed, rather than climbing up and down the ladder. The ambience and atmosphere of the cabin has changed completely, as we enter a new phase of life here at North End.

Just before 5:00 pm, Bernard stopped by with Greg on the back of his ski-doo. They stayed for an hour, sipping tea and chatting. Greg, about 15 years old, asked if we had any alcohol.

"No, we didn't bring any. We just have tea, coffee, hot chocolate, or powdered orange juice."

Greg had also been looking through my binoculars. "Can I buy these?"

"I need them, Greg. I can't sell them to you. I wouldn't have any binoculars myself, then."

It seems that Greg just wanted to take something home, almost like he wanted to purchase a souvenir of his visit to North End.

Just after 6:30, four other ski-doos arrived, carrying eight teenagers. None of them stopped, or even waved hello, but spent 15 minutes careening around the camp like a biker gang on Harley-Davidson motorcycles. It was bedlam. Bern certainly wouldn't like this, and neither did I. This wasn't the kind of changed ambience that we had been looking forward to this morning. We're now too accessible to town. The ice on Colville Lake needs to melt completely. Only then will we be safe from marauding ski-doos. Only then will tranquillity be restored to North End.

Eventually one of the ski-doos backed into the flagpole, and I could hear a sharp *crack*. All four ski-doos circled around the pole a few times and roared off. Perhaps they had come to celebrate May Day, and had simply arrived one day late. Our first unwelcome visitors were perhaps simply observing the traditional May Day spring festival that celebrates human fertility and the renewal of nature.

The festival originated with the celebration of the Roman goddess Flora and spread to other countries of the Roman Empire. May Day was particularly popular in England during medieval times. Activities centred around the maypole, a tree collected from the woods and brought to the village to celebrate the upcoming summer. Certainly everyone in Colville Lake knows about Bern's flagpole. Ski-dooing out to a standing flagpole would be a lot easier than dragging in a tree from the bush. Sure, that's it. Our visitors were not being unruly; they simply came to celebrate May Day with us.

Everyone, perhaps especially teenagers, feels the unmistakable presence of approaching spring. They, like Kathleen and me, are just naturally excited by the carefree future before us.

My understanding of traditional May Day, the May Day before Puritans promoted morality, is that many people participated in temporary sexual encounters while they were off cavorting in the woods. Because of puritanical influence, the English Parliament banned May Day in 1644. Irrespective of any ban, though, Kathleen and I would not be off in the woods playing sexual hide-and-seek on this belated May Day. The temperature at 7:00 pm, although comparatively warm, was only -2 degrees. We're still keeping our clothes on when outside.

Monday, May 3. A gray, chilly (-2 degrees at 5:00 pm), cloudy day, with a persistent northeast wind. We stayed mostly indoors, where Kathleen organized summer canoeing gear while I wrote in my journal. For the first time I'm beginning to feel genuinely restless and impatient with winter. Now that the weather has warmed, I wish for a continual progression of increasing heat and retreating snow. I particularly wish for more open water. I chafe at even the minor setback of today.

Kathleen spotted a group of Willow Ptarmigan huddled out on the lake.

I imagine that they too are disappointed with today, and also wish for the ground to reappear completely so that they can finally put their snow-white plumages away for the winter.

Tuesday, May 4. Another dull, gray day, much of which we again spent indoors. We sat quietly at the table reading and writing. In the afternoon we snowshoed out to the woodlot to retrieve the last of the kindling from the felled trees. Ski-doos had travelled up Woodlot Way. They had even turned west to rumble along our own, private Riverside Drive. We no longer live alone in an isolated, boreal forest.

The ground continues to expand everywhere and multitudes of trees and shrubby twigs have 'sprung up' in the middle of our snow trails. On the south-facing knoll below the flagpole, Prickly Saxifrage has sprouted new leaves beneath its bright red leaves of last year. The snow next to the shore below our cabin is melting. Soon, perhaps, open leads will develop, through which we can paddle our canoe. For the past few days a muskrat has taken up residence at the base of the hill below our cabin, and it often sits on a ledge of ice, sunning itself next to the open water.

Wednesday, May 5. A sunny, encouraging day. We walked without snowshoes up the lake to the valley of Winter Camp II, and then back on Winter Camp Walk. While in the valley, we saw a pair of Northern Goshawks, and we lunched, lying on bare ground, in the afternoon sun. We were warm, even at -6 degrees, as long as we sat sheltered from the strong, southeast wind.

Tommy and Terry visited in late afternoon. Tommy is living at the Tent Camp on the Big Island. Terry will be returning to town this evening, and we gave him our mail. Very little snowmelt occurred today, although even a little progress hastens the arrival of spring.

Thursday, May 6. Another day of cold, strong winds. Compared to the temperatures of February and March, however, the day was quite warm, with a high of -4 degrees at 5:00 pm. Nonetheless, we want thaw, and will be satisfied with nothing else.

We talked to Margaret during the seven o'clock radio call, as Bern has been away since April 30. She says that James and Sharon will be bringing our mail to the Tent Camp, so we plan to visit them tomorrow. We haven't walked to the Tent Camp since we dragged to town on April 15, nearly three weeks ago. Maybe this little excursion will help to raise our spirits. We need to get out more. I'm not saying we are suffering from the mythical cabin fever, but we do seem to be in a funk.

With Bern away, I hoped that Margaret might be willing to ease up on the daily requirement to call in. I still object to the regimen to be at home at precisely seven o-clock everyday. It's just too much routine and regimentation. And maybe Margaret would also like to be freed from the daily routine of receiving our call.

"You know, Margaret, we've been here over four months and nothing bad has happened. The days are warm, and it's much less likely that we'll get into any trouble. Why don't we call in every other day instead of every day?"

Her response was quick. She didn't even think about it. "No, it's best if you call every day. We need to make sure every day that you're OK."

Oh well, I tried.

Friday, May 7. A clear morning made to feel cold by the strong, persistent southeast wind. We dallied and lingered in the cabin, waiting for warmer, calmer conditions before heading out to the Tent Camp. After lunch we acknowledged that we had sunk to a pathetic state. We had become downright faint-hearted. Two months ago we happily went out at -30 degrees even with a strong wind. Now we seek shelter from the wind at only -5 degrees. We have become soft and timid. How quickly our perspective has changed to accommodate current conditions.

After a suitable self tongue-lashing, we set out for the Tent Camp at 12:45. Just before the first island portage, about 200 m up the trail, we saw a lone figure jumping up and down wildly, like a man swatting at a swarm of stinging bees. Everyone we had met since arriving at North End was invariably calm, no matter what the situation. No one ever became excitable or demonstrative. My first reaction was "what's a white guy doing way out here?" This thought struck me as somewhat ironic, as I myself was a white guy, and I was way out here. Irony aside, the agitated person up ahead was certainly not from around here.

As we approached, the man started coming up the trail toward us, carrying a briefcase, which confirmed my first impression. Has to be a white guy.

By then the stranger saw us, and waited for us to join him, where he stood beside his four-wheeler, which had become stuck in the deep snow next to the ski-doo trail.

"Hi," I said. "My name's Mike. This is my wife Kathleen."

The man held out his hand and said, "I know. My name's Jamie. I'm the resource conservation officer in Norman Wells, and was in town, so thought I would come out and visit you. My machine is stuck, though. I was going to walk the rest of the way. It's not very far is it?"

"No, not too far. So how come you're riding a four-wheeler?"

"Ski-doos break down a lot in warm weather. I'm more used to four-wheelers anyway, and it worked fine when I was on the ice on Colville Lake. I didn't expect so much snow though, after the Big Island."

"So did you happen to bring any mail for us? We were going to the Tent Camp to get mail that Margaret Brown said would be there for us."

"No, I was just coming straight to your cabin. I didn't stop at the camp. I do have a *Mackenzie Valley View* newspaper and an *Up Here* magazine for you, though."

"Thanks very much. It's always nice to get reading material. It's still about 2 km to our cabin, and the snow is deep in spots. Why don't we just help you get unstuck, and we can all go back to the Tent Camp?"

So with all three of us straining, we pushed the four-wheeler back up onto the hard-packed ski-doo trail and continued to the camp, where we enjoyed three hours of chatting and drinking coffee and tea in Tommy's wall tent. James and Sharon had moved their camp 1 km across the bay to where they are building a cabin on the mainland. They had left four pieces of mail for us, a primary reason for today's 12-km round trip.

The travelling conditions on the way out to the Tent Camp, even without snowshoes, were fairly good. The snow crust was firm, and we broke through only a few times. On our return to the cabin, however, the snow had softened in the plus two-degree heat, and we repeatedly broke through. Even so, we persevered without putting on our snowshoes. We're tired of using them, particularly as the lamp wick bindings seem to work themselves loose quickly in the warmer weather. And indeed, the days are definitely warmer. Even at 10:00 pm the temperature was still zero degrees.

Saturday, May 8. I'm willing to say that spring arrived today. The temperature remained warm overnight, falling only to -2 degrees. The cabin interior this morning was +8 degrees even before lighting the fire. The most excitement though, occurred when we went outside this morning and saw eight Herring Gulls sitting on the ledge of ice normally frequented by the muskrat. We listened all morning to the sound of their calls during flight, which undeniably announces to us that spring has arrived. How many more bird species must be on their way right now?

In the afternoon Tommy rode up on his ski-doo and asked, "Have you seen any geese or swans?"

"No, we haven't, but we have seen Herring Gulls."

"Well, I saw some geese fly over the Tent Camp this morning. You should see them soon."

Tommy wasn't interested in Herring Gulls. He was carrying a shotgun, and drove off looking for fresh, succulent meat. About 30 minutes later four Canada Geese arrived, and as we stood in the warm afternoon sun with our binoculars, we saw a shorebird on the edge of the ice. Too far away to know what species of shorebird, but it was probably a Greater Yellowlegs. A large pan of ice, the largest pan of ice so far, maybe 7 m in diameter, broke free from the shore and floated off down the Ross River. We reached our highest temperature of the winter, +6 degrees at 4:00 pm. A solitary housefly buzzed happily on the west-facing side of the cabin, soaking up the sun's warmth.

By mid-evening, 20 Herring Gulls sat on the edge of the ice, hunkered down, facing into the southeast wind. Behind the cabin, in the lower branches of a White Spruce tree, a small spider dangled in the air, spinning its web. We also saw a Northern Hawk Owl hovering near the top of the pole supporting the radio antennae wire. Although the Northern Hawk Owl is a resident species, we had not yet seen it this winter. It is as though the owl simply wanted to join the crescendo of life reappearing before our eyes.

Kathleen's feelings about the last two days are summarized below:

Yesterday it was obvious that everything had changed. Although the overnight temperature still fell below zero, and although we still gazed out at a frozen, white expanse on Colville Lake, I felt that winter was over. As we walked to the Tent Camp, the air felt warm despite the strong wind. People have been out and about for the last couple of weeks and yesterday we met Jamie, who told us that the ice moved 200

metres on the Mackenzie River at Fort Simpson a day or two
ago. Norman Wells should see movement in a week. The ice
bridges on the Peel and Mackenzie Rivers on the Dempster
Highway are closed. It is happening and you can feel
everyone's excitement. The snow is soft and wet. The sound
of dripping is everywhere, and puddles sit in the hollows.
The sun is setting close to midnight and daylight now extends
for 24 hours. The thaw we see today will only escalate. Yes.
Everything has changed.

Sunday, May 9. The day broke sunny and warm – zero degrees at 8:00 am. After breakfast we sat outside, feeling warm. Three Tundra Swans landed in The Narrows. Paddling season might arrive soon. I could wait no longer, and walked over to where my canoe had been resting upside down on log rails since February. Before shipping the canoe north I had taken out most of the screws that held the wooden gunwales to the plastic hull. Wood and plastic expand and contract at differential rates, and extreme cold occasionally causes cracking in plastic hulls if the wooden gunwales are too tight. I rummaged through our repair kit, found the small jar of screws, reattached the gunwales, and carried our canoe down to the shore.

We paddled twice around our little section of open water. We didn't stay out long, only about 15 minutes; but it was so exciting to finally be paddling.

A great deal more open ground appeared today, as did many more flies. Three formations of Tundra Swans, approximately 200 birds, passed overhead in the late afternoon, flying northward in loose, V-formations. Bohemian Waxwings also arrived to feed on juniper and Kinnikinnick berries on the south-facing knoll below the flagpole. Only two days ago these berries had still been buried by snow.

Ski-doos raced back and forth all day, although no one stopped by for tea, or to visit. They were all much too absorbed in their spring ritual of hunting geese and swans.

The evening was calm, clear and warm, at +6 degrees, and I paddled the canoe solo, from 10:30 to 11:30 pm. I drifted beneath a low-angled sun, staring into the mirrored reflection of open water. The muskrat eased itself off the bank, and swam to the opposite shore. Geese called overhead. I glided across the black surface of the water, mesmerized by rocks slipping silently beneath my passing canoe. Effortless, graceful movement. I have enjoyed snowshoeing, but I now want to paddle down the Anderson River to the Arctic coast.

[*Author's Note:* Yes, I now spend much of my time thinking about paddling to the Arctic coast, and of the previous canoe trips Kathleen and I have enjoyed in Canada's Far North. The next few pages summarize the allure, romance, adventure and true contentment that we always experience when paddling all alone down a remote, pristine river. If you wish, feel free to skip this reflective essay, jumping ahead to continue reading our winter story.]

Floating Free – An Interlude

My thoughts drifted back to our previous canoe trips in northern Canada, when Kathleen and I stood on float plane docks watching the deck crew cram our gear into the cramped cargo area of a Cessna 185. We would have just driven to the end of the road at Fort Smith, or Yellowknife, or Lynn Lake. I love the end of the road, and all that it signifies. Beyond the end of the road there is no more concrete – no more houses – no more incessant noise of machines and motors. Beyond the end of the road there still exists earth on which to walk. Beyond the end of the road there still exists natural sand beaches on which to camp. Beyond the end of the road there still exists pristine quiet within which to rest and to rediscover tranquillity. We became canoeists for all these reasons.

I especially remember the time we flew to Lynx Lake, at the outlet to the Thelon River. Our first trip to the North by ourselves. We would spend the next six weeks all alone, in a region about which we had no information and no guidebooks. Six weeks down an unknown river with no communities along its 950 km to Baker Lake on Chesterfield Inlet of Hudson Bay. A marvellous adventure that thankfully still exists in our modern world of insatiable, ever-expanding city-states chained together with permanently clogged six-lane highways.

No matter which river we travel, though, our canoe journeys are similar, and usually begin the same way. Kathleen and I climb into the loaded plane and fasten our seat belts. Moments later the plane lifts off the water, and banks gradually toward a distant northern horizon. Except for the loud drone of the engine, we fly in self-reflective silence. Below us, an exquisite jumble of lakes, forest and flowing water stretch peacefully toward the junction of earth and sky. Somewhere beyond that threshold, the Thelon or Coppermine or Seal or Snowdrift River waits for our arrival. The actual name of the river matters not at all. In fact, we could simply call it The River. We just want to be on a river, any river that flows to a distant northern horizon.

A few hours into the flight the forest thins and then nearly disappears. Just ahead, just beyond tree line, a sensuously curved lake emerges. The pilot descends toward its outlet, peering intently into the shallow, transparent water.

"No rocks," he declares confidently over the headphones. "We can land near shore."

A few moments later our pilot stands on the left pontoon, pushing the plane to shore with an aluminum pole. Kathleen and I jump lightly onto the sandy beach, and quickly help unload our gear and supplies.

The pilot usually then says something like, "Nice spot. Gotta go. Good luck."

These bush pilots always seem to be in such a hurry. They have goods to deliver. People to transport. Bills to pay. Our pilot poles the Cessna 185 back out into deeper water. Only a few minutes later the plane begins its taxi down the lake, and lifts lightly into the northwest wind. It circles back, flies low over our beach, tips its wings in farewell, and withdraws slowly toward the southwest.

People often ask us how we feel when the plane leaves us behind. People usually expect that we feel abandoned, forlorn, or apprehensive. We actually feel just the opposite. It is only now that our adventure can truly begin. It is only now that can we can enjoy a life of complete freedom and confidence that springs from the beauty of uncertainty. We feel liberated. We don't know where we will camp each night; but we know unquestionably that each day will end warm and dry in our tent. We don't know exactly when we will actually arrive at our destination; but we know positively that our paddling skills and experience will take us to the end of The River.

The River will be our home and constant companion for the next four weeks or so. We also know that for the next four weeks our health, success, happiness and safety will depend entirely on our own decisions and personal judgment. We have escaped the confinement, shackles and false security of modern society. We take no cell phones. No satellite phones. We acknowledge that such technology can provide a measure of safety; but the price is too high. Instant communication shrinks the wilderness. Instant communication obliterates the purity of isolated independence that we crave. Instant communication contradicts the freedom of personal responsibility. Instant communication would sap the strength that we derive from vulnerability.

We watch and listen to the float plane drone much too slowly toward the south. Suddenly it vanishes from sight and hearing, and we stand – all alone and confident – beyond the edge of our known world. Our spirits soar with excitement and anticipation. We stroll down the shore, which curves, like the delicate crescent of a new moon, toward the bottom of a small cove. At the end of this quiet embayment the shoreline turns gently east around a low bluff projecting into the lake. Here the lake narrows, and small undulations ripple its smooth surface. The River! Finally, after a long winter of preparing food, organizing gear, studying maps, dreaming, and just plain waiting, we are once again on The River.

We scramble up the 2-m bank onto the tundra, which sweeps away gently and elegantly to the northern horizon. The land, and all its inhabitants, basks in the calm, soothing warmth of the afternoon sun. At our feet lies a gracefully rolling prairie clothed in a thin mosaic of Alpine Azaleas, Cloudberries, Bog Blueberries, lichens and mosses. Like a true Garden of Eden, nurtured by immutable laws of nature, our gigantic, granite rockery extends forever outward in reassuring, timeless continuity. Every plant in its place, without human intrusion or interference. No pruning. No mowing. No fertilizing. Simple perfection. Horned Larks and Lapland Longspurs sing to us as we stroll, silently and side-by-side, to the lake's outlet – to the birthplace of The River.

We stand on the bluff point above The River. A gradually-sloping, white-sand beach fringed in White Spruce adorns the north bank. Just downstream The River turns to disappear northeast around an esker point, beyond which 30 days of unknown adventures wait for our descent tomorrow morning. I turn my gaze far beyond the esker point toward the distant northern horizon

– a tangible goal that will dominate our physical and our mental journey. The distances, however, are vast; and no matter how far or how long we travel each day, the horizon will continually recede before us. The secrets and beauty that are surely hidden just beyond this elusive destination will beckon to us throughout our entire journey. The perfect canoe adventure would be to paddle northward forever, without ever reaching the end of The River.

Eventually one of us breaks the languid stillness by pointing out that we need to make camp and cook dinner. I love the routine of camp chores. The regular, predictable sequence of activities provides immediate comfort and continuity in what is otherwise a completely unknown landscape. We lug the packs up onto the low ridge, away from the lake's shore. I dig out a fire pit in the sand, collect kindling and wood, and place a pot of water on the grate for tea. After putting up the tent, Kathleen joins me at the fire to prepare dinner. Throughout these mundane but necessary tasks, a proud family of Common Loons often promenades along our shore, yodelling confidently in their joyous freedom. I know how they feel. I too am very glad to be back in the North, far beyond the end of the road.

An inukshuk stands silently on the ridge overlooking the lake. Perhaps it was built to guide travellers to The River flowing out of the lake's outlet. So many Canadians tell us that they prefer to vacation in Europe, because of its long history and established civilizations. Canada, we are told, suffers by comparison. Conventional belief is that Canada has no old structures or history.

Such a blatant misconception is unfortunate and regrettable. Inuksuit have been erected at thousands of locations all across Canada, a truth that confirms our nation's very long history. I remember one time on Whitefish Lake, only one day's paddle from the overland route to the Snowdrift River. We had battled very strong headwinds all day, but made about 25 km before stopping at 6:30 in the evening. From our camp we looked across a channel toward an esker bathed in sunlight. This particular esker had occupied its position for 6,000 years, ever since the great glaciers melted. For much of that time this sinuous ridge of gravel and sand has been used by the Inuit as a base from which to hunt caribou that annually cross Whitefish Lake here, in water only one metre deep. As many as 10,000 native artifacts have been discovered on this esker, which makes it an enduring cultural site more permanent, and much older, than any of the grand edifices of Europe. Older even than the Great Wall of China. Older by nearly half again than the pyramids of Egypt.

The native peoples of Canada lived in a northern climate that did not permit agriculture and sedentary life. Permanent cities or homes would have been useless to a society that needed to travel seasonally to procure food such as caribou, seals, salmon, walrus and whales. The absence of highways, grand walls and grandiose churches in no way cheapens or diminishes the intensity and longevity of their civilization. On the banks of The River, we can still physically see and experience their camps and burial sites. Here on the banks of The River I can easily imagine the reverence these people must have felt for a homeland that provided all of life's necessities.

I often feel an emotional link to these original people of Canada's North. As they must have wondered long before me, I wonder what kinds of conditions Kathleen and I will experience on our journey. This is a special moment for all wilderness adventurers. A moment when everything is unknown. A moment when everything is also possible. How many rapids will we encounter? How many days will we paddle beneath warm sun or drenching rain? How often will we be confined to camp by the notorious winds that rise up out of the Arctic Ocean near the mouth of the Coppermine River, and then sweep diagonally across the continent to rest in the boreal forest at the foot of Hudson Bay? How many nights will we glide effortlessly across perfectly tranquil lakes, paddling by compass bearing beneath the soft glow of perpetual twilight?

At the end of our first night on northern canoe trips we generally seek the security of our tent soon after dinner. We rest on our elbows, drinking tea, and studying topographic maps. For seemingly the first time we realize that the maps indicate at least two dozen rapids between the beginning of The River and its mouth. We always seem to gloss over these potential difficulties when examining the maps at home.

Outside the tent, like embers fanned by a peaceful breeze, the crimson and ochre tundra glows softly beneath the slanting rays of a sun that will never set during our mid-summer sojourn on The River. A satisfied pair of Sandhill Cranes rattles happily from their nearby nest. Mosquitoes buzz harmlessly just beyond the protective netting of our tent doors. A slight breeze wafts warmly from the southeast. Sleep comes slowly and leisurely. Tomorrow we will finally descend The River! Our adventure is just beginning. Our story and its ending remain unknown.

The warmth of a new day slips through the open south-facing door of the tent and touches my face shortly before 5:00 am. I wake relaxed and excited. I eagerly pull on my nylon river pants, lace up my leather boots, and step outside. Except for mist that rises fleetingly from the lake's glassy surface, the entire world sits motionless, as though mentally preparing itself for the new day.

While Kathleen slumbers, I begin another ritual that brings stability and comfort. I collect a few handfuls of dead Crowberry, which had only recently been uprooted from its lakeside terrace by the irresistible power of ice struggling to free itself from the land. The fiery red, needle-like leaves easily flame at the touch of my match, and quickly ignite the twigs of willow placed on top. I soon add a few larger stems of spruce, arrange the grate over the developing fire, and retrieve our kitchen bucket from beneath the overturned canoe.

At the lake I fill a pot with water and place it over the fire. A few minutes later I toss a tea bag into the steaming, boiling bubbles and call out to Kathleen that the tea is nearly ready. I now open a baggy of bannock mixture, pour in 3/4 of a cup of water, and rewind the twist-tie. Twenty-five minutes later, I divide the golden, skillet-sized bannock into two sumptuous portions. I then cut my share into two pieces, and slice one of them open into its top and bottom halves. Kathleen performs the same surgery on her steaming breakfast. The containers of margarine and jam sit exactly halfway between us. For the next 30 minutes we lounge in the sunshine, devouring our bannock, sucking our fingers, smacking our lips, sipping our tea, and mumbling obvious, comfortable banalities. We have ample time to fully enjoy our breakfast, as there are no buses to catch, no meetings to attend, no deadlines or timetables to meet.

All the while, The River, ever patient, ever ready, continues to flow away from the lake's outlet. It's time to begin our adventure. It's time to be on The River. It's time to pack up and go.

Breaking camp provides yet another satisfying ritual. Kathleen had already stuffed our sleeping bags before breakfast. I now take down the tent while she washes and puts away the dishes, and boils another pot of water. Kathleen fills one thermos with tea and a second thermos with hot water for soup at lunch. We then pack and cinch the three canoe packs, and carry all our gear, including canoe, down the bank to the water's edge.

Hand-over-hand, across my thighs, I slide our canoe gently into the lake, where it floats, proud and high, poised to begin the imminent descent. We load the three packs into the centre of our canoe, and lodge one white bucket into the bow and a second white bucket into the stern. I place my fishing pole and folding saw along the left gunwale, forward of the stern cane seat. Kathleen positions the spare paddles along the right gunwale, rearward of the bow cane seat. We then fit the spray deck into place with snaps on the underside of the wooden gunwales. We string our binoculars around our necks, don our PFDs and paddling shoes, and step into the canoe.

We push off with our paddles from the lake's rocky bottom, and drift lazily outward from shore. For a few moments neither of us moves or speaks, as our canoe slides silently toward the opposite shore, where three Red-throated Loons wail bewitchingly.

"Are you ready?"

"Yes. Let's go."

Kathleen draws right while I apply a sculling draw on the left. Our canoe gracefully turns its bow to the east. With a few easy forward strokes we reach the outlet and moving water. Without a word we both rest our paddles across the gunwales. The River has been waiting for us. It reaches up, cradles our canoe in an affectionate embrace, and bears us away toward an unknown world far beyond the distant northern horizon.

For a few suspended moments we sit motionless, exhilarated by movement without effort, elated by the fluid, unceasing energy of The River. As though by magic The River carries us beyond the first bend, away from the outlet, away from our camp, and away from our past.

The River runs briskly between two eskers – long, sinuous ridges of sand and gravel deposited in melt channels within the massive glaciers that ruled this land only 18,000 years ago. Below us, submerged beneath the clear, vibrant, green water, lays a sheet of limestone rocks, sedimentary remnants of a great, Palaeozoic inland sea that covered this land 500 million years ago. To our right, scattered across the tundra, we see pink and gray granite outcroppings of the Canadian Shield, all that now remains of a magnificent mountain range that once rose majestically above this land 2.5 billion years ago.

Through all this geological upheaval and change, The River flows inevitably onward, confident in its strength – comfortable with its destiny. Kathleen and I now share that destiny, and feel that strength. Our canoe, The River and we have become indistinguishable. What befalls to The River will also befall to us. It is time to paddle, to accept our just portion of responsibility for the journey.

In unison, we extend our paddles forward, me on the left, Kathleen on the right. We plant our vertical blades fully into The River, and pull, top hand punching through the stroke. As the shaft passes our hips, we remove the paddles, feather the dripping blades forward, extend and plant again. Extend, plant, pull, remove and feather. Our muscles fall easily into the fluid routine of paddling. Forty-five strokes per minute; 2,700 strokes per hour; 16,200 strokes per six-hour day. Over the next 30 days Kathleen and I will both extend, plant, pull, remove and feather 486,600 times. We'll certainly be leaner and stronger by the end of the journey.

Rhythmically, hypnotically, we repeat the process throughout the morning – both of us absorbed in our private, personal communication with The River. A seductive morning moving across golden-green, shallow water, broken occasionally by black, impenetrable depths. Extend, plant, pull, remove, feather.

"Switch," Kathleen requests from the bow, to rest her paddle-weary side. Now I paddle on the right, Kathleen on the left. So satisfying in its simplicity. So rewarding in its effectiveness. Unnoticed, the morning and the distance pass away behind us.

"Look, Michael! Up ahead. I think I see a straight line of white across The River. That's gotta be a ledge. You didn't mention anything about a ledge last night."

I shrugged. "The maps didn't indicate any rapids or portages for about another six km. Let's pull out into that eddy on river left and have a look."

We angle our canoe toward the inside bend, just above where The River plunges over a 2-m drop. As our bow crosses the eddy line next to shore, Kathleen plants her paddle in a stationary draw, around which The River easily turns our canoe up into the calm water. We tie the bow line securely to a clump of riverside willows, and saunter downstream.

The limestone ledge extends all the way across The River. At the base of the drop, The River boils back toward the ledge in an infinite cycle of dangerous, re-circulating water that would likely trap a capsized swimmer. Time to portage.

Back at our canoe we leisurely unsnap the spray deck, lift the three canoe packs out onto the tundra, and change into our hiking boots. We have repeated this drill many times before, and the familiar routine seems pleasurable. Dare I say it? Another very comfortable, very reassuring routine. Kathleen attaches the paddles, fishing pole and folding saw to the green pack, and heads down the bank beneath her load. I soon follow with the light blue pack, carrying the two white buckets in my hands. Kathleen then returns for the dark blue pack. Moments later I arrive back at our canoe, which I lift onto my shoulders and soon deposit with the rest of our gear on the beach below the ledge.

After a brief rest, we change back into our river shoes. We then load the three packs into the centre of our canoe, and lodge one white bucket into the bow and a second white bucket into the stern. I place my fishing pole and folding saw along the left gunwale, forward of the stern cane seat. Kathleen positions the spare paddles along the right gunwale, rearward of the bow cane seat.

It was at the end of a portage just like this on the Starvation River, late one summer a few years ago, that we witnessed our most spectacular herd of caribou. They approached the right bank, and the leading members of the herd halted momentarily before plunging into The River. The rest quickly followed, in loose, single-file groups. From our secluded position, only 200 m away, we crouched, mesmerized by this greatest remaining spectacle of mammal migration on the North American continent.

An hour later, the last members of this swarming, purposeful herd scrambled up the left bank, shook The River from their coats, and continued across the tundra landscape toward their traditional wintering grounds. Seconds later the northern vastness again lay empty and still.

The River now sweeps forward in long arcs, and we run with the strength of the current from outside bend to outside bend. We paddle without speaking, as life on The River requires few words. We live in a physical realm of sun and sky, of water and horizon. Kathleen and I breathe the same air, and feel the same breeze upon our faces. Completely unlike our often-separate lives in Vancouver, on The River we are truly a couple, striving perfectly together toward a shared purpose and a common goal.

Simultaneously, we hear the tumult of an approaching rapid where The River narrows and falls through a sharply-curving S-bend. Together Kathleen and I concentrate on the same route through the rock-strewn boulder garden. Together, as though with a single pair of eyes, Kathleen and I see the same flashing, dissipating haystacks at the bottom of the bend, which signifies security at the end of this short stretch of white and foam.

The River now widens and flattens to meander slowly through a limitless landscape with neither beginning nor end. Transfixed in time and space, we float free in a breathless, sensory world – we exist simply and solely for the pleasures and demands of the moment.

We paddle slowly along the lee shoreline, assessing the many possible locations for lunch. We eventually select a small inlet formed by a sedimentary shelf jutting a few metres into The River. Smooth sandstone, scraped and polished by glacial ice, slopes gently upward from the water's edge. From shallow pools and crevices, prostrate, Net-veined Willows politely hold their fuzzy 'pussy-willow' flowers only a few centimetres above the very thin pockets of nurturing soil.

Kathleen pours a package of noodles into our cups and adds hot water from the thermos. A few minutes later, satiated with soup and crackers, we lie down on the smooth sandstone. With arms and legs splayed outward, and with hats pulled down to shield our faces from the sun, we bathe in the vibrant radiance of the Arctic summer. With the willows at our side, we share in the life-giving warmth of rock heated by the afternoon sun. I wonder how many people, both ancient and modern, have napped on our current lunch spot that we presumptuously called our own. I wonder about their dreams and visions as they progressed down The River toward their secluded world beyond the ever-distant northern horizon.

We return to our canoe and ferry upward and outward into the current. The River reaches up, takes hold of our bow, and swings us easily downstream. Above our heads, Arctic Terns whirl and dart like garden butterflies, and then suddenly dive steeply toward The River in pursuit of aquatic insects and the fry of trout and grayling.

The terns, perhaps the world's greatest wanderers, had arrived only weeks before us from the southern tip of South America, 17,000 km away. Like us, they had flown to the perpetual northern light that now shines upon The River. Like them, we had flown irresistibly north, not fully knowing our fate, but confident that The River would provide for all our needs and aspirations. Water for drinking. Fish for dinner whenever we might wish. Driftwood for cooking and warmth.

We continue paddling onward, again in contented silence. Even after a winter of inaction, our muscles already respond more willingly to the day's tasks. The physical exertion now feels exhilarating. Extend, plant, pull, remove, feather. Me on the left, Kathleen on the right. To the southeast, thunderclouds rise skyward in huge, flat-bottomed pillars. A portentous wind drifts across the tundra, but only slightly ripples the surface of The River, which rolls onward toward the secret world that waits beyond the ever distant northern horizon.

The River also brings excitement and challenge. Up ahead the land drops away, and The River pours through narrow, high banks that seemingly stand at the very edge of the world. We paddle cautiously along the inside bend of the left bank, round the point, and then see a 1-km-long island of gravel and willow that splits The River into twin sets of foreboding, turbulent ribbons of white. We eddy out, wrap the bow line around a large, streamside boulder, and hike down the bank to scout the rapids.

We walk single-file, without speaking, both of us independently assessing the cascading challenge before us. The River glows beneath the lengthening, sunlit shadows of early evening. Golden-green tongues of water surge through an armada of impassive, dark, angular, rocky outcrops. Curling sheets of foam sparkle throughout.

"What do you think, Kathleen? Do you want to run or portage?"

"I think we can run this, Michael; but let's have a look at the rest of the drop."

"I agree. The map shows a small cove where we might eddy out about halfway down."

We continue along the north bank, planning our intended route. "I think this rapid requires only two moves, Kathleen. First we need to make a strong ferry out to the eddy behind the large rock at the top of the rapid. From there we can drift by the first jumble of rocks next to shore. Then we need to drive hard back to the left to avoid the ledge in the centre of the channel."

Kathleen nods. "I was thinking the same thing. After that we should be able to sneak along the left shore. The rest of that entire stretch down to the cove seems to have downstream Vs between all the rocks."

We head back to our canoe, turning around frequently to memorize the changing perspective of our checkpoints throughout the run. "See that grey-ish-looking, pyramid-shaped rock? We've got to stay just right of that before beginning to head back left. If we head back any sooner, we'll never get through that first wall of rocks."

"I see it. Are you confident with our choice to paddle this?"

"Yes."

"Let's go, then."

Back in our canoe we stretch our spray skirts snugly over the cowling of the spray deck 'cockpits.' We glance back one last time down the rapid, pick up our whitewater paddles, and then sit quietly, facing upstream. Kathleen on the left, me on the right. As usual, at the beginning of every difficult rapid, my mouth dries like a discarded chunk of styrofoam baking in the summer sun. "It's your lean, Kathleen."

"I know. You just make sure you're powering hard when we cross the eddy line."

We take a deep breath and insert our blades fully into The River. With short, purposeful strokes, our canoe ratchets up to the top of the eddy. We cross the eddy line at full speed, angled slightly outward, both of us leaning lightly downstream. The racing current grabs the hull of our canoe, from bow to stern, and propels us outward, across The River, toward the mid-channel eddy below the entry rock. With a few forward strokes we rest safely in the haven of our first checkpoint. On either side of us The River churns in a nerve-jangling, clamorous din.

We cock our heads downstream, searching for the greyish-looking, pyra-mid-shaped rock. "There it is," said Kathleen, "but it certainly seems a lot more in river centre, and closer to the ledge than when we were standing on shore."

"Things always look different from The River. Do you want to leave the eddy on river right or river left?"

Seconds later we re-enter the rock-studded maelstrom, slowly working our way down to the greyish-looking, pyramid-shaped rock. We ride a narrow tongue of green water between two rounded boulders, slip past the greyish-looking, pyramid-shaped rock, and angle our canoe toward the left bank. The ledge looms ominously, its jaws wide open, only four canoe lengths below.

"Forward. Forward. More power!"

Knifing through the eddy below the greyish-looking, pyramid-shaped rock, our canoe speeds toward the left shore. "OK. Enough power. We're by the ledge. Let's straighten out."

We now run with the current along the shore, slowing our descent by side-slipping into eddies below scattered rocks that offer clear, obvious passages. Less than a minute later we easily glide into the shallow, still water of the welcome cove. Halfway through. Only 0.5 km to go.

I stand up to scan the rest of the rapid. "This doesn't look so bad, Kathleen. Not many rocks at all. Mostly shallow gravel bars, and some standing waves no more than a metre high. Do you want to get out and scout?"

"No. Let's just go."

Back in the current, The River rushes forward with unrestrained eagerness. Our canoe bounces and rocks as we romp through the haystacks toward the bottom of the island, which suddenly appears to our right. With a final burst of speed, accompanied by a climactic crescendo of water crashing over the bow, the current hurls us out of the rapid.

Our canoe floats casually away, into a world of calm and quiet. Seconds later the twin channels merge unceremoniously and The River resumes its inevitable passage toward my mystical world beyond the distant northern horizon.

Kathleen and I are genuinely pleased with ourselves every time we paddle such a rapid successfully. And I certainly understand why so many modern outdoor adventurers in documentaries, magazines and books commonly use phrases like 'beating' or 'defeating' a rapid. I am always disappointed by the popular notion, however, that wild places are a battleground between man and nature – a place to enhance human egos. The wilderness – and The River – simply exist; they do not pursue victory over human adversaries. I seek solace and sanctuary in wild places, and I wish that all visitors to Canada's North would simply allow nature to prevail, without being subjected to conquest.

Our challenges in rapids are uplifting, fulfilling and nurturing. Because we are generally alone, only our decisions matter. No external forces influence the outcome. Together we decide to run a rapid. Together we plan our route. Together we execute our plan. Entering the rapid we know – with only a very little doubt – that we will succeed. During the descent, our minds focus exclusively on the rapid. No time for multi-tasking. We are completely alive and absorbed by the moment, thoroughly committed to the single task at hand. Such is the immediate intimacy with time and place that we always enjoy when paddling a wild, Northern river.

Safely below a rapid, we know – without any doubt – that we, and we alone, have achieved our success. Very affirming. Very satisfying. We usually glance back upstream briefly, just long enough to imprint upon our minds the relative difficulty of what we have just paddled. The information will be essential for gauging future rapids that we will certainly encounter. Satisfied, we stow our whitewater paddles beneath the spray deck, take up our cherry wood, otter tail paddles, and resume the journey toward our mystical world that calls out to us from beyond the distant northern horizon.

"So, Michael. When do you want to start looking for a place to camp?"

"Any time now. I'm getting a bit hungry."

We beach our canoe, unsnap the spray deck, and carry our canoe packs, white buckets, fishing pole, folding saw, paddles and canoe up onto a tundra ridge where we can watch the nighttime sun roll along the northern horizon. While Kathleen sets up the tent and prepares our sleeping gear, I collect wood and create a kitchen area with smooth, flat stones for counter tops. We soon rest in the comfort of our flickering fire – sipping tea and dining on shepherd's pie.

Below camp, The River flows smoothly into twilight, murmuring softly against the cobblestone shoreline. Too exhilarated for rest or sleep, I stroll downstream along the ridge, eager to gain a preview of our unfolding future. The earthy, intoxicating fragrance of Northern Labrador Tea rises up from beneath my footsteps to saturate my magical universe. I always hate to step on plants; but you have to step somewhere, so it might as well be on Northern Labrador Tea.

I climb easily to the peak of a commanding hilltop. Before me, in all directions, stretches an endless panorama of rivers, streams and lakes too numerous to count – all of them waiting for me to paddle through their rapids or along their quiet shores. I look forward to tomorrow morning, to that electrifying moment when Kathleen and I will launch our canoe in The River, ferry out into the current, and then draw downstream toward the beckoning world, far away beyond the still distant northern horizon.

For 30 days I will live as people were intended to live – free and open. When thirsty, I will dip my cup into the sparkling, pure water. When hungry,

I will catch a fat trout or Arctic grayling. When tired, I will rest or sleep. When energetic, I will travel beneath a summer sun that circles tirelessly above all four horizons.

I turn to look at The River, now glowing cardinal-red beneath the midnight sun. I envy The River – living and laughing like an anarchist – wild and spontaneous. If only I could be so lucky to live my entire life with such abandon and purpose. If only Kathleen and I could always be in Canada's North – forever adventuring, forever strong, forever young.

I stand motionless as my shadow lengthens across the silent landscape. My silhouette falls away before me, spills over the ridge, and crosses the narrow, cobblestone beach. It hesitates momentarily, and then effortlessly slips into the water, where it flutters briefly on the surface before joining The River on its joyous journey toward its everlasting world beyond the forever-distant, northern horizon.

That's what it's like to be on The River – that's how I feel about being on The River. I love everything about being on The River. Everything, that is, except reaching the end of The River.

Only about six weeks from now Kathleen and I will be heading down the Anderson River, toward its distant northern horizon on the Arctic coast. Until then, back to our winter story....

Li^{n}yatisa Resumed

Monday, May 10. I woke at 3:00 am to stroll along Privy Path. The morning, like virtually all mornings since last February, was very quiet, very peaceful. Then, out of nowhere, a sudden, ripping noise fractured the silence, like low jets, roaring up overhead from the south. I whirled around, and called out to Kathleen. "The ducks are here!"

We quickly dressed and scurried down to the water, where American Wigeons, scaups and Mallards floated in The Narrows. During the day many more birds arrived, including American Robins, Snow Geese, Northern Pintail and one Rusty Blackbird.

At 10:00 am we headed out to Ketaniatue Lake along the Connector. Our trail had been packed firmly by hunters on their ski-doos, and we were able to travel easily even without snowshoes. While we rested at the height of land on Colville Ridge, three Vs of Snow Geese passed above our heads. As we gazed north we could see only a white, frozen landscape, yet waves of birds continued to press onward. Like our flight of faith that we would find a comfortable cabin last January 31, these birds advance onward with their flight of faith that open water will exist. Truly amazing, this spring explosion of life!

We lunched at Ketaniatue Lake, and then headed back up the Ross River along Riverside Drive. Between the lake and our cabin the river ran completely open, except for two wide, shallow sections, which also showed signs of breaking up. Large blocks of ice lay strewn along the banks.

This was the first and likely the last time we would travel the entire 12-km circle route that took us so long to establish. The snow was going quickly, and the travel along Riverside Drive proved to be very difficult. We worked harder than at any other time during the winter. Harder even than when we had originally broken new trail. The snow was only lightly crusted – just a thin mantle overlaying loose snow crystals saturated with water. Even with our snowshoes back on, we continually plunged below the surface. Every step forward required half-a-step back to lift and then shake off what seemed like a kilogram of wet slush that clung to the forward half of our snowshoes. When we arrived back at the cabin I was as tired as I can ever remember being. Perhaps I'm getting old. I'm certainly no John Rae when it comes to snowshoe travel.

Our home was now alive with the sounds of life. I stepped outside frequently to eavesdrop on the musical conversations of Herring Gulls, geese and ducks. Kathleen broke through a spider web as we walked to the flagpole to view American Robins foraging in the open grass. It seems like our new neighbours have always been here. Only a few days ago it seemed like they would never arrive. Today's high temperature reached +13 degrees at five o'clock. Winter is truly over.

Tuesday, May 11. I slept very well and rose reluctantly at 8:15 am. I couldn't stay in bed all morning, as there was much to do. I needed to write in my journal. I also wanted to sit in the sunshine. I wanted to drink tea. I especially wanted to watch for new birds arriving. Common Goldeneye and Green-winged Teal had sneaked in last night while we were sleeping. Throughout the afternoon, herds of caribou headed northeast, across Colville Lake, working their way slowly through the slush and weak crust.

After dinner Kathleen and I paddled 0.5 km into the bay below The Narrows, which has opened up much more in the last two days. We drifted silently past a resting muskrat, as sun glistened and sparkled on the nearly smooth water. A mink ran along beside the canoe, apparently curious about this strange, two-headed creature. We could hear the splash of paws in icy slush, and periodically he broke through the thin ice. American Wigeons flew upward from our canoe at the last moment, squeaking like plush toys as they fled. Lesser Scaups came in low over the water, and splashed down only 10 m in front of our canoe. Rusty Blackbirds foraged in grassy meadows along the bank, making a weak imitation of the much more musical Red-winged Blackbird.

Around 10:00 pm, three ski-doos approached from the north and stopped just outside our cabin door. The riders sat on their machines, apparently waiting to be noticed, waiting to be welcomed. "Hello, would you like to come in?"

"Yep." Our visitors sat down at the table, still not saying anything.

"Would you like some tea, or some coffee?"

"Yep."

"Do you prefer tea or coffee? We have both."

"We like both."

George had visited once before. Terry and Tommy had stopped by three times before, and we had also shared tea with Tommy at his Tent Camp on the Big Island. They and their friend Robert, whom we had not met before, were returning from a successful overnight swan and goose hunting trip to Ketaniatue Lake. Even while sipping from their mugs, they kept their shotguns ready, and constantly glanced through the window to see if any birds were passing by. We showed them our bird book, and they pointed out the species most preferred for eating. They were particularly fond of scoters, which they called 'black ducks.'

"Which ones do you like best?" I asked. "There are three species of scoters, and you can see in the book that two of them, the Surf Scoter and the White-winged Scoter both come to Colville."

Our friends peered at the book. "They're both black. They're black ducks."

I had to agree.

Throughout the visit all four men were generally quiet. They talked only about matters of importance. The Black Ducks should arrive in a couple of weeks. The caribou are moving out now. The ice on the main part of Colville Lake will be good for ski-doo travel for another month or so. Even then, few words were spoken. Just enough words to make the point. In fact, most of the northern native people we have met are generally quiet. Very different from most Southern people, or dare I say many white people, who seem to talk and laugh loudly all the time, who seem to be uncomfortable with silence. Sometimes when I'm at Southern gatherings I find myself subconsciously reaching for the TV remote, thinking momentarily that I could just turn loud people off, or at least quiet them down. But no, the din grows only louder with each passing minute, with everyone eventually talking at once, and no one listening to what is being said. Damn, I hate that.

Although generalizations are vulnerable to contradiction, it is my experience that native people don't feel the need to talk unless there is something to say. Even then, they tend to speak quietly. We have been reading Rene Fumoleau's book, *Here I Sit*. Fumoleau, an Oblate of Mary Immaculate, came to the Northwest Territories in 1953, where he served as priest. He was also a skilled photographer and an accomplished writer. His story *Back!* supports my point regarding the manner in which native people traditionally communicated. Fumoleau was in Fort Good Hope in December of 1976, and during the week the thermometer was stuck at the magical -40 degrees. The wife of the home in which he was staying explained that her family had just returned from trapping at Canoe Lake. Her husband and two (young) boys had come back by ski-doo, while she and two small children had flown back on a Cessna 185. Only her 15-year-old son Eddy remained out on the land, as he was charged with bringing back the dog team.

"Eddy? He left (camp) three days ago, he'll be here soon," she said.

Think about it. Canoe Lake was about 180 km away. No roads. No other people. No communication. A young boy all by himself. Travelling at -40 degrees. Managing the dog team. Setting up the tent every night. Feeding and caring for the dogs every night. All by himself. Minus 40. Any mistake could be his last.

Most modern, urban families today, under these circumstances, would be quite agitated, anxious and vocal. The Takalay family, however, continued to prepare dinner, continued to deal with the daily chores, continued to host their visitor and priest, Rene Fumoleau. All was calm, as though nothing was out of the ordinary, as though there was no reason to worry. "Eddy, he'll be here soon."

And then, during after-dinner tea, came the sound of dog bells as Eddy mushed up to the cabin. Eddy walked in, took off his parka, and without a word walked over to the wood stove to warm himself. Mrs. Takalay continued to watch her pot on the stove, while talking to Father Fumoleau. No commotion. No shrieking. After a few minutes, Mrs. Takalay turned to Eddy and said, "You came back."

"Yes, I came back."

Such simple words. Such quiet, dignified conversation and reunion between mother and son. Nothing more needed to be said. Fumoleau's story could have easily closed with the following words that a proud but humble mother and 15-year-old son were likely thinking, but left unspoken:

"Of course my son came back, he is a man."

"Of course I came back, Mother, I am a man."

Wednesday, May 12. The day again began sunny, calm and warm – plus 5 degrees at 8:00 am. Spring continued to erupt across the landscape, and the animals were all responding. A Red-breasted Merganser, a Slate-coloured, Dark-eyed Junco and a Mew Gull arrived just before breakfast. A Yellow-rumped Warbler (Myrtle race) flitted by just before noon, while an Osprey soared overhead.

As we ate our lunch on the south-facing knoll below the flagpole, a herd of approximately 250 caribou emerged from the bush just west of the cabin, skirted the open water, and walked along the south shore. We heard them before seeing them as they sloshed and slogged through the melting snow. Two of them actually broke through the ice, but immediately clambered back up out of the water to resume their journey north to their calving grounds.

In the evening, around 10:00 pm two male Sharp-tailed Grouse began to dance on the knoll below the flagpole. We had not known that our favourite open area on which to lounge also served as their lek. The males accompanied their strutting performance with a soft, pigeon-like cooing as they vied for the attention of females. When the Sharp-tailed Grouse are mating, who can deny that spring has arrived?

Much of the snow on Colville Lake has melted, and the ice is covered in shallow pools. Tommy told us that this water will drain off and the ice will remain strong enough for travelling for another couple of weeks. Narrow linear ponds marked the pathways where ski-doos had recently travelled. The melting snow also laid bare older trails that had been buried for more than two months. One of our first routes below the cabin was down the centre of a bay to a small island about 0.5 km away. We had abandoned this trail as unsafe when open water began to appear between the riverbank and the trail. Although unused since mid-March, this former route was once again clearly visible. Even Ron's ski-doo trail used only once, on February 17, reappeared nearly as intact and as fresh as the day it was packed down.

We paddled down the bay in the afternoon, forcing our way, like an ice-breaker, through two short, soft sections of ice. By tomorrow we should be able to reach the small island. As we passed by our muskrat friend, he sat with his head nestled in an ice nook, apparently disguising himself as a small log. Or he might simply have assumed, like a two-year-old playing 'peek-a-boo,' that if he couldn't see us, then surely we couldn't see him.

At 9:30 pm we sat outside on the south-facing bench next to the cabin. The heat reflecting off the wall felt as though it could be as high as 18 degrees, even though the ambient temperature was only +8 degrees. Robins called to us from the forest across The Narrows. American Wigeons wooshed like miniature jets low overhead. A pair of Canada Geese plummeted from the sky, honking loudly as they crash-landed into The Narrows.

Life can not possibly be any better than this. Returning to Vancouver will be difficult. Kathleen and I discussed our future. At one time, like many couples, we thought it would be nice to own recreational property. We now realize though, that ownership is not necessary for enjoyment. We don't own the cabin. We don't own the land. We don't own the caribou or the birds or the muskrat. We don't own any of what we see and experience everyday. Ownership would not make our experiences any more real or satisfying. Let the landlords own the property. Let Bern replace the sod roof on his cabins. Let Bern worry about guests burning down his cabin. Let Bern worry about vandalism. We will simply come to admire, to appreciate, and to bask in the beauty.

Thursday, May 13. During last night's radio conversation, Margaret reported that flickers had arrived in town, and warned us that flickers sometimes fly down the smokestacks of wood-burning stoves. "You should keep the damper closed when you're not using the stove."

We were skeptical. Why would a flicker, or any bird, want to fly down our smokestack? Yet, this morning we were awakened by a rat-a-tat-tat on our cabin roof. We stepped outside, and there he was. A male Yellow-shafted Flicker hammering away at our sod roof, right next to the smokestack! I immediately started the fire. No need to take any chances. I wouldn't like to open up the stove door to find a soot-covered flicker lying in the ashes.

This afternoon we paddled nearly to the bottom of the bay below the island, a distance of nearly 1 km. Only a 20-m stretch of slush blocked our route to where open water on the Ross River truly flowed. On the west bank, two streams rushed headlong out of the bush, spewing forth a yellow film of sediment over the decaying ice. When we returned to the dock, a molting male Willow Ptarmigan strutted along the bank, obviously proud of his striking new red comb. In the evening a black bear stood on a shelf of ice on the west shore, drinking from The Narrows. Suddenly startled by our presence, the bear retreated a short distance to hide in a clump of still leafless shrubs. The bear stared at us for a few seconds, yawned, and then slowly climbed the ridge.

Rushing streams, molting ptarmigan, yawning bears and flickers wanting to take up residence in our chimney. Spring rushes headlong into summer.

Friday, May 14. We paddled past the island this morning, and then broke through 15 m of slushy ice to reach moving water. Down the Ross River we went, eddying out behind the rock around which ice used to accumulate only three weeks ago. The seismic cut lines were free of snow. Even the snow trails that we used only last Monday were completely bare. Sheets of water poured over the land. Snowshoeing is finished for this winter.

The river ran swiftly, and we returned to the cabin by ferrying back-and-forth to take advantage of slower water and eddies on the inside bends. Even so, we needed short, quick strokes to prevent the water from pushing us back downriver. A very good morning workout.

After lunch we canoed down the river again. So good to be back in the canoe. Below the island, we slid past the rock and around the first bend, where many birds loafed on ice ledges or floated in the calm backwater. Swans, geese, Mallards, Northern Pintails, American Wigeons, scaups, goldeneyes and yellowlegs – a magnificent gathering – all of them sharing with us this exciting, warm and relaxing time of year.

Bonaparte's Gulls, American Coots and Oldsquaws arrived from the south today. The Oldsquaw's name refers to its constant chattering, as some sources say, 'like gossiping old women.' To me, the name had always sounded a bit unpleasant, and somewhat insulting to mature women, particularly to native women. And in fact, the year after we returned from the cabin, in 2000, the American Ornithologists' Union officially changed this bird's name to the Long-tailed Duck.

The Union had been petitioned by a group of biologists from the U.S. Fish and Wildlife Service in Alaska to change the name on the basis that the species was declining in numbers in Alaska, and conservation management plans required the help and cooperation of Native Americans. The biologists were concerned that the name Oldsquaw would offend Native Americans. Requests to change the name had been made to the Committee in past years by some who considered the word 'squaw' to be offensive. The Committee declined to consider political correctness alone in changing long-standing English names of birds but was willing in this instance to adopt the alternative name, Long-tailed Duck, which was used in most of the English-speaking world outside of North America.

Certainly Long-tailed Duck aptly and better describes the bird's appearance than does 'Oldsquaw.' There can be no doubt, though, that part of the reason for the name change was indeed political correctness.

In 2006, while I was serving as secretary of Paddle Canada, the executive was discussing whether or not to discontinue using the term 'Eskimo Roll' to describe the manoeuvre to right a capsized kayak. The word 'Eskimo' was originally used derogatorily by the Cree to describe their long-standing adversaries, the Inuit, as 'eaters of raw meat.' I pointed out that other long-standing names, such as 'Oldsquaw,' had also recently been changed. One of the executive members was an Inuit woman and an avid birder. She said that she didn't approve of the duck name change, "We still call 'em Oldsquaws." She paused for a moment and concluded, "Of course we call 'em Oldsquaws only until we shoot 'em, and then we just call 'em good eating."

This Inuit woman also recommended that Paddle Canada continue using the term Eskimo Roll: "All kayakers know what it means. Why make up a new word? Also, no one feels insulted by the historical implication of Eskimo. We are proud to be known as Eskimo."

I'm not implying that this story contains a moral. I just like the story, and saw this opportunity to tell it. If you need or want a moral, make one up, and send it to me.

Saturday, May 15. A clear but cool day – still -1 degree at noon, although the day eventually warmed to +8 degrees by late afternoon. A slight, but troublesome northwest breeze blew from morning until early evening.

After dinner we walked to Woodlot Way, which flowed like a river. We were stunned with the amount of boggy forest that had replaced our winter home. High shrubs had sprung up, seemingly from nowhere. Other than for no bugs and the scattered mounds of soft snow, we could have been walking through a summer boreal forest. The ridges of small hills were dry, as though snow had never existed. Yet, only seven days ago we were snowshoeing through a silent world that had just welcomed the year's first Herring Gulls. Since the morning of May 8, 25 species of birds have arrived, including a White-crowned Sparrow today. The air is alive with the sounds and sights of ducks and geese flying and calling overhead. Even plants are now displaying signs of spring. The aspen buds show fuzzy growth, as do the crowns of the anemones growing on south-facing slopes.

Sunday, May 16. After lunch we paddled down river nearly 2.5 km until we reached an ice-filled embayment just before the Ross River cuts through Colville Ridge. *En route* we saw a Barrows Goldeneye and a Horned Grebe. A vole ran along the ice margin, and what appeared to be an ermine darted very quickly along the bank. Our friend the muskrat has made a nest of sticks and mud. The river opens up more everyday. We wish that Colville Lake to our south would show similar signs of progress toward spring. There are still no shoreline leads.

The day had been sunny, calm and relaxing, with a high of +11 degrees at 5:00 pm. Before dinner we dozed and read against the south-facing wall. Throughout this week we have spent more time resting outside than inside the cabin, where it seems colder every day.

Late in the afternoon three hunters on two ski-doos went up Woodlot

Way, even though virtually no snow now exists there. They fired off at least 50 rounds in 30 minutes, and returned south without stopping to visit.

Monday, May 17. A cloudy day, with flakes of snow fleeing before a strong northeast wind; cold with a high of +2 degrees. We spent the entire day indoors, reading, writing and puttering. We organized our miscellaneous toiletry articles for the Anderson River canoe trip, and I revised the trip's itinerary, based on a starting point of North End, rather than the town of Colville Lake.

Much of the Anderson River flowed through land that belongs to various First Nations groups, and we had been required to apply for travel permits. Bern often advised groups on logistics of paddling the Anderson River, and he had asked us for a summary of the necessary paper work, which I prepared for him in the morning.

After lunch Kathleen again wrenched her back, only slightly, but as a precaution she spent the rest of the day in bed. We are both worried about her physical ability to sit in and to paddle a canoe for 6 to 10 hours per day. Her back problems hang over both of us like today's sombre, dark weather. Despite the coolness, though, melt continues. Open water at the outlet now begins 20 m above the south end of the dock. I look forward to paddling to town.

Tuesday, May 18. Another cold, cloudy day. The northeast wind continued to send snow flurries scudding southward across Colville Lake. I wrote in the morning, and then hiked over to Riverside Drive in the afternoon. The ridge just east of our cabin is now quite dry, and generally bare of snow. Last night the temperature fell to -6 degrees, and puddles of water along the trail had refrozen. We will probably endure 2 or 3 days of soggy bush travel once the temperature remains above freezing.

Tommy visited in the early evening, after returning from a successful swan hunt down the river. He reports that the ice dam just before the Ross River cuts through Colville Ridge now has several short leads, with much thin ice. I mentioned that we had seen our first bear just a few days ago.

"Do you have a gun?" Tommy asked.

"Yes, I have a rifle." I handed him my Browning .308.

"Nice. Lever action."

We enjoy a paddling day-trip. If the warm weather continues,
the Ross River will soon run free all the way to Ketaniatue Lake.

"I like it because I can keep one bullet in the chamber and four in the clip. I can get off five quick shots. It's also light. I can carry it easily."

Tommy nodded. "Many bears around soon."

Late in the evening, about 11:00 pm, the ice on Colville Lake itself finally began to stir. From far across the lake there came a groaning, as thick plates of ice shifted and pushed against each other. We stood outside for nearly an hour, listening to the ice sigh as it struggled to rise from its winter slumber. Periodically, sharp cracks, like rifle shots, shattered the softer moaning. The shots sounded like they were coming from near the western shore, and suggested that the plates of ice were beginning to pull apart along pressure ridges. Perhaps open leads along the shore will soon develop. When the lake ice begins to move, when the lake ice calls out to you, then surely paddling season must be near.

Wednesday, May 19. Another cool, snowy day, with a northeast wind. We again spent the day indoors, puttering, reading, writing and enjoying the birds. The point opposite our cabin is one of their favourite spots, as a shallow, pebble-strewn shoreline provides a variety of aquatic foods. Yellowlegs, Herring Gulls, American Wigeons and Mallards all feed there. The Bonaparte's Gull twirls and bobs like a phalarope. This evening, a male Common Merganser, a new spring arrival, joined the festivities.

Tommy, Wayne, Snowbird, Greg and his sister Estelle visited in the afternoon. Our cabin has become a destination, and we very much enjoy receiving visitors and chatting over cups of tea.

Bern returned after being away since April 30. During the evening radio conversation he said that, "Much warmer weather is just around the corner." He didn't provide any specifics about how much warmer, just 'much.' Today's high reached only -1 degree. Even ten degrees warmer sounds like 'much' to us.

Thursday, May 20. I'm beginning to feel somewhat restless and confined. The weather remains cool, and the ice persists. I don't care for this cool, gray, damp weather. I much prefer the cold, sunny, frozen days of February and March.

We paddled down river today and penetrated about halfway through the ice dam just before the Ross River cuts through Colville Ridge. The water has made inroads, despite the cool weather. If 'much warmer weather' returns, the river will soon run free to Ketaniatue Lake.

Red-throated Loons arrived today. Mew Gulls, with their childlike calls, fed off the point with the Bonaparte's Gulls, which are so endearing and unafraid. They are fast becoming Kathleen's favourite gull.

I mentioned to Bern that we had seen our first bear last Thursday.

"Do you have a gun?" he asked. "Once when I was out at the cabin a bear came right onto the porch. I had to shoot it with my 12-gauge shotgun."

"Yeah, I have a rifle. A .308."

"You better keep it loaded."

Darn, between flickers coming down the chimney and bears prowling on the porch, our cabin seems to be under siege.

Friday, May 21. Today was calm and warm, with a high of +7 degrees. We spent a very pleasant day hiking along Winter Camp Walk to the site of our second camp, and where we had also enjoyed Kathleen's birthday dinner. We strolled through the forest, on mostly dry ground. We lingered and stopped often. Cold no longer pushed us forward.

Our winter camp, previously so idyllic in the snow, was now nothing more than a shrubby bog, and very unappealing. When we camped here exactly two months ago, we had cleared the tent site of shrubs, had cut down several trees, and had hacked boughs for the tent floor. It seemed like we were having quite an impact on the site. Most of that activity, however, had occurred above snow more than one metre deep. Now that the snow had melted, virtually no trace existed of our having been here. Only a loose pile of cut wood, a few evergreen boughs, and some ashes left over from Kathleen's birthday fire.

I carried my rifle today. Not because of what either Bern or Tommy had said, but because I have been carrying a rifle since 1980, when we often backpacked in the Southern Chilcotin Mountains of British Columbia. One of our favourite hikes was into the Spruce Lake country on the May 24 weekend, which was usually our first trip of the year. By then the snow was melting, and the sub-alpine flowers were often quite spectacular. We commonly saw bears, both black and grizzly.

In the beginning, I never carried a rifle, and had been quite content to rely simply on being vigilant – always hanging our food – always cooking away from where we slept and always making noise when hiking along streams. One day a professional colleague of mine, who lived in the region, said that he would never travel in the Chilcotins in the spring without a weapon – that I was being foolhardy. Well, he didn't actually say foolhardy, but that's what he meant.

I still wasn't convinced, and to prove my point (to myself, mostly) I asked another colleague, Bert Brink, who was one of British Columbia's most renowned naturalists and outdoorsmen. I also considered him to be somewhat of a pacifist by nature. He was surely a lover of wildlife, and was also very familiar with the area.

"So, Bert, do you think I should carry a rifle when Kathleen and I go into the Chilcotins in spring?" I fully expected a lengthy answer, with premise, argument and conclusion. Bert, as an academic, was always very thorough.

"I wouldn't go in there without a gun," he said.

That was it. No further explanation. He wouldn't go in there without

I liked visiting my wood left over from our second winter camp.
In the Arctic, a man can never have too much wood.

a gun. If Bert wouldn't go without a gun, why should I? So I bought my Browning .308 lever action, and have been carrying it ever since.

I'm not a hunter, but practice every time we go backpacking or canoeing. I try to simulate a realistic situation. I find three cans and set them up about 3 m apart. I then walk away about 10 to 15 m, the distance at which I imagine I would begin shooting at a charging bear. I then wheel around, kneel, and fire quickly at all three cans. I have to say, with some pride, that I always hit the cans. And I mean always.

As yet, though, I am untested with any real action. But I'm not really worried about being attacked by a bear. In my life, while on the ground, at fairly close range, I have seen approximately 200 black bears, 40 grizzly bears and five polar bears. All the grizzlies left, usually running, as soon as they became aware of our presence. The polar bears didn't run, but then neither did they act aggressively. Only one of the black bears continued to sniff at our packs, even after we fired off a 'bear banger' noisemaker. Eventually, though, even this stubborn black bear left. I have never felt, even for an instant, that I needed to use the rifle for defense.

That being said, I am used to carrying the rifle. It is just another piece of gear, like my hat or sunscreen or bug repellent. I just always have the rifle. Today, however, I carried the rifle for an additional reason – to protect my own reputation. Suppose that we happened to startle a grizzly bear, who suddenly charged like a locomotive, knocked us both to the ground, and then slapped us around a few times for good measure. Suppose that the encounter proved fatal, and that we had not been carrying the rifle. Being dead is bad enough. Even worse would be for Tommy or Bern to stand over our bodies, shaking their heads and saying, "Crazy city people, they weren't even carrying a gun." I carried my rifle today to protect the reputation of all city people.

After visiting the winter camp we walked up the side stream to visit the Ravens that lived at the top of that ancient, gnarled spruce. We made no pretence at sneaking up the valley and fully expected the Ravens to challenge our approach, particularly since their eggs should have hatched by now. But no Ravens swooped down to defend their territory. No Ravens called out the alarm. When we reached the knoll, we stared, somewhat in disbelief at a short stump; the venerable, ancient spruce had been cut down. It seems that Sharon and James had harvested the tree for building their new cabin. We quickly headed back down the stream, feeling quite saddened.

We returned to Colville Lake via the picturesque little river valley that leads to the Teepee Site. We started cutting across the lake to the cabin, but immediately felt very nervous. The snow had completely melted off the lake, and the ice was filled with holes and cracks. Ponds of water lay up against the shore. The ice was probably still thick enough to support our weight, but we returned to shore and pushed our way through the muddy bush. Occasionally we were forced to wade through knee-deep streams, but eventually reached the cabin in a little more than two hours – very much a slog. Despite the warmth and the amount of standing and running water, though, there were still no mosquitoes or biting flies.

We finished the day with a paddle after dinner. The evening was very calm, and the ice continues to recede. I don't know how I can possibly return to Vancouver. I feel so comfortable, so natural, just wandering through the bush, with no one else around. I cannot have this feeling in my suburban home, on my fenced, 60 by 125-foot lot. In my backyard I can walk 25 paces south along the west fence, and then make a 90-degree left turn to walk 50 paces east. Another 90-degree left turn points me back toward the house, which I reach with another 25 paces. Ninety degrees left and another 50 paces bring me back to the starting point. How can I ever return to Vancouver?

Saturday, May 22. I re-stacked wood on the porch this morning. Based on consumption rates for the last 20 days, I estimate that this stack will last 30 days, with an additional five more days of wood still available 'on the ground.' This 'on-the-ground' wood is no longer below the orange tarp, which we have dried, folded and put in the storage cabin. I conservatively estimate that we have 35 more days of wood, with only 29 days to go, assuming a June 20 departure. If going to town takes seven days, then we have a 13-day surplus of wood. We're going to make it!

We paddled down the river in mid-morning, but were still blocked by ice in the same bay as before. After lunch, we spent most of the afternoon sitting in the sun, watching the mink, muskrat, voles, Bonaparte's Gulls, Mew Gulls and yellowlegs. A Red-necked Grebe arrived from the south.

Joseph and Martina, and their daughter Sonita, visited this afternoon. Joseph says that the ice on Colville Lake is still very thick, and will be safe for two more weeks – that we shouldn't worry.

"You can travel on the ice until it starts to look sooty. Then it's not safe." Martina invited us to visit them at their camp, where James and Sharon are building their new cabin.

Sunday, May 23. I awoke to new arrivals from the south this morning – four Surf Scoters (or should I say Black Ducks, to be consistent with local ornithology) were floating and diving off the grassy point. For the first time, many ducks, particularly American Wigeons, Mallards and scaups have moved above the lake's outlet. Perhaps there is some kind of fish or insect hatch that has lured these birds upstream. Or, perhaps these individuals are

Joseph and Martina had told us that the ice
should be safe for travelling for another two weeks.

recent arrivals, too late for the crowded, more preferable downstream locations. Or maybe they just want to be upstream.

We strolled through dry forest behind the cabin for an hour after lunch. We were warm and comfortable out of the wind, and we stretched out on the carpet-like ground cover of lichen and Kinnikinnick. Most of our previous experience in the North has been on canoeing trips in the summer, when vast swarms of mosquitoes, black flies and midges often dominate the landscape. We rarely just stretch out on the ground to rest. Perhaps for the first time ever we were truly comfortable while also being warm in the boreal forest. The Southern stereotype that equates the North with bugs is obviously somewhat inaccurate and misleading. In reality, bugs are present for only a relatively short time of the year.

I once read an account of an early European 'explorer' asking the native people how they dealt with bugs. The reply came, "what bugs?" I now understand that the reply had not been flippant, but merely reflected the fact that bugs are nonexistent for most of the year. When bugs are nonexistent, one does not need to deal with them.

We saw our first flower today – a Prairie Crocus blooming on the south-facing knoll below the flagpole. A beautifully bold blue statement of confidence that spring has indeed returned. 'Pussy willows' have also popped out on the willow trees, and small mammals are brimming with the energy of spring. Two muskrats mated 'on the fly' while swimming across The Narrows. Throughout the day we saw voles scurry across the ice, plunge into the water, and swim rapidly away from mink and gulls in hot pursuit. The land bustles with activity, yet the ice on Colville Lake persists.

Monday, May 24. The temperature fell only to zero last night, and three new species arrived: Pacific Loon, Tree Swallow and White-winged Scoter (or should I say Black Duck).

I spent three hours last night, from 11:00 pm to 2:00 am, watching six ski-doos racing back-and-forth across the lake, hunting ducks. If the ice is thick enough to support ski-doos, it should certainly be strong enough for Kathleen and me to go the Big Island. Our main problem will be getting from the shore to the ice and back again. In many places now the ice along the shore has melted or turned to slush. So every time we cross between ice and the shore we will likely get wet. There are seven such crossings each way today, one here at the cabin, two at each of two portages across islands *en route* to the Tent Camp, one at the Tent Camp itself, and one final crossing to the site where James and Sharon are building their cabin.

When we had planned for our Colville Lake adventure we were thinking primarily of winter and our summer canoe trip. We had packed mukluks, Sorels and hiking boots, none of which are appropriate for wet, spring conditions. Fortunately, there were two pairs of gum boots in the storage cabin that fit us pretty well. I'm sure that Bern and Margaret would be happy to loan them to us.

So after breakfast we headed south, up the lake, in our borrowed rubber gum boots. At first we both felt a little nervous about being out on the ice. It looked so blue, so different, without its mantle of snow. Puddles of water dotted its surface, while fissures and cracks zigzagged in haphazard directions. After only 10 or 15 minutes though, we both felt comfortable and confident in assessing the ice. We simply stayed away from the few sooty, black-looking sections. In most places, except near the shore, the ice was still nearly a metre thick.

Walking directly on ice, as opposed to snow, proved to be very easy, and we reached Joseph and Martina's camp in what seemed like no time at all. When we approached the shore, Estelle, Sunita and Jimmy were splashing and playing in the water, like children at any Southern summer beach during this holiday weekend celebrating Queen Victoria's birthday. Jimmy was dressed only in swimming trunks and tennis shoes, even though the temperature was likely only about +10 degrees. When they spotted us, all three children ran along the shore, and eagerly pointed out the best place for Kathleen and me to cross the open lead of water.

A few minutes later James arrived from town on his ski-doo. The open part of Colville Lake was still frozen solid, and racing across 34 km of ice on a ski-doo at only +10 degrees would be cold. James was dressed in his winter parka, with its fur-lined hood cinched tightly around his face. He made a striking contrast with the children wearing their summer outfits. It's difficult to know what to wear during the shoulder season.

We spent the warm afternoon chatting with Rita, Martina, Estelle, Sunita and Jimmy, and watching James, Frank, Joseph and Mike build the cabin. I very much admired and envied their practical skills. All the logs had been dragged in from the bush, and were de-barked, notched, and fitted entirely with hand tools. The men worked calmly, without drawn plans or blueprints. They had built cabins before. Everyone knew how to build cabins. Building cabins was easy. It would take them only a couple of weeks of part-time work, and the cabin would be ready.

We then headed 1 km west across the bay to the Tent Camp on the Big Island, where we enjoyed tea with Terry, Greg, Richard and Trudy before setting out for home late in the afternoon. The travelling conditions had changed substantially during the heat of the day, with much more open water and slush near the shoreline, and more pools of water out on the ice. All went smoothly and quickly though, until we stood on the shore of the last portage. This morning the ice had been solid, with an easy transition to the bank. Now the ice was transparent, thin, and like plastic. We could easily see to the bottom of the lake, through clear water about knee deep. Firmer ice out on the lake lay about 3 m away.

Estelle, Sunita and Jimmy point out the best place
for Kathleen and me to cross the open lead of water to reach land.

I pushed at the ice with my foot. The entire sheet wavered as one piece, but it seemed like we could cross. As we gingerly stepped out, the sheet buckled beneath our feet. We quickly backtracked, walked 20 m down the shore and found a safer place to cross over to firm, thick ice.

Back at the cabin, many, many, and I mean many ducks, now bathed, fed and rested off the grassy point. I suppose I could have tried to count them, but it didn't seem important at the time. Trust me, there were many, many ducks. Red-necked Grebes swam in courtship all evening, like synchronized water ballet dancers. Hour after hour they wailed and cackled loudly, and were quiet only when under water. The other ducks must certainly be weary of their incessant outpouring of affection for each other.

The day had been very successful. We had left some letters with Martina to mail when she returns to town, and the approximately 15-km round trip was pleasant and easy. We think the ice will be safe to travel for another week to 10 days. The day had also been very hot, reaching our highest temperature so far of +20 degrees at 5:00 pm. In fact, we complained about the heat. We're hoping for cooler weather. We seem to be very hard to please.

Tuesday, May 25. I can finally say, with absolute confidence, that our supply of firewood is no longer a concern. We don't need to burn much wood now. For the past three mornings, we have risen to a cabin interior already at +10 degrees. Then, with pieces of wood that only a week ago we would have considered too small, we have been able to warm the cabin to +20 degrees in only a matter of minutes. After about 90 minutes, when breakfast is finished, we stop adding wood for the rest of the day. From about 6:00 pm until 10:00 pm, the sun pours through our west-facing window, which helps maintain the cabin at a very comfortable 20 degrees for our evening cribbage game and popcorn snack.

We sat outside most of the day, on the south side of the cabin, out of the north wind, feeling warm and reading in the sun. I slipped between dozing and waking, listening to the ducks splash, display and court one another. It sounded very much like a suburban, municipal, swimming pool filled with excited, strutting, diving adolescents. Scoters (i.e., Black Ducks) and scaups continued to arrive, zooming in on their jet wings. Sixteen Tundra Swans, with heavy wing beats, circled and landed like Boeing 747s. The swans usually arrived in pairs, and once on the water they faced each other, elegant necks bent forward, wings outstretched, apparently giddy with their successful arrival. This display invariably excited the other swans, all of which immediately repeated the same dance. Later in the day most of the Tundra Swans lifted up into the north wind, momentarily hung in the sky like a cribside mobile, and then coalesced into a V heading north.

Kathleen's diary entry for today shows her satisfaction with our current life:

> *I don't think we could have a better spot to spend this time.*
> *Certainly the cabin is well made, and has everything we need*
> *in a home, but it is the location that makes our life here so*
> *very special. We sit on some of the first open water in the*
> *entire region, and we are surrounded by ducks, geese, swans*
> *and birds. It has been such fun to watch these creatures day*
> *by day, and to learn their personalities. About a week ago, a*
> *Bonaparte's Gull 'staked out' a small, shallow bay as his own.*
> *From the cabin, we can easily observe his breeding behaviour,*
> *which includes yelling very loudly if any intruders, including*

us, ever dare to enter his territory.

This morning I walked below the cabin, and sat down only one metre from the end of the point, which is marshy and shallow. In addition to the Bonaparte's Gull, Mew Gulls, Greater Yellowlegs, Rusty Blackbirds, American Robins and some ducks spend a great deal of time here. I set up my camera on the tripod, and sat all morning taking pictures with the 300-mm lens. All the while the birds simply went about their business as though I wasn't even there.

It is so wonderful just to sit here and watch. Swans with their necks in the water looking like blobs of snow. Red-necked Grebes doing their breeding dance accompanied with loud, harsh calls. Flocks of scaups arriving, sounding like jets overhead. Groups of 5 to 10 scoters diving and splashing. Barrow's Goldeneyes and American Wigeons swimming by in the calm, joined by little piles of ice floating downstream.

I like that last part, about watching bits of ice floating downstream. When we tell people back in Vancouver that we often just sat and watched ice floating downstream, they always look perplexed. I know they're thinking that it can't be interesting or exciting just to watch ice float downstream. Maybe you need to have been here since January 31 to enjoy watching ice float downstream. Or maybe you just need to live life at a slower pace, without deadlines and without 'to-do lists.' Watching ice floating down stream was very satisfying.

Our home here at the north end of Colville Lake is so peaceful, so relaxing, so alive, so brimming with the hope and jubilation of spring. In every way, life here is perfect. Again I ask myself, how can I ever go back to Vancouver? What could possibly be so powerful a draw as to lure me away from my personal paradise? How can I go back to live in an urban environment that I don't like, to work at a job I no longer enjoy, to earn money that I no longer need? Why should I go back? Why would either of us want to go back? Are we going back mostly because we are well paid? Will I betray my own happiness for the proverbial 30 pieces of silver? Am I so much a product of the material culture I claim to reject that I will become my own Judas? I already have every material possession that I need or want. There exists no reason for me to return to Vancouver. But yet I will go back, even though I want only to continue living in this natural, comfortable, vibrant landscape. Why am I going to go back?

Wednesday, May 26. The shoreline to the south of our cabin expands each day, and large blobs of snow melt in the water, literally before our eyes. The west bank of Colville Lake shows open water, and our dock on the north side of the point will soon be reachable by canoe.

After lunch, we put on 'our' gum boots and headed up Ketaniatue Connector into a cold (+7 degrees), overcast, north wind. The trail was very wet and marshy, with high willows all along the cut line. Very much a tedious hike and so different from our exhilarating, open, sunny vistas up the same route during winter. From Colville Ridge we could see that most of the many lakes to our north were still covered with ice. Ketaniatue Lake itself was open only at its 'narrows' and in the small bay at the mouth of the Ross River.

Many birds have now left. No more Canada Geese. No more Northern Pintails. No more goldeneyes. Sounds of life though, still filled the evening air. I sat outside facing the western sun, listening to the alarm calls of the Greater Yellowlegs – the soft one-note cooing of swans – the plush-toy squeaking of American Wigeons – the whistling of Surf Scoters (i.e., Black Ducks) taking flight – the cackling of Red-necked Grebes still enjoying their never-ending courtship – the distant wailing of a Common Loon. A mink scampered along the rim of the ice receding in South Bay. A lone Spotted Sandpiper tilted and bobbed in the shoals off the grassy point. Our canoe sits on shore, lashed to a small spruce tree. My entire world is comfortable, and lies in wait for the final disappearance of winter, which surely is now no more than 10 days away.

Thursday, May 27. During last night's radio conversation, Bern said that James would be bringing six letters for us to the new cabin site. So after breakfast of porridge and toast we headed south, 6 km up the lake, to pick up our mail. The ice around the shoreline, particularly on both ends of the two island portages, was now very thin and slushy.

On our return trip home in the afternoon, just as she was leaving the ice to get up on the shore of the last portage, Kathleen broke through, to just above her knee. A few minutes later we stood at the other end of the island portage, looking across the slush to the firmer ice beyond.

"I think we can cross this, Kathleen. It should be firm enough if we go slowly, and besides, the water is not too deep."

I moved out, and Kathleen followed. The ice felt very soft and plastic. About half way across (it always happens half way across, doesn't it?) the sheet quivered and bent, and then slowly began to settle below the surface. It all happened in slow motion. I kept expecting to hit bottom, but just kept sinking. Icy water poured into my gum boots. I kept sinking. The water reached my knees. I kept sinking. The water reached to the middle of my thighs before I finally stood on the bottom.

I turned around to look at Kathleen. "Don't come this way," I said. (I'm pretty good at pointing out the obvious.)

"Well where should I go?"

*As Alan had predicted, the plastic kids toboggan
was our most useful piece of winter gear.*

I pointed to a spot about 1 m to my right. "Right over there. You can plainly see that it's thicker there, and not nearly as deep. Go over there."

Yes, I realized, even then, how ludicrous my advice sounded. If the best route was so bleeping obvious, then why wasn't I over there, instead of standing here, on the bottom of the lake? Apparently I'm somewhat illogical, even irritable, when standing at the bottom of a lake in water up to my thighs. Did I mention that the water was really cold?

Kathleen moved to her right, and easily reached the firmer ice without breaking through. I pulled myself out of the water and back up on the ice without breaking through again. A few steps later I stood with Kathleen on the solid ice.

I had been pulling our plastic toboggan, which fortunately floats very nicely. Our supplies and change of clothes had remained dry. I towelled off and changed into a fresh pair of socks. Yes, it's now time to apologize to Alan for not immediately accepting his advice to get a kids plastic toboggan. We have used it virtually every day since arriving last January 31. We have used it to haul wood, to haul water, and to haul spare clothing and supplies on day trips. We have used it on snow, on ice, on land, and now even on water. Thanks, Alan, for being so persistent with your advice.

When we arrived home Kathleen prepared grilled cheese sandwiches and hot orange drinks. We sat outside in the sun, along the south-facing cabin wall, reading aloud to each other, savouring each letter, one sentence, one word at a time.

After lunch we paddled downstream, about half way to Ketaniatue Lake, before being blocked by a narrow, sooty barrier of ice. This section will open up in 1 or 2 more days. Most of the shoreline is free of ice. Most of the bush is free of snow. Most of the runoff rivers are now quiet trickles. For the first time, we were actually able to paddle to and land on the small island just north of our cabin. The land appears as summer. As usual, paddling back upstream to our cabin was a smidge more work than paddling downstream. It won't be long though, before we can continue to paddle downstream, all the way to the Arctic coast.

We feel like summer. The air is warm. Prairie Crocuses bloom on all the knolls and throughout the drier bush. The fragrance of Labrador tea fills the air. We saw one lonely bull caribou yesterday crossing the lake. He continually stopped to glance back, seemingly wondering where everyone else had gone, seemingly unaware that his herd had already departed for the spring calving grounds.

The Greater Yellowlegs and the Red-breasted Mergansers spent most of the evening in courtship. During consummation the yellowlegs are particularly noisy and unashamed, loudly proclaiming their union to the entire world. The two male mergansers often seemed more concerned with each other than with the single female that both of them desired. Every few minutes they would face each other, draw their heads inward toward their chests, and then spring out wildly like a spasmodic jack-in-the-box.

Spring is here, but the ice on Colville Lake persists.

Friday, May 28. A very relaxing, calm, warm day. In the morning we paddled down the river – sun shimmering on the water – heat on our backs – multi-coloured stones gliding beneath us – grassy reeds yielding to the flow of the current. I had brought my fishing pole, and we beached the canoe on river right, where we stood on mostly bare ground. I tried for nearly an hour to catch a fish by casting into the riffles, but with no success. This surprised me, as I fully expected to catch something. Lake trout, grayling and pike have emerged from the depths of frozen Colville Lake, and we have seen them basking in the warm shallows. The grayling and the pike will soon be spawning.

In the evening we strolled along the shore of South Bay, which now shows many places where the ice has come away from the banks. Even a male Mallard broke through when he tried to join his mate on the slushy pan of ice. A lone mosquito landed on my shoulder, and a pair of Arctic Terns arrived from South America. A yellow, prostrate potentilla began to bloom on flagpole hill. Spring continues onward.

Isolation and quiet have returned to the north end of Colville Lake. Most of the ducks, swans and geese have migrated onward. Long-tailed Ducks (Oldsquaws), White-winged Scoters (Black Ducks), a pair of Mallards and a pair of Tundra Swans still remain. A mated pair of Bonaparte's Gulls occupies our south dock and act as though they own it.

Ski-doos no longer roar up the lake. The weather is too hot, the ice is too soft near the shore, and too few ducks remain to hunt. We are happy and content, and bask in the long heat of the never-ending day.

We are now contacting Bern at 10:00 pm, so as not to interfere with our walks after dinner. During tonight's conversation, I mentioned to Bern that we saw fish in the Ross River, but I had not been able to catch any this morning. Bern said that late evening was the best time to catch fish, "And you don't have to go down the river. It's easy just to catch them at the outlet."

Immediately after the call, I went to the pier, and on the third cast caught a 60-cm, 2.5-kg lake trout. I look forward to tomorrow's dinner, although I always feel genuinely sorry for the fish, which is such a beautiful creature.

Saturday, May 29. We have much more wood than I originally estimated last Saturday. At that time I thought that we had enough wood on the ground to last just five more days. Our consumption rate has decreased substantially though, and we actually heated our cabin all week using only the wood on the ground, which will likely last another five days. We haven't even touched the wood stacked on the porch.

We have a wealth of wood. I no longer need to estimate how many more days of wood remain, and I feel real good about it. My neatly stacked and full woodpile brings me infinitely more satisfaction than looking at the current balance in my cheque book. Wood seems so much more valuable than mere numbers. Wood seems so much more tangible than mere scratches lined up in columns on a piece of paper. I can see my wood. I can touch my wood. I can smell my wood. My wood sits just outside my front door, within easy reach. My wood is a very 'liquid' asset. My wood makes me feel quite secure.

This morning we awoke to a strong southeast wind, which in the late morning blew off a large (200 m by 50 m) pan of ice below The Narrows and sent it crashing into the island. In late afternoon the wind increased, and reversed directions twice, sending the ice pan back to the main pack, and then north again to jam our route downstream, west of the island. Despite the strong wind, we now feel comfortable outside, without windbreakers, without long underwear. I wear only a single layer – a medium wool shirt. Warmth has replaced the bite of winter.

Throughout the day, hazy, billowy summer clouds rose upward. A brief rain shower, the first of the year, spilled lightly from the sky, and the earth smelled fresh and pure. By 9:00 pm the winds calmed and the sun filtered through broken clouds. A pair of Common Loons drifted in a golden shaft of light, moving without even a ripple, black heads turning regally and elegantly to monitor their summer kingdom of forest and water.

Sunday, May 30. Unable to sleep I stepped outside at 1:00 am and looked at the thermometer – still above freezing at +2 degrees. Our resident snowshoe hare hopped by, apparently unconcerned with, or perhaps accustomed to my presence. The hare's pure white coat had turned dirty brown and mottled. One would think that the hare would be too embarrassed to be seen in public, after dressing so elegantly all winter.

Two mosquitoes landed on me. A pair of Arctic Terns sat on the tips of adjacent spruce trees, bobbing precariously on leaders too slender to fully support their weight. Tree Swallows darted and swooped for mosquitoes out over Colville Lake to the south. Beneath the midnight glow of a sun just below the horizon, the ice no longer glistened white and shiny. Rather, it now reposed dull and gray, like a defiant, dying monarch. The 40-km, monolithic, implacable sheet of ice was finally starting to show its age. We are told that 'once it starts to go, it goes quick.'

Water begins to pool up on the ice in the south bay on May 30. Open leads expand along the shore. Break-up can't be too far away.

Kathleen worked most of the day repairing the mosquito netting that encloses the front porch. In the afternoon we sat on the porch, smug in our bug-free refuge. During dinner, however, the first significant insect attack of the year came from behind our line of defense, from inside the cabin. At first there were only a few flies, and we simply swatted in their general direction. Then there were scores of flies, and we took turns using our flyswatter in earnest. Then there were untold legions of houseflies emerging like black clouds from within the cabin walls. We spent 90 minutes surrounded and inundated by buzzing, annoying magnitudes of flies. Perhaps it was just a serendipitous hatching of eggs laid last fall. Or perhaps we had angered the insect gods by feeling so smug behind our mosquito netting.

Monday, May 31. For the first time this month, the temperature remained above freezing overnight, reaching a low of +2 degrees. In the morning we strolled over to the woodlot, where I found three small trees that had been felled last fall, recently emerged from beneath the snow. I spent the morning dragging them down Woodlot Way to the edge of the lake. I should be able to pick them up by canoe in a few more days, as the ice is now melting rapidly all along the shoreline.

We already have a complete stack of wood on the porch, and we don't need this new wood. But it seems that in the Arctic, a man, or at least this man, can never have too much wood. These three trees should provide at least 12 days of heat, which is all the time that we have left at the cabin, assuming that we spend a week in town and that we leave for the coast on June 20. When we arrived at the cabin last January 31, we found a complete stack of wood on the front porch. We will leave the cabin just as we found it, with a complete stack of wood on the front porch. This is how it should be.

It's hard to believe we have so little time left, just 12 days, in our beloved cabin, where we have been so happy and content. Our home base for snowshoeing expeditions – our front row seat for the return of the birds – our viewpoint for the changing of the seasons. We will miss this spot – physically, emotionally and spiritually.

In the early afternoon we lunched outside, in the sun, along the cabin's south-facing wall. A muskrat rippled the surface of South Bay. The rich resinous fragrance of Balsam Poplar filled the air. Catkins of Trembling Aspen burst forth. Chunks of ice broke free and floated away. Blue butterflies fluttered by.

In late afternoon a strong northwest wind rose, and battered our point for 2.5 hours. When it was all over, the ice in North Bay appeared defeated – only half its size of this morning, with a pocked, sooty colour. Even the ice in South Bay now seemed like it had lost its tenacious grip. It too has turned predominantly dark gray. Along the shore, east and beyond Woodlot Way, there were numerous open leads and pools – many more than this morning. A trip to town by the weekend seems possible, particularly since a light rain now (8:45 pm) falls, which will further saturate and weaken the disintegrating ice.

CHAPTER 11

Bemetegoxay

Tuesday, June 1. *Bemetegoxay:* 'The Month of the Ice Melting.' Early in the morning (1:30 am), I stepped outside into an overcast sky, and a brisk northwest wind, with a temperature of -4 degrees. The Northern Hawk Owl again sat on its radio antennae pole, feathers ruffling in the wind. He looked directly at me, with those intense eyes, and angular, menacing beak so characteristic of all owls. A red squirrel darted away along the edge of the cabin.

We rose for the day at 8:00 am to a very blustery, cloudy June. The temperature stood at only +2 degrees. After a breakfast of pancakes, Prem and maple syrup we organized all of our clothes and gear that we would need for the canoe trip, and then began packing away all our winter stuff to be shipped to either Vancouver or Inuvik. We don't yet know how we're shipping this winter gear and leftover food to Colville Lake, let alone to Vancouver or Inuvik. We can be ready in half-a-day though, when the opportunity arises.

After lunch, I walked over to Woodlot Way to saw up the three trees. Much of the shoreline is open, and the rest of the outer shore is pocked with pools and leads. The ice in North Bay shrank by another third today, and seems to be so fragile that it can't last more than two days.

By 8:30 pm the wind stopped and the sun returned. We eagerly strolled outside and lounged on the bench along the west-facing wall in front of the screened porch. Mallards, American Wigeons, White-winged Scoters (Black Ducks) and humans all drifted, basked or loafed, in mated pairs, enjoying the warmth of their own little corner of paradise. Whiskey Jacks, always insatiable, took chunks of cheese directly from Kathleen's hands. A giant northern pike swam in the grassy ice-free shallows off the dock in North Bay.

A squadron of Tree Swallows, after the day-long wind delay, took up their respective positions, like a baseball team taking the field, to circle, climb and dive for bugs over South Bay.

We stayed awake most of the night, enjoying the birds and the fantastic lighting. So interesting to remember that on our first morning last February 1, the sun rose nearly due south at 10:00 am. Now it rises nearly due north at 1:30 am.

Wednesday, June 2. We slept late, until 9:00 am, but awoke to a warmer, less blustery, clear day. After our bannock breakfast, we paddled east along the shore of South Bay, and for the first time reached beyond the storage cabin. We then swung southwest along the margin of the ice, and for the first time entered the cove beyond the point on the west shore of Colville Lake. Only 90 minutes earlier, this route had still remained blocked by a narrow isthmus of ice.

We then turned north, past the grassy point, and along the edge of the ice in North Bay, gliding slowly past Mr. and Mrs. Barrow's Goldeneye, who were resting on the ice. We paddled in the lee of the southeast wind, along the shore to which ice had still clung only two days ago. We circled the island, where pairs of Bonaparte's Gulls, Greater Yellowlegs, Mallards and Northern Shovelers had obviously built their nests – all eight birds became immediately agitated by our presence. We returned to the cabin for grilled cheese sandwiches, and exchanged our wool clothing for cotton shirts and nylon river pants.

The southeast wind continued strongly in the afternoon, and eventually caught a loose corner of the ice in North Bay. A 200-m long by 75-m wide pan swung outward, and eventually broke loose from the northwest shore. Thirty minutes later the pan had moved off down the Ross River. North Bay lay free of ice, except for a 10-m strip along the margin. Summer paddling season is nearly here, although the ice in South Bay seems so very intractable.

At 8:30 pm the southeast wind caught the edge of the remaining ice in North Bay and sent it in a slow spin, away from the shore, and out of the bay, which is now free of ice for the first time since October 7. Finally free of ice after nearly eight months.

Thursday, June 3. A burst of heavy rain woke me at 1:30 am. After a few minutes it stopped, and I stepped outside to a beautiful morning and the smell of freshly-moistened earth. Seven degrees and perfectly calm. The sunset/sunrise glowed on North Bay, which was dotted with moving Vs of ducks gliding slowly across its silent, motionless surface. Across The Narrows, a beaver swam along the west shore, and a Greater Yellowlegs foraged for aquatic morsels in the grassy, foreshore shallows. Only 12 hours earlier, a 75-m wedge of ice had filled the inner cove. Now the cove appeared as though it had never known any existence other than the relaxed, idyllic, languorous pace of a mid-summer millpond.

After pancakes and Prem for breakfast, during which we used the last of our maple syrup, we paddled along the east shore of South Bay, hoping that we could reach James and Sharon's new cabin. We were surprised at how much open water greeted us in the foot of the bay, but then were disappointed to be blocked by ice at the second rounded point, only 0.5 km south of our cabin. On our return, we stopped at the foot of Woodlot Way for a load of wood. During the morning the northwest wind had shifted to the southeast, and had blown the ice back into South Bay. All of the shoreline leads were now blocked by ice, and we were forced to disembark about halfway back to the cabin. We pulled our canoe up on shore, tied it to a tree and returned to camp overland through the bush.

By the time we had finished lunch the southeast wind had cleared the second rounded point of ice. We hiked back to the canoe, re-launched and continued paddling south. Just beyond the Teepee Site, a little over 1 km from the cabin, we reached completely ice-free water. We paddled easily to within 0.75 km of James and Sharon's cabin, until we were stopped by an expanse of ice from Colville Lake that stretched into the 1-km gap between the Big Island and the mainland. Satisfied that we would soon be able to reach the open part of Colville Lake, we returned home and were able to force our way through the weakening ice in South Bay all the way to our cabin.

As we sat enjoying our afternoon hot orange drink, two huge slabs of ice (20 m by 75 m) broke free from the foot of South Bay and rammed into the dock. Our access to Woodlot Way was now virtually free of ice. For the first time, I sensed in my gut, rather than simply knew in my head, that the great ice sheet was waning. We hope to go to town soon, and are eager for the ice to melt.

I felt luxurious today during our extended paddle. My new cherry wood, otter tail paddle looked so lustrous with its golden varnish, appeared so elegant with its symmetrical, elongated shaft and blade, and felt so smooth with its velvet-like wooden grain. The paddle flashed in the sunlight as it sliced through green, clear water, sending small whirlpools twirling away in its wake. The canoe leaped forward at its command, gliding silently while waiting for the next surge. So utterly beautiful, and so simply effective. To move peacefully along the shore while holding such a paddle in one's hands must surely be one of life's most sensuous pleasures.

Friday, June 4. We finished organizing gear to be shipped to Colville Lake and Inuvik, although we still don't know how this will happen. We are now wearing and using only what we will need for the canoe trip. We worried a little about putting away all of our wool clothes, but we felt comfortable and warm dressed only in tee shirts and nylon pants. The afternoon temperature reached +16 degrees, which is warmer than many of the days we normally encounter on Northern canoe trips.

We're both feeling more than a little sad that we will be paddling away from our cabin in a couple of weeks. Despite what I wrote in the *Floating Free Interlude*, I have changed my mind about wanting to paddle down the Anderson River to the Arctic coast. I realize now that two very distinct reasons explain my love for wilderness canoe trips: (1) the beauty and excitement of being on the river, and (2) the opportunity and reason to escape my comparatively unsatisfying life in Vancouver. Now, however, I no longer need this escape, as I'm already completely happy right here at the north end of Colville Lake. The canoe trip down the Anderson River will only take me away from what is arguably, at least for me, a perfect life. Damn.

Just after lunch we paddled nearly two km down the west shore of Colville Lake to the first island portage. We beached the canoe and walked across on bare ground. Bog Birch had leafed out nearly completely. The great ice sheet now wastes before our eyes, particularly with today's strong northeast wind. In the late afternoon, the sheet in South Bay swung around and split in two. Half the sheet floated off down the Ross River, while the other half plugged our access to the east shore.

Tommy, Richard, Greg, Shania and Kaila arrived by aluminum boat in the afternoon. Our first visitors not to come by ski-doo. At their invitation, we will visit the Tent Camp tomorrow. Assuming that the ice doesn't shift too much in the wind, we can now paddle all the way.

I had been a little worried about having five visitors, all drinking tea, and then using the outhouse, which is filled nearly to capacity. Kathleen and I never urinate in the outhouse, as everyone knows you're not supposed to urinate in the outhouse. But our visitors included three men and two women. I felt uncomfortable even thinking about asking them to just wander out into the bush. So I said nothing. But when I checked the outhouse later in the evening, the frozen urine had finally begun to thaw and subside! Our available capacity had increased by about four centimetres, which should give us enough room for the rest of our time here.

Most of the migrating geese, swans and ducks have moved on. Our home is quiet, except for the calls of summer songbirds. Only occasionally do we hear the shrill three-note alarm of the Greater Yellowlegs. The Bonaparte's Gulls must be on their nest as they no longer noisily defend 'their' dock. So far we have seen only a few mosquitoes, which haven't bothered us outside. We sleep easily at night when we kill the few mosquitoes that sneak past the netting on the porch.

Saturday, June 5. After laundry and lunch we paddled out in a continuing northeast wind to the Tent Camp. The ice had diminished by half overnight, and we found open leads all the way to the Big Island. Ice still packed the south shore facing the open part of Colville Lake, however, and we were forced to beach the canoe 100 m before reaching the trail leading up to the tent. At the camp we enjoyed whitefish steaks, trout chowder, huge bannocks, coffee and tea. These people live like I wish to live. Relaxing in their wood-warmed tent, eating and living from the produce of the land: fish, caribou, ducks. To me, it seemed an enviable, idyllic, rewarding and satisfying life. They know everything about their land. They know where the ice is thick. They know where the caribou pass and where the beavers build their houses. They know how the ice shifts during spring break-up, and when the mosquitoes emerge. Marie, the matriarch of Colville Lake, says, "The mosquitoes get bad when the big lakes thaw."

By the time we returned in late afternoon, the ice sheet had diminished by half again. By dinner the wind shifted to the northwest, and blew the remaining ice south up the lake, nearly out of sight.

The ice on Colville Lake proper, south of the Tent Camp though, remains only slightly pocked with pools of water. We probably won't be able to head to town until Thursday. Our hosts this afternoon advised us to go sooner than later: "Better to paddle when the ice moves as one sheet, before it breaks up into smaller pieces. Hard to tell where the wind will blow smaller pieces."

Sunday, June 6. We paddled down the Ross River, about 3/4 of the way to Ketaniatue Lake, before we stopped at the top of a long, swift, shallow rapid. We beached and walked the rest of the way, usually along trails, perhaps traditional travel routes. Small Wood Anemones bloomed in pleasing clusters along the upland edges of marshy sites. The wide leaf of a coltsfoot thrust upward through the moist ground. A Glaucous Gull, white as ivory, flew up and down the river. A large sheet of ice still blocked access to the narrows in Ketaniatue Lake; but it should break up in a few more days.

After dinner we dismantled and cleaned the wood-burning stove. Tommy and Greg stopped by for tea and coffee at 9:00 pm. They reported that the ice on Colville Lake proper, south of the Tent Camp, is beginning to break up. Depending on wind direction we should be able to leave for town on Thursday.

Monday, June 7. We paddled south to the Tent Camp this afternoon in calm and sunlight. The distant shoreline appeared tawny from last year's withered grass. The near shoreline fell away steeply below our canoe – beneath the clear water lay a fine mosaic of rounded stones, like a submerged Japanese rock garden.

Ice still dominated Colville Lake south of the Big Island. I doubt that we'll be going to town on Thursday. During our return to the cabin we faced a very strong headwind from the north, gusting toward us with ever-increasing strength. It was as though the wind had finally discovered that we have returned to the North with our canoe. Just like old times out on the Barrens, the wind swept out to greet us, to play with us, to thwart our aspirations of reaching our destination at the end of a paddling day.

Like the past three evenings, I went down to the pier with my fishing pole after the radio conversation with Bern. I was hungering for a trout dinner, but had been unsuccessful for three straight days. Not a bite. Not a nibble. After ten casts, again with no luck, I changed lures, from my favourite slim, flashy, gold Mepps spinner to a larger, bulky, red-and-white spoon. On the second cast I landed a 58-cm lake trout. I should have changed lures three days ago. Change is difficult for me though, and the Mepps spinner has always been a stalwart and dependable lure. I'm not receiving any endorsement fees from the makers of the Mepps spinner. I doubt that Mepps has ever heard of me. I just like their lure. I cleaned the fish, and took the entrails and head down the shore to the burrow where we had been leaving our food scraps all winter.

Tuesday, June 8. At 11:30 last night, while in bed, we heard scampering noises, seemingly inside the cabin. I stepped outside to discover our mink peering out at me from a tunnel it had recently excavated beneath our home, now also its home. Bern wouldn't like this. I asked him/her to leave, but (s)he only looked quizzically at me. I repeated my request, nay my demand, but again the mink demurred, albeit politely. I raised my voice; it cocked its slim head, and stared at me as if to say, "Why, only an hour or so ago you gave me a fish head at my burrow, and now you order me away? Why are you being like this?"

Nevertheless, I remained firm, and the mink finally ran out from beneath our cabin, where once again we could sleep without interruption. Still though, I felt a little selfish for not being able to share my space.

We idled away most of the day, sleeping until 10:30, lingering over breakfast, feeding the Whiskey Jacks, reading in the sun, sauntering through the still bug-free forest, cleaning the cabin, and imagining an ice-free Colville Lake. Tomorrow we will paddle to the Tent Camp for another look south, across the ice, across the lake, across to town. I am restless and eager to travel.

The diminutive Fairy Candelabras bloom in profusion about the cabin. Fragrant Mountain Wormwood sprouts along the south and west walls. The blue-purple petals of Lapland Rosebay are beginning to appear in the forest, where White Death-Camas leaves also extend skyward from a carpet of lichen. Dwarf Nagoonberry blooms along the shore near the south dock. Summer is here, but we wait for the ice on Colville Lake to be gone.

Wednesday, June 9. After lunch we paddled down to the Tent Camp.

For the first time we were able to paddle right to the trail, on the south side of the Big Island, that leads up to the tents. Children played and ran along the shore, acting very much like summer had arrived.

We shared tea and bannock, and talked about the ice. An east wind had blown the ice away from the east shore, just south of the Big Island. I mentioned again, as I do on every visit, that I want to paddle with the ice. That I want to be with the ice as it's breaking up. Finally Marie said, "Well, if that's what you want, why don't you just go, and see what happens? Here's some fresh donuts for your travel."

Marie was right of course. No sense paddling down here every two days just to look at the ice. We should just go and see what happens. We returned to our cabin, ate some grilled cheese sandwiches, packed up our tent, camping supplies and food, and headed back south at 6:30 pm. We stopped at 8:00 at the Tent Camp for coffee, and Marie gave us some smoked fish for our journey. We started out for town, along the east shore of Colville Lake, at 8:45 pm.

Four km later the ice lay rafted up against a narrow point that projected into the lake. No open leads. We forced our way to shore, beached the canoe, unloaded all the gear, and portaged 150 m across the tundra-like point, where Cloudberry and Bog Rosemary were beginning to bloom.

Just as we finished the portage, Richard, Tommy and Greg arrived in their aluminum powerboat, forcing their way through the thick ice. "We were out hunting," they said, "and happened to see you here."

Richard, Tommy and Greg had all been in the tent when we left about an hour ago, and didn't mention anything about a hunting trip. I think they had actually come mostly to check up on us, to make sure that we were OK. Nevertheless, they had just recently shot some Long-tailed Ducks ("Oldsquaws, until we shoot 'em, and then we call 'em good eating").

While Kathleen and I snacked on smoked fish, our three visitors prepared their dinner. Their approach to camp cooking differed markedly from ours. We would normally prepare a small fire pit encircled with stones. I would then collect some small, medium and larger diameter pieces of wood, which I would saw into appropriate lengths. If I had known how, I would then gut and de-feather the birds and put them in a pan over a grate on the fire. This method sounds good, but in reality is unnecessarily complicated.

Our three visitors made no fire pit encircled with stones. They simply dragged in a large pile of wood of all and various dimensions and set them on fire. Then, with small sticks, they impaled each of the birds through the throat, placed them around the perimeter of the blaze, and sat back to enjoy their tea. Bits of fire began to run off away from the camp. No one seemed concerned. The bush was still too wet for a wildfire to break out. After about 30 minutes the birds were declared done. The seared feathers rubbed away easily from the charred skin. The birds were then 'opened' with a knife, and the guts simply fell out. This simple approach required minimum effort with very few supplies. Just a knife and some matches. No grate. No pots and pans. No axes. No saws. Quite opposite to the high-tech approach used by most urban visitors to the wilderness.

After an enjoyable hour of conversation and tea, Kathleen and I paddled away into absolute calm and quiet. The midnight sun, still high above the northern horizon, shone hot upon our backs. The calls of Common Loons and Oldsquaws beckoned us south. We slid between the sunlit, golden shore-line on our left and the white, silent, rotting ice sheet to our right. So often I had dreamed for an evening exactly like this, and now I was awake in my own dreams. I nearly laughed out loud with the sheer joy of being alive at that moment – in that place.

We stopped at 1:30 am and set up our tent in a well-used camp on an open terrace overlooking the lake. At 2:30 we fell asleep instantly, serenaded by the calls of White-crowned Sparrows. I slept soundly, without waking, until 11:45 am.

Thursday, June 10. We awoke to a sunny, calm, warm morning. Just like yesterday morning, we still live at Colville Lake. But our life differs very markedly from yesterday. Now that we live in a tent rather than a cabin, our senses are so much more alive, so much more a part of our surroundings. We are no longer walled off from the natural world. We see and hear Arctic Terns diving and plunging into the lake. We hear ice shards tinkling in the distance. We hear waves caressing our cobblestone beach. We feel the touch of a gentle breeze on our faces as we cook breakfast bannock over a fire that crackles so very reassuringly. And still no mosquitoes. Again I ask, how can life be better than this?

After breakfast we paddled toward the next point, 5 km away, to see how far we could get before being blocked by ice. This east/west point extended even farther into Colville Lake than the previous icebound point, and through our binoculars at breakfast we thought that we could 'see' ice blocking the shoreline.

"Let's just go and have a look," we said. "No need to pack up. We probably won't be able to get through anyway."

Ninety minutes later we rounded the point in a 100-m wide lead of open water, and could see apparently unending open water down the shoreline to the next distant point. We returned to camp, now knowing that barring a major wind from the northwest, we can probably reach town tomorrow.

We sat in front of the campfire sipping tea. Should we leave for town now, at five o'clock? If so, we would arrive when everyone was sleeping. Should we rest until midnight, and then head out? I love paddling beneath the midnight sun, and we would reach town around 7:00 am, just in time for breakfast. Or should we get a few hours sleep first, and put on the water early by 2:00 am, before the wind has a chance to block the open lead? We don't know what we'll do. And that's the beauty. There is no night. There is no day. There is no right way. There is no wrong way. For now, we'll just sit by the fire, periodically poking in more logs. We'll head to town when we feel like it. No later, and certainly not before.

Friday, June 11. We headed down the east shore, south toward the point, just after breakfast, about 10:00 am. Again we found open water, with nearly 150 m between the shore and the ice sheet. A mild northwest wind now helped push us forward. We continued paddling around the point, toward the next point, 2.5 km away, where ice clogged our route, and lay rafted up, in large broken chunks against the shore. We beached in a small cove within the icy jumble, and walked along a ridge covered in scattered spruce and Bog Birch to assess the situation.

Again, Northern Labrador Tea smelled so very sweetly as we surveyed the ice, which extended nearly 1.5 km in an impenetrable barrier. We returned to the boat, and relaxed on shore, sipping tea, and gnawing on smoked whitefish. We concluded that unless the wind shifted to the southeast, to push the ice offshore, we would likely need to camp in a small clearing 200 m up into the bush.

We heard a motor approaching from the north, and twenty minutes later Richard, Tommy and Greg landed for coffee and conversation. They reported

As we canoe to town on June 11 we are blocked by ice
blown toward our east shore by the northwest wind.
We beach the canoe and wait for the wind to shift.

that the northwest wind was moving the ice back on to the east shore of
Colville Lake. The open leads through which we had paddled so easily only
hours ago were now clogged with ice; our visitors had spent most of the morning forcing their way through. We lounged for a few minutes, and then they
continued south to drop off some gear at an intended camp, slowly struggling
through the pack with their powerboat.

We followed 10 minutes later in their broken lead, which was already
closing up. Only half way through, 100 m from shore, the ice squeezed shut,
and held us firmly. We knew that the powerboat would be returning soon,
so we sat patiently, listening to the candled ice of a new spring. In mid-
winter, the surface of the snow is colder than lower in the profile. As the
days become warmer in spring, the temperature gradient in the snow cover
reverses; the surface is now warmer, and melts during the heat of the day.
Water then drains down through channels in the upper snow crystals, which
turn into long, vertical cylinders called ablation needles. The result produces

a musical tinkling when these prism-shaped needles rub against each other. It was as though we were sitting in a giant field of wind chimes, as we swayed back and forth in the gentle breeze.

Fifteen minutes later the powerboat returned, and again opened up a narrow, chaotic, serpentine route. Richard, Tommy and Greg wished us luck as they crunched their way north, and we slowly paddled south through the closing lead. Only two canoe lengths from open water we again became hopelessly mired as a thick, unbroken chunk of ice fell into the last remaining lead. Thirty minutes of ramming, poking, rocking, prodding, banging, and prying eventually freed us from the pack, and we once again paddled into open water.

The next point lay only one km away. By now we were suspicious of all points, which seem to collect ice like magnets. Our suspicions proved correct, for as we rounded the point, ice completely filled the 1.5-km, shallow, scalloped bay to the south. We paddled back to the north side of the point, where we beached, collected firewood, and prepared and ate our cheese and pasta dinner. We then strolled along the ridge, where Cloudberries, Bog Rosemary and Lapland Rosebay bloomed among the tussocks of Northern Labrador Tea. We climbed up an open, tundra-like terrace to stand before a low, four-sided picket fence. Inside, the single wooden cross marked a grave that had been beautifully located to overlook Colville Lake. To the south, toward town, we could see nothing but unbroken ice. Kathleen and I returned to the canoe along the bay, along a shoreline that had no open leads. We seemed to be stuck.

The wind continued to blow from the northwest, and Kathleen wondered if we should just set up the tent and camp for the night.

"I don't know," I said. "It's not a great place to camp, I'm not really sleepy or tired, and I don't feel like putting up the tent. Maybe the wind will shift."

"It's been blowing in the same direction all day, Michael. It's already eight o'clock, and there's no sign that the wind is letting up. I don't want to put the tent up either, but I don't want to just sit on the shore all night."

On one of Richard's visits to our cabin we had mentioned how spectacular the Northern Lights had been for most of February and March. Richard commented that "when a man is all alone on the winter trail, he can whistle for the Northern Lights to come closer."

South, toward town, still more than 25 km away,
we see nothing but unbroken ice.

"So you know, Kathleen, if Richard can whistle for the Northern Lights to come closer, then maybe I can whistle for the southeast wind to blow."

I whistled meekly, not wishing to challenge the universe. We sat and watched tiny bits of ice floating along the shore. Moments later they stopped, then reversed their direction and twirled back up the shoreline as the wind shifted to blow from the southeast! Large rafts of ice out on the bay now showed lee water along their margins. Arctic Terns began diving into what must be small patches of open water on the still ice-filled bay to our south. Red-breasted Mergansers and scoters (Black Ducks) landed and fished in slivers of leads. Twenty minutes later the entire shoreline opened up as the pack drifted out from shore.

It's not possible to know why the wind shifted just as I whistled. Kathleen says that she was simultaneously praying for the wind to shift, meaning that the experiment was confounded. Also, there was no 'experimental control,' in that we had no data for what would have happened without either whistling or praying. All I can say is that I whistled, Kathleen prayed, the wind shifted, the ice moved, open leads appeared, and we continued our journey south to town at 9:00 pm.

We rounded the point to enter the shallow, scalloped bay that still contained some ice at its north end. We sluiced our way through gray slush, forced our way through disintegrating, candled rafts, wedged our way through cracking chunks, and in only 20 more minutes paddled away into open water, now apparently without end.

We canoed snugly up against the shore in the lee of the continuing southeast wind. The calm lake surface reflected the shoreline dunes and stunted spruce, which glowed in the midnight sun. The gray, brooding ice lay harmlessly 200 m to the west. Perhaps we will reach town tonight. At 12:30 am we again encountered very thick, nearly unbroken ice on the cape 5 km east of town. We powered into and up onto a 25-cm-wide crack, where we rocked up-and-down and back-and-forth until the ice surrendered, split open, and allowed us to pass.

We continued west, along the south shore, now expecting to reach town. At 2:00 am we approached the headlands, which lay encased in ice. We paddled along the entire margin of the pack, hoping to find a route through. No passage existed, however, and we turned back to shore just in time, as shifting ice was already closing in behind us. We rammed through and beached the canoe at the ski-doo trail, 1.5 km from town, at two-thirty in the morning.

We walked into town, almost expecting an enthusiastic reception. The town site was empty though, almost deserted; everyone seemed to be either away or in bed. We returned to the canoe and began unpacking. By 5:00 am we had completed portaging all our gear to Bern Will Brown's compound. Still no one up to greet us. No one to invite us in. What should we do? It didn't seem right to disturb anyone. So we just strolled around town, between Bern's lodge and Robert and Jo-Ellen's house, hoping someone would look out their window and see us. We had made several circuits by 6:00 am, but still no one had seen us. We played on the swing set. Still the town remained quiet and asleep. We made several more rounds.

Finally, at 7:00 am, we heard rustling in one of the lodge's cabins. On our next pass, the curtains were open, and Margaret's sister, Agnes, who was in town working and preparing meals at Bern's lodge, spotted us. At 7:30 we were seated at the table in the main dining room, dining on a fantastic breakfast of eggs, bacon, toast, juice and coffee. Thank you, Agnes!

I thoroughly enjoyed the past two days. I loved seeing, playing with, and being with the ice. I savoured paddling beneath the marvellous light of midnight. I am very satisfied to know that I can still paddle all day, throughout the night, and yet still have enough energy to portage 2.5 hours across boggy ground. We had left the Tent Camp on the Big Island on the evening of June 9 'just to see what happens.' What happened was a fantastic two days. Thank you, Marie!

Saturday, June 12. We spent the day wandering around town, greeting people who now know us from all of their visits since duck hunting season began. It seems that we have been accepted as part of the community. Everyone knew of our trip and progress to town because of 'Native Radio.' All were happy to see that we had arrived safely.

People were disappointed though, that we had wandered around town for three hours in the early morning, just hoping that we would be spotted. Agnes said that, "We were worried about you. Bern said not to worry. That you were fine. That you knew what you were doing. That it's a nice time of year, and you were probably just camping. But we were worried. You could have knocked on any door in town, and people would have let you in."

We could have knocked on any door in town, and people would have been happy to let us in. It never occurred to us that we could have knocked on any door in town. Think about it. We could have knocked on any door in town. Even on the doors of people we didn't know, and they would have welcomed us in. I am reminded of another of Rene Fumoleau's stories, entitled *Dene Christmas*. Father Fumoleau had arrived in Fort Good Hope [Radeli Koe] in June of 1953. Here he met John, a Dene in his early twenties. Father Fumoleau admired John's art, and asked John to draw the Christmas Story as though it had happened in Fort Good Hope. The two men agreed that the drawing should feature local and native themes, in that Joseph and Mary would arrive by a toboggan pulled by four dogs. Mary and Joseph, after finding no room in town, would pitch their tent on the other side of Jackfish Creek, where Jesus would be born.

After a week, Father Fumoleau asked John how the drawing was coming along. "I've been thinking about it a lot," John said. Another week went by and John said he was still working on the drawing. Weeks turned into months and Father Fumoleau asked John directly if the drawing would be ready in time for Christmas.

"I don't think so," John replied. "I mean, that drawing doesn't make any sense to me."

"Oh?"

"You see, if Mary and Joseph had come to our village, they could have walked into any Dene house, and the people would have said, 'Come on in, you're welcome.' "

I'm also reminded of the time Kathleen and I came off the Coppermine River in 1995. We had hoped to stay several days in the small, predominantly native town of Kugluktuk on the Arctic coast, but there was no vacancy in either the small hotel or the two bed and breakfast establishments. No campground existed. No public toilets. No fresh water.

Disappointed, we went to the airline company to book a flight out of town, back to Yellowknife. As we told our story a young native man helping in the back room came to the front desk and said, "You can stay in my house. I will be away hunting caribou for the weekend. Just come on in and make yourself comfortable." We had never met him before. We were complete strangers. Yet we were being invited in without even having to knock.

I felt a little ashamed of myself. I had walked around in Colville Lake for three hours early in the morning without knocking on any doors. Although I felt courteous at the time, my behaviour could also be considered insulting to a community that had been worried about our safety.

Emails, phone calls and dinner at the lodge completed our day. At 8:00 pm, 36 hours since leaving our last camp on the east shore of Colville Lake, we crawled into bed and instantly fell asleep.

Sunday, June 13. An uneventful day in town. Emails. Phone calls. After church we walked to the airstrip, up on the terrace east of town. From there we could see that all the ice has been moved offshore by the continuing southeast wind, which blows more strongly with each hour. The route to our cabin along the east shore of Colville Lake gapes wide open. We hope to leave Tuesday morning.

This afternoon Bern volunteered to come to North End by powerboat to take all of our winter gear back to town. Now we just need to make arrangements to get the gear from Colville Lake to Inuvik.

Monday, June 14. More emails and phone calls in the morning, after which we became tourists by buying an original oil painting from Bern. We also commissioned Sharon to make some moosehide slippers for Kathleen. Sharon said the slippers should be ready in four or five days, and that James would bring them out to our cabin. We told her that we didn't have $100.00 in cash – that we had only about $45.00 left. "Would a cheque be OK? Is there anyone in town who would cash a cheque for us?"

"I don't need the money now. Just give James a cheque when he comes out."

In the afternoon Bern and I sat on his veranda, smoking his cigars, enjoying the sun and listening to children playing, splashing and laughing in the water, sounding very much like the migrating ducks and geese of mid-May.

Periodically Bern called out to passersby: "Why weren't you in church yesterday?" And, "Be sure to go for that job interview tomorrow." It seemed a little paternalistic to me. We white people on the porch of the largest home in town, smoking cigars and admonishing the parishioners. I know that Bern meant only the best for the people of Colville Lake. After all, it was his responsibility as a former priest and as their current deacon to offer secular advice and to provide spiritual leadership. Yet I felt a little uncomfortable. The passersby also appeared somewhat unreceptive.

After dinner, we watched a little TV with Bern. The news stories seemed irreconcilably arcane and divorced from our lives. We had heard some news over the winter, on the CBC network, as we listened to the morning weather reports on our battery-operated radio. Sometimes the reception was good, particularly if we wrapped the antennae in tinfoil. Most times, though, the reception was poor. Occasionally we heard of the war in Kosovo. The media, understandably, were quite excited by the war. If we had been home, in Vancouver, we also might have been excited by the war. We would have discussed it with friends, argued its merits with family, presented our opinions to casual acquaintances. We would have talked about the war as though our opinions mattered, as though our opinions were based on fact, rather than on mere hearsay streaming out to us on the radio or television.

In our cabin at the north end of Colville Lake, however, we realized that our opinions about the war in Kosovo mattered to no one. We realized that our opinions about the war were based almost solely on conjecture and ignorance. We realized that our opinions about the war in Kosovo would not change the war's outcome. We realized that the war in Kosovo did not affect our lives at the north end of Colville Lake, any more than our lives at North End affected those who lived in Kosovo. We were worlds apart, in the literal sense. I am reminded of the anecdote of the remote Chinese peasant who professed that he did not care about the Emperor or his policies. "But do you not fear the Emperor's power?" he was asked. He shook his head no, and replied, "The Emperor's power is like that of the sun. It is far away."

Kathleen and I sat outside in the evening, and for the first time, the mosquitoes became annoying.

Tuesday, June 15. We enjoyed another one of Agnes' sumptuous breakfasts of eggs, bacon, toast, juice and coffee at the lodge. Three other guests joined us at the table, including a representative from North-Wright Airways in Norman Wells, with whom we made arrangements to fly our winter gear from Colville Lake to Inuvik. Our business in town was now complete, and we set out for home at 10:30 am. The cape no longer lay encased in ice, which was barely visible far to our west. We paddled around the point into a warm, southeast breeze, barely aware of the mosquitoes clinging to our backs, and flitting about our heads.

The shallow lakeshore mirrored the puffy-clouded, sun-drenched sky above. A golden-green light suffused through the placid water, penetrating easily to the sandy bottom half-a-metre below our canoe. Cloud shadows hypnotically wavered and played on the sandy rills. Our rhythmic strokes took us from one hour to the next, one ice-free point to the next. All the while we paddled as though in a trance, not daring to stare too closely or too long into the amber water, whose shifting, shimmering patterns threatened to seduce us into a prolonged stupor.

About halfway down the east shore we stopped for dinner between two points where the shore gradually merged with the land. Open, park-like stands of spruce had beckoned to us, inviting us to linger on carpets of flowering Kinnikinnick and Crowberry, crunchy layers of lichen and soft layers of deep green moss. We resisted the temptation to camp in what was certainly the best campsite between town and the north end of Colville Lake. We were too close to home to stop now. Only 25 km to go.

We paddled on, in open water, where only five days ago we had battled thick rafts of often impenetrable ice. The temperature hovered at +30 degrees. Increasing swarms of mosquitoes brought out the DEET repellent. Summer had arrived with an unbridled passion.

By 10:30 pm we neared James and Sharon's new cabin. We paddled down the east side of the Big Island in its protected, calm water. Near its shrub-covered northern extension hordes of mosquitoes forced a temporary halt to apply generous amounts of DEET to our exposed arms and face.

At the exact moment of midnight, just like Cinderella, we beached our canoe in front of our cabin. We were home. Only 13.5 hours to paddle approximately 40 km, and we felt relaxed and energetic. We seem to be in better physical shape than we thought.

Much had changed since we left six days ago. The Trembling Aspen and Balsam Poplar tress had leafed out. Red Bearberry had sprouted thick leaves. Prickly Saxifrage, Northern Comandra and arnica were all blooming. Even at midnight, the temperature of our cabin interior registered +22 degrees. Mosquitoes buzzed about our heads all night. Summer has arrived. In many ways, today was the first day of our canoe trip down the Anderson River to the Arctic coast. Our winter adventure – our sojourn into icebound isolation has ended. Vancouver threatens us in the not too distant future. I feel disconsolate, and wish we could return to last January 31, when Kathleen and I first stood on the ice, all alone, surrounded by silence, trepidation and excitement.

Wednesday, June 16. A day spent cleaning up, washing clothes, repairing gear and studying our maps of the Anderson River. Over the course of the winter we had accumulated six bags of garbage, mostly cans. We had burned all paper and cardboard garbage in the wood stove, and had given most of the organic garbage to the mink that lived in the burrow along the east shore north of our cabin. I had assumed that Bern would be taking our garbage back to town, but during last night's radio conversation he said, "No, just burn it. You'll find a garbage dump, in a pit about 100 yards northeast of the cabin."

I found the garbage dump, and spent a couple of hours flattening and then burning the cans. Six bags of garbage aren't very much for five months, certainly much less than we would have accumulated in five months back in Vancouver. But I didn't like the idea of leaving my garbage here at the north end of Colville Lake, which seemed so pristine. This spot didn't deserve garbage. In reality, though, it doesn't make much difference whether my garbage gets dumped in town or here at the cabin. It's still garbage. It has to go somewhere. It's my garbage, and it's my responsibility to deal with it.

The weather was unbearably hot to be outside, particularly in front of a hot fire. Only last Wednesday morning the overnight low was -2 degrees. Tonight's low should be +10 or +15. Kathleen strung mosquito netting above our bunks; hopefully, tonight's sleep will be uninterrupted and more relaxing.

Thursday, June 17. Very hot today at twenty-eight degrees. Much too hot to be comfortable. We spent most of the morning in the dim, shuttered coolness of the storage cabin organizing and labelling all of the bins. We still had nearly $400.00 of food left, which we are donating to Bern for transporting everything back to town. We labeled one bin of odds-and-ends for Robert and Jo-Ellen, in appreciation for their hospitality when we were in town. Everything else, except the sled, we labelled 'Inuvik by North-Wright Air.' We had been disappointed in the sled's performance, and had asked Bern to sell our sled for whatever price he could get. Any price would be better than paying to have the sled flown to Inuvik. I would perhaps even consider just giving the sled away.

I don't expect many takers, though. People in town hadn't been overly impressed. "Too heavy," they said. More importantly, people here don't drag sleds by hand. They pull sleds by ski-doo. People here have places to be and work to do. Power gets it done faster. I'm sure that people had been a little bemused by our desire to do everything the old-fashioned way – dragging sleds and paddling canoes. Why would anyone drag sleds or paddle canoes unless they had no choice? During our last day in town, Jo-Ellen told us that one of the girls in her class had asked her, "Mrs. L [Jo-Ellen's last name was Lyslo], are those white people really poor? They don't even have a kicker for their canoe." No, I don't expect many offers to buy our hand-pulled sled.

Throughout the rest of the day we mostly sat outside on the dock, enjoying the cooling southeast breeze, which also kept most of the mosquitoes grounded. Loons called to us from the opposite shore, and I caught a whitefish for dinner. These last days at our cabin are calm and relaxing. Yet they are also tinged with sadness. We wish to continue forever, just as we are today – living in this moment, in this beautiful spot beyond the end of the road, north of the Arctic Circle.

Friday, June 18. We awoke at 10:45, after staying up until after 1:00 am. Even then I went to bed reluctantly, believing, for no apparent reason, that I 'should' sleep. The most enjoyable part of the 'day' though, is during the night, when the air is cool, and the land glows softly. Our bodies seem to have adjusted naturally to sleep 'late' in the unending light of summer. The concept of 'late' though, is so fraught with value and subjectivity. In reality, we did not sleep 'late,' but actually rose exactly on time. We woke when we wished to wake, when we were ready to wake. We slept timelessly, and then woke to resume life exactly where we had left off before going to bed.

The day continued hot and muggy, until mid-evening. And then the thunderheads rose to subdue the sun's glare. Colville Lake became placid, and a cool breeze blew in from the thickening blackness to the west. After two days of foreplay, the climax came. Lightning split the sky, and penetrated to the very depths of the earth. Crescendos of release rolled across the land. I felt calm, energized, satisfied. The air smelled immaculate and the wind brought renewal from beyond the horizon. Such sweet violence. Such delicious mayhem. I sat on the porch enraptured by the prehistoric purity of the unrestrained, passionate, electrical union between heaven and earth. A gentle rain followed.

Saturday, June 19. Our last day at the cabin. Our last day of life at North End. Distant gunshots from hunters chasing geese and swans woke me, and I stepped outside at 4:30 am. I stood alone and silently outside on the south dock. A Bald Eagle soared majestically above Colville Lake. A beaver swam confidently through The Narrows of the outlet. A northern pike broke water aggressively in the shallow warmth off our north dock. Palpable, quiet sorrow at leaving an idyllic winter of solitude and adventure. In a little over 24 hours we will paddle away forever from our cabin. It will then be the end. Sadly, this is the end – the end of what has been the most satisfying period of my entire life.

I went back to bed, and a few minutes later heard a boat approaching from the south. Even before we could dress, James stood outside, knocking on the door.

"Would you like some tea?"

"Maybe one cup, but I gotta get back. I have your moccasins."

"Great. So that was a hundred dollars, right? Sharon said that a cheque would be OK."

"No, I need cash or a money order."

I understood that cash would be preferable to a cheque, but I was surprised that James would suggest a money order. Not a lot of banks here at the north end of Colville Lake.

"We don't have that much cash, James. Sharon said a cheque would be fine. She said I should make it out to her. I hope that's OK. It's the best we can do."

James didn't seem entirely happy, but there was no other choice. He took the cheque and immediately headed back south.

About 11:00 pm, Richard and Charlie stopped by in their powerboat on their way to Legententue Lake, to scout the area for moose, and to do a little hunting.

"Would you like some tea?"

"Yep."

This was Charlie's first visit, and he looked around our cabin with interest as he waited for the tea water to boil. His gaze quickly settled on our airtight wood stove, very small by comparison to the much larger stoves usually found in Colville Lake homes. Kathleen poured the tea, and all four of us took a sip. Charlie set his mug down, looked at me, and asked, "So, you stay warm last winter?" No direct criticism of our stove. Just a rhetorical question to suggest that in the future we might want to consider getting a larger stove.

They asked if we still planned to leave tomorrow, and wondered where we intended to camp. I spread out the maps and pointed out the places on our intended itinerary, including our first camp in the narrows at Ketaniatue Lake.

"That's not a good place for camping. Willows too dense and tall." Richard pointed to another spot, on a point about 4 km beyond the narrows. "This is the first good spot for camping. You should camp here."

We drank a few cups of tea, and said goodbye to Charlie and Richard just after midnight.

Sunday, June 20. I awoke at 9:00 am, and strolled up to the storage cabin to start bringing our canoe packs down to the water. Suddenly a voice rang out, "Hi!"

Charlie was calling out to me from Flagpole Hill, and soon stood beside me, out of breath.

"We broke down. Kicker stopped working. Been running all night. Bugs real bad."

"Come on in for pancakes and coffee."

A few minutes later Richard joined us for a full breakfast in a crowded, happy cabin. I wondered how they planned to get back to their camp, which was on the Big Island. I was wondering if perhaps there was a boat at James and Sharon's. They would need a boat. Even getting down to James and Sharon's through the bush would be difficult. They would need a boat. I assumed that they would ask for Bern's boat, and Bern had specifically asked me not to loan any equipment or gas. I decided to meet the problem head on.

"How are you getting back to camp?"

"By boat."

"I don't think you should take Bern's boat. He says he has no gas. You should take our canoe."

Richard and Charlie accepted the offer and paddled away at 11:00 am, Richard in the stern, stroking strongly.

At 12:30, an aluminum boat approached, towing our canoe behind. Two older men that we had never met before stepped out onto the dock and began tying up. I waited until they finished.

"Would you like to come in for coffee?"

"Yep."

Our visitors sat down at the table while Kathleen brewed up more coffee. We talked of our trip down the Anderson River.

"Lot of bears on the river. You have a gun?"

I showed them my Browning .308.

"Nice lever action."

"You know, everyone here says that the lever action is nice, but no one but me has a lever action. All of you have bolt action rifles. If lever action is nice, then why don't you have lever action rifles?"

*On June 20 we began our 550-km trip down the Anderson River
to the Arctic coast. It marked the end of what had been
the most satisfying period of my entire life.*

"Lever action might jam."

Another example of the diplomatic approach used by the people here. Sure, my lever action was nice. Just not as nice, in their opinion, as a bolt action. This was the first time that I had asked for their advice, so it was the first time that the advice had been given. Very diplomatic.

One of our guests then commented, "We were surprised when you came to town last winter over the ice. Why, we asked ourselves, would anyone camp out on the ice in the middle of the lake? We know that Eskimos camp out on the ice. So if Eskimos camp on the ice, then maybe other people can also camp out on the ice." Our guest paused, and then concluded, "But here at Colville, we have trees, and we like to camp in them."

I took this as a diplomatic suggestion that in the future I shouldn't choose to camp out on the ice. Camping in the trees is safer, and more sheltered from winter storms.

After finishing their coffee, our guests mentioned that they hadn't been in the cabin for a very long time.

"We liked being here," I said. "It's a great cabin. Very well made. Just like the lodge he built in town. It's beautiful. Bern has a lot of skills. I wish I had his skills."

Our guests looked around a bit, and then one of them spoke slowly and softly.

"I cleared the land for this cabin. I built the cabin. The people built Bern's lodge in town, to help the priest. The people were here before Brown, not the other way around. Colville Lake was here before Brown."

I was stunned by this quiet, unexpected, somewhat undiplomatic out-pouring. But I could see their point. Bern is famous in the North, and I think deservedly so, for reasons I have already presented. But in reality, many Southerners, many whites have come north and become famous for doing es-sentially what the indigenous people have done for millennia; building cab-ins, surviving in the bush, being part of an isolated community, creating art. The Southern whites have become famous because their achievements have occurred in an environment considered strange or unusual from the Southern, urban perspective. Fair enough. But the accomplishments of Southerners, the success of 'newcomers,' the fame of men like Hornby, Brown and Rae have sometimes been promoted by media that overlook or otherwise ignore the contributions of the indigenous population.

As all four of us walked back to the dock I asked what would happen to the cabin after Bern is gone. "After all, he's getting on in age. He's 79 this year."

"Maybe we should burn it down. Priests aren't supposed to marry, aren't supposed to start businesses."

Finally, at 2:30, our gear was packed, and both cabins locked and shut-tered – just like we found them last January 31. Kathleen and I wandered one more time around the compound. We walked along Laundry Lane and Lower Cabin Crescent. We sat below the flagpole and looked south across the wind-rippled surface of Colville Lake. I could have cried without too much prompting. I sighed deeply as we slowly made our way back past our cabin with its wood stacked neatly, 2 m high on the porch. We continued down the hill to our loaded canoe, which bobbed slightly in the afternoon breeze.

We looked at each other. What could we say? "It's over. It's time to go."

I felt no joy, no excitement – only loss. Kathleen and I stepped into the canoe and paddled away toward the Arctic coast. We could not bear to look back.

Down A Country Road

Kathleen and I reached the Arctic Ocean by canoe on July 15, and two days later flew in a chartered Cessna 185 back to Inuvik, where Alan and Marilyn welcomed us 'home.' We drove our van to the Finto Hotel, where we looked forward to hot baths and restaurant meals. I pulled into the empty parking lot, stopped near the front steps, and turned off the engine.

"You can't park here, Michael."

"Why not?"

"There's a sign. No Parking."

This wasn't going well. We'd been back in 'civilization' for only five minutes and already I felt irritated and out of place.

My discomfort increased as we drove south to Vancouver, particularly when we entered the three lanes of afternoon commute traffic crawling across the Iron Workers Memorial Bridge toward our home in North Vancouver. This wasn't going well at all.

Soon after returning to our positions at the University of British Columbia, Kathleen and I gave a slide show about our life at Colville Lake. After the presentation one of my colleagues commented that, "It must be hard to come back, Mike."

"No, Jim," I replied. "It's more than *hard*. It's *impossible* to come back. I don't think I can do this anymore."

I was right. I could no longer accept office walls, meetings and schedules. My stomach knotted every time I approached campus for another day of work. I sometimes became irritable and short-tempered. I tired easily. I often struggled for hours to complete even a short memo. I missed my quiet, unfettered life at Colville Lake.

In September of 2002, I turned 55 and gladly accepted the generous buy-out offered by my sympathetic dean, Moura Quayle. One year later, Kathleen and I sold our suburban home in North Vancouver and moved to a one-acre, oceanside retreat on Pender Island, approximately halfway between Vancouver and Victoria. Here we intended to live a rural lifestyle, with days devoted to ocean paddling, walks on forest trails to coffee shops, gardening and 'doing as we pleased.'

At first Kathleen and I were very happy. We both believed that we would never leave Pender Island, a place considered by most of our friends and family to be among the best locations one could live in Canada. But during summer, tourists sped along the narrow, winding island roads, while sea-doos and power boats roared past our bucolic home. During winter, rain and gray skies blotted out the sun, seemingly for weeks at a time.

By January of 2006 we could no longer ignore the irresistible call of Canada's peaceful North. We longed to walk on frozen rivers beneath the winter sun. We wished to know once again the exhilaration of seeing the ice finally release its grip on the frozen landscape. Break-up at the outlet of Colville Lake had been tremendously exciting, but our original plan back in 1998 had been to witness break-up on a large river, such as the Yukon. Dawson City had always been a favourite place for us to visit during summer. Could we possibly find a winter cabin to rent on the Yukon River near the historic gold rush town of Dawson?

During a conference call with my fellow executive members of Paddle Canada, Trevor Braun, in Whitehorse, gave me the phone number of Tommy Taylor, who owned a cabin on the right bank of the Yukon River, 12 km downriver from Dawson City. I called the next day.

"How much to rent your cabin from approximately April First to break-up?" I asked.

"How 'bout we make a deal," Tommy replied. "You look after my 29 sled dogs, and you can stay for free."

Although not what we had in mind, the adventure appealed to us. Actually, we called Alan first, to get his advice about the difficulties of tending to the needs of 29 sled dogs, as we were a bit reluctant.

"It's a great opportunity, Mike," he said. "It will be an adventure."

We arrived in Dawson City on March 30, at -25 degrees, and travelled by ski-doo the following morning to our cabin.

We spent the next six weeks wearing our mukluks, walking on the river, enjoying the ever-lengthening days, and of course, feeding the dogs. Each day Kathleen and I butchered slabs of caribou and moose, sawed up frozen fish, and cut wood to boil four large pots of food over an open fire. Although we had never owned pets before, we thoroughly enjoyed the company of our huskies, each of whom had a distinct personality. The dogs also seemed to enjoy our company, particularly at feeding time. We hold very fond memories of seeing and hearing their contentment, when they howled in unison, with full bellies, from atop their doghouses.

Break-up on the Yukon River occurred in front of our cabin on May Ninth. Truly spectacular to see an ice sheet more than one metre thick and nearly 1 km wide grind and groan its way down river, with open water following behind. Within an hour our world transformed from winter to summer, from icy silence to flowing life. Two gulls, riding residual blocks of ice, appeared proud, smug and content as they floated down the river. We wished that we could float with them forever northward, but reluctantly returned to Pender Island two weeks later.

In August of 2007 the thought of another soggy winter on the West Coast seemed too depressing and daunting. I contacted another executive member of Paddle Canada in Winnipeg to inquire about lakeside cabins. Cameron White said it would be easy to find such a cabin in northern Manitoba, "the true Lake District of Canada."

A week later Marilyn Fehr called to ask if we would be interested in coming to Inuvik, from September to early February to house-sit and care for their five sled dogs. Wow! Of course. Who wouldn't want to enjoy a winter in Inuvik? Alan had spent the previous year in Ottawa, at the request of his employer, Parks Canada, learning French. His 'stay' had been extended, but his current dog and house sitters were no longer available. We packed up the van and arrived in Inuvik on September Twenty-fifth.

Even though Alan and Marilyn's five dogs lived in the bush a few kilometres outside of town, caring for them proved remarkably easier than our previous assignment of 29 dogs. Nearly every day we released them from their chains to let them run free and wild along snow trails, and we came to know them as individuals. I should also say that we quickly developed a very strong 'fondness' for Brownie, Grey, Patsy, Sailor and Slick.

Marilyn and Alan's Christmas letter in December indicated that Alan had accepted an offer from Parks Canada to become superintendent of Saskatchewan's Prince Albert National Park. The letter further indicated that they would be looking for a home near the town of Prince Albert, and would not likely be able to find a property large enough for their dogs.

Now this was very bad news. In places like Inuvik, lots of people have dogs. And people who have dogs generally have lots of dogs. Brownie, Grey, Patsy, Sailor and Slick were all either nine or eleven years old. People who had dogs would not want to take our dogs, which were too old to work. Alan and Marilyn might be able to find a home for one or two dogs. At best our family of dogs would be separated. At worst, Brownie, Grey, Patsy, Sailor and Slick would experience the 'normal' fates of such old dogs in Inuvik: to be 'put down' or sold to polar bear guides as 'cannon fodder' to surround and distract the bear for wealthy hunters. These alternatives were unacceptable, not only to Kathleen and me, but also to Marilyn and Alan.

Certainly, we thought, Alan and Marilyn should be able to find a property near Prince Albert that would be large enough for Brownie, Grey, Patsy, Sailor and Slick. Kathleen and I decided to review the Multiple Listing Service website on the Internet. We would find a home and property large enough for Marilyn, Alan, their four boys, Brownie, Grey, Patsy, Sailor and Slick.

We spent the next few days in front of the computer monitor, intrigued by how inexpensive Prince Albert property was compared to Pender Island. Out of curiosity, we began to search more rural areas in central Saskatchewan. Damn! They are giving property away in Saskatchewan. Moreover, central Saskatchewan enjoys a 'real' winter. When the snow arrives in the fall, it stays until spring. Sunny skies predominate year-round.

Slowly Kathleen and I began to realize the obvious. We didn't need to return to Pender Island. We didn't need to endure the soggy West Coast. *We* could move to Saskatchewan. *We* could enjoy our personal winter paradise. *We* could provide a home for Brownie, Grey, Patsy, Sailor and Slick.

So that's how it came to be that Kathleen and I traded one acre on Pender Island for 565 acres near Preeceville, a small community of 1100 people in east central Saskatchewan. Marilyn and Alan are living just north of Prince Albert, with Patsy, who has become a pampered house dog. Brownie, Grey, Sailor and Slick still live in the bush, near our house, and spend winter days mushing with Kathleen and me along our Aspen Parkland trails and across the frozen shores of Loch Lomond.

Oh, by the way, I remained cancer-free at my tenth anniversary of surgery in 2008, and no longer need to report for an MRI. Even so, my leg has never completely healed. It remains weak. I sometimes stumble, and periodically I experience stabbing pains along my sciatic nerve. Kathleen's back occasionally gives her problems. These discomforts though, are trivial, almost meaningless. Life is very good. Kathleen and I spend a lot of time wearing our mukluks, and walking along crunchy, snowy trails beneath crisp, blue skies and a golden, Saskatchewan sun.

REFERENCES

Bastedo, Jamie. *Reaching North: A Celebration of the SubArctic*. Red Deer College Press, 1997.

Christian, Edgar V. *Unflinching: A Diary of Tragic Adventure*. John Murray, Ltd., London. 1937. Republished as *Death in the Barren Ground*. 1980. G. Whalley (ed.).

Conover, Garrett and Alexandra Conover. *A Snow Walker's Companion: Winter Trail Skills From the Far North*. Ragged Mountain Press. 1994.

Fumoleau, Rene. *Here I Sit*. Novalis, Saint Paul University, Ottawa. 1995.

Grey Owl. *Tales of an Empty Cabin*. Key Porter Books, Toronto. 1998.

Jason, Victoria. *Kabloona in the Yellow Kayak: One Woman's Journey Through the Northwest Passage*. Turnstone Press. 1995.

Kephart, Horace. *Camping and Woodcraft: Handbook for Vacation Campers and for Travelers in the Wilderness*. MacMillan Co., NY. 1960.

McGoogan, Ken. *Fatal Passage: The Untold Story of John Rae, the Arctic Adventurer Who Discovered the Fate of Franklin*. Harper Collins, Toronto. 2001

Pielou, E. C. *A Naturalists' Guide to the Arctic*. University of Chicago Press. 1994.

Savishinsky, Joel S. *Trail of the Hare: Life and Stress in an Arctic Community*. Gordon and Breach, New York. 1974.

APPENDIX 1
Arrival of Birds From the South

W inter resident birds seen regularly during our stay included Gray Jay, Willow Ptarmigan, Boreal Chickadee, Common Raven and Sharp-tailed Grouse. We first saw a Pine Grosbeak on March 31, although it might also have been a winter resident. Other likely winter residents included the Northern Hawk-Owl, which we first saw on May 8, and the Spruce Grouse, which we first saw on May 10.

April 12	Bald Eagle	May 14	Long-tailed Duck (Oldsquaw)
April 26	Snow Bunting		American Coot
May 5	Northern Goshawk		Bonaparte's Gull
May 8	Herring Gull	May 15	White-crowned Sparrow
	Lesser Yellowlegs	May 16	Horned Grebe
	Greater Yellowlegs		Barrow's Goldeneye
	Canada Goose	May 19	Common Merganser
May 9	Tundra Swan	May 20	Red-throated Loon
	Bohemian Waxwing	May 22	Red-necked Grebe
May 10	Mallard	May 23	Surf Scoter (Black Duck)
	American Wigeon	May 24	Tree Swallow
	Lesser Scaup		White-winged Scoter
	Rusty Blackbird		(Black Duck)
	Snow Goose		Pacific Loon
	American Robin	May 25	Common Loon
	Northern Pintail	May 26	Fox Sparrow
May 11	Common Goldeneye		American Tree Sparrow
	Green-winged Teal		Spotted Sandpiper
May 12	Red-breasted Merganser	May 27	Yellow Warbler
	Slate-colored Dark-eyed Junco	May 28	Arctic Tern
	Yellow-rumped Warbler	June 2	Northern Shoveler
	(Myrtle race)	June 6	Glaucous Gull
	Mew Gull	June 11	Short-eared Owl
	Osprey		
May 13	Northern Flicker (Yellow-shafted race)		
	Molting Willow Ptarmigan		

Temperatures During Our Stay

Maximum and minimum temperatures were determined with repeated readings of our thermometer hanging on the northwest corner of the cabin. True maxima and minima might have differed slightly.

Date	Max. C	Min. C	Max. F	Min. F	Comments
January 31	-19	-19	-2	-2	Sunny; Calm
February 1	-19	-19	-2	-2	Snow
2	-19	-19	-2	-2	Windy
3	-35	-44	-31	-47	Northern Lights
4	-25	-38	-13	-36	Light Snow
5	-21	-43	-6	-45	Morning Sun
6	-24	-28	-11	-18	Light Snow
7	-31	-42	-24	-44	Northern Lights
8	-30	-40	-22	-40	Sunny; Calm
9	-26	-30	-15	-22	Northern Lights
10	-43	-44	-45	-47	Northern Lights
11	-29	-45	-20	-49	South Wind
12	-26	-40	-15	-40	Northern Lights
13	-19	-40	-2	-40	South Wind
14	-14	-37	7	-35	Variable Cloud
15	-15	-38	5	-36	Sunny; Calm
16	-11	-15	12	5	South Wind
17	-8	-16	18	3	Southeast Wind
18	-6	-8	21	18	Southeast Wind
19	-14	-18	7	0	Clear; Calm
20	-12	-22	10	-8	Light Snow
21	-14	-30	7	-22	Light Snow
22	-18	-25	0	-13	Fog then Sun
23	-14	-17	7	1	Cloudy
24	-11	-17	12	1	Light Snow
25	-12	-22	10	-8	Sunny Breaks
26	-14	-22	7	-8	Morning Cloud
27	-15	-21	5	-6	Morning Cloud
28	-19	-30	-2	-22	Sunny
March 1	-15	-33	5	-27	Light Snow
2	-13	-31	9	-24	Snow

MICHAEL D. PITT

Date	Max. C	Min. C	Max. F	Min. F	Comments
March 3	-24	-27	-11	-17	Northwest Wind
4	-24	-30	-11	-22	Northwest Wind
5	-26	-36	-15	-33	Northern Lights
6	-26	-40	-15	-40	Northern Lights
7	-23	-42	-9	-44	Northern Lights
8	-28	-42	-18	-44	Northwest Wind
9	-24	-39	-11	-38	Northern Lights
10	-18	-41	0	-42	Northern Lights
11	-5	-37	23	-35	Northern Lights
12	-1	-8	30	18	Sunny; SE Wind
13	-4	-14	25	7	Evening Snow
14	-13	-18	9	0	Northern Lights
15	-6	-12	21	10	Fog & Cloud
16	-8	-12	18	10	Afternoon Sun
17	-5	-11	23	12	Cloud & Snow
18	-9	-18	16	0	Sunny Afternoon
19	-7	-24	19	-11	Sunny
20	-5	-27	23	-17	Northern Lights
21	0	-22	32	-8	Southeast Wind
22	0	-12	32	10	Sunny; Calm
23	0	-7	32	19	Snow Flurries
24	-3	-15	27	5	Snow Flurries
25	-6	-13	21	9	Strong NW Wind
26	-16	-22	3	-8	NW Wind; Snow
27	-16	-25	3	-13	Evening Snow
28	-27	-38	-17	-36	Sunny; NW Wind
29	-22	-41	-8	-42	Sunny; NW Wind
30	-20	-43	-4	-45	Sunny
31	-12	-40	10	-40	Sunny; SE Wind
April 1	-5	-19	23	-2	Strong SE Wind
2	-8	-14	18	7	Strong North Wind
3	-8	-23	18	-9	Northern Lights
4	-3	-26	27	-15	Strong South Wind
5	-2	-24	28	-15	Northern Lights
6	-4	-17	25	1	Northern Lights
7	-12	-22	10	-8	Morning Snow
8	-10	-21	14	-6	Northern Lights
9	-4	-31	25	-24	Sunny & Calm
10	-4	-28	25	-18	Northern Lights

Date	Max. C	Min. C	Max. F	Min. F	Comments
April 11	-2	-24	28	-11	Variable Cloud
12	-3	-20	27	-4	Cloudy
13	-6	-16	21	3	Morning Snow
14	3	-23	37	-9	Northern Lights
15	3	-20	37	-4	Snow
16	In Town				
17	In Town				
18	In Town				
19	In Town				
20	In Town				
21	In Town				
22	-4	-10	25	14	Sunny; NW Wind
23	-6	-14	21	7	Snow; NW Wind
24	-8	-24	18	-11	Northwest Wind
25	-4	-12	25	10	Variable Cloud
26	-10	-23	14	-9	Sunny; NW Wind
27	-11	-29	12	-20	Sunny; NW Wind
28	-4	-23	25	-9	Sunny; SW Wind
29	-1	-22	30	-8	Snow
30	2	-16	36	3	Snow; SE Wind
May 1	2	-6	36	21	Cloudy
2	0	-9	32	16	Cloud; East Wind
3	-2	-8	28	18	Strong NE Wind
4	0	-9	32	16	Cloudy
5	-3	-12	27	10	Sunny; SE Wind
6	-4	-14	25	7	Sunny; SE Wind
7	2	-7	36	19	Light Snow
8	6	-2	43	28	Sunny
9	7	-6	45	21	Sunny; SE Wind
10	13	-6	55	21	Sunny; SE Wind
11	12	-3	54	27	Sunny; SE Wind
12	14	-2	57	28	Sunny; SE Wind
13	17	-3	63	27	Sunny; East Wind
14	8	-3	46	27	Cloudy; East Wind
15	8	-6	46	21	Sunny
16	11	-8	52	18	Sunny; Calm
17	2	-5	36	23	Cloudy; NE Wind
18	0	-6	32	21	Snow Flurries

MICHAEL D. PITT

Date	Max. C	Min. C	Max. F	Min. F	Comments
May 19	-1	-6	30	21	Snow
20	4	-8	39	18	Light Snow
21	7	-9	45	16	Sunny; Calm
22	10	-7	50	19	Overcast; Calm
23	12	-6	54	21	Sunny
24	20	0	68	32	Cloudy; Calm
25	16	-3	61	27	Variable Cloud
26	10	-1	50	30	Snow Flurries
27	13	-3	55	27	Sunny; Calm
28	16	-4	61	25	Sunny; Calm
29	16	-3	61	27	Rain Showers
30	16	0	61	32	Variable Cloud
31	18	2	64	36	Thunder; Rain
June 1	11	0	52	32	Cloudy; NW Wind
2	13	1	55	34	Evening Rain
3	20	4	68	39	Morning Rain
4	16	3	61	37	Variable Cloud
5	6	1	43	34	Cloudy; NE Wind
6	13	-2	55	28	Sunny; SW Wind
7	15	3	59	37	Sunny; NW Wind
8	12	3	54	37	Variable Cloud
9	12	-2	54	28	Sunny
10	In Town				
11	In Town				
12	In Town				
13	In Town				
14	In Town				
15	In Town				
16	26	24	79	75	Sunny; NE Wind
17	28	14	82	57	Sunny; SE Wind
18	26	19	79	66	Evening Rain
19	22	15	72	59	Sunny; NW Wind
20		12		54	Paddling North

MICHAEL D. PITT

Michael D. Pitt

B orn and raised in California, Michael D. Pitt immigrated to Canada in 1975 to accept a position at the University of British Columbia as a professor of grassland ecology in the Faculty of Agricultural Sciences, where he eventually served as associate dean for eight years. In 1981 he married his wife Kathleen, who worked at the university as an administrator in Information Technology Services.

The lure of a rural lifestyle, however, with golden sun reflecting on winter snow, inevitably proved irresistible. Kathleen said goodbye to commute traffic, deadlines, memos and office walls in 2000. Michael escaped 18 months later. They now live on 565 acres in the Aspen Parkland near Preeceville, Saskatchewan, where sled dogs Brownie, Grey, Sailor and Slick help them operate *Meadow's Edge Bed & Breakfast.*

Kathleen and Michael Pitt are authors of *Three Seasons in the Wind: 950 km by Canoe Down Northern Canada's Thelon River,* published in 1999.

CPSIA information can be obtained at www.ICGtesting.com
Printed in the USA
LVOW011213221211

260692LV00006B/355/P